"*Measuring What Matters in Peace Operations and Crisis Management* addresses the recognized need to better understand the impact of external interventions in conflict environments. It highlights the need to identify appropriate measures of effectiveness from the perspective of recipient populations so as to enable international actors to better comprehend the significance and impact of external interventions. This book is an important and timely contribution to the ongoing debate on the role of international actors in promoting peace and stability."

– Martti Ahtisaari, Chairman, Crisis Management Initiative
(2008 Nobel Peace Prize laureate)

"*Measuring What Matters in Peace Operations and Crisis Management* provides a clear and detailed guide through the largely uncharted territory of evaluating increasingly integrated endeavours in response to conflict and crisis. This will be an invaluable resource for practitioners, policy-makers, and scholars alike. In breaking new ground in its sophisticated attempt to capture, analyze, and suggest the way ahead for this complex and multidisciplinary field, this contribution is both timely and significant – a must-read for all concerned."

– Alex Bellamy, co-author of *Understanding Peacekeeping*

"The evolution of international intervention in support of global peace and security has created complex environments in which multiple stakeholders operate in common spaces. An expanded understanding of roles, responsibilities, and capabilities through the lens of tradespace enables improved planning and enhanced cooperation and effectiveness in the field. *Measuring What Matters in Peace Operations and Crisis Management* provides an insightful perspective into performance enhancement and the measurement of success."

– Douglas Coates, Director, RCMP International Peace Operations Branch

"The most important question peacekeepers need to keep asking themselves is what kind of impact we are having on the communities we are mandated to serve and protect. The painful truth is that our missions have often caused harm or failed to prevent suffering. *Measuring What Matters in Peace Operations and Crisis Management* focuses on measuring the consequences of our operations is thus a highly welcome, timely, and relevant contribution that comes at a time when peace, stability, and crisis management operations are being fundamentally reviewed and questioned. It is a pioneering study that covers an important gap in the field, and it should be on the required reading list for all those responsible for the planning and management of peace operations."

– Cedric de Coning, Research Fellow, ACCORD and
Norwegian Institute of International Affairs (NUPI)

"*Measuring What Matters in Peace Operations and Crisis Management* provides some much-needed clarity to the debate on measuring performance of complex interventions. It recognizes that even the most coherent and well-thought-out strategy can be undermined by a lack of benchmarks and tools that can be used to measure the extent to which strategic and functional objectives have been achieved. This is particularly true for conflict-ridden and fragile environments where there is limited indigenous capacity to assist in the formulation of a strategy at the outset of an intervention. This book will be of great value to both policy-makers and practitioners supporting multi-dimensional peace operations. Moreover, it provides some useful and practical tools that this area is so desperately in need of – particularly in linking security development policy with security development realities on the ground."

– Ann Fitz-Gerald, Centre for Security Sector Management, Cranfield University

"A groundbreaking book that provides a comprehensive treatment of measuring success for missions that is of critical importance. The author challenges how we think about what we do when we strive to achieve sustainable peace and security. This information is valuable for those who work on international missions, for the governments and citizens who support them, and, most importantly, for the affected communities in disrupted states."

– Alan Okros, Professor, Deputy Chair: Command, Leadership & Management, Canadian Forces College

MEASURING WHAT MATTERS
in Peace Operations & Crisis Management

SARAH JANE MEHARG

CENTRE POUR LE
MAINTIEN DE LA PAIX
PEARSON
PEACEKEEPING CENTRE

School of Policy Studies, Queen's University
McGill-Queen's University Press
Montreal & Kingston • London • Ithaca

Copyright © 2009 School of Policy Studies, Queen's University at Kingston, Canada

SCHOOL OF
Policy Studies
Queen's UNIVERSITY

Publications Unit
Policy Studies Building
138 Union Street
Kingston, ON, Canada
K7L 3N6
www.queensu.ca/sps/

All rights reserved. The use of any part of this publication for reproduction, transmission in any form or by any means (electronic, mechanical, photocopying, recording or otherwise), or storage in a retrieval system without the prior written consent of the publisher – or, in case of photocopying or other reprographic copying, a license from the Canadian Copyright Licensing Agency – is an infringement of the copyright law. Enquiries concerning reproduction should be sent to the School of Policy Studies at the address above.

Library and Archives Canada Cataloguing in Publication

Meharg, Sarah Jane
    Measuring what matters in peace operations and crisis management / Sarah Jane Meharg.

Originated as a multi-phased research project undertaken by the Pearson Peacekeeping
    Centre, 2007-2009. Written by Sarah Jane Meharg, with contributions from other
    authors.
Includes bibliographical references and index.
ISBN 978-1-55339-228-6 (pbk.).—ISBN 978-1-55339-229-3 (bound)

    1. Peacekeeping forces—Evaluation. 2. Humanitarian assistance—Evaluation.
3. Crisis management—Evaluation. 4. Conflict management—Evaluation. I. Queen's
University (Kingston, Ont.). School of Policy Studies II. Pearson Peacekeeping Centre
III. Title.

JZ6360.M43 2009   355.3'57   C2009-901525-0

Cover designed by Kathryn Robicheau

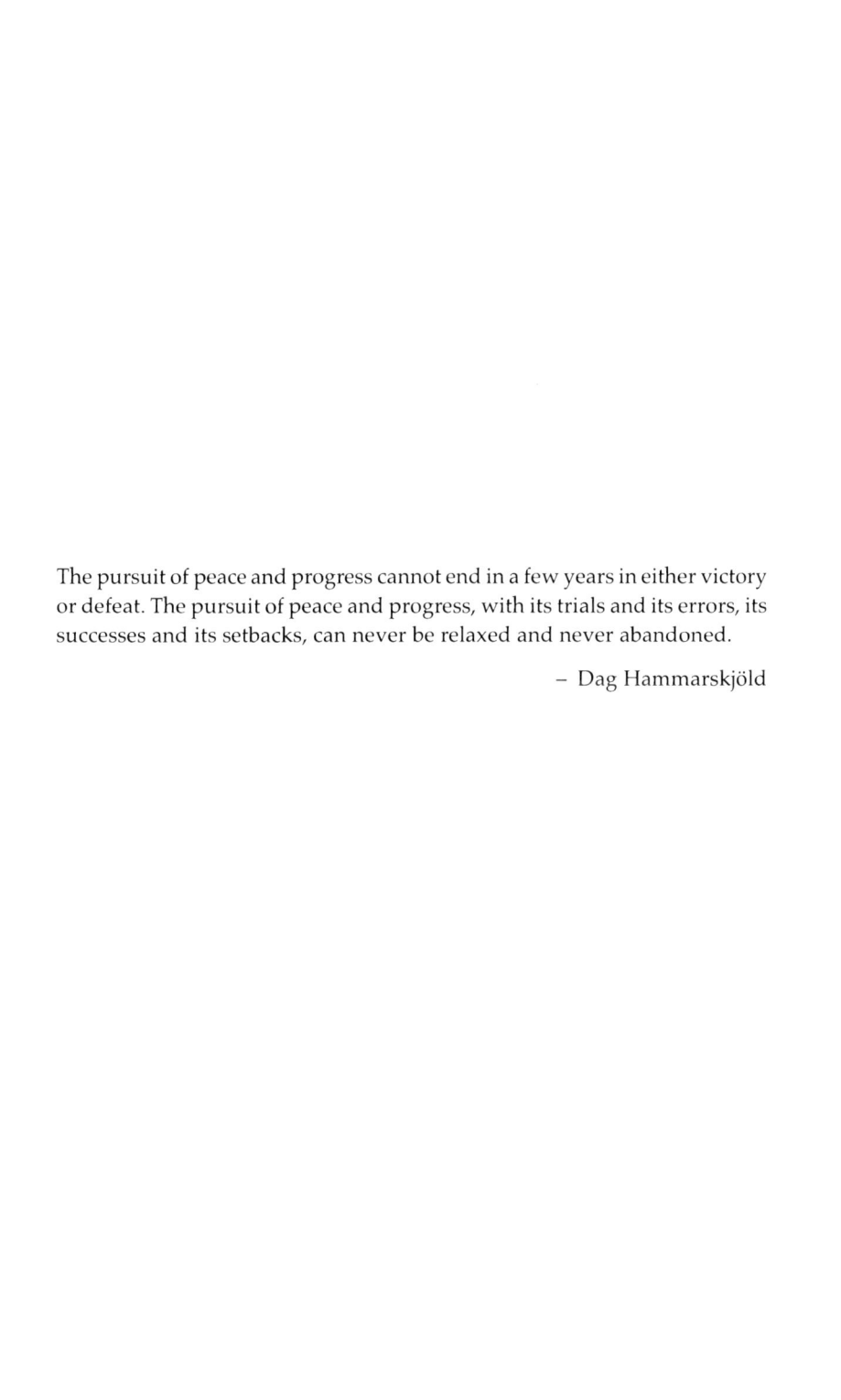

The pursuit of peace and progress cannot end in a few years in either victory or defeat. The pursuit of peace and progress, with its trials and its errors, its successes and its setbacks, can never be relaxed and never abandoned.

– Dag Hammarskjöld

Contents

Tables, Figures, Maps	ix
Foreword	xi
Acknowledgments	xiii
Introduction	1
Methodology, and How to Read This Book	19

PART I. Worldviews and Paradigm Blindness

CHAPTER 1:	Trade-Offs and Play Spaces	27
CHAPTER 2:	Theories of Intervention	45
CHAPTER 3:	The Language of Measuring	57
CHAPTER 4:	Mechanisms and Tools	89
CHAPTER 5:	Measuring Success in Bosnia-Herzegovina	129

PART II. Measuring What Matters

An Epistemic Community		151
CHAPTER 6:	Peace Operations and Crisis Management: Not Just Benign Tasks but Political Acts	153
	RORY KEANE	
CHAPTER 7:	Trends and Challenges in Measuring Effectiveness in the Humanitarian System	159
	JOHN BORTON	

CHAPTER 8:	The Art and Science of Assessing Iraqi Security Force Performance	169
	KEITH HAUK and STEPHEN MARIANO	
CHAPTER 9:	Measures of Effectiveness: Examining the United Kingdom in Afghanistan	177
	STUART GORDON	
CHAPTER 10:	Measures of Effectiveness for Peace Operations and Crisis Management	183
	DAVID CHUTER	
CHAPTER 11:	Significance of Impact Assessment: A New Methodology	189
	EMERY BRUSSET	
CHAPTER 12:	An Organizational Perspective on Measuring the Effectiveness of Crisis Management	203
	KRISTIINA RINTAKOSKI	
CHAPTER 13:	Measuring Effectiveness in Peace-Building and State-Building	209
	JAKE SHERMAN	
CHAPTER 14:	Practitioner Perspectives and Policy Options	215

PART III. Entering a Common Tradespace

CHAPTER 15:	Measuring Success in a Common Tradespace	229
CHAPTER 16:	Emerging Trends in a Common Tradespace	243
Conclusion		255
Appendices		263
Bibliography		271
Author Biography		283
Contributors		285
Index		289

Tables, Figures, Maps

Tables

1.	The Results Dichotomy	34
2.	ALNAP's Evaluation Typology	77
3.	Tactical Conflict Assessment Framework Questions	180
4.	Inputs, Output, Outcome, and Significance of Impact Chain	198
5.	Intervention Worldviews	218

Figures

1.	Boots, Suits, Sandals, and Badges	2
2.	The Spectrum of Operations	4
3.	Abraham Maslow's Hierarchy of Needs	32
4.	A Cross-Sector Comparison of Principles and Effects	38
5.	The Linear Chain of Logic	59
6.	Understanding Measurement	62
7.	Disarmament, Demobilization, and Reintegration Measures of Effectiveness	63
8.	Effects-Based Approach to Operations	63
9.	Doing the Right Things, or Doing Things Right?	65
10.	The Rolling Process	66
11.	The Lessons Learned Process at the Peacekeeping and Stability Operations Institute	68
12.	An Example of a Web-Based Lessons Learned Approach, Center for US Army Lessons Learned	69
13.	The Performance Measurement Process	72
14.	A Performance Measurement Framework	72
15.	The Evaluation Process	75
16.	Logical Framework (LogFrame)	95

17. Essential Tasks Matrix: An Excerpt 99
18. Effects Assessment Report Using the "Red-Yellow-Green" Military Assessment Scale 102
19. Lines of Operations Using Effects 103
20. Mission Analysis Process 104
21. Levels of Attribution and Influence 105
22. Joint Assessment Mission Matrix 109
23. Reflecting on Peace Practice: Four-Quadant Matrix 114
24. Military Deployments in Global Peace Operations 119
25. IDRC's Outcome Mapping Approach 121
26. Bombs, Doves, Ups, Downs, and Sides 122
27. Thermometer Imagery 123
28. Traffic Light Colour Coding 123
29. Permissive, Non-Permissive, and Grey Zone Environments of International Interventions 134
30. A Formula for Sustainable Change 137
31. Effects Diagram, Afghanistan Evaluation 192
32. The "Black Box" in Impact Evaluations 193
33. Evaluation Concept Overview 195
34. Government Departments Approach Interventions from Different Perspectives 234

Maps

1. ZIF Crisis Prevention and Peace Operations 2008 117
2. A Detailed View of the ZIF Map 118
3. Mapping United Nations Missions 120

Foreword

Political risks certainly exist when we engage in evaluation and assessment. Good leadership entails responsibility, and with responsibility comes the uncomfortable process of identifying the strengths and weaknesses of an organization's ability to meet its mandate and its donors' requirements and to serve the wider good.

This is all the more important when an organization such as the Pearson Peacekeeping Centre (PPC) works at the international level supporting the effectiveness of peace operations.

Honest and transparent evaluation of performance, as well as the longer-term verification of programs, projects, and intervention activities, are the challenges we face in this era of accountability and transparency. As stakeholders involved in peace operations and civilian crisis management come together to contribute to global peace and security, one salient truth transcends all areas of our collective work: we need to know where we are in order to know where we are going. Evaluating and assessing our work will help us as we travel this particular path. This tenet has informed my own work at the Pearson Peacekeeping Centre.

I was hired in 2005 to lead the PPC through a period of transition and to strengthen the centre as the premier research-led training, education, and capacity-building organization contributing to the effectiveness of peace operations. My first order of business was to conduct a complete and transparent evaluation of the PPCs structure, systems, policies, values, and staff. I accomplished this task with the assistance of the PPC staff and a third-party agency that collectively walked us through the self-assessment process.

Making the great, the good, the bad, and sometimes the ugly (but fixable!) realities of the PPC public knowledge was a leadership decision. Our goal was to build upon our core strengths and address our weaknesses head on through internal reflection as well as through public criticism. Our process of self-assessment was educational, enlightening, and challenging. The challenges were not mine alone but were also carried by my staff, former staff, and the wider network of supporters and advocates who had put their hearts and souls into our NGO during their tenure at the centre. For some, this task proved too difficult, and they self-selected out of the process. For others, the process was an opportunity for new visions and change. With time to reflect and assess, the staff at the centre adopted a new mission and new perspectives on how the Pearson Peacekeeping Centre impacts ongoing change in the international arena.

The PPC took this important step in 2005-06 and gained institutional strength and awareness during the process. The centre positioned itself to contribute to measuring the effectiveness, progress, and success of peace operations by conducting the primary field research resulting in this book, *Measuring What Matters in Peace Operations and Civilian Crisis Management*, and in the compendium training module and practitioner's handbook.

Greater leadership in the area of assessment and evaluation is required among the sectors contributing to peace operations. I began with my organization, and I encourage you to do the same for the benefit of sustainable global peace and security.

Suzanne Monaghan
President, Pearson Peacekeeping Centre

Acknowledgments

This book is a result of a multi-phased research project undertaken by the Pearson Peacekeeping Centre (PPC) from 2007 to 2009. My sincerest thanks go to over eighty people in nine countries who participated in interviews in support of this book and the research project outcomes: a training module and handbook for peace operations and crisis management practitioners. Participants involved in this study represented a wide range of sectors involved in international interventions, including development, defence and security, humanitarianism, war-affected locals, government, the private sector, think tanks, civilian policing, and academia. Thank you – especially to my colleagues in Bosnia-Herzegovina – for your willingness to discuss your experiences of effectiveness, progress, and success.

From the interview participants emerged key thinkers able to grasp the difficult topic of measuring what matters in international interventions. These few were asked to contribute short vignettes to the book to highlight their experience in this area of emerging practice. My utmost gratitude is conferred on Emery Brusset, John Borton, David Chuter, Stuart Gordon, Stephen Mariano, Keith Hauk, Jake Sherman, Kristiina Rintakoski, and Rory Keane for their willingness to ponder the topics under examination in this book. It was an honour to work with such a diverse, dedicated group of experts. Like most information-age projects, we worked together via distance, from points as far away as Baghdad, Italy, the United States, France, England, Belgium, and Finland.

I offer my thanks to PPC president Suzanne Monaghan and the rest of our staff for supporting this worthy research initiative, and to Christian Leuprecht and Arthur Sweetman, Queen's University School of Policy Studies, for their interest in partnering with the PPC on this initiative.

My sincerest appreciation goes to PPC vice-president Ann Livingstone for having a compelling vision of the importance of research-led training and education for peace operations. Only with this vision will practitioners be able to thoroughly evaluate and critically assess international peace operations activities and their impending effects, whether good or bad.

A book is a team effort and never the work of one person. Although solo activity was my bread and butter, I was not alone. A debt is owed for the research support of Stephanie Blair, Michael Hehn, Stefanie Landry, and the amazing Melanie Paradis. Gratitude is due to Mark Howes, Val Jarus, and Kathryn Robicheau for their keen eyes and quality control, without which this volume would be less than it is. As for the behind the scenes support, I am truly blessed.

Finally, to all recipients of international peace operations interventions and crisis management, thank you for your continued patience while the international community re-evaluates its motivations for intervention and identifies how to measure what really matters to you.

Sarah Jane Meharg

Introduction

The international community is coming of age.

It has graduated from a divergent group of agenda-driven actors into a community of practice and is now attempting to adopt comprehensive norms, standards, and codes that will see it through to the next stage of evolution: a common tradespace. The international community's ability to contribute to tenable global peace depends on an ability to work within this space – to do the *right* things, at the *right* times, in the *right* ways, using the *right* means – and to accurately assess collective progress and success.

The doctrine of the international community offers guidance for comprehensive norms, standards, and codes that will transform interests, values, services, and products into a common *tradespace*. The notion of a tradespace is a collocation of the terms *trade-off* and *play space* and is a framework for analyzing the complex resources, costs, and provisioning involved in very large projects with multiple stakeholders, objectives, and interdependent variables. Trade-offs are an exchange of one thing in return for another, especially the relinquishment of one benefit or advantage for another considered to be equally or more desirable; play space is the area bounded by the functionality and purpose of those stakeholders involved in that space.

Tradespaces are multi-variant interdependent spaces recognized for a collection of processes that span multiple sectors in which stakeholders each have their own core objectives. The concept is aptly suited to peace operations and civilian crisis management because these activities require *inter*-stakeholder processes to reach an equilibrium state that is stable, resilient, and maximizes effectiveness, progress, and success for principal stakeholders, including members of war-affected publics. Understanding operations through the lens of a tradespace makes research difficult, as traditional research calls for a sectioning-off of processes and phenomena within a space. This is counter-intuitive to the interrelated nature of the tradespace being researched.[1]

Deciding upon right things and accurately assessing our collective and cumulative success may be yet a long way off. Deep ontological divides exist between the sectors of peace operations and civilian crisis management. There is little agreement as to what projects, aims, objectives, and outcomes make up peace operations and civilian crisis management. Peace operations for the United Nations are different from the European Union's remit for civilian crisis management, and coalition activities in Iraq do not fall under the rubric of peace operations. Yet the sectors that conduct peace operations and civilian crisis management are similar – even shared. It could be assumed, falsely, that the sectors involved in peace operations and multinational civilian crisis management activities have common ontology; the ontological divide between the sectors, however, is great. As the international community shapes its own tradespace, there is no illusion that the sectors of military, security, governmental, humanitarian, police, and private sectors will adopt similar ontologies or worldviews to inform their collective crisis interventions. The so-called 3D approach (development, diplomacy, and defence) representative of the whole of government of military, diplomatic, and humanitarian organizations and civilian police is aptly described as "boots, suits, sandals, and badges" (Figure 1).

FIGURE 1
Boots, Suits, Sandals, and Badges

Understanding ontological divides will be a requirement within the new tradespace. Dana Eyre, former senior advisor for USAID in Iraq, suggests: "Unity of understanding is more important than trying for unity of command in the complex tradespace of peace operations and civilian crisis management."[2] The challenge, however, is that success must first be measured and assessed in order to inform decisions regarding the *right* things, at the *right* times, in the *right* ways, using the *right* means. Herein lies the rub. How exactly do we define success? If we define it differently, is there any opportunity to agree on success within the common tradespace? Answering these questions may be dependent upon identifying what our goals and objectives are in peace operations, and what stakeholder strategies exist for achieving them.

Evolution towards this point has been marked. Stakeholders involved in international peace operations and civilian crisis management – namely, defence and security, civilian police, humanitarian organizations, international organizations, governments, host nations, and the private sector – have matured their structures, praxis, policies, guidance, and accountability, leading towards effectiveness with the broadly shared intention (albeit unconscious) to eventually enhance the *comprehensive* efficacy of peace and security management within a shared operational space. International multi-lateral interventions are increasingly integrated and multi-functional, encouraging stakeholders in various sectors to provide services across sectors through many tasks and activities within the spectrum of operations, including security, governance and participation, humanitarian assistance and social well-being, economic stabilization and infrastructure, and justice and reconciliation.

Along with the development of these public services contributing to the global common goals of peace and security has come the privatization of these services. The coupling of the private and public sectors in these social capital endeavours has produced a robust *peace economy*.[3]

The shared operational space is overlaid with the spectrum of operations – typically perceived as a linear model by the international community – and is divided into three dominant areas of activity:

1. *Intervention*, characterized by suspension of hostilities; stabilization agenda; non-permissive environment
2. *Peace Operations and Civilian Crisis Management*, characterized by transitional operations; cessation of armed conflict; reconstruction and short-term quick impact agenda; quasi-permissive environment
3. *Peacebuilding and Development*, characterized by consolidation operations; sustainable peace and prosperity agenda; permissive environment

The spectrum of operations (Figure 2) informs the international systems of intervention, yet it does not support thinking about intervention as a common tradespace in which this collective community seeks to stabilize security and formulate tenable peace and accurately assess progress and success. The complexity of our security environment requires a new, sophisticated analysis of the efficacy of intervention programs.

The key question is how we are to measure the success of integrated, multi-functional international operations. This type of question forces clarification of the purpose, aim, and objectives of peace operations and civilian crisis management. Perhaps as in most scientific endeavours, peace operations and civilian crisis management cannot be defined until it is determined how they will be measured. Measures of success, therefore, clarify the purpose, aim, and objectives of international interventions. Unless we determine what success looks like at the beginning – for the international community and the members of the public – we cannot determine the scope and definition of peace operations and civilian crisis management.[4] Measurement comes first. Yet such scientific rational processes are linear imaginings, and it is not clearly understood how they can be applied to measuring significant changes in people affected by conflict and calamity.

FIGURE 2
The Spectrum of Operations

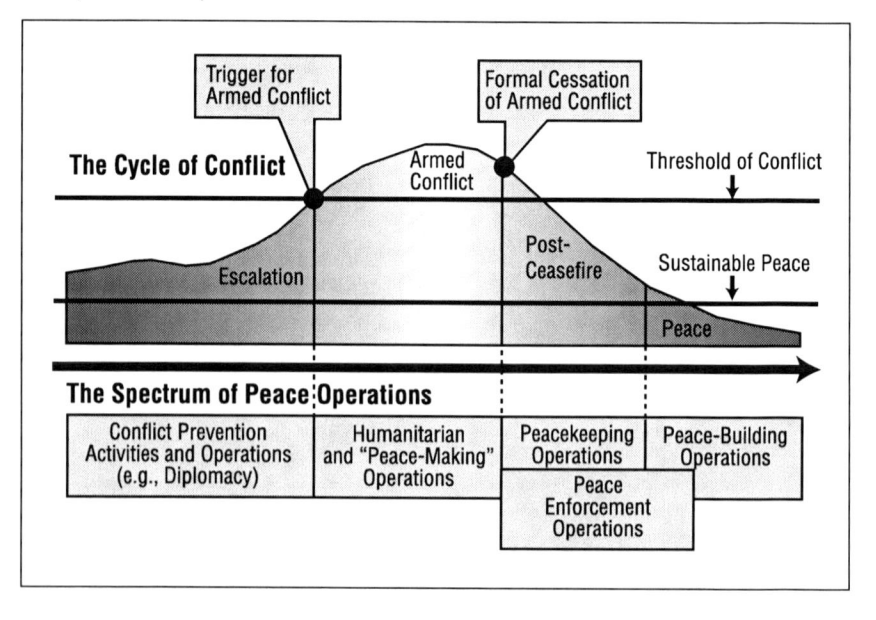

The success of peace operations is relatively easy to determine at the macro level.[5] Lives are being saved, or they are not. Stability is either present, or it is not. And the operation is either facilitating democratic transformation, or it is not. However, perceiving operational success as black and white progress towards peace and stability seems overly simplistic, especially in the global security environment – categorized by most theorists and practitioners as incalculably complex.

The *human condition* is virtually impossible to measure. Typically referred to in humanitarian and development literature as *human development and well-being*, in this context the human condition is the state of socially constructed influences construed from cultural, physical, economic, spiritual/religious, psychological, ideological, and political elements. These elements inform our lives and the way we relate to our contexts, and determine with which contexts we have a reflexive relationship. According to an anonymous United Nations program officer, "We don't know what [success] looks like. We can't agree on what it means. And the metrics of success are all different in each mission and sector."[6] When attempting to measure the human condition – whether it is worsening or improving – are there metrics that capture such change?

Some would argue yes, while others would say that metrics are numbers and scores, which by nature do not adequately address attitudinal, behavioural, or societal change – in other words, the postwar human condition. Militaries are ill-equipped to measure the human condition, and change cannot be attributed to Newtonian cause and effect linear dynamics. Said one interview participant involved in this study, "Militaries are very able to conduct internal audits of performance, yet our available systems are ill-equipped to audit change in war-affected members of the public. There are other ways to measure the human condition, and these are generated from the policing, humanitarian, and development sectors, because these sectors are the interface with local populations." As Eugene Bonventre, a colonel in the US Air Force, argues: "That such measurements will never be perfect and causal relationships will never be definitively proven should not preclude attempts to develop practical assessment techniques."[7] All measuring systems have innate technical limitations, which explains in part the difficulty in reaching a consensus on verification methodologies among the sectors of peace operations and civilian crisis management.[8]

Yet when it comes to international interventions, we are able to identify what *does not work* much more easily than *what does work*. The media seems to have a particular capacity in this regard. So too do war-affected citizens, such as those in Bosnia-Herzegovina, who can clearly articulate the dismal failures of the international community in their own backyard but have difficulty describing successes.

Worrisome for watchdogs, no standard fiscal reporting mechanism or performance measurement mechanism exists that can track obligations and expenditures of national intervention activities in places like Iraq, Bosnia, and Haiti. There remains no way to assess real costs, only targeted expenditures, no way to assess real-time progress, only targeted goals. The lack of field-reporting capacities and capabilities and of performance management systems makes it impossible to accurately portray the status of each sector, the overall assistance efforts, or the effectiveness of those efforts in peace operations and civilian crisis management. According to the Center for Strategic and International Studies (CSIS) in Washington, DC, peace operations and civilian crisis management theory and practice have advanced considerably over the last few years, yet the international community still lacks progressive, pragmatic, cost-efficient, and reliable models for measuring the success of their activities in conflict-affected environments.[9] Britain's Department for International Development unequivocally states that current systems for assessing project performance offer no way of identifying success in moving towards post-conflict goals.[10] A system is required that shows the connections between mandates, goals, and activities; that reflects more rigorous thought processes; that illustrates that planners have explicitly considered conflict dynamics and the potential positive and negative impacts of intervention activities in conflict environments.

The RAND Corporation, an American think tank, suggests that even though many peace operations and civilian crisis management activities involve several of the same stakeholders, it is difficult to find consistent and comprehensive data on all but the dominant activities, such as reconciliation or national army training projects. Most data sets are incompatible and do not lend themselves to comparative analyses across sectors, nor do they accurately assess progress in the majority of activities in post-conflict environments. Attempts to quantify outcomes of complex processes fail because of the unavailability of precise statistical measures; limited data sets, if they are attainable at all, inhibit firm conclusions of progress. According to the Active Learning Network for Accountability and Performance in Humanitarian Action (ALNAP), the quality of measuring systems remains underdeveloped and calls for a more sophisticated, high-quality process in order to have a lasting positive effect on improving learning, accountability, and performance in sectors involved in civilian crisis management.[11]

Other strategists argue that there are no meaningful metrics for measuring progress, and fewer meaningful government reports on progress in Iraq and Afghanistan.[12] Governments continue to use outdated methods for reporting results, publishing progress reports "long on noble rhetoric and short on useful content."[13] This reality is reflected in the deficiencies of the results-based measuring frameworks – employed by many governments – which prevent moving beyond monitoring activities to measuring the significance of the impact of such activities.[14] In the absence of metrics, maps, and useful analyses, there is undue reliance on a preponderance of positive anecdotes from the field to further justify interventions. When realistic evaluation is employed, the results are often non-transferrable. For example, specific activity-level improvements at the micro level do not necessarily transfer to macro successes. Their specificity in scope, scale, and localized approach cannot suggest what is occurring overall. The opposite also holds: macro successes cannot be transferred as local successes. There are no absolute measures of whether intervention operations, programs, and activities have worked.[15]

Challenges to the Tradespace

Incompatibilities between sectors and stakeholders, such as funding, worldviews, values, and mandates, impede flexibility, adaptability, survivability, scalability, modifiability, and robustness within the common tradespace. Most of the literature on peace operations and civilian crisis management suggests that three major sectors are involved in intervention: development, diplomacy, and defence. There are other sectors, of course, including policing, humanitarianism, government, private industry, finance, and academia. Each can be further unpacked to expose heterogeneous – not homogenous – sectoral stakeholders, motivated by sophisticated worldviews that inform their interventions. For example, the humanitarian aid and assistance sector alone can be subdivided into a mosaic of powerful actors informed by a religious agenda (Islam, Judaism, Christian), small and good-hearted organizations (Clowns without Borders), and the morally concerned (Amnesty International, Oxfam, CARE, Mercy Corps), among many other agendas and perspectives on humanitarianism. Each sector embodies intervention at different scales and levels, nationally and internationally, and each must contend with being painted by the same brush as those with which it shares a perceived sector. Outsiders think that other sectors are homogenous; this is not the reality.

Although rarely considered as stakeholders by the others, the host nation and its various publics, also motivated by unique *weltanschauungen*, are gravitational forces in the forward progress of intervention activities. And, as in the example above regarding the myth of homogeneity within the humanitarian sector, others too see the host nation and its population as a homogenous entity.

Enormous funding disparities exist between the development of organizations such as NATO and the rest of the stakeholders of peace operations and civilian crisis management. With trillions of dollars spent in the last fifty years on improving the systems of command, control, communication, coordination, and information technology, it is not surprising that other sectors have fallen behind the defence sector in terms of planning and measuring progress. Militaries' ability to measure success is for the most part far superior precisely because of the funds spent on development and multinational experimentation. In fact, funds spent, in theory, put western militaries at a superior advantage when compared to other stakeholders such as civilian police or international organizations like the ICRC, even though all are members of the international community of stakeholders involved in managing crises. Yet despite the time and funds invested, western militaries with their planning systems and metrics are no more able to accurately measure progress in peace operations and civilian crisis management than national development agencies such as DFID, USAID, and CIDA, or international organizations like the ICRC and ALNAP.

Understanding the values, principles, and theories that inform standards and mechanisms for measuring what matters is a keystone of the common tradespace. Fundamentally, if we understand what drives us to do our work and to measure that work, then we can better comprehend the dynamics of the complex environment instead of being victim to it. It is difficult, however, to change our perspectives regarding what we do and how we measure our successes. Our perspectives are laden with values, principles, and our individual and organizational identities.

According to Ralph Keeney, an American expert on value-focused thinking, values are what we care about. He suggests that value-focused thinking is critical in situations where there are real, important, and complex decisions to be made with no clear solution at hand.[16] This implies that the examination of stakeholder values can inform the process of measuring. On the other hand, militaries are concerned with measures of effectiveness (MOEs), which they understand as what is *wanted* rather than what must be done or what needs to be achieved. Steve Flemming, a defence scientist with Canada's Department of National Defence, observes that "the planners who typically produce initial MOE programs are engineers, and they tend to start at the wrong end – with what *can* be measured, rather than what *should* be measured."[17] Flemming goes on to say that the defence sector thinks that by measuring effectively they are actually making the change they are measuring.

Perhaps a part of the challenge is that some of the sectors involved in peace operations and civilian crisis management are seen as having lofty goals and vague mandates[18] rather than mandate-specific operational goals such as in the security and defence sectors. Not-for-profits, non-governmental organizations in the humanitarian and development sectors, and even the police sector get poor marks from military planners who see their own work as logical and rational, and that of other sectors (with whom they are now sharing the operational space) as soft, flaky, and loosey-goosey in terms of the ability to measure success. Not surprisingly, humanitarian and development NGOs see their military colleagues as "group-thinking Neanderthals"[19] with no ability to consider the qualitative aspects of intervention. Yet ALNAP's founder, John Borton, argues that humanitarians themselves have taken a long time to adopt a client-centric approach to their interventions, and by default, their performance measuring, whereas the military field of civil-military co-operation has advanced its client-centric approach nearly to the levels of psychological operations (e.g., winning "hearts and minds" campaigns). Militaries involved in peace operations and civilian crisis management (vis-à-vis combat operations and counter-insurgency efforts) have adopted military planning methods in their reconstruction and stability operations, which demand that measures of success are determined before campaign activities begin. James Embrey, the General Pershing Chair of Military Planning and Operations at the US Army War College, suggests that it "just makes sense that you do this thinking before you start the campaign, because it causes you to question, 'Should I do X if I can't know if it's making a difference?' as well as 'When higher-ups [headquarters] (and Congress) ask how we're doing on the path to victory, how do I answer their question (without winging it)?'"[20]

For western militaries, measures are outcome based (measuring effectiveness in changing conditions toward the desired conditions) as well as internal efforts based (measuring performance). Measuring effectiveness, progress, and success in combat operations is best done using military planning methods, as they are the most able to connect measures with mandates in order to achieve strategic intent and overall goal achievement. However, in peace operations and civilian crisis management, unlike in combat operations, it is the human condition that is being measured. Achieving intended effects, whether for increased security or for democratic governance, is the reason that intervention activities are undertaken.

As sector constituencies – the donors whom stakeholders report to – become more aware of the constraints within war-affected environments, their interest in success increases. As members of war-affected publics become principals in approaches to peace operations, their involvement in measuring what matters requires empowerment and encouragement.

All sectors need to measure intervention activities to identify gaps in effectiveness according to the principals involved – including citizens, donors, and the global commons.[21] The quality and consistency of evaluations and audits appear to be directly related to the level at which an organization is held to account by its constituencies, such as donors, governments, and citizens. In other words, attempts to verify success are completed only if and when an organization is held accountable for its actions, has incentives for measuring, or is a learning organization that values lessons and practices to improve future intervention activities. And of course, if there are resources, materiel, and staff specifically dedicated to conducting measuring, reporting, and evaluation, there is a higher likelihood of those activities being completed as a part of an intervention itself.

Moreover, sectors' objectives are different, which affects intervention outcomes. Although they intend different outcomes with their intervention activities, the ways in which success is measured along the way could be a rallying point for clashes of intervention titans. Many NGOs fall into the category of non-profits, being known to track their performance using over-simplistic performance metrics related to their mission, such as funds raised, tonnes of food distributed, number of immunizations administered, number of refugees repatriated, number of police and judges trained. But, as John Sawhill and David Williamson argue, these metrics do not measure the real success of an organization in achieving its mission.[22] There are few, if any, adequate methods to measure the achievement of organizational or program objectives, because of their sweeping, broad nature. Sawhill and Williamson offer an excellent example to illustrate their point: CARE USA's mandate is "to affirm the dignity and worth of individuals and families living in some of the world's poorest communities." And in the authors' words, "Try to measure that!"

From an outside-looking-in perspective, the major stakeholders involved in peace operations and civilian crisis management tend towards similar approaches to intervention activities and measuring the success of such activities. However, the values informing their approaches are distinctly different, even divergent. Militaries focus on end states rather than interim processes, while humanitarians focus on continual and consistent beneficiary access rather than exit strategies. Civilian police, under UN auspices, approach their work through a mentoring-training or crime-reduction lens, while most private sector actors are focused on efficiency towards profitability. Military personnel tend to see humanitarians as hostages of fortune, forever perpetuating their business and seeking the next crisis to assuage, while humanitarian non-governmental organizations tend to perceive private security companies as mercenaries, and see uniformed military personnel as to be avoided at all costs.

There are two dominant modalities for measuring success. The first measures outcomes and is fixed upon goal attainment and achieving end states. The second measures process and focuses on ways to shape the environment so that intervention activities can lead to goal achievement. It would be over-simplification to suggest that the military and defence sectors focus on the former while the humanitarians and development field focus on the latter, but this is not always the case. The security perspective does have a predilection for finding better, more meaningful metrics to measure progress in non-traditional state-building environments in which militaries find themselves at work. The prevalence of the combat-centric perspective wanting better, clearer, more meaningful metrics for peace operations and civilian crisis management is a hangover from traditional war fighting, and this method is not applicable to state-building activities. Metrics are useful in combat: numbers count, because numbers save lives. Such metrics are far less meaningful in complex operations, yet the quest for the holy grail of metrics continues.

Establishing the right metrics and indicators as measures of success, or building the capacity to conduct measurement, is tied to the values, principles, assumptions, and philosophies of intervention. The RAND Corporation and others suggest that establishing performance metrics is vital so that policy-makers can objectively assess success and failure during nation-building missions and make mid-course corrections if necessary.[23] The US Government Accountability Office, on the other hand, recommends that a performance management system be designed to better assess progress toward achieving goals and to provide a basis for planning future reconstruction.[24] Some argue that stakeholders involved in complex operations would benefit from using the same system to more completely communicate performance information to decision-makers in home governments and, eventually, tax-paying constituencies.

Although stakeholders of peace operations and civilian crisis management have developed progress reporting frameworks based upon metrics and indicators, these tend either to measure internal project progress – almost like an audit – or more vaguely, to measure external progress according to the perceived impact of a project. Hindsight is always 20/20, and most evaluations – including lessons learned and best practices – come *after* the completion of an intervention activity. This highly biased process can turn a blind eye to failures while spin-doctoring successes. Lessons learned and best practices are not a measurement system and may not capture the impact of interventions on people. Available measuring frameworks are not compatible between stakeholders and sectors, and range in utility, purpose, and application, resulting in less than comprehensive determinations of success in peace operations and civilian crisis management. Success is cumulative. It is achieved not by reaching one's pre-determined targets but through a cumulative process of successes.

The Complex Environment

We live in uncertain times. And uncertain times lead to constant change in our systems, policies, and processes. Our ever-changing security environment – which some refer to as complex – is causing the international community to think and act differently. One swift Google search illustrates this point perfectly. Articles on international relations, and more specifically security and defence, refer to the ever-changing and dynamic *complex* security environment. With most media messages, we read that life in the twenty-first century will be characterized by complexity, instability, and change, as well as globalization, dynamicism, and evolution. If constant change is the future, how then is success to be measured in a context of change?

The hallmark of measuring anything is stability. A stable system can be measured; a constant application of policy can be measured; a consistent approach can be measured. Science has shown that stability is the key to repeating any type of experiment or process. From a scientific perspective, an environment of instability creates different results every time. Instability means that variables are introduced and removed throughout a process. In an unstable environment, measuring is not verifiable. In a crisis environment there are few if any constant variables, and our ability to conduct multi-variant analyses is limited at best, especially when the evolving human condition is part of the environment being analyzed. If the benchmarks against which intervention activities are compared or measured become outdated because of the multi-variant environment, what hope do we collectively have of measuring our success to verify the efficacy of interventions? This suggests that failure to measure success occurs with a rapid rate of change. Correctly measuring success may forever suffer because of the attempt to catch up to reality.

Some see this period in our history as an opportunity to respond innovatively to constant change. If this period is considered as an opportunity rather than a constraint, then there are opportunities to adjust the ways in which success is measured in places like Afghanistan, Haiti, and Bosnia-Herzegovina. These adjustments may even have application on a national scale, where change seems to occur less quickly than in the international arena. Perhaps our collective hand is forced to progress our thinking beyond linear dynamics – simple cause and effect equations – towards non-linear approaches that better reflect the reality of the complex environment.

At the same time that the peace and security environment is in flux, so too the transformation from industrial age thinking and systems continues towards information-age thinking and systems. This transformational opportunity also serves as a process for shrugging off the constraining systems, policies, and processes of outdated modalities designed for a prior age dependent upon Newtonian cause and effect mechanics.

In such an environment of change and so-called complexity, there may be little room for standards and mechanisms that worked well with yesterday's reality but have less relevance and utility in today's environments. What, then, can stabilize the application of our processes regarding international intervention activities in an environment known for its fluctuations, inconsistencies, and absence of rules-based relationships?

The positive news is that measuring success in general has become more deeply ingrained in some sectors, in particular the humanitarian sector. It is probable, as many of the participants interviewed for this research project have forecast, that as more data is developed, considered, and shared across sectors, there will be a convergence around optimal comprehensive verification methods of activities related to peace operations and civilian crisis management.

Conceptual Clarifications

Some conceptual clarifications should be made at the outset of this discussion.

1. Despite significant forward progress in the field of evaluation related to cause and effect relationships and the correlation of program success to linear-dynamic relationships, these lessons have not fully been transferred to peace operations and crisis management assessment and measuring. Although third-party evaluators, who have benefited from significant progress in their field, conduct formal evaluations of bilateral intervention programs in conflict-affected regions, the broadly defined indicators of success for peace operations and crisis management limit the utility of cause and effect correlation for measuring success, progress, and effectiveness. The indicators used to measure progress in state building, governance, and well-being are not clear and may not be transferable to other contexts. This lack of clarity is an impediment to fully adopting the progress related to cause and effect attribution in the field of evaluation.

2. Although there are limitations to cause and effect measuring, the intellectual conceptualization of linking intervention inputs (our activities) with outputs and outcomes is a useful exercise.

Understanding at some level that there are linkages – albeit remote, in some respects – between our activities and sustainable peace may cause interventionists to be more critical about the unintended consequences of intervention activities in conflict-affected environments.
3. When thinking about policy, it is important to consider *change* in relation to *resources* and *political will*. Change related to peace operations and crisis management occurs in relation to these two other factors.

This book is about tradespace stakeholders' worldviews, practitioners' views of modalities of measuring intervention activities, available mechanisms and tools suitable to measuring progress in a tradespace framework, and policy options to inform comprehensive progress in peace operations and crisis management. The goals of this book are fourfold.

First, it undertakes to highlight stakeholder worldviews to increase understanding and improve synergies among those that share the international intervention tradespace. How we measure our activities drives how we do our activities. This book presents the argument that the principals involved could benefit from a deeper understanding of the theories, concepts, philosophies, and assumptions of the other stakeholders with whom they share space in the peace operations and civilian crisis management environment.

Second, this book examines the modalities of measuring success through the lens of the agents who plan, implement, and live with the results of peace operations and civilian crisis management.

Third, it provides an overview of the mechanisms and tools for measuring effectiveness, progress, and success within the tradespace. Various linear cause-and-effect mechanisms are presented – results-based management, measures of effectiveness, LogFrames, essential task matrices – which attempt to reduce complex intervention activities to simple success stories. Much work has been done since 2003 in developing mechanisms and tools for measuring the success of interventions, yet there is little understanding of the reasons behind such developments, and perhaps worse, few applicable *field-ready* tools for practitioners to measure their impact on people within complex systems.

Fourth, the book presents a series of policy options as a way to verify our collective successes in a globalized and inclusive international tradespace through the strategic exercise of measuring effectiveness normed against organizational requirements *and* the priorities of war-affected citizens in post-conflict societies.

This book is not about metrics, indicators, benchmarks, or measures; nor does it delve into the scientific theories of analysis best suited to capture information in the field. It develops a discourse constructed from practitioner perspectives rather than offering a rigorous canvassing of scholarly opinion in this area of inquiry. The aim was to canvas those *working in* peace operations and crisis management rather than those *studying* these operations.

The international community has become preoccupied with measuring the effectiveness of its activities in war-affected environments.[25] This focus is partially motivated by a need to calculate the costs of these very expensive ventures; often activities have not been as successful as intended. Some stakeholders are interested in measuring the effectiveness of their work in places like Afghanistan; those stakeholders who witness the realities in the field are compelled to make the goals, plans, and systems of interventions more effective. Other stakeholders may be reticent to discover whether their military, policing, diplomatic, developmental and humanitarian activities are ineffectual – or worse, whether they have negative effects on citizens recovering from armed conflicts and other calamities.

The problem of measuring success is not a failure of poor indicators or metrics – as yeoman's work continues to be done on this front by organizations like USIP, UN, OECD-DAC, and NATO – but is partially caused by the worldview held by many working in the international system that there is an answer "out there" to explain what is going on in interventions. The answer, it is perennially believed, once found, will allow us to solve the problems of an insecure world.[26] This linear worldview may become an insurmountable obstacle towards relevant intervention policies and approaches and the further maturation of a common tradespace in which progress can be charted. An emerging epistemic community grapples with these difficult questions and contributes to the maturation of the shared processes and policies that connect the sectors in international interventions, confronting territoriality and allowing for increased trade-offs between sectors.

There is no right or best approach to intervention, and therefore no right approach to measuring success. To commit to one way, or a best way, undermines the validity of stakeholder approaches to alleviate the effects of war, and undermines making progress towards tenable peace. The *right metrics* or the *right way to measure* are not "out there" waiting to be discovered by military planners or humanitarian evaluators. There are only better ways to think, and this is what matters in measuring peace operations and civilian crisis management.

Measuring what matters – our *worldviews* – informs our approaches, our policies, and the operational environment. While my friend Mike Pryce would say "military *planning* becomes a way of thinking," I contend that "understanding *thinking* becomes a way of planning" (therefore, measuring). The new complex environment seeks our understanding and a quantum leap of faith – not our metrics – to generate the urgent forward momentum required to measure sustainable results. Leadership may be invaluable in shedding outdated thinking and assuming new thinking appropriate to the complex environment. Only by understanding our worldviews and concomitant failures and successes will we be able to swiftly adopt the necessary sea change required in the race to strengthen weakened states, prevent bloodier violence, and promote tenable peace in our interconnected, complex world.

Then, and only then, will the international community have come of age.

Notes

[1] As a reader, you are invited into this ambiguous tradespace, where there may be more questions than answers and more challenges than solutions. However, this book is a guide to navigating the interconnected tradespace in a way that is meaningful to measuring the interventions that occur there.

[2] Dana Eyre, personal communication during the Civilian Crisis Management Initiatives 2007 Annual Conference, Brussels, Belgium.

[3] Charles T. Call also makes this point: "The burgeoning peacekeeping and peacebuilding industries cost billions of dollars each year, mostly in places where wars have ended but sustainable peace remains questionable" ("Knowing Peace When You See It," 174). The application of business language to the peace sector remains unacceptable to some stakeholders. Considering local recipients of intervention activities as *clients*, basing intervention decisions on *market demand*, and building *business cases* and *business plans* to encourage donors to support humanitarian projects have all been considered as fouling the often morally driven work undertaken for the betterment of humanity. However, as the 1990s ended and the twenty-first century began, it became clear that humanitarianism, development, peacekeeping, peace-building, and crisis management had indeed become *industries* generating their own economies. Governments began assessing their own international development programs through auditing and management tools; peacekeeping operations became influenced by monitoring and evaluation modalities; and humanitarian interventions were measured against performance indicators.

[4] Often, success and progress are used interchangeably in theory and field practice. As progress is inexorably considered as a *positive* rather than a *negative* progress, it is synonymous with *success*, which is commonly conceived of as the progressive realization of a worthy goal.

[5] Center on International Cooperation, Annual Review of Global Peace Operations (2006).

[6] Anonymous personal communication, 2008.
[7] Bonventre, "Monitoring and Evaluation," 72.
[8] I have been researching this topic since 2005. My firm was contracted by the Canadian Forces Joint Operations Group to develop a *measures of effectiveness system* for the Canadian provincial reconstruction teams (PRTs) conducting reconstruction activities in Afghanistan. The focus of the project was to develop a progress measurement framework for the 3D approach to reconstruction operations. The project included a network-centric command and control system with effects-based operations logic applicable to reconstruction efforts. To date there are no strategic guidelines in use for PRTs, and each participating nation uses this peace operations mechanism differently. Consequently, PRTs are ad hoc and experimental because they do not have clearly defined objectives and performance measures that assist in determining their accomplishments. See Office of the Special Inspector General for Iraq Reconstruction (OSIGIR), *Review of Effectiveness*, ix. Militaries are now doing humanitarian and development work through PRTs and often refer to their short-term projects as Quick Impact Projects (QIPs). Based on experience in Iraq, the US Army has even developed the Commander's Emergency Response Program (CERP), which is a fund that permits military leadership to conduct pseudo-development projects in the field as it sees fit. According to experts, the use of CERP has caused capacity-building problems across Iraq, enabling the US military to perform tasks that properly belong to local and provincial governments (ibid., ix). According to the interview participant at the UNDPKO, militaries are very good at QIPs, but as soon as NATO leaves Afghanistan, QIP projects will stop, allowing other power-brokers such as the Taliban to fill the void. Comparatively, OCHA is committed to long-term development and is not supportive of military PRTs and QIPs. The development sector thinks of the PRT approach to peace and security as informed by daily needs and short-term thinking (anonymous communication, 2008). A report released by the Office of the Special Inspector General for Iraq Reconstruction supports this perspective, recommending that PRTs should have clearly defined objectives and performance measures and clearly defined milestones for achieving these objectives, should link ways and means, and identify accountability frameworks (OSIGIR, *Review of Effectiveness*, x). The debate about the efficacy of peace and stability created through PRTs is ongoing.
[9] Barton et al., *In the Balance: Measuring Progress in Afghanistan*.
[10] Department for International Development (DFID), *Interim Strategy for Afghanistan*.
[11] ALNAP, *Evaluating Humanitarian Action*, 3.
[12] Cordesman, "Missing Metrics," 3.
[13] Ibid.
[14] Banerjee, "Development for Afghans," 6.
[15] Pawson and Tilley, *Realistic Evaluation*.
[16] Keeney, *Value-Focused Thinking*, 22.
[17] Steve Flemming, personal communication, 2008.
[18] Sawhill and Williamson, "Measuring," 1; also Meharg, *Helping Hands*, 129.
[19] Meharg, *Helping Hands*, 126.
[20] James Embrey, personal communication, 2008.

[21] Sawhill and Williamson, "Measuring," 1.
[22] Ibid.
[23] Jones et al., *Establishing Law and Order*.
[24] United States Government Accountability Office (USGOA), *Afghanistan Reconstruction*.
[25] The following examples highlight this point from a Canadian perspective. In September 2007, Canadian General Ray Henault hosted the NATO Military Committee Conference. The conference provided an opportunity to exchange ideas on sustaining and improving NATO's high readiness forces as well as developing better criteria to measure progress and effectiveness for operations, including Afghanistan. The conference examined strategic aspects of NATO operations and capabilities from a long-term perspective. In October 2007 Canada's Defence Minister Peter MacKay announced that Canada's commitment to NATO required the development of better criteria to measure progress and effectiveness for operations, especially in Afghanistan. The point was echoed in the Government of Canada's Manley Report on Afghanistan (2008), which suggested that to achieve success in theatre, the Canadian government needed to elevate coordination in Ottawa among Canadian departments and agencies engaged in Afghanistan for better efficiency and effectiveness. On 4 February 2008 the appointment of the Canadian commander to NATOs RC-S in Kandahar, Afghanistan, Major General Marc Lessard, was announced. Lessard suggested that his priorities would be coordinating or harmonizing operational aspects of governance and development within the overall security framework. And on 29 February 2008, NATO Secretary General Jaap de Hoop Scheffer maintained that continued discussions must be held on the effectiveness of the International Security Assistance Force operation in Afghanistan and what is needed to achieve success for NATO and the international community as a whole. Interestingly, these examples are representative of the international community's seizure upon this critical topic of the twenty-first century.
[26] A modification of David Hawkins's reference to the perennial quest for *the* answer, from *Power vs. Force*, 25.

Methodology, and How to Read This Book

This book bridges policy-making and field practice related to measuring the success of peace operations and crisis management. It is intended as a learning tool underpinned by applied research; it uses real opinions from real people to illuminate the modalities of measurement used by stakeholders. The worldview of stakeholders becomes apparent in the pages that follow and is useful in informing policy, processes, and future intervention activities.

This book is written for those interested in better understanding stakeholder approaches to measuring progress in peace operations and crisis management. More specifically, these people include:

- humanitarian practitioners
- military and defence stakeholders
- civilian police
- government representatives
- policy-makers
- private sector
- donors
- students of international relations (peacekeeping, crisis management, peace operations)
- members of war-affected publics

The research culminating in this book does not include all the mechanisms and tools available for measuring progress, nor were all persons working in this field contacted or interviewed. The research, however, did attempt to include a cross-section of multinational, multi-sectoral, and multi-stakeholder approaches to measuring progress in peace operations and crisis management.

The Pearson Peacekeeping Centre

Primary field research for this book was funded and conducted between 2007 and 2008 by Canada's Pearson Peacekeeping Centre (PPC), whose core funding comes from the Government of Canada as well as other international sources. The PPC is a not-for-profit, Canadian-based institution dedicated to improving the effectiveness of peace operations around the world. Using a multidisciplinary and activity-based learning approach, the PPC teaches and trains those who serve in conflict zones, including civilians, military personnel, and police officers. Since its inception in 1994, the PPC has trained over 17,000 people from more than 150 countries, and it has inspired the creation and development of similar training organizations in nearly one hundred countries. This track record has earned the centre an internationally distinguished reputation that brings credit to Canada from around the world. The PPC's mission to enhance the effectiveness of peace operations through training, research, and capacity building reflects the values that are cherished by Canadians, such as human rights, the rule of law, international stability, collective security, and diplomatic primacy. The PPC's highly capable staff, active alumni, and community of facilitators is composed of academics, senior military and police officers, humanitarian experts, and diplomats and has attracted an impressive roster of international clients such as NATO, the UN Department of Peacekeeping Operations, the Canadian Government, the German Ministry of Defence, and the Inter-American Defence College.

To keep pace with the constantly evolving field of contemporary peace operations, the centre works diligently to identify, analyze, and incorporate emerging trends and best practices into its learning products. It conducts applied research in the peace and security domain through primary field research, seminars, high-level consultations, and international conferences, and by incorporating a diverse array of interdisciplinary perspectives including anthropology, cultural geography, ethics, history, conflict analysis, and economics. The centre has a dedicated team of generalist researchers with a wide breadth of experience, so that they can examine research materials with a multi-faceted lens. This allows the PPC to provide a neutral space for dialogue – a safe space where difficult questions about peace and security can be posed and unpacked. Our research team regularly collaborates with other academic institutions, policy-makers, international organizations, and development groups to ensure that the PPC remains at the leading edge of new developments in the peace operations community.

The PPC is currently unique within the peacekeeping community of practice because it is the only known institution with a 75 percent female staff representation, making Canada a world leader in supporting the only female-led peacekeeping organization in the world and fulfilling some requirements outlined in United Nations Security Council Resolution 1325 on women, peace, and security.

Methodology

Interviews

Interviews were the primary source of information in support of this book. The purpose of the interviews was to identify the realities of measuring progress as understood by the people who work in peace operations and crisis management, including those who live in war-affected areas long after the end of operations.

Three series of interviews took place. The first set (twenty-nine) took place in Bosnia-Herzegovina in March 2007 using a research team. The second set (twenty-one) took place in Belgium, France, England, and Norway from February to March 2008 using a research team. The third set (thirty) were carried out in Canada and the United States (or via telephone to the United States) from April to November 2008 by the lead researcher. In total, eighty interviews of key elites were completed in nine countries.

Semi-structured interview methods were used, based upon a series of questions intended as a starting point for each interview. Participants were provided with the summary of interview questions a few days prior to the interview. The summary of interview questions can be found in Appendix A. The actual questions varied between interview participants at the discretion of the interviewer(s) in order to address the issues and topics most relevant to the participant. Some interviews focused on particular practitioners' experiences while others were more technical in nature.

The interview process was somewhat constrained by time and limited resources; however, the interest level in the topic of measuring effectiveness proved to be a high priority, and therefore most people accepted our invitations to participate in an interview in support of the project.

Data Collection

There were two different tracks for data collection. The first was a result of the interviews. As individual participants referred to what they considered to be important reports, studies, evaluations, lessons learned, books, criteria, principles, and standards, these were then pursued and included in the study. The second track was a general literature search, especially on stakeholder approaches to measuring their activities in peace operations and crisis management and relevant theory in support of this activity.

Book Organization

The first section of the book is a broad examination of who is involved in measuring intervention activities, what they are measuring, and why they are measuring in these ways. Chapter 1 examines the "state of play" in the field of measuring in peace operations and crisis management, along with some of the terminology and definitions commonly used in the field. Chapter 2 examines theories of intervention that support various mechanisms and tools. Chapter 3 reviews the language of measuring, while chapter 4 offers an examination of some of the existing mechanisms, tools, projects, and databases of indicators, systems, and standards for measuring what matters. Chapter 5 offers narratives from those who measure, and also from locals who judge effectiveness and success of international interventions with a different lens.

The second section reviews stakeholder approaches to measuring through a series of vignettes by eight stakeholders involved in measuring intervention activities. The vignettes in chapters 6 to 13 are learning tools that examine worldviews, modalities, and discourse through the examination of field realities. Understanding the approaches presented is critical to understanding the political realities of peace operations and crisis management; because such realities effect the currency and traction of policy, these vignettes are intended to generate knowledge that can counterpoint the scholarly literature and theory in this field of inquiry. Contributors include Rory Keane, John Borton, Keith Hauk, Stephen Mariano, Stuart Gordon, David Chuter, Emery Brusset, Kristiina Rintakoski, and Jake Sherman. (For more information on the contributing authors, please refer to the last pages of this book.) Chapter 14 concludes the vignettes by summarizing the lessons, best practices, and realities in "executive summary" style for policy-makers and practitioners. This chapter also identifies policy options for the stakeholders involved in peace operations and crisis management divined from the previous chapters and vignettes. In essence, this chapter identifies what others need to know about alternate ways of thinking about progress, effectiveness, and success of intervention activities.

The third and final section of the book presents lessons learned and best practices that could inform the next steps of measuring peace operations and crisis management in the comprehensive (and complex) present environment. Chapter 15 discusses the environment in which intervention activities are occurring and focuses on the theory of the comprehensive approach and its practicalities that are intended to increase the effectiveness, progress, and success of our activities in such environments. This chapter aims to distinguish when comprehensive measuring could make a difference, and when it should not be employed in peace operations and crisis management. Chapter 16 examines multi-sectoral best practices and next steps in measuring what matters in peace operations and crisis management. The conclusion frames a comprehensive approach to measuring what matters. Some practical distinctions for practitioners are made to serve those involved in intervention activities in understanding the other stakeholders involved in peace operations and crisis management.

Supported Learning

This book and its supporting research are an integral part of the measures of effectiveness *handbook* and *training module* available through the Pearson Peacekeeping Centre at www.peaceoperations.org. Measuring is a practical process, dependent upon various philosophies, concepts, theories, and worldviews, and the handbook and training module become the practical leaning tools through which this process can be better understood. These tools are intended for those thinking and working in this area, and those interested in learning more about how other stakeholders manage this process to improve their interventions in war-affected environments.

A website of additional links is available at www.peaceoperations.org/measuring. It includes a compendium of the mechanisms, tools, and documents listed in this book.

Online Applied Research Cluster

The Pearson Peacekeeping Centre has set-up an online applied research cluster workspace to advance the field of inquiry of measuring effectiveness, success, and progress. This workspace is used by practitioners, scholars, and policy-makers like you for networking, learning, and engaging with other practitioners who are advancing the field of measuring, monitoring, and evaluating international interventions.

You can participate in this members-only workspace by invitation only. If you would like to participate, send an email request for an invitation to the Huddle workspace:
smeharg@peaceoperations.org

https://my.huddle.net/workspace/4750624

PART I

Worldviews and Paradigm Blindness

CHAPTER 1

Trade-Offs and Play Spaces

> We need to know how "social order" is possible to better understand our worldviews, concepts, theories, and principles.[1]

Weltanschauung: *Weltan*-what?

Weltanschauung is the German term for worldview. It is understood as a framework of ideas, systems of knowledge and beliefs through which individuals interpret the world and interact with it. It is a *wide world* perception understood from the perspective of an individual, group, community, or professional/stakeholder sector, including cultures, subcultures, religions, communities of practice, ethnic groups, political and ideological groups, and even *imagined communities*.[2] The particular view of the world makes activities, experiences, and circumstances meaningful to those who hold it. Different *weltanschauungen* exist in the world's diverse cultures. Although *weltanschuuungen* are considered as mental models, philosophies, or ideologies, they are more than that. They are interactive, reflexive frameworks that allow those who hold them to interact with their environment in a way meaningful to them and to their community of practice.

How stakeholders *imagine* their work informs their contextual perspectives. How we view the world is how the world responds to us. We are in a reflexive relationship with our world: how *we* see it is how it *is*. Stakeholders function in the context they see and create – they are all functioning in different worlds. This concept is useful in understanding why stakeholders intervene in crises, and why they measure their successes in particular ways. Stakeholders translate their worldviews into practice differently, and this difference can cause much aggravation, even hatred and fear, among and between stakeholders and sectors working towards the attainment of peace and security within an increasingly globalized, yet sovereignty-constricted international community.

Western Worldviews

Rudyard Kipling's 1899 poem "White Man's Burden" presents a Eurocentric view of the world in which non-European cultures are seen as childlike in comparison with the high culture and civilized developments of Europe.[3] Kipling critiques a view that suggests that white people have an obligation to promote cultural development in underdeveloped regions and to support this development through the promotion and provision of western healthcare, education, government systems, and policies, amongst others. The White Man's Burden, informed by Christian notions of charity, has been viewed in its interpretations as racist and imperialistic or, alternatively, philanthropic. In Christian theology, charity is love and is the greatest of virtues. Love is understood as unlimited kindness to all people, which exemplifies the human spirit and therefore reflects the nature of God. This type of love resides in the will rather than in the emotions and informs Christian attitudes of assisting those less fortunate. The notion of charity is reciprocal in nature; it includes the love of self as well as the love of one's neighbour. It is translated into the principle of the Golden Rule: Do unto others as you would have them do unto you.

The idea of imposing western systems upon regions that have their own traditional ways has long been debated by those who believe that it is a duty to do so, and those who believe it to be abhorrent to impose such ways. Charitable volunteerism and giving are considered as obligations for those more fortunate, and are loaded with symbolism informing motives in intervention activities.

Interventions by the West, specifically the North Atlantic Treaty Organisation (NATO), the United Nations (UN), and other collective security coalitions, are criticized as being neo-colonial in nature. Colonialism is the extension of a state's sovereignty over another nation's territory, which historically has been exploited in ugly and greedy ways that have caused severe cultural, social, religious, economic, and political knock-on effects in the colonized state.[4] Colonizers are powerful hegemons that have tended to impose foreign systems, practices, and traditions upon those they perceive as underdeveloped and even primitive. Colonial hangovers tend not to be easily shaken off in the aftermath of the departure of the colonial power. Whether neo-colonialism has been veiled by peace operations and crisis management activities is debatable – however, those who experience contemporary interventions such as educated Bosnians did during the 1990s argue that intervention is indeed a form of neo-colonialism. Although this may not be what the interveners intended, this is how it was perceived. One could say that neo-colonialism, veiled as peace operations, does not have the obligations that historic colonialism had to its so-called subjects: provision of medical care, education (even though it was a foreign education imposed through a new language), and religion (even though it was an imposed God). Such obligations rarely came with a tolerance of vernacular practices, languages, traditions, and rights; in fact, the mindset of the colonizer was to relieve people of these vernacular ways. Contemporary intervention activities suggest that there remains a high level of intolerance for local practices and systems such as non-western forms of governance and leadership.

Although the idea of cultural imperialism appears as an outdated modality informing contemporary interventions, it is very much a part of the *weltanschauung* of those intervening in war-affected environments through peace operations and crisis management mechanisms. Crises – whether human made or natural – and resulting interventions allow an entry point into a perceived underdeveloped or broken system that the West is intolerant of (otherwise understood as a failed, failing, or fragile state). This is the case in Afghanistan and Iraq, where the international community imposed westernized and centralized government structures and democratic practices where none existed prior to invasion in 2001 and 2003. The charitable worldview informs intervention and is coupled with geopolitical and economic interests of the twenty-first century hegemons.

The opportunities and constraints of sovereignty have come to the fore in the environment of globalization. The 1648 Treaty of Westphalia created an international system whereby states became the central unit of analysis. A state is a political organization of society made up of the institutions of government. The state is a form of human association distinguished by its purpose, the establishment of order and security; its methods, the laws, and their enforcement; its territory, the area of jurisdiction or geographic boundaries; recognition by other states; and finally, by its sovereignty.

Sovereignty is the effect of a state having absolute and final legal authority over all matters within its defined territory. A sovereign government is not accountable to any power outside of itself and has the authority to manage both foreign and domestic affairs. Sovereignty provides a buffer or barrier between states that keeps out intruders into the internal affairs of one another. In reality, sovereignty can and has been compromised because no state government has unrestricted and unrestrained power in either external or internal matters within contemporary international affairs. International factors such as economic globalization or armed conflict may be impossible for one state to control by itself. Furthermore, if a particular national government commits egregious crimes against its own citizens, the international community has occasionally intervened in that state's internal affairs for humanitarian purposes, as, for example, in Kosovo in the former Yugoslavia.

The international community has spent the past century agreeing on standards of the human condition which states are bound to uphold for their people. Values such as the *rule of law* and *human rights* are espoused as essential elements in secure, stable, and prosperous states and are evidenced by universal characteristics that include democratic elections, transparent courts and corrections systems, absence of ethnic, racial and religious persecution, and various freedoms such as those of movement, speech, and religious practices. Emerging universal standards are also evidenced by access to health care, education, transportation, and technology and are contributing to the continued development of the doctrine of the international community. The absence of these standards of quality of life, coupled with egregious human rights violations, is an impetus for intervention based on post-Westphalian theory espoused by most members of the international community. However, these reasons do not necessarily cause powerful hegemons – such as China or the US – to intervene. Rather than an historic colonial ideology that foregrounds the values of the colonizer as superior to those of a people under colonization, the interconnected and interrelated international community of states sees the values it subscribes to as those that connect all peoples – universal rights and freedoms. This evolving doctrine, as presented in 1999 by Tony Blair, the former British prime minister, is built upon a foundation of theory that includes the White Man's Burden, Christian charity, and cultural imperialism, but it moves considerably beyond these points of reference and advances to include the collection of states that make up the international community. Proponents of the doctrine of the international community suggest that it is difficult to argue against the ideology that all people deserve the right to live without want and deserve to have their rights protected so that they remain outside of the realm of persecution and fear so common in environments experiencing contemporary armed conflict. The doctrine of the international community is *value imperialism* as a modality of intervention in the twenty-first century, which has progressed beyond the cultural imperialism of yesterday. To promote the inclusion of failing states into the international community by imposing a set of commonly held universal rights and freedoms upon their systems, politics, economies, strategies, and territories provides benefit to those who support this ideology. Adopting wayward countries into the sisterhood of states moving towards peace and security writ large transcends *interests* and moves towards shaping our environments with the *application* – rather than the *imposition* – of universal standards.

Just War theory is the essence of the doctrine of the international community that subscribes to the values of an interconnected and interdependent world. Just War theory offers a framework in which war and use of force can be justified upon moral grounds. Just War is not based upon territorial ambitions but on values. Although not directly informing peace operations and crisis management, Just War suggests that if the international community – or some other collective security organization – is threatened by an aggressor, the right to engage in warfare only exists if the damage being inflicted by the aggressor is lasting, grave, and certain; if other means, such as diplomacy, have failed; if the use of arms is not more destructive than the good intended; and if success against the aggressor(s) is inevitable.

Building upon notions of increased connections and dependencies between and among states, the human security paradigm has provided a lens through which to understand global vulnerabilities at a different scale from that of traditional national security hinged upon state sovereignty. The human security thesis counts the lowest global denominator – the individual – as the most important in understanding security as a form of peace and stability. The development of human security itself was created from a convergence of research fields interested in the development-security nexus, which argued that the bottom of Abraham Maslow's hierarchy of needs (Figure 3) is the place to consider development and security as linked concepts leading towards self-actualization at the top of the hierarchy.

Human security, with its best-known tenets of "freedom from fear" and "freedom from want," informs some level of every peace operation and crisis to be managed. The value of human security is the foundation of the principle to protect when such securities are undermined by state authority. The Responsibility to Protect, developed in 2001, is policy

FIGURE 3
Abraham Maslow's Hierarchy of Needs

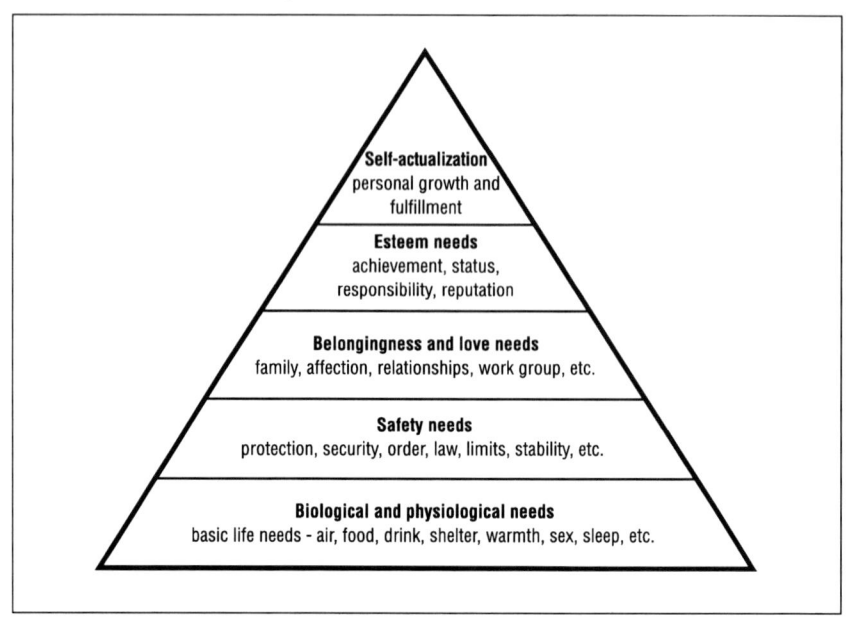

```
                    /\
                   /  \
                  / Self-actualization \
                 /  personal growth and  \
                /      fulfillment        \
               /----------------------------\
              /       Esteem needs           \
             /     achievement, status,       \
            /    responsibility, reputation    \
           /------------------------------------\
          /      Belongingness and love needs    \
         /  family, affection, relationships,     \
        /            work group, etc.              \
       /--------------------------------------------\
      /               Safety needs                   \
     /   protection, security, order, law, limits,    \
    /                  stability, etc.                 \
   /----------------------------------------------------\
  /         Biological and physiological needs           \
 /   basic life needs - air, food, drink, shelter,        \
/              warmth, sex, sleep, etc.                    \
--------------------------------------------------------------
```

guidance regarding interventions undertaken for humanitarian reasons. In the event that a state is not evidencing the values shared by the international community, the guidance argues that there is a moral right to intervene to provide protection to those assaulted by egregious violations. This is a *normative* approach to intervening in state affairs – what *should* be done by the international community, namely the United Nations – and is not necessarily widely supported in practice, because, among other reasons, it is seen as an expression of universal morality, which, it is argued, does not exist.[5]

Examples of Just War theory and Human Security theory illustrate the worldviews brought into war-affected environments. These are two examples of the different assumptions driving intervention activities.

The existing doctrine of the international community can offer guidance to stakeholders for engaging across sectors within a common *tradespace*. Tradespaces are those spaces bounded by shared processes among agents within that space; thus the term becomes relevant to international interventions as we collectively seek to maximize effectiveness, progress, and success of activities leading to sustainable peace.

Shared approaches and processes do not necessarily mean agreement upon common objectives or *unity of effort* – as is so often put forward by military thinkers. Rather, they may mean a lateral approach to decision-making informed by commonalities including theory and language. Lateral sharing among sectors may increase a *unity of understanding* between stakeholders.

The international community increasingly is responding to crises involving failing, failed, and post-conflict states, natural disasters, and complex emergencies. Peace operations and civilian crisis management are activities that aim to do more than suspend hostilities to create a secure environment in which longer-term development initiatives can take hold. These operations offer a spectrum of military, economic, political, and cultural activities that result in the stability in a region.

Peace operations and civilian crisis management are catch-all phrases that include the traditional remit of peacekeeping, as well as more contemporary variations on this theme such as post-conflict and post-disaster reconstruction, state building, peace building, transitional operations, reconstruction and stabilization operations, humanitarianism, and short-term development interventions.

Along with these variations in operations has come a cadre of different goals and objectives, which in turn has caused momentum for measuring. The impetus to measure the effectiveness of such activities – to discover whether activities are fiscally sound and bring about their intended effects – is of importance to most principal stakeholders. The underlying message suggests that there is a prevalent way of thinking that, like an audit, attributes ineffectiveness to wasteful spending and misallocation of funds.

The Active Learning Network for Accountability and Performance in Humanitarian Action (ALNAP) notes three major constraints for humanitarians that are applicable to the other stakeholders involved in peace operations and crisis management.[6] Conflicts polarize perspectives so that the same events are often subject to different interpretations, reducing the objectivity of evaluations. Data and information are difficult to access in many crisis situations. High staff turnover and short rotations can prevent consistent assessment of progress. Most sectors involved in intervention have large turnovers of staff; even militaries are challenged by the six-month rotational period in the theatre, which detracts from consistent data collection and internal information sharing. The exception to this limit would be civilian police – especially high-ranking police – deployed on peace operations and other international missions for up to two years. Their rotational period is much longer than their military counterparts, thus improving their capacity to gather data consistently and to share information. Post-conflict interventions, perhaps most relevant to aid and assistance agencies, typically occur in extremely disordered conditions that lead to rapid changes in circumstances, mandates, and conflict dynamics, all rendering evaluation difficult.[7]

A major challenge posed to those reporting on progress is the relative ease with which tangible things can be counted, measured, and confirmed, whereas intangibles such as attitudinal shifts, behavioural changes, and governance are not easily corroborated (Table 1). Although often the more important elements of tenable peace and security, these intangible aspects of intervention activities are not easily documented because of the constraints of mechanisms and tools used for measuring. Numbers of buildings reconstructed, kilometres of roads refurbished, and other tangible, quantitative results are more easily relayed.

TABLE 1
The Results Dichotomy

Tangible Results	Intangible Results
Easy to measure	Difficult to measure
Easy to see	Difficult to see
Easy to calculate	Difficult to calculate
Incontrovertible	Controvertible

Within other sectors involved in peace operations and civilian crisis management, the challenges go beyond standardization and are inhibited by lack of information-sharing and by stove-piped departments and agencies reporting progress using different reporting mechanisms, standards for evaluation, and metrics and indicators. Organizations complete reports on activities for donors funding such activities; evaluations are a different method of measuring processes and impacts.

The absence of relevant and useful measuring systems for stakeholders to assess their intervention activities makes it impossible to determine if the intended and unintended effects are being caused by their activities and to what standard. Stakeholders attempting to improve reporting mechanisms understand that such improvements must adequately address the two challenges of measuring what matters: financial efficiency and intervention efficacy.

Members of the international community – namely, the United States and the United Kingdom as well as the World Bank and the ICRC – have experienced the political fallout of failed peace operations and civilian crisis management activities. Inadequate frameworks to measure progress of intervention activities have translated into a political hot pursuit to create better metrics, indicators, databases, matrices, audits, and reporting mechanisms. As early as 2003 there was a shift towards better assessment of progress to provide a basis for planning future crisis interventions. This shift was observed in the United Nations, the World Bank, Britain, Canada, the United States, NATO, and the European Union.

The impetus in the United States is attributed to overspending and fund misappropriation in Iraq during the occupation. Government watchdogs called for increased accountability requirements to analyze the progress and management of services and funds, and to identify major factors obstructing advancement of interests in war-torn environments and the achievement of policy objectives. In March 2008 the Agency Co-ordinating Body for Afghan Relief (ACBAR) published a report stating that the "international aid effort in Afghanistan is in large part 'wasteful and ineffective,' with as much as 40 percent of funds spent going back to donor countries in corporate profits and consultant salaries."[8] Other challenges include the short lead time for humanitarian action in response to human or natural disasters. These types of intervention lack objective statements and indicators in planning documents against which evaluations later occur. Other sectors such as military, civilian police, and development agencies have more lead time in planning and implementing interventions in crisis environments and should have clearer plans and implementation strategies. Think tanks and government reports have recommended the establishment of performance management plans and evaluation systems as well as better metrics and indicators, comparable to other international standardization processes such as international auditing practices or International Standardization Organisation (ISO) business management.

Military Perspectives

Having the ability to measure the effectiveness of something gives the illusion of control over it. Western militaries put emphasis on designing metrics for their operations in order to control those operations. Military planners put much effort into designing measures of effectiveness and getting the metrics *right*, with less development of the capacity to measure the *right* phenomenon. If they have the metrics right, logic suggests that they must be doing the right activities. A presentation by Colonel Denis Thompson before he was to head up the Canadian Forces in

Kandahar, Afghanistan (2008), highlights this perspective. Col Thompson maintained that measures of effectiveness were the military command tool that he planned to use to address three distinctions in the field: (1) *Local perceptions*, mapped against human geography; (2) *Nature and intensity of security incidents*, measured by operational research of existing data to identify trends; and (3) *Measuring results*[9] of useful reconstruction delivered, underpinned by the economic status of ordinary people. From his presentation, and perhaps prior to the reality of field operations affecting his perspective, Col Thompson was confident that measuring the effectiveness in these three areas would offer him a useful command tool to make alterations to operations as required in order to create the biggest impact for both Afghans and Canadians. Whether or not this was his field experience is yet to be determined; however, it is clear from his presentation that militaries share the worldview of their ability to control their environment.

According to Lieutenant General David Leakey, director general of the European Union Military Staff in the Council of the European Union, Brussels, there is no benefit from a humanitarian practitioner's perspective to measuring outcomes, because activities are part of the peace industry. To do a good job would mean being out of a job, which is not the purpose of the peace industry. Yet the peace industry is, theoretically, an industry that is supposed to work itself out of a job. Locally based international community (IC) workers are also in this category; they want their IC organizations to stay in Bosnia-Herzegovina in order to stay employed, because they have no intention of going to Afghanistan or the next hot spot in which they would be asked to work for their IC organization. According to Leakey, militaries have more intention to measure than humanitarians, but in his opinion no one wants to actually measure their own activity effectiveness except the locals and constituent publics involved.

Perhaps the western military worldview is shifting, based on the changing context of intervention activities. Col Eugene V. Bonventre, US Air Force, suggests that the motive behind US Department of Defense (DoD) involvement in humanitarian assistance (HA) through the Overseas Humanitarian, Disaster and Civic Aid (OHDACA) programs is "to mitigate the effects of natural and man-made disasters, to shape the environment in which DoD operates by providing access to critical areas and by influencing civilian populations, and to improve the capacity of vulnerable nations to better prepare for disasters."[10] As we will see, this type of pseudo-humanitarianism is counter to the humanitarian worldview and creates increased tensions between the sectors involved in peace operations and crisis management.

Humanitarian Perspectives

> It is not only what we do, but also what we do not do, for which we are accountable.[11]

As early as the 1960s, communities of practice were formed in the various sectors involved in disaster relief and international peacekeeping efforts.[12] In time, humanitarianism developed core principles to inform its work. The principles for humanitarian action fall into three scales: primary, secondary, and tertiary.

Primary Principles

Humanity: Upholding the right of all persons to receive and give assistance.

Impartiality: Providing humanitarian assistance in proportion to need and with respect to urgency, without discrimination based upon gender, age, race, impairment, ethnicity, and nationality or by political, religious, cultural, or organizational affiliation.

Secondary Principles

Informed Consent: Ensuring that the intended beneficiaries, or their representatives, understand and agree with the proposed humanitarian action and its implications.

Duty of Care: Ensuring that humanitarian assistance meets or exceeds recognized minimum standards pertaining to the well-being of disaster survivors.

Witness: Reporting on policies or practices that affect the well-being of disaster survivors.

Tertiary Principles

Transparency: Ensuring that all relevant information is communicated to intended beneficiaries or their representatives and other specified parties.

Independence: Acting under the authority of the governing body for the agency and in pursuit of the agency's mandate.

Neutrality: Refraining from giving material or political support to parties to an armed conflict.

Complementarity: Operating as a responsible member of the humanitarian assistance community.

Humanitarian principles are a "framework of principles derived from International Humanitarian Law which is intended to guide and position humanitarian agencies in assisting and protecting those outside the limits of war in ways that are both ethical and practical, that also places obligations onto parties to the conflict and attempts to regulate the conduct of a conflict."[13] According to *the Humanitarian Accountability Partnership* (HAP), "the essence of humanitarianism is about acting upon the moral obligation to express solidarity with those living in distress and suffering, even in situations when an ideal response is impossible. On many occasions the best possible humanitarian action may be incomplete but still worthwhile."[14] Militaries involved in humanitarianism, however, seek to shape the environment in which they operate by influencing civilian populations and providing access to critical areas.[15] The humanitarian sector is motivated to adhere to primary, secondary and tertiary *principles*, while western militaries are motivated to achieve primary, secondary and tertiary *effects* through their effects-based approach to operations (Figure 4). Higher order or higher level principles are the primary principles, while lower level principles are considered to be tertiary.

There remains an assumption in many countries that humanitarian aid and disaster relief is essentially *charitable* work, and therefore anything that is done in the name of helping victims is acceptable, regardless of unintended consequences or knock-on effects of such work. The belief

FIGURE 4
A Cross-Sector Comparison of Principles and Effects

Humanitarian Sector

Primary principles: Humanity, impartiality

Secondary principles: Consent, duty of care, and witness

Tertiary principles: Independence, transparency, neutrality, and complementarity

Security and Defence Sector

Primary effects: Establish security

Secondary effects: Influence behaviours, attitudes

Tertiary effects: Win hearts and minds, shape environment that humanitarian volunteerism is immune to codes and standards still clings to disaster relief work. According to the International Federation of Red Cross and Red Crescent Societies, "All NGOs, big and small, are susceptible to ... internal and external pressures. And as NGOs are asked to do more, and the incidence of complex disasters involving natural, economic, and often military factors increases, the need for some sort of basic professional code becomes more and more pressing.[16] The Code of Conduct for the International Red Cross and Red Crescent Movement and NGOs in Disaster Relief (Code of Conduct) was developed in 1994 by eight of the world's largest disaster response agencies in response to the burgeoning community of NGOs involved in disaster relief.[17]

The Code of Conduct is voluntary and self-policing. It outlines ten principles for NGOs to adhere to in disaster response work. It also sets out the relationships that agencies working in human-made and natural disasters should seek with donor governments, host governments, and the UN system. The "Principle Commitments" are:

1. The Humanitarian imperative comes first.

2. Aid is given regardless of the race, creed or nationality of the recipients and without adverse distinction of any kind. Aid priorities are calculated on the basis of need alone.

3. Aid will not be used to further a particular political or religious standpoint.

4. We shall endeavour not to act as instruments of government foreign policy.

5. We shall respect culture and custom.

6. We shall attempt to build disaster response on local capacities.

7. Ways shall be found to involve programme beneficiaries in the management of relief aid.

8. Relief aid must strive to reduce future vulnerabilities to disaster as well as meeting basic needs.

9. We hold ourselves accountable to both those we seek to assist and those from whom we accept resources.

10. In our information, publicity and advertising activities, we shall recognise disaster victims as dignified human beings, not hopeless objects.[18]

The Organisation for Economic Development Co-Operations and Development Assistance Committee (OECD-DAC) Criteria serve as a compass for many interventionists and evaluators. As outlined by the

Nordic Consulting Group and Channel Research in a 2008 report, the criteria are:

Relevance: concerned with assessing whether a project is in line with local needs and priorities, as well as donor policy (or policies).

Appropriateness: the tailoring of humanitarian activities to local needs, increasing ownership, accountability and cost-effectiveness.

Effectiveness: measures the extent to which an activity achieves its purpose or whether this can be expected to happen on the basis of the outputs.

Efficiency: measures the outputs, both qualitative and quantitative, achieved as a result of inputs. This generally requires comparing alternative approaches to achieving an output, to see whether the most efficient approach has been used.

Connectedness: refers to the need to ensure that activities of a short-term emergency nature are carried out in a context that takes longer-term and interconnected problems into account.

Coherence: the need to assess security, development, trade and military policies as well as humanitarian policies, to ensure that there is consistency and, in particular, that all policies take into account humanitarian and human-rights considerations.

Coverage: the need to reach major population groups facing life-threatening suffering wherever they are.

Impact: looks at the wider effects of a project – social, economic, technical and environmental – on individuals, gender- and age-groups, communities and institutions. Impacts can be intended and unintended, positive and negative, macro (sector) and micro (household).

These principles heavily influence the humanitarian sector's way of approaching interventions too.

Prior to the 1990s, the notion of evaluation and results-based management methods was not mainstreamed discourse within the humanitarian system of stakeholders. According to Lara Olson, one of the lead researchers on the RPP project, "We discovered that there were no formalized mechanisms for capturing lessons learned or best practices from NGOs engaged in peace work broadly defined by the NGO humanitarian sector."[19] According to John Borton, founder of ALNAP, the humanitarian sector lacks a mechanism capable of providing an overall assessment of its performance. Since the mid-1990s, the humanitarian sector has seen a range of quality and accountability initiatives. As Borton suggests, standards, codes, and professional norms have been developed relating to particular aspects or thematic issues within the humanitarian sector.[20] Some of these developments have rallied around coordination of action and timeliness of delivery, and both Olson and Borton agree that the wider peace-building and humanitarian sectors have become increasingly systematized, self-aware, and self-critical since the early 1990s. This transformation towards a sector-wide logic has changed the face of humanitarianism. With this change has also come more thoughtful approaches to measuring the effectiveness, progress, and success of humanitarian activities within the operational environment of peace operations and crisis management and the significance of impact upon local populations.

Local Perspectives

Most sectors have been slow to acknowledge the importance of the views and opinions of its *clients* – the populations affected by conflicts and natural disasters. The millions of people affected by contemporary armed conflicts and large-scale crises such as earthquakes, famines, and mass population movements are referred to in many different ways as *intervention stakeholders*. There have been shifts in some sectors that move the so-called *beneficiaries* or *affected populations* to the centre of the decision-making and implementation process, yet few studies seek to understand their unique worldviews and how these impact the effectiveness and success of operations.

Beneficiaries (also referred to as *primary stakeholders*[21]) are the end-users of an activity – those who supposedly derive benefit from an intervention. Beneficiaries are the affected population or the group who are to benefit directly from the assistance or services provided by others; they are those considered to derive benefit from a program. The term beneficiary, mainly used by the humanitarian sector, is loaded; it suggests that those receiving aid and assistance derive positive benefits from intervention activities and does not consider the possible negative consequences of aid and assistance. Military personnel typically refer to this group as *locals*. *Recipients*, by comparison, are the sub-agencies or NGOs involved in dispersing humanitarian aid and assistance. This term is mainly employed by the humanitarian sector but is adopted by other sectors in referring to those whom they are directly assisting. *Clients* generally refers to the end-users of a program, service, policy, or product. The client is the same as the recipient/beneficiary. The term *recipient populations* refers to plural, heterogeneous publics. Other modalities that categorize citizens and are informed by stakeholder worldviews include *us and them, indigenous people, victims, insurgents, terrorists, affected people, host nation, end-users,* and *primary stakeholders*.

As agents of change, war-affected people have much to contribute to the success of interventions. In an interview, Glenn MacPhail, retired member of the Canadian Royal Mounted Police, said that policing success and progress is constantly evaluated by locals. "They will tell you if they don't like something. Unfortunately police do not sit and listen to locals. Some will say 'Since I was on the drug file in Toronto, I know about drugs, therefore I will do the same thing here in Bosnia.'" Police would be well served to ask questions of the locals, MacPhail suggests, because "it is better if police are not experts, because they become better listeners. In Bosnia before the war, Yugoslav police had four years of police high school, then four years of police university, compared to our six months of training! And we are trying to tell them what to do! We need to appreciate local systems."[22]

According to evaluation expert Emery Brusset, evaluations need to be shared with the population that was a part of an evaluated intervention project – especially in peace building, where the recipient communities are the focus of evaluation.[23] Mary Kaldor's London-based Human Security Project (HSP) suggests that this gap is the *perspective deficit*. The HSP realized that although many internal assessments were completed – peer reviewed and otherwise – among mission stakeholders in war-torn environments, there were no assessments related to the locals *by* the locals. When assessments, reporting, and evaluation are completed, most locals never have a chance to review the reports. Recipients need to have access to hard copies of evaluation documents, as they typically have no Internet access and cannot access evaluations electronically.[24]

Studies have been completed on perceptions of war-affected populations experiencing a peacekeeping operation, such as the external study completed in 2005 by BERCI International in the Democratic Republic of the Congo. This report was part of a larger study commissioned by the Peacekeeping Best Practices Section of the Department of Peacekeeping Operations as part of a wider effort to measure public opinion in populations where UN peacekeeping operations are based.[25] In addition, chapter 5 of this book highlights Bosnian perspectives on the peace operation and subsequent crisis management that population experienced in the mid-1990s.

Conclusion

Worldviews – *weltanschauungen* – become important elements in understanding the environment in which we are intervening. They inform the problems we choose, the questions we ask, and the measures we establish to verify our activities. The security and defence sector sees the intervention theatre as controllable and securable; humanitarians see it as impartial, neutral, and independent; the development sector could see it as a long-term investment that leads to sustainable peace and prosperity; primary stakeholders and locals may see it as war-ravaged, debilitating, and traumatic. All may be correct.

Summary Points

- Worldviews are useful ways to understand why stakeholders intervene in crises and why they measure their successes in a particular way. Stakeholders translate their worldviews into practice differently, which can cause misunderstandings among sectors working towards the attainment of peace and security.

- The existing doctrine of the international community can offer stakeholders guidance for engaging across sectors within a common *tradespace* – those spaces bounded by shared processes among agents within that space. Thus the term becomes relevant to interventions as the international community collectively seeks to maximize effectiveness, progress, and success of activities leading to sustainable peace.

- Tangible things can be counted, measured, and confirmed more easily than intangibles such as attitudinal shifts, behavioural changes, and good governance. Many of these intangible elements are often the more important contributors towards tenable peace and security; however, they are not easily reported on because of the constraints of measuring mechanisms better suited towards tangible things.

Notes

[1] Steve Flemming, personal communication, 2008.

[2] Benedict Anderson argues that a nation "is imagined because the members of even the smallest nation will never know most of their fellow-members, meet them, or even hear of them, yet in the minds of each lives the image of their communion" (*Imagined Communities*, 6). The same is true for most communities to which people subscribe.

[3] Kipling's now famous poem was first published in the British magazine *McClure's* in 1899 as a sardonic response to the American takeover of the Philippines after the Spanish-American War.

[4] Arguably, there may be some positive examples of colonization and their positive knock-on effects. Bosnia-Herzegovina, according to Valery Perry (personal communication, 2007), may fall into the quasi-protectorate bilateral category of an imperial power exercising control. Yet, so-called good examples may be in the eye of the beholder.

[5] David Chuter, personal communication, 2008.
[6] ALNAP, *Evaluating Humanitarian Action Using the OECD-DAC Criteria* (2006).
[7] Ibid.
[8] Boone, "World News: Afghan Aid," 2.
[9] Thompson understands "measuring results." See Cordesman, *Armed Nation Building*.
[10] Bonventre, "Monitoring and Evaluation," 66.
[11] Molière, French playwright, 1622–1673.
[12] The International Council of Voluntary Agencies (ICVA), founded in 1962, is a global advocating alliance of humanitarian and human rights NGOs for humanitarian action. ICVA provides a means for the collective body of its members to work together to effect change, and also assists members to improve their own work through access to initiatives and tools that help to increase quality and accountability.
[13] ALNAP, *Annual Review 2002*, 212.
[14] *HAP 2007 Standard in Humanitarian Accountability and Quality Management*, 6.
[15] Bonventre, "Monitoring and Evaluation," 66.
[16] IFRCRCS, *Code of Conduct*.
[17] Prior to 1994 there were large international outfits involved in disaster relief. These organizations had deep field experience and decades of professional development upon which to inform their work in war-affected areas. The conflicts in Rwanda were a trigger point for this relatively stable sector. Bloody images of conflicts in Bosnia, Rwanda, and Haiti spirited around the world by CNN and the Internet inspired a legion of fresh, immature, and unprepared NGOs to arrive in the same environments in which the larger international organizations were relieving the effects of the disasters. The commotion that ensued had never been experienced before. Misinformation, redundancies, and lack of standards resulted in inefficiencies, ineffectiveness, and chaos. Prior to this period no accepted body of professional standards or code of behaviour existed to guide the practice of disaster relief for those providing such relief.
[18] IFRCRCS *Code of Conduct*.
[19] Lara Olson, personal communication, 2008.
[20] Borton, "Inventory of the Principal Projects," 1.
[21] ALNAP, *Evaluating Humanitarian Action*, 19.
[22] Glenn MacPhail, personal communication, 2008.
[23] Brusset et al., "Collaborative Learning Projects."
[24] Kaldor, *Human Security*.
[25] BERCI International, *Peacekeeping Operations in the Democratic Republic of the Congo*.

CHAPTER 2

Theories of Intervention

> From time immemorial, man has tried to make sense of the enormous complexity and frequent unpredictability of human behaviour. A multitude of systems have been constructed to try to make that which is incomprehensible comprehensible. To "make sense" has ordinarily meant to be definable in terms that are linear – logical and rational.
>
> But the process, and therefore the experience, of life itself, is organic – that is to say, nonlinear by definition. This is the source of man's inescapable intellectual frustration.[1]

An examination of some of the theories of intervention can assist us in making sense of the complex conflict environment, which may in turn help to assuage some of the intellectual frustration caused by our collective approaches to these environments. This summary will support a deeper understanding of stakeholder *weltanschauungen* in peace operations and crisis management.

Development theory is a mixture of interdisciplinary social science approaches that consider how desirable societal or cultural change is best achieved. Development theory is informed by other schools, including modernization theory, dependency theory, worlds systems theory, state theory, and cognitive psychology theory. To begin, modernization theory says that development can be achieved by following the steps and methods taken by developed countries.[2] This theory applies a linear, sequential, structured model that suggests that an underdeveloped country must do the things that other countries have accomplished to be developed.

Specific things must be done to reach an end state. The perfect mixture, sequence, and structure must be discovered and applied to a developing nation in order to achieve development to international standards. Developed states (usually western) are considered as the catalysts for the development of countries through the implementation of various mechanisms. Modernization theorists understand that linear and sequential development strategies can be applied to bring developing nations onto so-called *equal footing* with developed nations at a rate much faster than the developed nations themselves took to achieve their own status.[3] This paradigm stems from Newtonian cause-and-effect, industrial-era thinking and does not consider the advent of information technologies; transformative change; interconnectedness of global structures such as economies, religions and politics; influence of organized crime and corruption; and exponential growth cycles that are the hallmarks of the information age of the twenty-first century. Conversely, *dependency theory* frames the relationship between developed and developing countries as relational, in that developed countries achieved their status on the backs of underdeveloped countries. One cannot exist without the other.

World systems theory argues that development and industrialization are not concomitant processes and can be – even should be – separated from one another. This separation allows for culturally appropriate internal growth to occur, rather than the development of inappropriate industry.

According to *state theory*, politics and economics are entwined and therefore individualize the timing and levels of development attained. Important to understanding stakeholder approaches, this theory offers that state stability is the key to development. When state institutions are stabilized – and the hallmarks of development are actualized – a country has the ability to develop along its own path.

Systems theory is an interdisciplinary field of science that studies the nature of complex systems. More specifically, it is a framework by which one can analyse and/or describe any group of objects that work in concert to produce some result. Systems theory comes out of 1920s biology science, which sought to explain the interrelatedness of organisms in ecosystems. Systems theory serves as a bridge for interdisciplinary dialogue between autonomous areas of study, as well as within the area of systems science itself.

The *change model*, developed by psychologist Kurt Lewin, is a helpful concept for understanding the forces that keep a system's behaviour stable.[4] This model is used by psychologists to better understand change among people, including extreme examples such as prisoners of war. Understanding international intervention activities through this model is useful because it suggests that when local forces that strive to maintain status quo in a war-affected environment and the people interested in seeking change are about equal, current behaviours are maintained. In this state, no change is adopted. There is a perpetuation of status quo behaviour and attitude – which can undermine the goals of intervention activities and the needs of war-affected people. If interventionists can modify the balance in their favour, less tension is created in local systems and people. It thus becomes easier for interventionists to implement planned change and therefore *transition towards transformation* in a society.

Change theory is distinct from *theory of change* (ToC). According to Edgar Schein, a professor of management at MIT, some aspects of Lewin's change theory applicable to cross-cultural learning and larger scale societal change have some application in peace operations and crisis management. Schein suggests that any important changes involve the examination of deep cultural and sub-cultural assumptions. However, from a psychological perspective, it is difficult to change cultural assumptions; therefore change may be better understood as learning. Considering change through the lens of learning allows for societies to change through enlarging and broadening rather than through the elimination or replacement of cultural elements. Change itself often means the outright elimination of a belief system, which is threatening to individual identity, community identity, and cultural practices. Change can be uncomfortable – even traumatic – for most people: "Just adding a driving force toward change often produced an immediate counterforce to maintain the equilibrium. This observation led to the important insight that the equilibrium could more easily be moved if one could remove restraining forces since there were usually already driving forces in the system. Unfortunately restraining forces were harder to get at because they were often personal psychological defenses or group norms embedded in the organizational or community culture."[5]

However, the notion of *learning* allows for cultural beliefs to be augmented, expanded, and adapted to new globalized norms or regional practices. Because change (or learning) cannot occur without *learners*, it is crucial, according to Schein, that people be involved in any kind of shifts in cultural beliefs.

The foundational goals of peace operations and crisis management are attitudinal and behavioural change in recipient populations that allow for tenable peace and security. Planned change – which is the intention of most interventions – cannot occur unless the counter-forces (psychological defences and cultural norms) are addressed through a logical chain methodology. *Change management* applies a logical chain methodology of transition, which directly addresses the "people" side of change and has a useful application in creating attitudinal and behavioural change in war-affected environments. According to Jan Tucker, "Change management theories effectively support how to deal with developmental and transitional change, but are less effective at dealing with successfully implementing transformational change." Tucker identifies the three types of change that occur most frequently in organizations as *developmental, transitional,* and *transformational*:[6]

1. *Developmental change* occurs when a company makes an improvement to its current business.

2. *Transitional change* replaces existing processes or procedures with something that is completely new to the company/sector. Corporate reorganization, mergers, acquisitions, the creation of new products or services, and the implementation of new technology are examples of transitional change. The future of the organization is unknown when the transformation begins, which can add a level or discomfort for employees.

3. *Transformational change* occurs after the transition period. Transformational change may involve both developmental and transitional change. It is common for transitional and transformational change to occur in tandem. When companies are faced with the emergence of radically different technologies, significant changes in supply and demand, unexpected competition, lack of revenue or other major shifts in how they do business, developmental or transitional change may not offer them the solutions they need to stay competitive. Instead of methodically implementing new processes, companies may be forced to drastically transform themselves.[7]

The types of change distinctions outlined above are useful in understanding the ways in which sectors are transitioning in their thinking regarding their intervention activities. When implementing their projects, practitioners can consider their work through the lenses of transitional change and transformational change to convey their motives to recipients and beneficiaries in the field.

Change management processes include:

1. Creating a change management strategy (assessment)
2. Engaging elites as change leaders (sponsorship)
3. Building awareness of the need for change (communications)
4. Developing skills and knowledge to support the change (education and training)

5. Helping people move through the transition (coaching, mentoring)
6. Developing methods to sustain the change (measurement systems, incentives, and reinforcement)

Change management has come to the fore in corporate and governmental sectors. Influenced by corporate change structures, change management has to do with people and transitions towards new ways of doing business. This type of transformation can be understood through Lewin's change theory and has applicability as a philosophy supporting transition operations within the rubric of multinational peace operations and crisis management. Taking its cue from change theory, change management acknowledges the importance of overcoming inertia in organizational or community thinking and installing new concepts. This process is referred to in many different ways, including:

- unfreeze – change – freeze
- ADKAR (Awareness, Desire, Knowledge, Ability, Reinforcement)
- holding on – letting go – moving on
- homeostasis – dying – rebirth

In other words, change requires people to let go of ideas and adopt other ideas. Change management is a series of methods that leads organizations through this often difficult transition. Many sectors involved in peace operations and crisis management have not been accustomed to think in terms of change management, and rarely has this corporate and governmental process been self-applied in security and defence, by civilian police, the UN, and humanitarian and development agencies. We often want recipients in war-affected areas to embrace our intentions for change, yet the international community has shown reticence to undergo change management within its own institutions and organizations, even while it promotes change within nation and state building initiatives in war-affected environments.

Theory of change (ToC), as distinct from change theory, is a planning and evaluation method for social change. It incorporates long-term goals and identification of measurable indicators of success and formulates actions to achieve goals. ToC is a roadmap that is closely linked to results/outcomes-based planning approaches such as results-based measurement (RBM). The Canadian International Development Agency (CIDA) employs RBM as a comprehensive, life-cycle approach to management that integrates business strategy, people, processes, and measurements to improve decision-making and to drive change. The approach focuses on getting the right design early in a process, implementing performance measurement, learning and changing, and reporting on performance. This planning and results-oriented approach highlights successes and lessons during implementation of an intervention activity. It tends to map a causal pathway by specifying what is needed for goals to be achieved. It also requires the articulation of underlying assumptions that can be tested and measured. And it changes the way of thinking about initiatives from what an organization is doing to what an organization wants to achieve.

According to Lara Olson of the University of Calgary, former co-researcher for the project Reflecting on Peace Practitioners (RPP) and co-author of the results in *Confronting War: Critical Lessons for Peace Practitioners*, the RPP research discovered that agencies and groups involved in the study were not aware of the driving principles behind their own programs and activities – what the project refers to as *underlying assumptions*. Portions of study were really uncomfortable for some of the peace-building agencies because the study examined assumptions. It found that theories of change were under-examined by agencies, despite their importance as drivers of agency programs. Olson and her team captured various theories of change through workshops and case studies. Referred to as "assumptions" by the RPP researchers, the theories, values, and principles informing agency decisions to intervene were captured by asking the critical question "Why are you doing what you are doing?" Olson argues that these things are often so implicit within an organization that they are rarely, if ever, examined; there are no organizational policies that dictate assumptions. The RPP research team found a distinction between sectors regarding the sophistication of understanding intervention assumptions.[8]

Even though results-based management offers the opportunity to shift away from what an organization is doing to what an organization wants to achieve, Steve Flemming, a defence scientist with Canadian Department of National Defence, observes that "the planners who typically produce initial measures of effectiveness programs are engineers, and they tend to start at the wrong end – with what can be measured, rather than what should be measured."[9] In other words, Flemming argues, they attempt to measure what they know they can achieve rather than what they want to achieve. David Hawkins, author of *Power vs. Force*, points out the relevance of nonlinear dynamics in this process: "The world conventionally assumes that the processing of problems requires starting from the known (the question or conditions) and moving on to the unknown (the answer) in a time sequence following definite steps and logical progression. Nonlinear dynamics moves in the opposite direction: From the unknown (the nondeterministic data of the question) to the known (the answer)! It operates within a different paradigm of causality. The problem is seen as one of definition and access rather than of logical sequence."[10]

Linear sequencing, however, is the dominant force in the evaluation of results within the international community. Theory of change links actions to results. This is the most common linear planning method in the development field. It is a useful tool in tactical-level intervention activities to incorporate the interests of locals into program planning and implementation in permissive environments. In this way, theory of change informs the linear measuring mechanisms employed in peace operations and civilian crisis management that serve as performance auditing tools against which projects can be measured from beginning to end.

Other theories that inform the international community's interests in intervening in state affairs include conflict prevention, conflict resolution, theories of peace, and social contract theory. Each is duly informed by the value-based principles of collective security, collective defence, human rights, civil liberties, freedom, democracy, governance, and equality. *Value-based principles* are aspirational in nature, and can be ideologically based, such as democratic liberal values. In addition, there are also a series of practice-based principles, including "Do No Harm," reduction of discrimination, reinforcement of the state as a priority, coordination with donors, security-development nexus, avoidance of exclusionary activities, and "operate quickly yet focus on the long term." *Practice-based principles*, on the other hand, inform the ways in which theories of intervention are operationalized. These include coherence, harmonization, whole of government approach, comprehensive approach, transition, capacity building, and the conflict sensitive approach. These values and principles have shaped the doctrine of the international community through both conflict-specific agreements as well as generic intervention guidance documents. Intervention-specific documents that the international community continues to rally around include the *General Framework Agreement for Peace in Bosnia and Herzegovina (Dayton Peace Accords)* (1995), *Bonn Agreement* (2001), *Cotounu Agreement* (2003), the *European Union Africa Strategy* (2005), *Afghanistan Compact* (2006), and the *Afghanistan National Development Strategy (2006)*. Generic guidance documents include the *University Declaration of Human Rights* (1948), *International Covenant on Economic, Social, and Cultural Rights* (1966), the *Brahimi Report* (1999), *In Larger Freedom – Millennium Development Goals* (2000), *Paris Declaration on Aid Effectiveness* (2005), and the *United Nations Peacekeeping Capstone Doctrine* (2008).[11]

Effectiveness, efficiency, accountability, and sustainability have become the measurement and reporting meta-narratives of twenty-first century peace operations and crisis management. The *Paris Declaration on Aid Effectiveness* (Paris Declaration) and the *OECD DAC Principles for Good International Engagement in Fragile States* contributed to the doctrine of the international community, motivating many states to follow suit by adopting the emerging meta-narratives informing intervention in the common tradespace (effectiveness, efficiency, accountability, and sustainability). France's Cooperation Framework Agreement (DCP) adopted an approach focused on coherence, predictability, coordination and ownership, similar to the watchwords of accountability, effectiveness, and sustainability of USAID, OECD DAC, and many UN departments.

In many interviews in support of this research project, the Paris Declaration was hailed as a seminal document informing international community thinking regarding indicators and progress.[12] Its purpose is to provide guidance to reform the ways in which the international community delivers and manages aid in the context of the UN Millennium Declaration and Millennium Development Goals.[13] The Paris Declaration discusses aid effectiveness through the implementation of good practices, such as:

> Strengthening partner countries' national development strategies and associated operational frameworks (e.g., planning, budget, and performance assessment frameworks).
>
> Increasing alignment of aid with partner countries' priorities, systems and procedures and helping to strengthen their capacities.
>
> Enhancing donors' and partner countries' respective accountability to their citizens and parliaments for their development policies, strategies and performance.
>
> Eliminating duplication of efforts and rationalizing donor activities to make them as cost-effective as possible.
>
> Reforming and simplifying donor policies and procedures to encourage collaborative behaviour and progressive alignment with partner countries' systems and procedures.
>
> Defining measures and standards of performance and accountability of partner country systems in public financial management, procurement, fiduciary safeguards and environmental assessments, in line with broadly accepted good practices and their quick and widespread application.[14]

Although these recommendations are specific to aid and development, similar concepts are embedded in the rationale for the comprehensive approach to peace operations and multinational crisis management. While these concepts may not suit the worldviews of stakeholders in some sectors involved in international interventions, they have informed the tradespace in which international interventions occur, whether preventative, *interventative*, or developmental.

Of significance to the present study is the Paris Declaration's focus on establishing indicators, timelines, and targets against which to measure progress, in order to further spur cumulative progress and to consistently track such progress over time. The Paris Declaration states that measuring progress is the touchstone of aid effectiveness.

The *conflict sensitive approach* has emerged from the growing consciousness of the international community of states that subscribe to a core set of values. There is an increased recognition of the unintended consequences, or impacts, of intervention. This approach is built upon the *Do No Harm* principle,[15] understanding that any intervention activity can have adverse, even fatal, consequences in war-torn environments. The Do No Harm notion was derived from the Hippocratic oath to eliminate questionable motives and unintended negative consequences of development work. Practitioners suggest that there has been a growing awareness among development, peace-building, humanitarian, and even military stakeholders of the need to go beyond Do No Harm, to seek to have a positive impact on the conflict context. The conflict sensitive approach involves the examination of potential impacts – whether positive or negative – on the conflict context and a reduction of the unintended negative consequences of intervention activities.

In 1999, Tony Blair, the former British prime minister, presented a set of values intended to explain why the international community of states chooses to intervene. This set of values, principles, and practices has become known as the *Doctrine of the International Community*, an explicit recognition that states' values and interests are mutually dependent and that national interests are to a significant extent governed by international collaboration. According by Blair, "We live in a world where isolationism has ceased to have a reason to exist. By necessity we have to co-operate with each other across nations. Many of our domestic problems are caused on the other side of the world ... We are all internationalists now, whether we like it or not. We cannot refuse to participate in global markets if we want to prosper. We cannot ignore new political ideas in other countries if we want to innovate. We cannot turn our backs on conflicts and the violation of human rights within other countries if we want still to be secure."[16]

Interconnected financial markets and economies, environmental change, and challenges to peace and security are global challenges that require intense international cooperation. Veronica Cody, deputy director general, Civilian Crisis Management, Council of the European Union, agrees: "We are experiencing an international order based on effective multilateralism."[17] The Doctrine of International Community is based upon the principles of transparency, standardization, codes of behaviour, and innovation between stakeholders for the prevention of conflict and creation of peace. Values include liberty, the rule of law, human rights, and open societies. The doctrine suggests that the spread of these values makes the collective community of states more secure. Further, according to Blair, "People are no longer interested in intervention for intervention's sake – they want to see progress where their values and dollars are put to the test."[18]

As these doctrines, discourses, and modalities suggest, the international community that intervenes in the world's most egregious calamities has matured into a community of practice motivated by a spectrum of intervention theories and practices. This community of unlikely partners attempts to adopt comprehensive norms, standards, and codes that will see it through to the next stage of evolution: a common tradespace.

Summary Points

- Intervention and worldviews are informed by theories including development theory, world systems theory, change theory, and theory of change.
- The Paris Declaration on Aid Effectiveness is considered a rallying document for practitioners, involved in measuring progress of intervention activities.
- Linear sequencing is the primary framework used in the evaluation of results of international interventions.

Notes

[1] Hawkins, *Power vs. Force*, 53.

[2] The notion of *development* is generally applied to countries. A developed country is one that has attained the western-style standards of free market economies, industrialization, social programs (medical, educational), democratic governments, and human rights guarantees for its citizens. Secondary standards include rule of law, transparent and legitimate governance structures, and particular freedoms such as speech and religious practice.

[3] In 2007 the French government underwent a review of its policy concerning fragile state interventions. The Direction Générale de la Coopération Internationale et du Développement released the *Fragile States and Situations of Fragility: France's Policy Paper*, which presents a case for careful intervention: "Fragile states, especially those emerging from a conflict, need aid… that can meet the longer-term challenges, over and above the need for immediate stabilisation. Yet donors have to keep up with fast-moving changes on the ground and struggle to adjust and provide the adequate, relevant and effective assistance in good time. They get caught between two – contradictory – sets of interests, *viz.* that of the

country's authorities and that of the donor community searching for an intervention consensus... And especially when it comes to fragile countries, interventions at any stage should take into account the entire process and not just part of it" (3).

[4] Smiley, "Planned Change in Organizational Development."
[5] Schein, "Kurt Lewin's Change Theory."
[6] Tucker, "Types of Change."
[7] Ibid.
[8] Lara Olson, personal communication, 2008.
[9] Steve Flemming, personal communication, 2008.
[10] Hawkins, *Power vs. Force*, 46.
[11] Whether conflict specific or generic, each document was referred to by the participants involved in this study.
[12] According to a delegate of the French Ministère des Affaires Étrangères, the ministry has a number of instruments that are used to enhance the relationship between society and state in fragile environments. The social compact theory informs the ministry in its engagement with such societies, and they use the OECD DAC principles for engagement with failed and failing states, as well as the Paris Principles on aid effectiveness for additional guidance. Of significance to the French government is legitimacy and state/local ownership in the areas in which they intervene.
[13] For more information on the goals, go to http://www.un.org/millenniumgoals/.
[14] "Joint Progress toward Enhanced Aid Effectiveness," 1.
[15] Anderson, *Do No Harm*.
[16] Reynolds, "Blair's 'International Community' Doctrine."
[17] Cody at CMI 2007 Conference, personal communication.
[18] Reynolds, "Blair's 'International Community' Doctrine."

CHAPTER 3
The Language of Measuring

The language used to describe the assessment of peace operations and crisis management can cause misunderstandings between stakeholders. Although there are traditional definitions for the concepts used in the evaluation of intervention activities, especially at the national government levels, these definitions have not been transferred to or understood within many sectors working in international interventions. In exploring the language used by practitioners, this chapter (1) illustrates the multifaceted definitions of the same/similar terms; and (2) examines some of the cross-cutting understandings between sectors that may have utility in informing the common tradespace of international community interventions.

As in other professions, the terms used to describe effectiveness, progress, and success frame sectors. In peace operations, however, what one sector understands as effective or successful is not the case for the others. According to Charles T. Call in *Knowing Peace When You See It: Setting Standards for Peacebuilding Success* (2008), the different paradigms of peace held within the community of stakeholders involved in peace-building and crisis management mean that there is no way to establish effective peace strategies because there is no agreement about what is being measured.[1] Similarly, using the term *evaluation* to a professional evaluator can leave you running for cover! The military language of measures of effectiveness, metrics, lines of operation, lessons learned, and effects-based approaches to operations is vastly different language from that used by development agencies, which refers to logical chains, LogFrames, inputs, outputs, outcomes, results and impacts. Police refer to assessments and evaluations, whereas humanitarians refer to impact evaluations and reporting. There are even misunderstandings within sectors, let alone across them.

Ted Itani, ICRC senior personnel, argues that having a common language and lexicon among stakeholders – even within the NGO community – can support measuring the effectiveness of activities. For example, he maintains that even the International Committee of the Red Cross (ICRC) and the International Federation of Red Cross and Red Crescent Societies (the Federation) do not share the same language. Itani suggests that if the ICRC and the Federation can agree on some terms (between and among stakeholders), that would be a move in the right direction.[2] Understanding the breadth and scope of the terminology used in the field of measuring is daunting but critical in navigating the emerging tradespace.

When participants in this research were asked what terminology their respective organizations used to describe measurement – particularly measures of effectiveness – their answers were varied. There were some commonalities as well as differences among and between the sectors. The responses add relevance to the literature on measuring effectiveness, evaluation, and results-based measurement and to other ways stakeholders understand the language of measuring.

Cause and Effect

Causality implies a relationship between two phenomena: the *cause* and the *effect*. Without the cause, the effect would not have occurred, and therefore one somehow has caused the other to happen. *Intervention Logic* analyses the expected effects of intervention in a logic system of causal relationships. These presumed causal relationships are often depicted in cause-and-effect diagrams (impact diagrams) or as result chains, both showing the expected causal relations between phenomena. The *Logical Framework* (LogFrame) is the most common of the planning tools used in development field, and its use is widespread in the humanitarian sector as well. Stuart Gordon has also introduced the LogFrame to military colleagues working in the UK's Provincial Reconstruction Teams in Afghanistan. Please refer to Gordon's contribution in chapter 9.

When measuring cause and effect relationships in peace operations and crisis management, *displacement* and *additionality* become important in measuring progress related to behavioural and attitudinal changes in people. Displacement refers to the negative effects of an intervention activity, which can cancel out any positive effects of that same activity. This effect has been referred to as the *unintended consequences* of peacekeeping[3] and *doing harm*.[4] Measuring mechanisms and tools must account for the unintended consequences of activities. Intervention activities can cause behavioural change based upon perceived incentives for local populations. Yet incentives are not proven to lead to long-term behavioural changes in recipient populations recovering from conflict.[5] The nature of interventions is incentive based in relation to host countries and war-affected people, which can cause behaviour changes – albeit ones lasting as long as the incentives and/or intervention presence – which can lead to changes in policy. *Additionality* examines whether a cause induces intended effects that would otherwise not have been reached without the intervention activity.[6] In other words, is an intervention activity the cause of the consequence? Traditionally, it has been important that evaluations attach importance to the causality of the relation between the intervention activity and the observed effects.[7]

In his famous study *Power vs. Force: The Hidden Determinants of Human Behaviour* (2002), David Hawkins offers some approaches to cause and effect relationships that may initiate the re-evaluation of the ubiquitous Newtonian causal measuring approach employed by the international community. He argues that within the *observable* world, causality has conventionally been presumed to work in the following manner (Figure 5), A → B → C. This is called a deterministic linear sequence, and he likens it to billiard balls sequentially striking one another.[8]

The implicit assumption in causality is that A causes B causes C. However, Hawkins's research suggests that causality operates in a completely different manner. In the linear model of causality, there are *unobservable* phenomenon applying pressure to the A and the B and the C. These unobservable phenomenon result in the sequence A → B → C, which is an observable phenomenon within our world. Most problems we attempt to deal with exist on the observable level, yet there are few studies on the

FIGURE 5
The Linear Chain of Logic

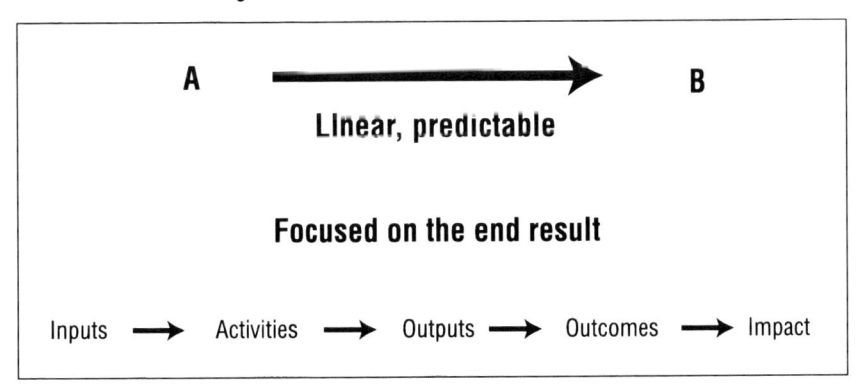

unobservable phenomenon out of which the A → B → C arise. The bureaucratic systems within the international community, in fact, attempt to fit the multi-dimensionality of conflict and calamity into two-dimensional measuring models based upon a cause and effect system of analysis – the logical chain modality. Such linear dynamics cannot begin to capture the variances and unpredictability of the non-linear conflict environment in which the international community intervenes.[9]

Effectiveness

There is no agreement of what effectiveness is, yet the term is ubiquitous in international aid, defence and security, and civilian policing. It can, however, be examined in terms of outputs, outcomes, effectivity, goal attainment, cost-effectiveness, and macro impact.[10] In other words, many things can be measured against effectiveness, such as time, materiel, personnel, resources, and funding. Effectiveness includes not only the extent to which an intervention objective has been achieved but also the positive and negative side effects, which are unintended and unplanned. Brusset et al. suggest that effectiveness is defined by the connection between outcomes intended (i.e., project objectives) and outcomes achieved.[11]

Effectiveness is the term commonly used to refer to the goal attainment of a measure, thus relating the outcome of a process to its original goals. In other words, an intervention is said to be effective if the outcomes match the goals.[12] Evaluation of effectiveness is impossible unless objectives are clear and measurable.[13] Too often objectives are either not specified or are specified in a way that is vague and incapable of being used as the basis for deciding whether or not the policies are successful. Objectives should be quantified and become explicit targets.[14] The Organisation for Economic Co-operation and Development (OECD) suggests that evaluators need to be part of the design of any intervention to accurately set the objectives. Measuring the effectiveness of an intervention requires clear, explicit, and quantified objectives.[15] Mosselman and Prince argue that effectiveness would be the percentage to which the objectives of the intervention have been reached. In fact, effectiveness relates a project's outcome (or effects) to the project's goals.[16] Evaluation, however, must go beyond the simple goal-attainment of a measure, and focus on the processes that contribute to the attainment of the intervention activity goals. In other words, evaluations need to examine whether goals have been reached as well as bring together the stakeholders involved so that the evaluation looks beyond effects of an intervention activity and gives due attention to the network of actors involved in the policy measure and the processes that invoked these effects.[17]

Emery Brusset, the founder of Channel Research, a Belgium-based evaluation company, argues that the dominant philosophy driving the measurement of progress and success of intervention activities may not be the best one to support the goals of the international community in crisis-affected areas. He posits that the measurement methods most appropriate in crisis environments are based upon the Chinese philosophy of *conducive condition*, not the Greek philosophy of *creating end states*. It is better to focus on the influence of dynamics rather than on creating the ideal situation. Brusset asks: "What is 'effectiveness' according to Chinese philosophy? It is to combine forces in a way which leads to a favourable outcome." Perhaps this philosophy underpins the comprehensive approach intended to increase the effectiveness of our activities in peace operations and crisis management.

Measures of Effectiveness and Progress

For those who are not trained military planners, the terminology of measuring effectiveness and measuring performance can be confusing. For example: "DPs are used to develop MoPs which, in turn, are used to develop MoEs which depend upon the environment and which, in turn, are used to develop MoFEs. Each MoM could be a MoP or an MoE."[18]

Even if the acronyms were spelled in full, this statement is not easily understood. Moreover, different militaries and the groups within these militaries see this description differently and attribute their own logic to the chain of related concepts. What hope do other stakeholders have of understanding the measuring logic underwriting military missions?

Measures are by nature quantitative, not qualitative.[19] The literature on measures of effectiveness (MOE) generally defines them as combinations of key indicators from multiple sectors used to determine overall progress toward attaining mission objectives.[20] An objective is exactly what will occur, how it will be accomplished, and to what standard of performance.[21]

Measures are the standards by which the success of a system is determined. There is no universal definition of this concept,[22] and this is particularly true in the sectors involved in peace operations and crisis management. Measures of effectiveness (MOEs) are standards against which the capability of a solution to meet the needs of a problem may be judged. The standards are specific properties that any potential solution must exhibit to some extent. MOEs are independent of any solution and specify neither performance nor criteria. MOEs are based on the perspective/viewpoint of a stakeholder and help to manage the implementation of an intervention activity.[23] Unlike audits, MOEs are understood as being external to a system and measure effectiveness of the outcomes of the system/activity. An MOE is a tool designed to help establish whether a system, when developed as a solution to a problem, performs the mission required of it by stakeholders.[24] Measures of performance (MOPs) are measured against efficiency and are internal to a system. Like audits, they are designed to measure the performance of the system itself.[25] Conversely, MOEs are also considered as a part of the doctrinal cycle and are used to calibrate only internal activities, rather than the effectiveness of an activity according to external (but affected) actors, including locals.

Figure 6 helps map out the modalities of measuring.

FIGURE 6
Understanding Measurement

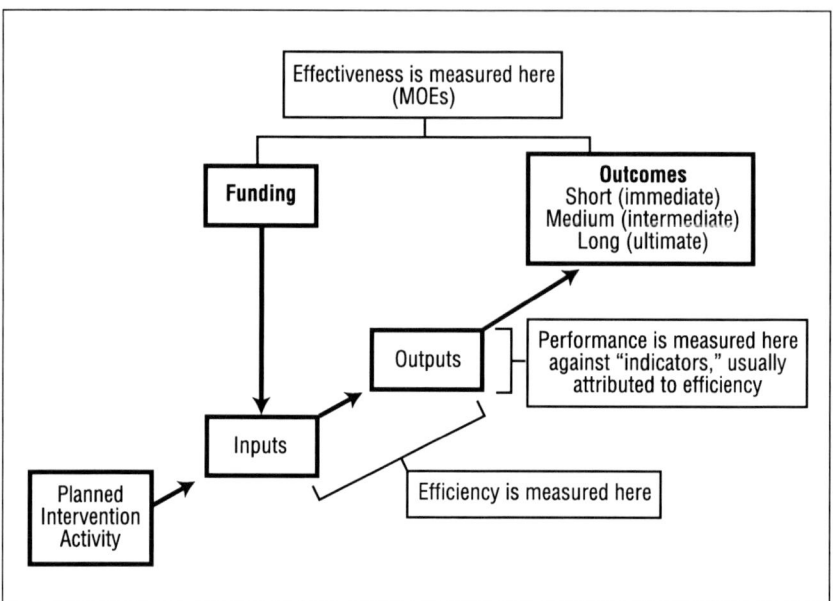

Source: Mosselman and Prince, *Review of Methods*, 24.

Measures of effectiveness allow for qualitative data analysis but are most often applied to evaluating quantitative data such as numbers of people, type and quantities of supplies/money, and time, as illustrated in Figure 7.

Effects-based measuring tends to oversimplify qualitative data and narrative approaches to phenomena, as well as give a false sense of positive impact due to the concept of "effectiveness." Figure 8 illustrates this point.

FIGURE 7
Disarmament, Demobilization, and Reintegration Measures of Effectiveness

Project	Measures of Effectiveness	Impacts
DDR	• 42,300 soldiers demobilized in 17 months • 39,121 light weapons registered and destroyed in 18.5 months • 11,008 ex-combatants retrained and reintegrated in communities of origin	• Reduced number of trained men with weapons • Stabilization of security environment • Strengthening of local economies through retraining and new forms of employment

Source: Meharg, "Measuring the Effectiveness of Reconstruction and Stabilization Activities," 39.

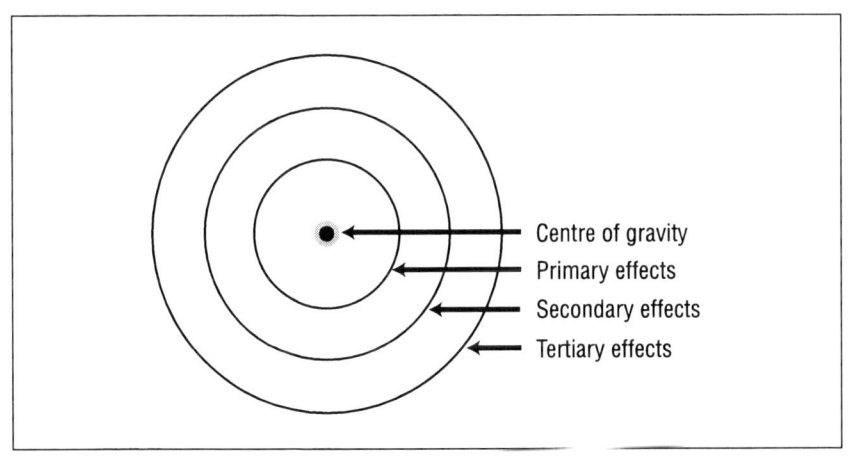

FIGURE 8
Effects-Based Approach to Operations

[Diagram: concentric circles labeled from innermost outward: Centre of gravity, Primary effects, Secondary effects, Tertiary effects]

Measures of effectiveness is a purely military term which has not yet "bled through to other government departments or influenced international civilian-led organizations and NGOs," says Ian Higginbotham of the Canadian Department of Foreign Affairs and International Trade.[26] In Mike Dziedzic's experience at the United States Institute for Peace (USIP), the term *is* used; however, *measures* is preferred over *metrics*, which is a decidedly military-centric approach to measuring progress. Likewise, the language of achieving *effects* is also common in Dziedzic's experience, yet the notion of *effects-based operations* is not part of civilian peace and security thinking.[27] "MOEs may not be the right terminology for this practice. MOEs may be the worst way to describe the activity of measuring,[28] suggests Colonel André Harvey, Canadian Forces.

Lieutenant Colonel David Last, a professor at the Royal Military College of Canada and a member of the Canadian Forces, argues that the language of measuring progress has shifted and that defence and security stakeholders are rallying around measures of effectiveness because of the term's utility as a framework for emerging operations. Last suggests that MOEs have emerged out of US Civil Affairs through a process of "institutional justification."[29]

According to Col John Agoglia, former director of the US Army's Peacekeeping and Stability Operations Institute and trained in the art of planning, *military planning* is not *measures of effectiveness*. MOEs are built upon polling, group surveys, and expert opinions, and these elements are not military planning. A significant part of intervention is planning. Within planning, the discourse of "doing the right problem versus doing the problem right" is a modality that influences military planning systems (Figure 9). The discourse suggests that in any activity an essential first step is to ensure that the right problem is being studied (and by extension, the right questions are being asked, and the right measures are chosen for evaluating the problem). When the right problem is being studied within a particular *problem space*, decision-makers are presented with sounder options. Choosing the right problem, asking the right questions, and choosing the right options to solve/mitigate a problem are all directly linked. According to this linear, scientific way of thinking, structuring problems in this way allows for the right measures to be used in evaluating the solution.[30]

Col Agolgia argues that some military planning experts are incapable of properly designing MOEs: "Just because you are a planner doesn't mean that you can do MOEs and MOPs!" He goes on to state that measures of effectiveness are not a sideshow but a core competency of those involved in this aspect of operations. People need to be trained to do this work, and "we need much more understanding and rigour." Col Agoglia says that people are becoming more aware of the linkages between assessment processes and measurement of effectiveness.[31]

Kristiina Rintakoski, of the Crisis Management Initiative in Finland, says that MOEs are a western military construct (i.e., in the United States, Canada, Britain, NATO) and are a retrospective tool that gauges an activity to inform the next steps. MOE is a new term for European civilian organizations, and she reiterates that the term comes from the United States and is not yet a part of the European lexicon, except for NATO because its lexicon is informed through its ally partners.[32] The European

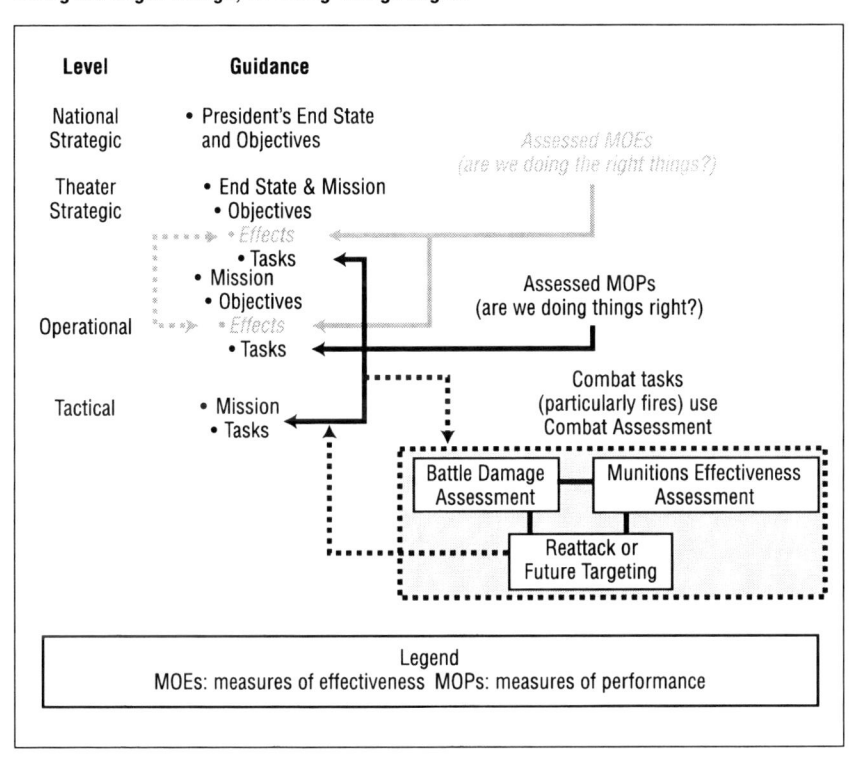

FIGURE 9
Doing the Right Things, or Doing Things Right?

Level	Guidance	
National Strategic	• President's End State and Objectives	Assessed MOEs (are we doing the right things?)
Theater Strategic	• End State & Mission • Objectives • *Effects*	
Operational	• Tasks • Mission • Objectives • *Effects* • Tasks	Assessed MOPs (are we doing things right?)
Tactical	• Mission • Tasks	Combat tasks (particularly fires) use Combat Assessment

Battle Damage Assessment — Munitions Effectiveness Assessment
Reattack or Future Targeting

Legend
MOEs: measures of effectiveness MOPs: measures of performance

Source: US Joint Warfighting Center, *Commander's Handbook*, iv-10.

Union (EU) continues to develop its civilian crisis management structure and policies through the maturation of the European Security and Defence Policy (ESPD) (2003–04). However, the concept of benchmarking for measures of effectiveness has not yet gained traction in the EU. According to Alexander Blyth, EU JUSTLEX, the EU started with the political strategic intent for the mission, from which a concept of operations and an operational plan were developed but this process did not cascade down into benchmarking and / or lessons learned, as it would have with military planners. MOEs were hit and miss. The response regarding success was mixed from those who were involved in those early missions.[33]

Says Blyth, "In 2003, the EU ESDP engaged in civilian crisis management. It began with fact-finding missions. The Joint Action gave the strategic political direction, which then informed the detailed planning. This then informed the CONOPS [concept of operations]. This then informed the OPLAN [the operational plan]. Therefore, these plans have to cascade down and in doing so must create effectiveness indicators – but this is *not* done. The OPLAN never got beyond broad objectives. Outputs and outcomes are often quite subjective and are based on perceptions of those on the ground.[34]

"The Concept of Operations is supposed to transform the political strategic intent into operational goals, but as said earlier, there is no definitive mention of MOEs. Measures of Effectiveness should be referred to as a must in the Joint Action (JA). The CONOPS should add more detail to the intent stated in the JA; then the OPLAN should definitively spell out each MOE (exactly what is to be measured, how, and the timeline). MOEs are time sensitive and are a 'rolling process' that must return or connect to the strategic intent and overarching operational plan. There needs to be much more of a link between MOE theory and practice"[35] (Figure 10).

Until recently, says Blyth, "there has been no real evidence of MOEs and benchmarks from the field. I believe the EU drives the measures based on their norms and does not include what the local perceptions are. Often, MOEs are driven centrally, and through the second and third pillars of the EU. National agendas (such as unilateral projects in Iraq) drive the norms for measures and measurement. In the last year or so there has been increased attention to growing professionalism, accountability, and the requirement to measure. Together these three points point inexorably to engaging MOEs."[36]

In military thinking there are two modalities concerning measures of effectiveness. In the first modality, there are those who evaluate to feed

FIGURE 10
The Rolling Process
MOEs are time sensitive, a rolling process that must return or connect to the strategic intent and overarching operational plan.

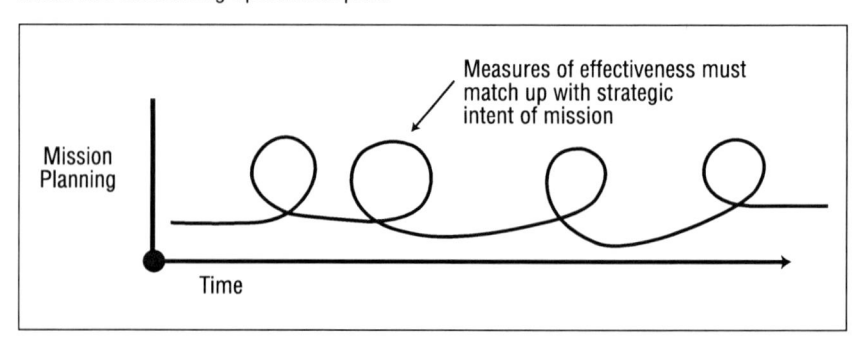

into lessons learned to improve response and performance. Militaries, and many civilian-led sectors involved in peace operations and crisis management, refer to *lessons learned* and *best practices*, with the recent addition of *interim lessons identified*, when measuring their missions.[37]

Veronica Cody, deputy director general, Civilian Crisis Management, Council of the European Union, suggests that the notion of lessons learned has really evolved over the past few years and is now accepted within the European Union as the critical step in improving crisis management missions. This is an internal exercise, retrospective in nature and only used as a validation process. Western militaries have substantive lessons learned (in the UK, *lessons learnt*) and best practices, which are induced to inform their decision-makers on what to modify next time around the post (see Figures 11, 12). But a high-ranking EU military rep observes that he has never seen anyone in the military (Italian or otherwise) read a learned lesson from a previous mission.[38] Similarly, the humanitarian sector has a system of capturing lessons but no way to learn from them. ALNAP's *Annual Review 2002* indicates that the number of evaluations of humanitarian action being undertaken has grown rapidly since 1994. Evaluations explicitly and implicitly identify lessons within the findings and conclusions; subsequent evaluations are then able to detect the extent to which lessons identified in previous evaluations have been addressed over time (i.e., properly learned). With the cumulative increase, it is becoming more common to find evaluations referring back to lessons identified in previous evaluations but seemingly *not* learned.[39] It appears that, in most sectors, evaluations reveal lessons but fail to engender learning that results in improved effectiveness, progress, success, and overall learning.

The second modality suggests that military planners follow a performance planning process. This is an ongoing process that informs a cyclical relationship between mandate – strategy – indicators.[40]

Both these modalities are internal measurement methods and do not consider the "external" measuring that moves beyond the traditional military operations remit to include *significance of impact*.

Inputs, Outputs, Outcomes, and Impacts

All logic chains assume a cause and effect relationship between inputs, outputs, outcomes, and impacts. Mike Dziedzic, of the United States Institute for Peace, emphasizes the difference between outcomes and impacts. He suggests that a series of dependent and independent variables must be identified during the intervention planning process to best assess the relationship between outcomes and impacts.[41]

68 *Measuring What Matters in Peace Operations and Crisis Management*

FIGURE 11
The Lessons Learned Process at the Peacekeeping and Stability Operations Institute, US Army

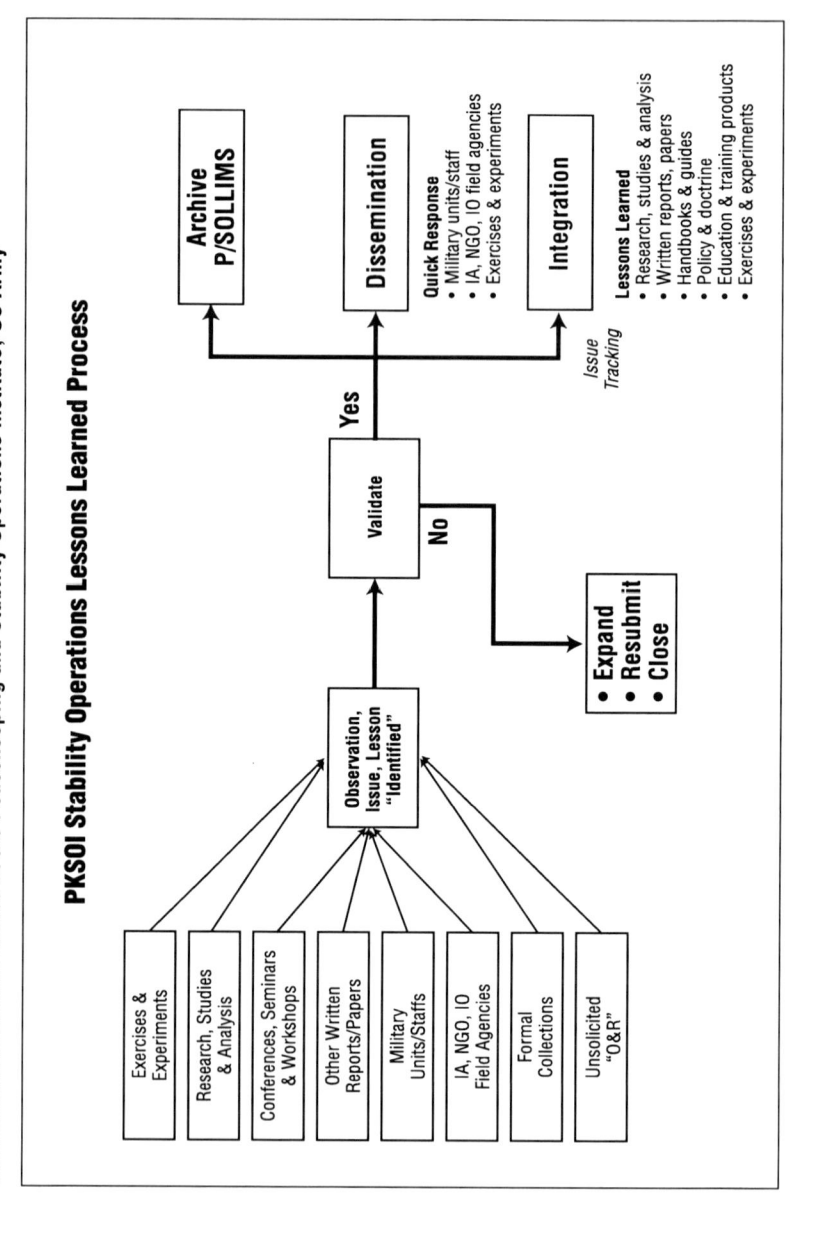

PKSOI Stability Operations Lessons Learned Process

Inputs to "Observation, Issue, Lesson 'Identified'":
- Exercises & Experiments
- Research, Studies & Analysis
- Conferences, Seminars & Workshops
- Other Written Reports/Papers
- Military Units/Staffs
- IA, NGO, IO Field Agencies
- Formal Collections
- Unsolicited "O&R"

Validate:
- Yes → Archive P/SOLLIMS, Dissemination, Integration
- No → Expand, Resubmit, Close

Quick Response
- Military units/staff
- IA, NGO, IO field agencies
- Exercises & experiments

Lessons Learned
- Research, studies & analysis
- Written reports, papers
- Handbooks & guides
- Policy & doctrine
- Education & training products
- Exercises & experiments

Issue Tracking

The Language of Measuring 69

FIGURE 12
An Example of a Web-Based Lessons Learned Approach, Center for US Army Lessons Learned

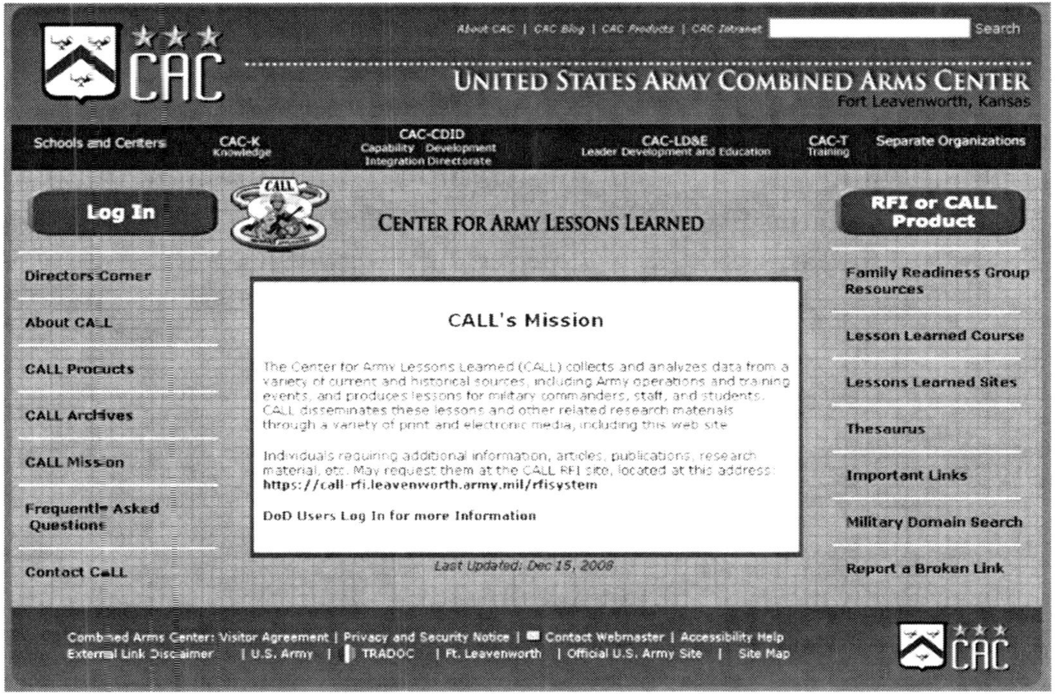

Source: United States Army Combined Arms Center. The Center for Army Lessons Learned (CALL) website: http://usacac.army.mil/ca2/call/mission.asp. Accessed 20 February 2009.

Inputs are the resources that are provided by donors, implementers, and beneficiaries. Inputs are commonly calculated as the financial, materiel, and time resources available to start and complete an intervention activity. *Outputs* are the direct effects resulting from a program and are usually definable quantities, most easily monitored over time and space[42] – for example, increases in something, higher numbers of something, or better something.[43] *Outcomes* are something that follows as a result of a consequence from the outputs, and can also be considered as the use made by the beneficiaries of an output.[44]

Two types of *impacts*[45] are relevant to measuring peace operations and crisis management. *Instrumental impacts* show a clear connection between a particular activity and a specific outcome, such as a change in infant mortality rates. *Conceptual impacts* are less tangible, advancing knowledge and informing decisions but without showing a direct link. Evaluations that measure instrumental impacts can directly affect decision-making and influence changes in an intervention activity under review. According to John Baylee, Asian Development Bank, "Evidence for this type of utilization involves decisions and actions that arise from the evaluation, including the implementation of recommendations." Evaluations that measure conceptual impacts have indirect influences on activity review. Conceptual impacts generate knowledge and increase understanding in a particular area and in a more generalized way.[46] "Conceptual use occurs when an evaluation influences the way in which stakeholders think about a program, without any immediate new decisions being made about the program. Over time and given changes to the contextual and political circumstances surrounding the program, conceptual impacts can lead to instrumental impacts and hence significant program changes."[47]

Peace operations and crisis management practitioners have been measuring instrumental impacts within a political context requiring success and progress related to intangible conceptual impacts such as well being and governance in war-torn societies. Impact can also be understood by total impacts and marginal impacts. Total impacts would see the creation or cancellation of a peace operation in its entirety, while measuring marginal impact would see the continuation of an operation for a period of time or the adjustment of a mandate to respond to the context in which an operation was occurring.

Impact is last in the logical chain of *input-output-outcome-impact*. Impacts are the consequences of an outcome, and the change triggered by the use of an output.[48] In the French government's *Guide to Evaluations*, the Ministère des Affaires Étrangères suggests that an impact characterizes a project that, beyond its expected effects, has an influence in other fields or at another level.[49] Further, the cumulative term for output-outcome-impact is *result*. This cumulative term is the essence of results-based measuring, as developed by Canada's International Development Agency in the 1990s. Notions of *significance of impact* have come to the fore in recent years, resulting from the discovery that not all impacts are created equal in peace operations and crisis management.

While efficiency is understood by the French government as a project in which the effects justify the expenditure incurred, others understand it less as a measure of funds well spent than a measure of the outcome achieved compared with a given output; efficiency thus revolves around identifying issues of opportunities used or missed (wasted). As Claude Fandre, head of the Evaluation Department of France's Ministère des Affaires Étrangères et Européennes, suggests, *effectiveness* is understood as *efficacy* in the French language, which has a decidedly different meaning in English.[50] Generally, however, *efficiency* is the term commonly used for relating outputs to inputs. A process is efficient if it requires relatively small inputs to produce a certain amount of output. If a process produces relatively small outputs compared to inputs, it is said to be *inefficient*.[51]

Performance Measurement and Performance Management

Performance measurement and management are underpinned by efficiencies. According to John Borton, the founder of ALNAP, the origins of performance measurement lie in the Industrial Revolution and the advent of large-scale manufacturing processes. The focus at that time was on increasing the efficiency of individual workers and was conceived primarily in terms of volume and cost and thereby productivity.[52] Since the mid-1980s, says Borton, the development of performance measurement and performance management has increased significantly and now includes measures such as quality, speed, flexibility, and dependability. As antiquated accounting-based performance mechanisms were replaced with balanced, multi-dimensional, non-financial, external, and forward looking performance measures, the *Balanced Scorecard* method was born. The expansion of such private industry performance measurement methods into the public sector has had positive results. Public sector endeavours have benefited by increased transparency, improved performance, organizational learning, and improved intelligence and services.[53]

Figure 13 shows the process of performance measurement, where each performance outcome becomes the foundation for the next outcome, and so on in a chain formation.

If a program's goals, objectives, and performance indicators have been carefully constructed, measurement will be a relatively mechanical

FIGURE 13
The Performance Measurement Process

Target →	Baseline →	Indicators →	Actual →	Review
End state or performance expectations	Conditions existing at outset of an activity	Performance, quantitative and qualitative	Assessment, monitoring, and reporting of actual end state	Comprehensive overview

Source: Meharg, "Measuring the Effectiveness of Reconstruction and Stabilization Activities," 37.

process. However, because there is no way to completely eliminate subjective judgment from any decision-making process, measurement must rely on agreed-upon systems or stakeholder consensus. Regardless of the clarity of a performance indicator, interpretations of the degree of achievement may vary. This variation may be minimized by careful wording of the performance indicators, but it may not be possible to completely eliminate varying opinions.[54] Moreover, any sophisticated form of measuring human conditions, or "soft" indicators, becomes challenging due to the complex nature of human relationships, psychologies, and unknown consequences of activities. A typical performance measurement framework is shown in Figure 14.

The various peace operations and crisis management activities within the security, governance, economic, judicial, and civil society sectors typically use performance indicator measuring systems, by which activity targets/projections are compared with actual project status.

FIGURE 14
A Performance Measurement Framework

Results	Performance Indicators	Data Sources	Reach and Beneficiaries	Collection Methods	Collection Frequency	Responsible
Impact						
Outcomes						
Outputs						
Resources						

Source: CIDA, *Results Approach*, 74.

Every organization requires three kinds of performance metrics: 1) metrics to measure its success in mobilizing resources; 2) metrics to measure its staff's effectiveness on the job; and 3) metrics to measure its progress in fulfilling its mission.[55] According to Sawhill and Williamson, the first two sets of metrics are relatively easy to create, while the third – an organization's progress towards its own mandate – is the most difficult, yet the most crucial. The authors refer to the mandate of CARE USA as a good example of a rather lofty goal: to affirm the dignity and worth of individuals and families living in some of the world's poorest communities. This mandate is replete with qualitative terms such as *dignity* and *worth*, as well as quantitative terms such as *individuals, families,* and *poorest*. For CARE USA to confirm whether it is fulfilling its mandate, it has three options in measuring success. It can:

- Narrowly define its mandate so that progress can be measured directly (in fact, making its mission quantifiable);
- Invest in research to determine whether its activities actually help to mitigate problems or promote benefits in accordance with its mission;
- Develop micro-level goals that if achieved would imply success on the macro-level.[56]

Borton posits that many lessons for the humanitarian sector can be gleaned from the opportunities and constraints experienced by the public sector in its adoption of performance measurement and performance management systems. Specifically, "efforts to measure performance should seek to limit themselves to overall measures showing trends in performance at a very aggregate level and that great care should be taken in using such measures as a means of controlling performance."[57]

Interestingly, Borton discovered that the humanitarian sector adopted evaluation methods at least a decade prior to its development of a framework for measuring overall performance.[58] In contrast, the opposite sequencing has been the norm in the private and public sectors, as well as in other peace operations sectors including defence and security. Militaries commonly use performance measurement and performance management within their planning and implementation activities and are only recently turning to assessments, monitoring, and overall evaluations of their activities. A potential explanation for this phenomenon within the humanitarian sector is that aid and assistance are not finite activities with specific goals, while military activities are planned as finite, with goals relating to an overall mission mandate. In addition, the humanitarian sector is described as many autonomous organizations, while multinational troops contributing to UN operations are directed under a status of force agreement (SOFA).

David Beer, chief superintendent, Royal Canadian Mounted Police, and former police commissioner of MINUSTAH,[59] maintains that civilian police performance is difficult to measure: "Who does it? Who pays for it? What period of time? Is performance compared against the security mandate?" Beer says these types of questions can structure the performance to be measured. "Performance measurement is about managing expectations," and in his experience, "expectations for policing are never met ... The true measures of success take time, and we don't have the time. Better questions may be: What was it like then? What is it like now? What are the changes? We need to start with objective measures: Who have you trained? How many have you trained? Did the training match up with the government's needs? This then moves into subjective measuring."[60]

Beer concludes that the only true measures of success are 1) transparency (such as fair trials, etc.), 2) accountability, and 3) sustainability. "However, we are never there long enough to see these things. Yet these three things are the only things that matter in the long term." He says, "In Haiti, which was my mission, whenever I felt like we were infringing on local cultures, I had to ask if we were doing things referring to these three measures. When police groups asked for Cadillac police vehicles rather than Volkswagen police cars, I had to question this against the three measures, because they wouldn't be able to afford the long-term maintenance, gas, and mechanics for expensive vehicles."[61]

Evaluations

Evaluation is a process, a professional field of expertise, and also a form of reporting. (See Figure 15.) Evaluation is generally completed internally and retrospectively;[62] an evaluation is retrospective by definition. Evaluations are understood in the literature as "periodic reviews of program activities, outcomes and impacts with an emphasis on lessons learned."[63] They are meant to offer a systematic and reliable assessment of the effectiveness of activities in a broader spectrum of interventions. Because results often take time to take effect, evaluations can be done years after an intervention activity has concluded. *Monitoring* is a term used to assess ongoing activities, in a continual, systematic collection, analysis, and use of data during the course of a project[64] whereas evaluation is used to assess activities after they have been completed. Evaluation studies an activity's impact and sustainability long after the project has been completed.

Monitoring and Evaluation (M&E) is the process of evaluation that is built into a project. It typically has its own budget line and is embedded into

FIGURE 15
The Evaluation Process

| Inputs | → | Outputs | → | Outcomes | → | Effects / Impacts |

Compliance and legal checks, audit

Monitoring/management

Mid-term review

Final evaluation

Ex post evaluation

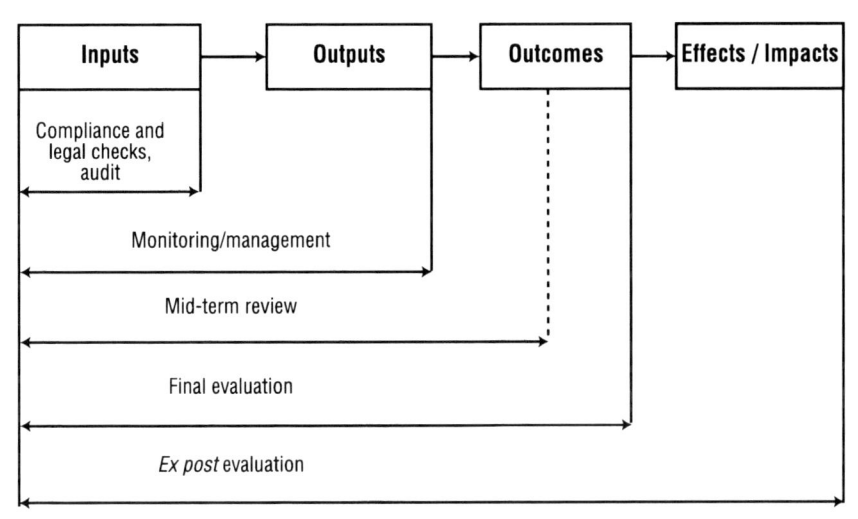

Source: French Ministry of Foreign Affairs, Evaluation Unit, http://www.diplomatie.gouv.fr/en/IMG/pdf/399_Int_Guide_eval_EN.pdf. Evaluation Guide 2007, 10.

various stages of a project's life cycle. Monitoring studies, however, follow a group of subjects for a longer period, analyzing how certain characteristics such as behaviour change over time. These types of evaluation are time and resource consuming as they require long-term investment by interveners.

Sometimes evaluations are completed before the end of an intervention activity and can offer judgment about the expected effects of an activity."[65] *Ex-ante* evaluations are carried out before the completion of an activity, *ex-nunc* evaluations during the life cycle of an activity, and *ex-post* evaluations after the activity's completion. Ex-post evaluations are the most common among stakeholders, asking, "What went right and what went wrong?"

The most familiar type of ex-post evaluations are lessons learned and best practices.[66] Since 2002 there has been a shift away from use of the term *lessons learned* to *best practices*. Although the notion of best practices is a military construct, it has emerged in the broader security and defence sector in which the NGO Crisis Management Initiatives (CMI) is involved. CMI considers best practices as a way to inquire into the efficacy of security and defence activities and apply such practices to future interventions. CMI uses a best-practices framework by inquiring how activities were successful, when/where they occurred and in what contexts, and how the successful effects of such interventions can be replicated in a similar way to ex-post evaluation questions.

Emery Brusset of Channel Research, which conducts third-party evaluations of bilateral intervention projects, offers that measures are informed by current public policies. Public policies are informed by principles such as the importance of *rule of law* and *security sector reform*, which become the terms of agreement, for example, in an ICRC mandate. Guidance also informs the process of evaluating, and Brusset says that Channel Research draws guidance directly from the OECD-DAC principles of relevance, coherence, and sustainability, as well as the principles of the Overseas Development Institute (ODI)[67] and Britain's ALNAP.[68] Some organizations, such as Germany's GTZ, have their own evaluation guidelines. Channel has also drawn guidance from the ICRC, NORAD guidelines, and USAID to conduct its comprehensive evaluations.

Impact assessments track change in a society as it relates to an identifiable source or set of factors. Brusset presents his systematic approach to evaluations. It takes three to four months to fully complete the studies for assessments and evaluations. If a multi-country study is undertaken, a period of approximately eight months is dedicated to the evaluation. Channel Research provides supplementary assessments of intervention activities meant to augment internal evaluations (or self-evaluation). As many organizations do not have time frames or end states built into their work, Channel Research's job becomes more complex. Typically, eight months to a year are required for peace-building projects to see "results"; impact assessments – a longer-term evaluation – can sometimes go on for two years. The time frame is dependent upon the client.[69]

Impact evaluation is the systematic identification of the effects – positive or negative, intended or not – on recipient populations and their environments caused by a given activity (usually within the development sector). Impact evaluation helps in gaining a better understanding of the extent to which activities reach the poor and the magnitude of their effects on people's welfare. This method is usually an aggregate of a range of methods, including large-scale sample surveys, small-scale rapid assessments, participatory appraisals, group interviews, key informants, case studies, and available secondary data.[70] This measuring system is informing the emerging methods for evaluating peace operations and crisis management interventions.

Helpful to the present study is ALNAP's evaluation typology (see Table 2) that differentiates between the types of evaluative reports of humanitarian action intended to reflect their different objectives and functions.[71]

TABLE 2
ALNAP's Evaluation Typology

Audit
An assessment of the degree to which an organization or its output conformed to stated objectives and/or international norms.

Conference, Workshop, or Seminar
Conference/workshop/seminar reports reviewing humanitarian action

Evaluation
A systematic and impartial examination of humanitarian action intended to draw lessons to improve policy and practice and enhance accountability. It has the following characteristics:
- It is commissioned by or in cooperation with the organization(s) whose performance is being evaluated.
- It is undertaken either by a team of non-employees (external) or by a mixed team of non-employees (external) and employees (internal) from the commissioning organization and/or the organization being evaluated.
- It assesses policy and/or practice against recognized criteria: efficiency, effectiveness/timeliness/coordination, impact, connectedness, relevance/appropriateness, coverage, coherence, and, as appropriate, protection.
- It articulates findings, draws conclusions, and makes recommendations.

Follow-Up Study
Study following up the implementation of evaluative study's recommendations.

Good Practice Study
A study intended to establish what constitutes good practice (sometimes referred to as best practice) in the provision of humanitarian assistance.

Lessons Study
A study initiated by an organization with the explicit objective of identifying lessons within that organization, but falling outside the full evaluation definition. A process that may be facilitated by external consultants but is generally internal.

Real-Time Evaluation
An evaluation that is carried out while a program is in full implementation, and that simultaneously feeds back its findings to the program for immediate use.

Review
An assessment (internal or external) of humanitarian action falling outside the full evaluation definition. Included in this category are internal reviews, impact assessments, mid-term reviews, monitoring activities, policy reviews, and operational research.

Summary
The summarized version of an evaluation or review, either prepared by the report authors or the commissioning agency, for dissemination in parallel with or instead of the full report.

Synthesis Report
An analysis of a series of evaluations to form an overall picture and assessment of the projects, programs, policies, or organizations that have been evaluated.

Many options are available within this typology; each is useful in understanding progress, success, and effectiveness. ALNAP's typology can inform decision-makers as to the best form of assessment required to address progress.

Evaluations generally support mandate extensions and funding increases. The notion of *validation* underpins this type of evaluation. In other words, evaluations are conducted to validate the pre-planned goals achieved through an intervention activity. *Goals* are an overall statement of intent and are broad, timeless, and unconcerned with particular achievements within a specified time period.[72] Because most goals – referred to in the development sector as *benchmarks*[73] – are not dependent upon attitudinal or behavioural changes in recipient populations, and because they *are* dependent upon controlled project variables (such as number of people trained, tonnes of food allocated, money spent), evaluations can be conducted when clear goals are present in an activity. Evaluations are more difficult when clear goals are absent from a project or were poorly envisioned during its planning phases. Notions of progress are absent in evaluations; however, *coherence* frames evaluations in the development sector.[74] Evaluations are distinctly different from the mechanisms used to measure progress.

The language of evaluation is measurement and validation, yet this field now places increased emphasis on *verification* as the modality for assessing intervention activities such as peace operations and crisis management. Verification is a process of reviewing, comparing, and testing to establish and document that a project meets a standard or specified requirement. By contrast, *validation* refers to meeting the needs of the intended beneficiary, recipient, or donor. The wider field of evaluation is beginning to move away from measuring the success of a project's mandate and to move towards the assessment of the broader situation in which a project is operationalized. In addition, as Emery Brusset points out, there is a shift in the language and meaning of evaluations in his field. This shift suggests that evaluation has become about verification, *not* measurement, and that it is evidence based, *not* measurement based.[75] Resource-heavy evaluations that require expertise, time, and money are not popular within the humanitarian sector. Based on ALNAPs findings, evaluations of the humanitarian sector are not as easy as other stakeholders would suggest. There is a heavy weighting on results rather than processes; Brusset examines this distinction in chapter 11.

Professional evaluation firms such as Channel Research implement in their work the OECD language of *input, output, outcome,* and *impact* through the broad, development-related principles of relevance, coherence, and sustainability of aid and assistance. These three principles are key to verifying intervention activities, whether they occur in the humanitarian, development, or defence and security sectors.

Auditing

Financial auditing has recently come of age. In 2005, the International Financial Reporting Standards (IFRS) were adopted by the European Union, with others to follow, including China, Japan, and India. According to industry experts, with the advent of the IFRS the barriers to a true global accounting language have now disappeared.[76] When the IFRS were originally conceived in 2001, it would have been considered as fantasy for other non-western countries to adopt them. Now, Europe and the United States, although they still use the generally accepted accounting principles (GAAP), are no longer able to pull economic strings as they once did, as the standards apply to them as well as the newcomers, which include over one hundred countries.

Auditing, a term most often applied to financial compliance, is applied to international policing missions in terms of compliance to international standards, policies, procedures, and rules.[77] Yet many stakeholders cringe at the use of the term, thinking it crass and inappropriate for measuring progress.[78] Crass or not, the term appears to have some appeal. On 22 April 2008, I attended a pre-deployment presentation by Colonel Denis Thompson before he was to head up the Canadian Forces in Kandahar. Col Thompson dedicated half of his presentation to something he referred to as the *audit trail* – in his words, a process that allows Canadians to understand how well their money is being spent to create a positive effect in Afghanistan. Applying auditing to operations shifts CF peace operations activities into the public realm, allowing for a semblance of transparency for those footing the bill for stabilization and reconstruction.[79] However, it may be flawed logic to use cost effectiveness as a significant measure or indicator attributed to success and positive impact.

Standards

A *standard* is a reference point that allows comparisons. Standards are sets of criteria, guidelines, or best practices.[80] According to the International Standard Organization (ISO), a standard is a "document, established by consensus and approved by a recognized body, that provides, for common and repeated use, rules, guidelines or characteristics for activities or their results, aimed at the achievement of the optimum degree of order in a given context." Standards should be based on the consolidated results of science, technology, and experience, and aimed at the promotion of optimum community benefits.[81] Of importance to this definition is the fact that standards are adopted and formally agreed upon by a community of practice. Further, all manner of fields have developed standards, including medicine, architecture, social work, psychology, logistics, library science, waste disposal, and hydrology. Standardization has benefited the development of these fields while allowing for creativity and good judgment in their application. The development of standards is an integral part of the evolution towards a common tradespace, and many movements are afoot attempting to develop standards for sustainable development,[82] humanitarian aid and assistance, private industry, and government interagency approaches, amongst others.

Charles Call questions the application of the notion of standard setting to the wider peace-building field of practice. "Given the ongoing constraints confronting international agencies engaged in peacebuilding," he asks, "does it make sense to hold a standard that will very rarely be met?"[83] However, Ted Itani, a senior officer with the ICRC, maintains that the Sphere standards are a good starting point in the process of measuring progress within the humanitarian NGO sector.[84]

Substantive evaluation standards developed through the Joint Committee on Standards for Educational Evaluation (JCSEE) are widely used in the evaluation field. The four basic JCSEE standards are utility, propriety, feasibility, and accuracy. It is noteworthy that these standards help potential evaluators and program planners identify their values, perspectives, and rationale *in advance of* implementation, so that they are aware of value judgments built into the evaluations. These standards are meant to guide the methodology, design, and implementation of evaluations.[85]

Metrics, Indicators, and Benchmarks

Jason Ladnier, a defence scientist working with the US government, says that he gets into trouble with his military colleagues when he uses words such as *metrics* in a loose way.[86] Says Ladnier, military planners take their language very seriously.

Measures of effectiveness are usually in the form of *metrics*, which are specific indicators that are measured to assess an intentional impact over time on the physical or social environment. Metrics are most often used with a series of scores and numbers, and indicate impacts that are easy to measure. Metrics are about managing expectations and avoiding getting an education on the ground, which helps to prevent doing harm. We must do no harm, or at least do *less* harm, by devising smarter metrics.[87] Linking metrics with a mission is fundamental in measuring effectiveness, progress, and success.[88] More important, perhaps, is confirming the validity of metrics within the context being measured. Ladnier observes, "It is important to do a 'gut check' with people in the field on the metrics themselves. For example, if people 'don't feel safe,' but the military 'feels safe,' we need to develop methodologies that account for the feeling of safety versus the indicators that tell us things should be safe."[89]

Jennifer Hazen, a consultant with the Small Arms Survey, says that *benchmarks* are the language of the United Nations, and the term *indicator* is heard from the donor side, such as OECD-DAC. Indicators are quantitative or qualitative measures of standards used to correlate or predict the value or measure of a mission, program, system, or organization.[90] Hazen says that the UN does use indicators to determine whether benchmarks are reached. Indicators assess if an activity that donors have funded was successful, whereas benchmarks are used to identify key steps that need to be achieved, and to provide a roadmap for measuring progress. Indicators have been used as a way of marking achievements that are necessary in order to enable the exit strategy of a peacekeeping mission.[91] The World Bank Operations Evaluation Department identifies performance indicators as measures of inputs, processes, outputs, outcomes, and impacts for project, programs, or strategies. When supported with sound data collection such as formal surveys, analysis, and reporting, indicators enable managers to track progress, demonstrate results, and take corrective action to improve service delivery. Poorly defined indicators are not good measures of success, whereas if they are designed correctly from the outset of an intervention, they can be an effective means to measure progress towards objectives. *Outcome indicators* – or impact indicators – measure the extent to which an activity contributed to the overall goals of a program.[92]

Indices of key performance indicators are available in most industry sectors; however, this is not the case for peace operations and crisis management. The set of indicators (mortality rates, disease rates, food distribution, etc.) used by humanitarians to determine their levels of success are not shared by militaries distributing aid to fill the so-called aid gap. Various index-type databases exist to support humanitarianism and development, including the Standardized Monitoring and Assessment of Relief and Transition (SMART), DARA's Humanitarian Response Index, World Bank Governance Indicators, and the ICRC's Annual World Disasters Report. As militaries are concerned with winning hearts and minds through humanitarianism, they use a different set of indicators (behaviour changes, attitudinal changes, number of violent attacks, etc.) to measure their success. According to Michael Dziedzic of the United States Institute for Peace, the Metrics Framework for Assessing Conflict Transformation and Stabilization (MPICE) is fifteen years ahead of the data available on indicators of peace and conflict. The framework, in effect, has been developed before the data has become available to input into it, while in other fields such as the health sector, there are available databases of indicator information to plug into measurement systems. Ian Higginbotham concurs with Dziedzic's comment: "My experience in Health Canada suggests that there are clearer indicators of performance; therefore it is easier to measure success, progress, and change."[93] Few of the traditional list of indicators for conflict and societal recovery fully grasp the objectives of peace operations and crisis management. What are the realistic indicators to measure? Mary Kaldor suggests that traditional epidemiological and health indicators are the best ones to indicate change, because micro-indicators are indicative of progress at the macro level.[94]

John Borton of ALNAP identifies the utility of key performance indicators to identify areas of success and failure within particular sectors. The annual compilation of results in a particular sector provides that sector with an overall picture of its performance, which can be compared against that of previous years to identify trends. Members of a sector can then benchmark their own results for the various key performance indicators, with the industry averages or norms thereby indicating areas where they exceed objectives or fall short of them.[95] Some sectors are more able to quantify their indicators, while others – such as those that "improve" the human condition – are much more difficult to quantify in pure terms.

Indices are not always helpful tools. Historically, the assessment of states – and therefore of the potential interventions required – was done through the lens of *failure*. States were indexed based upon their failure to provide health, education, food, and water, as well as their failure to contain disease such as HIV-AIDS. They were also prioritized based on their levels of democratic values and ideologies. The higher a state was ranked, the closer it came to being a fragile, failing, or failed state.[96]

Numbers vs. Narratives

Words do not suffice in measuring success, while numbers do not suffice in capturing ground truth. It is difficult to capture or convert the experience of people into numbers and scores, and easier through narratives and descriptions. However, the world we live in has a short attention span. When politicians have the choice between using statistics or narratives, they expound the numbers when related to a short-term output (30 insurgents killed; three wells dug; 243 girl children attending school; 1.5 million immunized against polio).

The study of measures has traditionally divided them into two types: quantitative and qualitative. Significant misunderstandings exist within the field of peace operations and crisis management about what these two types are and what they mean. The attributed meanings fall between essential and inadequate at best. There is deep distrust between the schools that believe statistics are omnipotent discount narratives, opinions and experiences are irrelevant, and the schools that believe words capture truth and numbers, scores, and measures are simplistic in conveying ground truth.

In their 2004 review for the European Commission on methods for measuring the effectiveness of state aid to small and medium enterprises, Mosselman and Prince observe, "In general, qualitative methods are simplest and cheapest, but have limited explanatory power. Quantitative methods that use a control group are best suited for measuring effectiveness, but are also more expensive and complex."[97] Stuart Gordon agrees with this conclusion, arguing, "To date, MOEs have tended to be largely quantitative, focusing on such things as numbers of projects or amount of money allocated, rather than trying to gauge underlying effectiveness.[98] Higginbotham suggests that there is a way of complementing qualitative, volume-based data by administering *open field* surveys to recipient populations. This triangulates indicators and allows the grouping of qualitative indicators with quantitative ones to create more meaningful information and perhaps a more meaningful evaluation of activities.

This issue is further underpinned by the authors of *A Monitoring and Evaluation Framework for Peace Building* (2006), who suggest that most donors – here specifically peace-building donors – are interested in quantitative approaches to assessing progress in the projects they fund:

> It is understandable why donors would like to adopt a set of "objective indicators," but purely quantitative approaches to evaluating peace building projects face at least three major challenges. First, they depend on reliable and up-to-date data on such factors as demographic displacement and behavioural or attitudinal change, which are particularly difficult to find in divisive conflicts. Second, they have difficulty in determining the distinction between programme contribution and social change: between contribution and attribution. It is unreasonable to claim a peace building programme is unsuccessful if the background conflict continues, and equally unreasonable to claim success if background tensions improve … The third challenge is that "measures like the number of people who have participated in sessions is not telling them what they really want to know."[99]

The authors argue that qualitative approaches are equally ineffective. Traditionally, there has been an over-reliance on informal approaches such as ad hoc interviews and weak methodologies for gathering meaningful narratives to evaluate peace-building projects. Moreover, as most are unsure of how to generate objective measurement from qualitative assessment approaches, there is a greater focus on using dressed-up numbers, scores, and measures to report to donors on progress. Thus, "the tension between quantitative and qualitative approaches tends to be exaggerated."[100]

The strength of qualitative techniques is that they describe the processes behind the results. However, they are unable to tell to what extent an intervention activity achieves its goals. Another weakness is that this method focuses on "first-order effects" only; such effects are merely the means through which goals should be achieved. Moreover, qualitative methods are not always neutral and do not necessarily allow for proving causal relationships between activities and effects. A solely qualitative methodology provides inadequate information regarding impacts and is not rigorous as a core method of evaluation. This method was considered by Mosselman and Prince to reveal the process rather than the effectiveness of an intervention activity. Similarly, evaluations that are conducted prior to the implementation of an intervention activity (ex-ante evaluations) are not considered neutral and cannot take account of an activity's negative or positive consequences.[101]

On the same theme, purely quantitative evaluations do not evaluate effectiveness because they cannot tell what the results of the intervention activity are or how the results are achieved. This type of method focuses on *zero-order effects* and therefore fails to provide a *reality check* because it does not gather insights on the performance of the activity in the field.

Mosselman and Prince go on to suggest that quantitative evaluation of first-order effects is a stronger approach because it is simple and efficient. This method must be based on a survey among recipients of the intervention activity. However, the authors point to weaknesses including the lack of a benchmark, relative subjectivity, and the ignoring of second- and third-order effects. They clearly state that the absence of a control group (benchmarks) is the downfall of any evaluation method. Leading from this, a more effective evaluation method includes a quantitative approach to first- and second-order effects with a control group and/or benchmarks. This method considers the positive and negative effects that could otherwise be eliminated from an evaluation if only first-order effects are considered.

Moreover, and a logical conclusion to their comparison, the evaluation method, which provides a quantitative approach to first-, second-, and third-order effects based on econometric models as well as a variety of qualitative and quantitative data sources, has some major advantages because it is better able to prove causality and the negative and positive consequences of an intervention activity. Of course, there are other methods – including the "goal free program evaluation." However, these ventures are prohibitively expensive and time-consuming.

These positions, of course, are extremes, yet the underlying beliefs – and beliefs they are – inform the mechanisms and tools used for measuring effectiveness, progress, and success in peace operations and crisis management. Numbers do not suffice in measuring success, while words do not suffice in capturing ground truth. The better mechanisms and tools (those that tell us something about an intervention that is useful to planners, and for informing the next intervention) balance quantitative and qualitative approaches to best measure project outcomes against the backdrop of the so-called clients – the recipient populations.

Summary Points

- Although other professions and sectors have standardized vocabulary for assessment and evaluation, this is not the case for most of the sectors involved in international peace operations and crisis management.

- Coupled with distinctly different worldviews, the lack of standardization of language reduces the ability of stakeholders to understand one another's intervention activities and the mechanisms and tools used for measurement.

Notes

[1] Call, "Knowing Peace When You See It," 173–94.
[2] Ted Itani, personal communication, 2008.
[3] Aoi et al., *Unintended Consequences*.
[4] Anderson and Woodrow, *Rising from the Ashes*.
[5] The following example is useful in understanding incentives and behavioural change: When a war-affected Afghan village existing under quasi-Taliban rule is asked for information by NATO forces in exchange for a new village well, their information may conform to what they think the forces want to hear. When the NATO forces depart the region, the village easily reverts to Taliban protection in return for information and/or assistance against the foreign forces. In an insecure environment such as many parts of rural Afghanistan, incentives can be a part of survival but do not lead to lasting behaviour changes.
[6] Mosselman and Prince, *Review of Methods*, 29.
[7] Ibid., 23.
[8] Hawkins, *Power vs. Force*, 46.

[9] Ibid.
[10] Mosselman and Prince, *Review of Methods*, 45.
[11] Brusset et al., "Collaborative Learning Projects," 15.
[12] Mosselman and Prince, *Review of Methods*, 25.
[13] Ibid., 23.
[14] Ibid.
[15] Ibid.
[16] Ibid., 24.
[17] Ibid., 25.
[18] Campbell, "Measures of Effectiveness," 12.
[19] Emery Brusset, personal communication, 2008.
[20] Bonventre, "Monitoring and Evaluation," 68.
[21] Ibid., 67.
[22] Noel Sproles, "Coming to Grips with Measures of Effectiveness," 54.
[23] Ibid.
[24] Sproles, "The Difficult Problem ," 146.
[25] Ibid.
[26] Ian Higginbotham, personal communication, 2008; Veronica Cody, personal communication, 2008; Claude Fandre, personal communication, 2008.
[27] Mike Dziedzic, personal communication, 2008.
[28] André Harvey, personal communication, 2008.
[29] David Last, personal communication, 2008.
[30] John Agoglia, personal communication, 2008.
[31] Ibid.
[32] Kristiina Rintakoski, personal communication, 2008.
[33] Alexander Blyth, personal communication, 2008.
[34] Ibid.
[35] Ibid.
[36] Ibid.
[37] Veronica Cody, personal communication, 2008; Kristiina Rintakoski, personal communication, 2008.
[38] Anonymous, personal communication, 2008.
[39] ALNAP, *Annual Review 2002*, 12.
[40] Veronica Cody, personal communication, 2008; John Agoglia, personal communication, 2008.
[41] Mike Dziedzic, personal communication, 2008.
[42] Brusset et al., "Collaborative Learning Projects," 4.
[43] Mosselman and Prince, *Review of Methods*, 24.
[44] Brusset et al., "Collaborative Learning Projects," 4.
[45] Davies et al., "Assessing the Impact of Social Science Research."
[46] Baylee, "Maximizing the Use of Evaluation Findings," 1.
[47] Ibid.
[48] Brusset et al., "Collaborative Learning Projects," 4.
[49] Direction Générale de la Coopération Internationale et du Développement, *Guide to Evaluations*, 43.
[50] Claude Fandre, personal communication, 2008.
[51] Mosselman and Prince, *Review of Methods*, 24.

[52] Borton, "Literature on Performance Measurement," 1.
[53] Ibid., 3.
[54] Hatfield, "Developing Performance Measures."
[55] Sawhill and Williamson, "Measuring What Matters."
[56] Ibid.
[57] Borton, "Literature on Performance Measurement," 4.
[58] Ibid.
[59] MINUSTAH is the United Nations Stabilization Mission in Haiti (Mission des Nations Unies pour Stabilisation en Haiti).
[60] David Beer, personal communication, 2008.
[61] Ibid.
[62] Emery Brusset, personal communication, 2008; Claude Fandre, personal communication, 2008.
[63] Bonventre, "Monitoring and Evaluation," 66.
[64] Kristiina Rintakoski, personal communication, 2008.; and Bonventre, "Monitoring and Evaluation," 66.
[65] Mosselman and Prince, *Review of Methods*, 36.
[66] Ibid., 35.
[67] The Overseas Development Institute is a leading independent think tank on international development and humanitarian issues. The Humanitarian Practice Network (HPN) at the ODI is an independent forum where fieldworkers, managers, and policy-makers in the humanitarian sector share information, analysis, and experience. HPN Network Papers examines in depth specific issues and experiences in the humanitarian field.
[68] John Borton is one of the vignette contributors (see chapter 7). The founder of ALNAP, Borton is an influential thinker in the field of humanitarian performance.
[69] Brusset et al., "Collaborative Learning Projects."
[70] World Bank, *Monitoring and Evaluation*, 22.
[71] For more information on ALNAP and its evaluation reports database, go to http://www.alnap.org/resources/erd/erd.htm
[72] Bonventre, "Monitoring and Evaluation," 67.
[73] Claude Fandre, personal communication, 2008.
[74] Ibid.
[75] Emery Brusset, personal communication at CMI Workshop, 2007.
[76] Bruce, "Barriers Fall," 2.
[77] Glenn MacPhail, personal communication, 2008.
[78] Mike Cessford, personal communication, 2008.
[79] Denis Thompson, personal communication, CANADEM-hosted public presentation, 2008.
[80] Bonventre, "Monitoring and Evaluation," 67.
[81] International Organization for Standardization, *ISO/IEC Guide 2*.
[82] AccountAbility is at the forefront of engaging the development community in dialogue about investing in standards for sustainable development. See Litovsky et al., "Investing in Standards for Sustainable Development."
[83] Call, "Knowing Peace When You See It," 183.
[84] Ted Itani, personal communication, 2008.

[85] ALNAP, *Evaluating Humanitarian Action*, 72.
[86] Jason Ladnier, personal communication, 2008.
[87] Ibid.
[88] Sawhill and Williamson, "Measuring What Matters "; Leakey, personal communication, 2008; Alexander Blyth, personal communication, 2008.
[89] Jason Ladnier, personal communication, 2008.
[90] Bonventre, "Monitoring and Evaluation," 67.
[91] Jennifer Hazen, personal communication, 2008.
[92] Bonventre , "Monitoring and Evaluation," 68.
[93] Ian Higginbotham, personal communication, 2008.
[94] Mary Martin, personal communication, CMI Workshop, 2007; Ted Itani, personal communication, 2008.
[95] Borton, "The Literature on Performance Measurement," 4.
[96] A fragile state is a low-income country noted by weak state capacity and legitimacy, causing susceptibility to crises. Fragility is characterized by extreme inequality, lack of access to health and education, fragmented security organizations, marginalization of racial or ethnic minorities, and susceptibility to institutional failures. According to indices such as the World Bank's Country Policy and Institutional Assessment, almost fifty countries are falling behind the achievement of the UN's Millennium Development Goals. There is an evolution away from the use of the term "fragile state" towards "resilience," because fragility is a negative label. OECD now uses the term "resilience" and applies the term "fragile" less often. Resilience, although itself a label, is a more positive one than failing or failed states (Stephan Massing, Rory Keane, and Claude Fandre, personal communication, 2008). Donors as well as implementing agencies are shifting away from measuring fragility because potential countries have used fragility to their own benefit to coerce more money from donors.
[97] Mosselman and Prince, *Review of Methods*, 80.
[98] Stuart Gordon, personal communication, 2008.
[99] PricewaterhouseCoopers LLP, *A Monitoring and Evaluation Framework for Peace Building*, 8.
[100] Ibid.
[101] Mosselman and Prince, *Review of Methods*, 90.

CHAPTER 4

Mechanisms and Tools

The current mechanisms, tools, and systems for measuring intervention activities are expensive in terms of time, labour, and resources, and typically attempt to measure outputs rather than longer-term outcomes and results. More suitable mechanisms and tools (those that tell us something about an intervention that is useful to planners and that have transferable lessons to inform the next intervention activities[1]) balance quantitative and qualitative approaches to best measure sustainable project outcomes for war-affected publics. This chapter examines some of the sector-specific mechanisms and tools that could be relevant to the common tradespace.

The Humanitarian Sector

Sphere Standards

Established in 1995, People In Aid is a member-run international network of development and humanitarian assistance agencies whose goal is the relief of poverty and suffering. The organization's purpose is to enhance the impact of its members through better people management and support. For People In Aid, the impact and effectiveness of relief and development operations depend upon the quality of staff and volunteers and the support an agency gives them. The organization was created to fill a human resources gap to support those intervening in war-affected environments. Its Code of Good Practice is considered to be the hallmark human resource (HR) guidance in the effective management and support of humanitarian aid and assistance workers.

A few years after the creation of People In Aid, the Sphere Project was launched in 1997. A group of concerned humanitarian NGOs, along with the Red Cross and Red Crescent movement, set out to standardize some of the ad hoc processes that directly affected the alleviation of human suffering. According to the project, Sphere is a handbook as well as a consultative process and is committed to the keystone principles of quality and accountability. The Sphere *Handbook* is updated through consultative processes, and practitioners can access updated iterations to be available periodically.[2] As the use of the handbook has matured, and the international community of stakeholders has continued to transform towards a common tradespace, the Sphere project is now providing a mechanism by which other Humanitarian Quality Standards – such as those developed by ALNAP and others – can become "companion" standards to the Sphere Project Humanitarian Charter and Minimum Standards in Disaster Response.

Humanitarian Accountability Partnership

The Active Learning Network for Accountability and Performance in Humanitarian Action (ALNAP) was established in 1997, following a multi-agency evaluation of the Rwanda genocide. ALNAP is a collective response by the humanitarian sector, dedicated to improving humanitarian performance through increased learning and accountability.

ALNAP is conducting a feasibility study of the mechanisms for assessing and reporting on the overall performance of the humanitarian sector. The network suggests that such a mechanism could be of substantial benefit to the sector and could reinforce and support efforts to improve humanitarian performance. Its project process is highly consultative and transparent in order to achieve buy-in from humanitarian stakeholders early on in the process. ALNAP has adopted a project to think through overall performance of the humanitarian sector in a systematic approach because their raison d'être is seeking ways, means, and ends that lead to accountability and performance within their sector.

The Rwandan genocide spurred the development of the doctrine of the international community, including the establishment of various institutes such as the Humanitarian Accountability Partnership (HAP) in 2003. A perceived "accountability" gap was identified regarding the ways in which humanitarian stakeholders responded to war- and disaster-affected environments, including lack of standards, perceived legitimacy issues, and the unintended consequences of humanitarian aid and assistance. HAP was created to promote the achievement of the highest principles of accountability through self-regulation by its members and has established a Standard of Humanitarian Accountability and Quality Management so that the people affected by crises can hold aid agencies to account. By adhering to the HAP standard, a humanitarian aid agency makes itself accountable to disaster survivors for the quality of its humanitarian work.

In addition to the principles of humanitarianism,[3] HAP has developed a series of Humanitarian Quality Management Benchmarks, which are intended to be applied in tandem with the Sphere standards. The benchmarks are

- humanitarian quality management
- transparency
- beneficiary participation
- staff competencies
- complaints handling
- continual improvement

These benchmarks for aid and assistance delivery provide an aspirational framework through which small and medium sized agencies can work.[4]

Evaluation of Humanitarian Action

According to ALNAP, there has been a move towards streamlining evaluations so that they are more effective and meaningful within the sector. Evaluation of Humanitarian Action (EHA) has been developed as a systematic and impartial examination of humanitarian action intended to draw lessons to improve policy and practice and enhance accountability. In EHA, evaluations are commissioned by or in cooperation with the organization whose performance is being evaluated; they are undertaken solely by external evaluators or by a mix of staff and external experts; they are assessed against recognized criteria such as the OECD's Development Assistance Committee (DAC) criteria; and lastly, they are articulated through findings, conclusions, and recommendations for the purpose of improving policy, practice, and accountability within the sector.[5]

Human Security Project

The Human Security Project (HSP) adopted a set of six principles that became the benchmarks of this assessment framework methodology. The principles are

- primacy of human rights
- legitimacy
- bottom-up approach (accountability beyond consultancy)
- effective multilateralism
- non-regional approach
- clear strategic direction

HSP discovered that the principles, loosely defined, could become benchmarks of success. The principles are an operational framework as well as benchmarks and a methodology. Having a robust assessment framework does not suggest that one size fits all missions, but the HSP argues that some benchmarks are universal. Measuring progress is easier to conceptualize when principles are the benchmarks, because it is easy to identify when principles are not met or upheld. For example, it is easier to measure *insecurity* than *human security*.[6]

Inter-Agency Whole-of-Government Sector

Metrics Framework for Assessing Conflict Transformation and Stabilization

Metrics Framework for Assessing Conflict Transformation and Stabilization (MPICE) was developed by the United States Institute of Peace (USIP) with the input of several partners including the Peacekeeping and Stability Operations Institute (PKSOI) and the US Army Corps of Engineers. The purpose of the project was to establish a system of metrics to assist in formulating policy and implementing strategic plans to transform conflicts and bring stability to war-torn societies. MPICE was developed to provide feedback to policy-makers to determine the effectiveness of intervention strategies. The project focuses on establishing better, more effective steps in peacemaking.[7]

According to Michael Dziedzic, a senior program officer at the United States Institute for Peace, and main author of the MPICE metrics framework and user handbook, theory and practice are brought together to enable policy-makers and practitioners to track progress towards self-sustaining peace in conflict zones. With three years of development, which included many different US government departments, think tanks, and academic institutions, over 800 metrics were established in support of conflict transformation and the achievement of viable peace. These metrics provide both a baseline assessment tool for policy-makers to diagnose potential obstacles to stabilization prior to an intervention and an instrument for practitioners to track progress from the point of intervention through stabilization and ultimately to a self-sustaining peace.[8]

This metrics system is designed to identify potential sources of continuing violent conflict and instability and to gauge the capacity of indigenous institutions to overcome them. The intention is to enable policy-makers to establish realistic goals, bring adequate resources and authorities to bear, focus their efforts strategically, and enhance prospects for attaining an enduring peace.[9] As well, a software tool supporting the metrics framework was developed to aggregate, statistically correlate, and display the data. The system has been beta-tested in the Sudan, Afghanistan, and Haiti; other applications include Guinea, the Balkans, and the Philippines.

Results-Based Management

In 1996 the Canadian International Development Agency (CIDA) adopted *results-based management* as its main management tool for measuring how, why, when, where, and for whom it was spending Canadian tax dollars, and who was benefiting from the expenditures. It adopted the new system to improve the impact of its work and to achieve increased efficiency, effectiveness, and accountability in achieving that impact.

Results-based measuring is now used by many government departments and agencies, including the European Commission Humanitarian Aid Office (ECHO), which applied a results-based measuring system (RBM) to its Humanitarian Intervention Plans in Afghanistan in 2002–03.[10] RBM is usually employed as a tool to gauge the impact of spending and resource allocation over a period of time in a particular program or activity. These systems use a mixture of quantitative and qualitative data for formal reporting of results.

CIDA's system of results-based management aims to

- define realistic expected results, based on appropriate analyses;
- clearly identify program beneficiaries and design programs to meet their needs;
- monitor progress towards results and resources consumed, with the use of appropriate indicators;

- identify and manage risks, while bearing in mind expected results and the necessary resources;
- increase knowledge by learning lessons and integrating them into decisions; and
- report on results achieved and the resources involved.[11]

This system, however, continues to be redeveloped because it does not capture the required levels of granularity or relevance for future planning. It also indicates direct connections between planned and unplanned activity results or, in other words, intended and unintended consequences, both positive and negative. Those involved in reconstruction or long-term development refer to this system as *performance monitoring plans* that are built on a foundation of *implementation planning*. *Performance reporting* is a result of the data embedded in performance monitoring plans.

Logical Frameworks

The Logical Framework Approach (LFA) is a management tool mainly used in the design, monitoring, and evaluation of development projects. Theory of change is the underpinning concept of results-based measuring and logical chain assessment tools (see Figure 16). This tool is also widely known as Goal Oriented Project Planning (GOPP) or Objectives Oriented Project Planning (OOPP). Developed by Leon J. Rosenberg in 1969, LFA is a project methodology widely adopted by bilateral and multilateral donor organizations.

Within the LFA methodology is the *Logical Framework* – more commonly referred to as a *LogFrame* – which is a tool within the broader methodology. The LogFrame is a management tool used to improve the design of interventions, most often at the project level. It involves identifying performance indicators at each stage of the results chain (inputs, outputs, purpose, and goal) as well as their causal relationships and the assumptions or risks that may influence success and failure. It facilitates planning, execution, and evaluation of an intervention.[12]

The LogFrame takes the form of a 4 x 4 project table. The four rows are used to describe four different types of events that take place as a project is implemented: the project activities, outputs, purpose, and goal. The four columns provide different types of information about the events in each row. The first column provides a narrative description of the event; the second lists one or more objectively verifiable indicators (OVIs) of these events taking place. The third column describes the means of verification (MoV) where information will be available on the OVIs, and the fourth column lists the assumptions. These are external factors that are

FIGURE 16
Logical Framework (LogFrame)

Start work on the Project Summary and Assumptions (Columns 1 and 4). Return to Columns 2 and 3 later.

Step 1: Define the Goal
What is the wider sector or programme goal? What overall need or problem are you trying to address? The goal does not change. It is effected by other factors outside the project. A group of projects may share a common goal.

Step 2: Define the Purpose
What is the rationale for what is planned? What impact do you hope to make? How will the client/user benefit? The purpose often relates to how outputs will be used or implemented. The purpose maybe effected by factors outside your project.

Step 3: Define the Outputs
What will be the measurable end results of the planned activites? What results will the activity be directly responsible for? Given the necessary resources, the management team will be directly accountable for the outputs.

Step 4: Define the Activities
What will actually be done to achieve the outputs? This is a summary presentation showing what needs to be done to accomplish each output.

Step 5: Verify the Vertical Logic
Use the if/then test to check cause and effect. If the given activities are carried out, will the stated output result? And so on up Column 1.
As design and implementation progress, return to the logframe and update it. Changes to assumptions, activities and outputs are certain to happen.

Column 1: Summary - Hierarchy of Objectives	Column 2: Objectively Verifiable Indicators (OVIs)		Column 4: Assumptions and Risks
Goal			
			6e Goal Assumptions
Purpose			
			6d Purpose Assumptions
Outputs			
			6c Output Assumptions
Activities			
			6b Activity Assumptions
			6a Critical Conditions

Step 6e: Define the Assumptions
What external factors are needed for, or may prevent, the long-term sustainability of the activity? Action: Redesign the plan. Evauate your assumptions.

Step 6d: Define the Assumptions
If the activity's purpose is achieved, will this in fact contribute to solving the original problem/need, i.e. the goal? If No, then redesign the activity. If Yes, then state clearly the assumptions you have made to reach this view. Action: Redesign the plan. Evaluate your assumptions.

Step 6c: Define the Assumptions
If the outputs were produced, would the purpose be achieved? What assumptions, outside the control of the activity have been made about the achievement of the outputs? If the risk or assumptions are too great, then redsign.z Action: Redesign the plan. Evaluate your assumptions.

Step 6b: Define the Assumptions
Check your logic. Will the completed activities lead to achievement of the outputs? Are all the resources needed to achieve the outputs? What assumptions, outside the control of the project have been made? If the risk or assumptions are too great, then redesign. Action: Redesign the plan. Evaluate your assumptions.

Step 6a: Define the Assumptions
Include here anything that must happen before the activity can commence.

Source: Department for International Development (DFID), recreated from http://www.dfid.gov.uk/ubs/files/toolsfordevelopment.pdf. *Tools for Development*, March 2003, chapter 5, 5.8.

believed to potentially influence (positively or negatively) the events described in the narrative column. The list of assumptions should include those factors that potentially impact the success of the project but cannot be directly controlled by the project or program managers. In some cases these may include assumptions that if proved wrong will have major negative consequences for a project. Good project design substantiates its assumptions, especially those with a high potential to have a negative impact.

The LogFrame is based upon a temporal logic model that runs through the matrix. This takes the form of a series of connected propositions:

1. If these activities are implemented, and these assumptions hold, then these outputs will be delivered;
2. If these outputs are delivered, and these assumptions hold, then this purpose will be achieved;
3. If this purpose is achieved, and these assumptions hold, then this goal will be achieved.

The series is viewed as a hierarchy of hypotheses, which introduces the essence of a scientific method to non-scientific endeavours such as peace operations and crisis management.

Ian Higginbotham of the Canadian Department of Foreign Affairs and International Trade (DFAIT) points out that measuring is not a simple task and the story is never as black and white as what can fit into the LogFrame boxes. Although DFAIT uses a positive-outcome approach to measuring its activities, like most stakeholder approaches to LogFrames, the process remains an internal rationalization of its own activities.[13] The World Bank suggests that LogFrames can ensure that decision-makers ask fundamental questions and analyze assumptions and risks; however, if the process is managed rigidly, the result is stifled creativity and innovation. If used inappropriately and in a heavy-handed manner, the LogFrame eliminates the dynamism of projects and becomes a static tool that does not reflect changing conditions. Although these disadvantages may be warranted at a headquarters or government agency level, they are not useful in the field where circumstances, resources, and time are under complex pressures.

Colonel Brad Bergstrand, a senior military advisor with the Peacekeeping and Peace Operations Group, Stabilization and Reconstruction Task Force (START), Canadian Department of Foreign Affairs and International Trade, says that START self-evaluates using the results-based measurement process. Because START supports other government agencies, it evaluates its support to other implementing agencies, recipients (NGOs), and beneficiaries (affected peoples) through a process of consultations. START has adopted a common approach to understanding outcomes. Within its RBM approach, it measures three types of outcomes of its activities: immediate outcomes, intermediate outcomes, and ultimate outcomes.

START has come to the realization that it can only measure *immediate* outcomes in today's complex environment. This may be because the fledgling organization was established in late 2005 and requires a period of maturation before it can measure longer-term outcomes related to its projects. It needs time to mature and adopt a blended approach to measuring the efficacy of its activities, based on its inter-agency arrangement. However, it can be argued that unless they are involved in a war-affected environment for the long-term, no sectors or stakeholders are able to understand, let alone measure, ultimate outcomes.[14]

Like Bergstrand, Higginbotham confirms that DFAIT is bound to the results-based measuring philosophy, which employs the logical framework model of inputs, outputs, and outcomes. DFAIT's system is referred to as the *Results Based Performance Framework* (RBPF), and Higginbotham says that it is the reporting tool used on just about every project at DFAIT at annual strategic and country theme level reporting. DFAIT distinguishes between short, medium, and ultimate outcomes, a similar approach to START's immediate, intermediate, and ultimate language. DFAIT uses indicators that are both qualitative and quantitative; each indicator has a source and method that supports baseline data and targets. Baseline data are measures of specific indicators that exist prior to project implementation.[15] Says Higginbotham, "At the highest level we have the Results Based Management and Accountability Framework (RMAF), which has its own set of indicators and uses a five to ten year timeframe to measure results. All program-level minutiae are plowed into RMAF."[16]

In most sectors, success means achieving defined targets. Higginbotham says that DFAIT's definition of success is meeting its targets, but intuitively it asks the appropriate question: "But how do we come up with these targets? And, how do we measure them?" Getting at the root of the target question is the key to measuring. If the wrong questions are asked regarding a project, the wrong indicators will be measured. If this is the case, the questions require re-evaluation.

Based on his experience, Higginbotham believes that few practitioners are willing to attribute hard numbers to targets, so it becomes difficult to measure success.[17]

Inter-Agency Framework for Conflict Analysis in Transition Situations

The US government initiative *Inter-Agency Framework for Conflict Analysis in Transition Situations* (2004) resulted from the Joint UNDG-ECHA Working Group on Transition. The implementation plan called for a framework for a common contextual analysis for the causes of conflict. Having such a framework, it was claimed, would help organizations to "understand and overcome the structures that lead to violent conflict in the first place and promote a coherent and integrated response."[18] The framework, one of the first tools available for an integrated approach to conflict interventions, offers a way to commonly understand the drivers of conflict and the capacities for peace in a particular intervention context.[19]

Post-Conflict Reconstruction Essential Tasks

In 2005 the US Department of State's Office of the Coordinator for Reconstruction and Stabilization (S/CRS) published its *Post-Conflict Reconstruction Essential Tasks*. This document, developed through consultations with reconstruction and stabilization practitioners and interagency working groups, is based on the Joint CSIS/AUSA Post-Conflict Reconstruction (PCR) Task Framework.[20]

The task matrix (see Figure 17) in the document provides a framework applicable to assessing macro-operations in war-torn environments. The matrix is intended to evolve and become more precise when engaged in the feedback loop between theorists, planners, and practitioners. Divided into five technical sectors with corresponding sectoral tasks, it provides an organized framework through which to better understand the various tasks necessary to achieve the environment in which positive peace and development may flourish. According to S/CRS, these five main reconstruction and stabilization sectors and corresponding activities in a war-torn environment require concerted efforts in order to transition towards intended liberal-democratic outcomes. The five sectors are security; governance and participation, humanitarian assistance and social well-being; economic stabilization and infrastructure; and justice and reconciliation. Each has three goals: initial response, transformation, and fostering sustainability.[21]

- The *security* sector's goals are to establish a safe and secure environment; develop legitimate and stable security institutions; and to consolidate indigenous capacity.

- The *governance and participation* sector's goals are to determine governance structure and establish foundation for citizen participation;

FIGURE 17
Essential Tasks Matrix: An Excerpt

	INITIAL RESPONSE **Goal:** Develop mechanisms for addressing past and ongoing grievances	TRANSFORMATION **Goal:** Initiate the building of a legal system and process for reconciliation	FOSTERING SUSTAINABILITY **Goal:** Functioning legal system accepted as legimate and based on international norms
Legal System Reform			
Legal System Reorganization	• Develop strategy to rebuild criminal justice system • Identify countries that can serve as models and sources of expertise	• Promote laws fostering judicial independence and transparency • Review role of judge and prosecutor and promote role of defence lawyer • Foster and develop ethical and independent behavior	• Institutionalize new structures and responsibilities
Code and Statutory Reforms	• Review current laws and resolve questions of applicability • Abolish provisions incompatible with international standards of human rights	• Facilitate discussions leading to new codes	• Implement legal code reform through legislation • Establish consultative mechanism(s) with international organizations, governments and NGOs
Participation	• Create and strengthen legal aid and NGO groups • Channel citizen input into law-drafting process • Translate interim and important laws into local languages	• Initiate public dialogue with all sectors of civil society on legal form	• Provide oversight and monitoring of code implementation
Institutional Reform	• Assess court administration capability and resources	• Incorporate credible local leadership • Develop reform plan to strengthen court administration capabilities and resources	• Finance and implement reform plan • Resolve backlog of cases in old system so that new system has an opportunity to take root
Human Rights			
Abuse Prevention	• Monitor vulnerable groups and act pre-emptively to deter human rights abuses; implement effective warning mechanisms	• Support local capacity to resolve conflict and prevent abuses	• Fold "abuse prevention" efforts into larger judicial and social programs
Capacity Building	• Assess capacity of indigenous communities, human rights, and other groups; engage local communities, consult leaders	• Foster support for/establish mechanisms and local capacity to protect human rights and resolve conflict; support citizen advocacy organizations	• Create mechanisms for organizing human rights and other NGOs; design processes for government/NGO interaction on human rights

Source: US State Department, http://www.state.gov/s/crs/rls/52959.htm, V-4.

promote legitimate political institutions and participatory processes; and consolidate political institutions and participatory processes.

- The *humanitarian assistance and social well-being* sector's goals are to provide for emergency humanitarian needs; establish a foundation for development; and institutionalize a long-term development program.

- The *economic stabilization and infrastructure* sector's goals are to respond to immediate needs; establish a foundation for development; and institutionalize a long term development program.

- The *justice and reconciliation* sector's goals are to develop mechanisms for addressing past and ongoing grievances; build a legal system and process for reconciliation; and cause the functioning legal system to be accepted as legitimate and based on international norms.[22]

These tasks, loosely defined, also become the benchmarks of progress in war-affected environments.

The matrix format is easy to appropriate, yet may not represent the complexity of reconstruction and stabilization nor the underlying themes, motivations, and theory required to understand the stakeholder sectors and related tasks. In particular, the relationships between tasks and the corresponding results of relationships are not encoded in the essential task matrix. The ever-changing political, economic, and cultural environments, along with war-affected populations, further problematize the matrix's potential oversimplification.

The Grid of Fragilities (French Government)

The notion of fragility has come to the fore in French intervention discourse. An interview participant working for the French Ministère des Affaires Étrangères suggested that as all states have their own levels of fragility, even France, they have to be careful in choosing what they say and what they do on this subject. Like many governments involved in supporting development, the Ministère de Affaires Étrangères has developed a cadre of tools to help assess levels of fragility and inform when and how the French government intervenes. The French government refers to one particular tool as the "Grid of Fragilities." This tool identifies gaps in stability or, in other words, fragilities within a state.[23]

The Grid identifies failures and inadequacies, not successes or capacities, and is the counterpoint to the understanding of OECD's Stephan Massing of *resiliency* as a notion for framing capacities.[24] Massing suggests that OECD use the term resilience, which is the opposite of fragility, arguing that resilience is a better label because it is positive, whereas fragility is negative. Massing stresses that "we must think about how terms are used by donors and beneficiaries/recipients."[25]

However, the French development department has not yet adopted the resilience label, and has developed a methodology based on fragile state indices coded through its Grid of Fragilities. The Grid, along with its supporting document, was validated in December 2007 and continues to be developed; however, the interview participant indicated that it was not fully functional as of March 2008.

According to this ministry employee, metrics and indicators are *fixed*, and his department is uncomfortable with this because of the "process of objectification" that occurs when using such systems of analysis. Instead, the Grid, which was developed using indices, is employed through an exchange between the field level and the development office in Paris regarding any specific fragile environment of importance to French national interests. The Ministère de Affaires Étrangères wants the information in the matrix to come from the ground, rather than being a top-down approach with a focus on micro data (rather than macro). The defence attachés of the French Interior Security also submit information for inclusion in the Grid process. Once the Grid is completed, they meet and discuss the results. The results are returned to embassies for action in the field. This then sets additional priorities for development work and engagement with partners in the countries in which France is working.

Security and Defence Sector

Effects-Based Operations

Effects-Based Operations (EBO) – known also as Effects-Based Approach to Operations, or EBAO – is a planning methodology for the conduct of military operations. A military planning tool generated in the United States, it is now being embraced by other allies including Britain and Canada, as well as regional organizations like NATO. The concept of EBO is not new and is based on an historical military tradition of shaping the will of an adversary. EBO is most effective in its adaptation of "network-centric warfare, technological, and real-time communications linking all aspects of war fighting into a shared situational awareness and shared understanding of command intent to achieve a unity and synchronicity of effects that multiplies the power of military forces."[26] This planning methodology maximizes efficiency and minimizes wasted efforts in the pursuit of goals.[27] (For examples of tools, see Figures 18, 19, and 20.) EBO is intended to influence the thinking and behaviour of an adversary in order to reach an envisioned effect.[28]

FIGURE 18
Effects Assessment Report Using the "Red-Yellow-Green" Military Assessment Scale

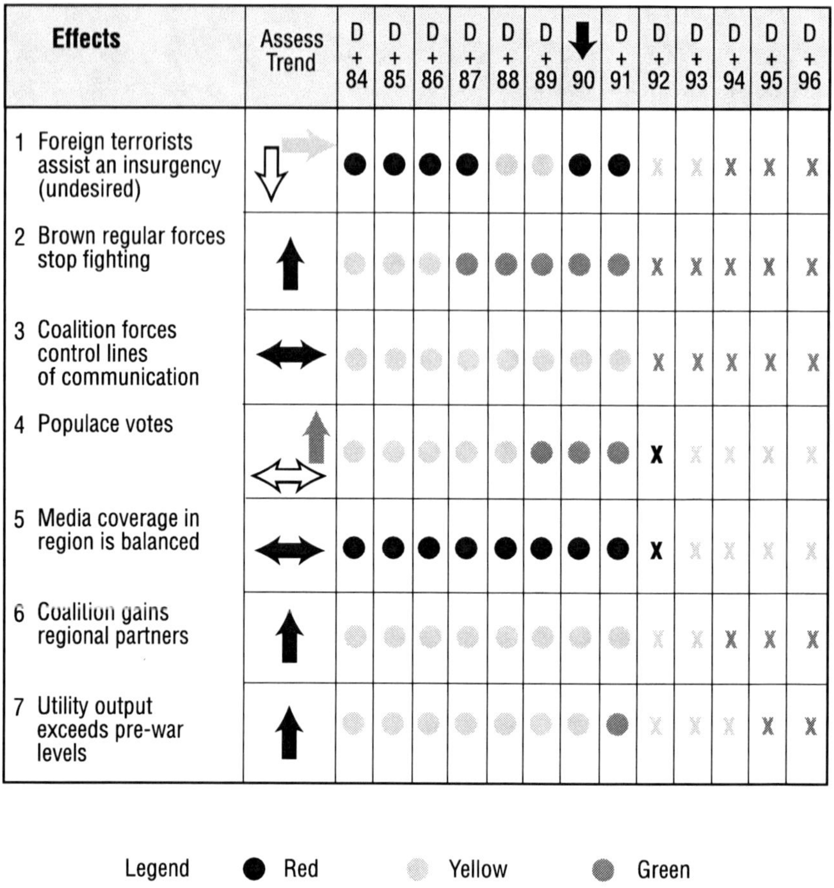

Effects	Assess Trend	D+84	D+85	D+86	D+87	D+88	D+89	D+90 ⬇	D+91	D+92	D+93	D+94	D+95	D+96
1 Foreign terrorists assist an insurgency (undesired)	⬇	●	●	●	●	◐	◐	●	●	X	X	X	X	X
2 Brown regular forces stop fighting	⬆	◐	◐	◐	●	●	●	●	●	X	X	X	X	X
3 Coalition forces control lines of communication	⬌	◐	◐	◐	◐	◐	◐	◐	◐	X	X	X	X	X
4 Populace votes	⬆⬌	◐	◐	◐	◐	◐	●	●	●	X	X	X	X	X
5 Media coverage in region is balanced	⬌	●	●	●	●	●	●	●	●	X	X	X	X	X
6 Coalition gains regional partners	⬆	◐	◐	◐	◐	◐	◐	◐	◐	X	X	X	X	X
7 Utility output exceeds pre-war levels	⬆	◐	◐	◐	◐	◐	◐	◐	●	X	X	X	X	X

Legend   ● Red   ◌ Yellow   ◐ Green

This chart is an example of how a joint force headquarters might track progress towards attaining desired effects. It indicates progress for previous days (the current day is D+89) and provides a forecast for future days. Note that undesired effects (Effect #1) also can be tracked in this manner. Task performance helps determine progress towards attaining a desired effect.

Source: US Joint Warfighting Center, *Commander's Handbook*, iv-14.

Mechanisms and Tools 103

FIGURE 19
Lines of Operations Using Effects

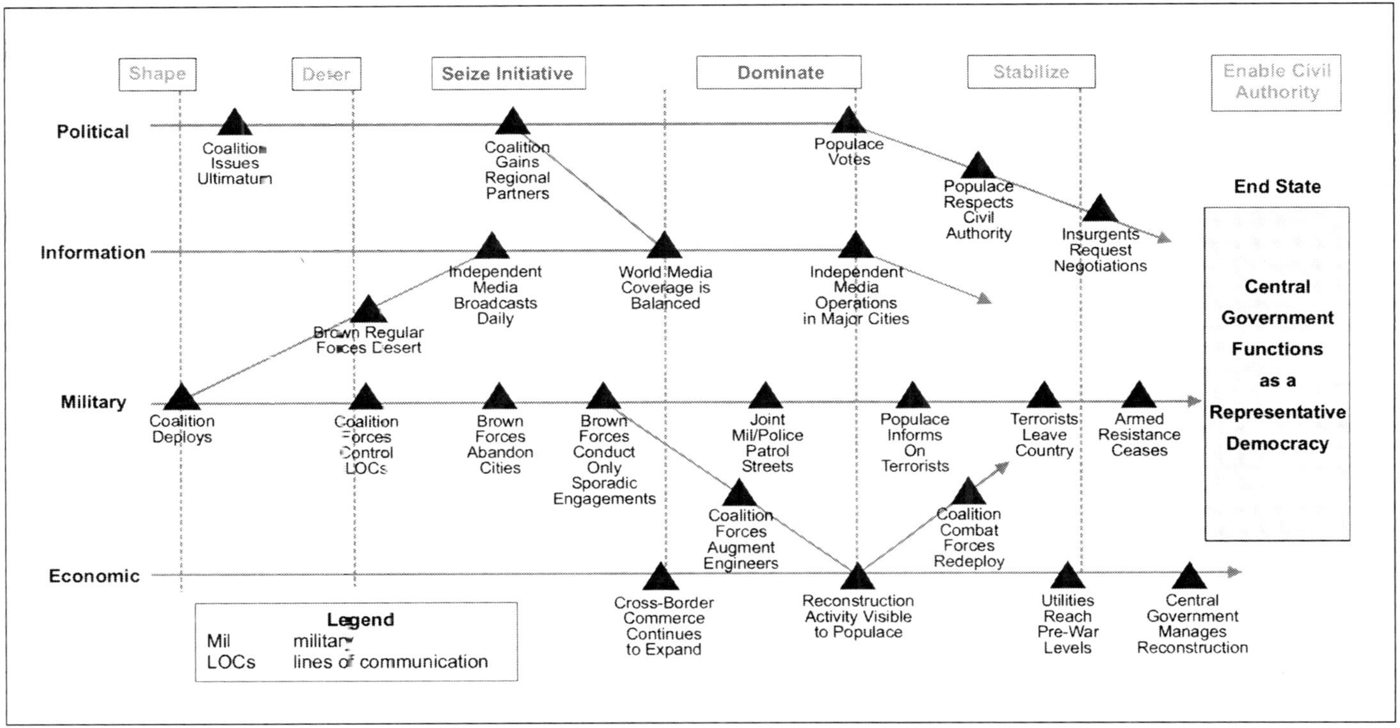

Source: US Joint Warfighting Center, *Commander's Handbook*, iii-21.

FIGURE 20
Mission Analysis Process

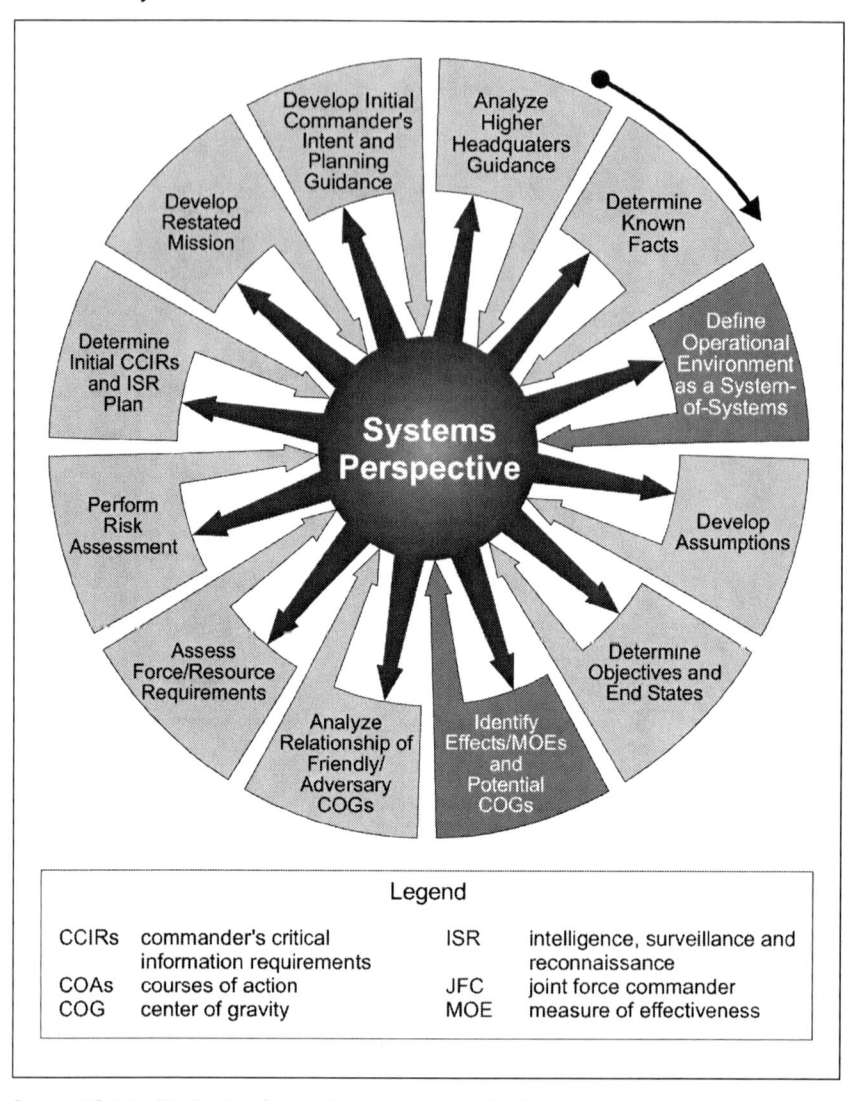

Mission Analysis Process wheel with "Systems Perspective" at center, surrounded by the following steps:
- Analyze Higher Headquaters Guidance
- Determine Known Facts
- Define Operational Environment as a System-of-Systems
- Develop Assumptions
- Determine Objectives and End States
- Identify Effects/MOEs and Potential COGs
- Analyze Relationship of Friendly/Adversary COGs
- Assess Force/Resource Requirements
- Perform Risk Assessment
- Determine Initial CCIRs and ISR Plan
- Develop Restated Mission
- Develop Initial Commander's Intent and Planning Guidance

Legend

CCIRs	commander's critical information requirements	ISR	intelligence, surveillance and reconnaissance
COAs	courses of action	JFC	joint force commander
COG	center of gravity	MOE	measure of effectiveness

Source: US Joint Warfighting Center, *Commander's Handbook*, iii-3.

In theory, there are some commonalities between EBO planning for military operations and the measurement of effectiveness in peace operations and crisis management environments. As with EBOs, successful peace operations and crisis management MOEs must be supported by an integrated whole of government approach that is capable of understanding the conflict environment as a complex system of systems.[29] A typical mission analysis process identifies effects and MOEs and can be applied to analyzing peace operations and crisis management.

Emery Brusset, Channel Research, presents a similar yet distinct effects-based approach incorporated in evaluation thinking. According to Brusset, Channel Research evaluates the influence of initiatives. Influence can be defined as how far the effect of an initiative extends (Figure 21).

FIGURE 21
Levels of Attribution and Influence

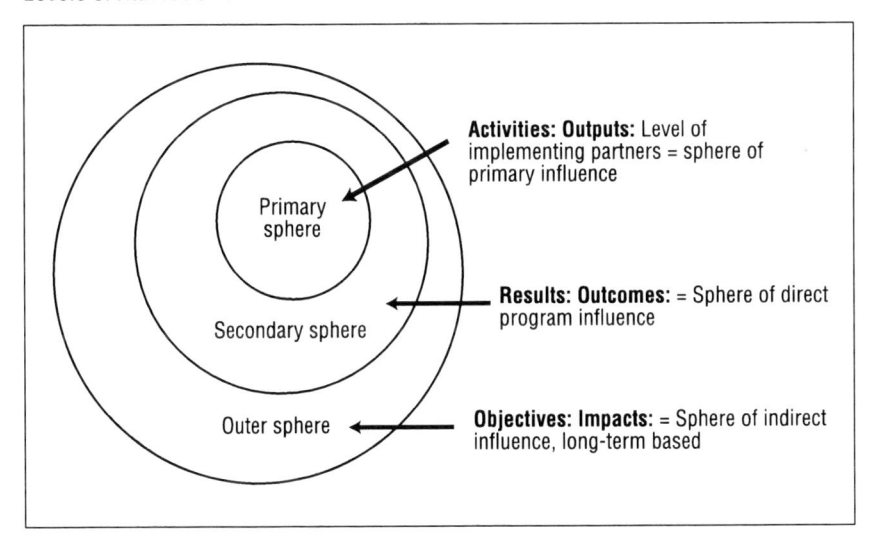

- **Activities: Outputs:** Level of implementing partners = sphere of primary influence
- **Results: Outcomes:** = Sphere of direct program influence
- **Objectives: Impacts:** = Sphere of indirect influence, long-term based

Primary sphere / Secondary sphere / Outer sphere

Source: Modified from Brusset, *Evaluation of Conflict Prevention*, 4.

Assessment of Governance Quality Indicators

As the US military became operational in Afghanistan, civil affairs teams found it necessary to assess governance quality in key Afghan cities. From this need emerged a measuring system, *Assessment of Governance Quality Indicators (AGQI)*. It was clear from the validation process that AGQI provided information that could be fed back into the cycle of PRT strategies and projects. Because AGQI monitored progress over time in a statistically valid manner, the tool empowered teams to better understand conflict-affected peoples and their needs. The system has non-military applications and could also be incorporated into a larger system of measures of effectiveness for operations in Afghanistan, conducted through an interagency approach.[30] This measuring system, although limited by its military application and intent, is a good example of sound social science methodologies integrated into the realm of peace operations.

Operational Research Methods

According to Dortmans et al., in the operational research field there is an established hierarchy of measures (or metrics) for testing concepts. Metrics are divided into three categories, each with three subordinate measures:

1. Feasibility
   a. Is the concept achievable?
   b. Is the concept affordable?
   c. Is the concept acceptable?

2. Applicability
   a. Does the concept have desired properties?
   b. Is the concept able to integrate?
   c. Does the concept meet needs?

3. Viability
   a. Is the concept reasonable?
   b. Is the concept sensible?
   c. Is the concept logical?[31]

Operational research theorists maintain that with these three metrics, all measures can be assessed for their appropriateness to a project. Asking these questions can provide a strong beginning to any stakeholder planning process. It is important to note that these metrics are for internal use only, to establish the efficacy of a study, rather than for release to a client, beneficiary, or recipient.[32]

The *Soft Systems Methodology* (SSM)[33] suggests that investigations of a concept/idea are formulated through a structured approach with the aim of providing a common understanding of the system of interest. This approach is ideal for exploring broadly defined fields or studies, such as elements of peace operations and crisis management activities.

In the SSM approach, issues are identified through a consideration of six factors in the context of the problem space (or the environment in which a concept will be implemented). They are:

C – Customer
A – Actors
T – Transformation
W – Worldview
O – Owner
E – Environment

These factors are then combined into a description of the system, which produces a root definition, or objective, from a particular perspective. What is interesting about this system is that it foregrounds the worldview that is driving a particular concept/project/idea.

Within operational research, various methods and techniques exist to understand the process of questioning within the problem structuring process. These include rich pictures, Faustian trees, soft systems methodology, the commercial products IDEF0 and iThink/STELLA, influence diagrams, strategic options development and analysis, Zwicky cubes, elimination of field anomaly relaxation combinations, strategic choice approach, and robustness analysis.

Development Sector

Rapid Appraisal Methods

Rapid Appraisal Methods are quick, low-cost ways to gather the views and feedback of beneficiaries and other stakeholders, in order to respond to decision-makers' needs for information. The World Bank Operations Evaluation Department suggests that these methods are flexible and cost-time efficient – a boon for most non-governmental and humanitarian agencies with limited resources – yet the findings resulting from this method are specific to communities and localities and thus cannot be aggregated to inform wider processes. Due to the informal nature of this method, the results are less credible than formalized data-gathering methods such as surveys.[34] According Mary Ann Zimmerman, of the US Department of State's Office of the Coordinator for Reconstruction and Stabilization (S/CRS), "In my days in the development world, we used to use Rapid Rural Appraisals, which were an attempt to find information in a reasonable amount of time and with reasonable results, and usually from a local-population perspective. This was qualitative information gathering, as well as sociological factors, and the military still needs to figure this out.[35]

Lieutenant Colonel David Last, a political science professor at the Royal Military College of Canada, comes to the same conclusion as Zimmerman, suggesting that the Rapid Assessment Process (RAP) commonly used in development projects may be a meaningful process to incorporate into peace operations and crisis management. Last is a proponent of adopting successful assessment methods from other fields and applying them to assessing operations to support peace, such as security sector reform activities. Last describes how RAP is used in peace operations by using a police training project as an example:

RAP is an iterative process, with a short cycle. We identify a problem, launch a multi-disciplinary team to examine it, and report with ground truth from multiple perspectives within a matter of weeks. The process recommends solutions to immediate problems. We try to implement the solutions with the help of local actors. These actions have (we hope) some impact, though it isn't immediately clear what the impact is. So we launch another team, consider a training assistance visit, which identifies the need for police training. On the strength of its recommendations, a training centre is established and generates graduates. Six months later the effectiveness of the graduates is evaluated, specific problems identified, and corrective action taken. The lessons are applied in other regions, but additional research teams are needed to confirm that they have been effectively applied.[36]

Civilian Policing Sector

Joint Assessment Mission

In 2003 the Joint Assessment Mission (JAM) was deployed to Timor-Leste to assess the Timor-Leste Police Service (TLPS) in five key areas:

1. Assess the handover of executive authority to the TLPS in relevant districts;
2. Assess progress against a timetable for the development of the TLPS;
3. Assess current TLPS capacity;
4. Recommend strategies to address the TLPS's needs; and
5. Develop a TLPS capacity building program.

During the consultative processes, the JAM compiled a significant amount of information that required ordering and standardization. To accomplish their assessment, the mission devised a methodology in the form of a 3 x 3 matrix (Figure 22). The matrix model enabled the three core organizational components to be assessed against the three critical institutional strengthening components:

Core Organizational Components

    Personnel: all civilian and police human resources

    Resources: materiel and informational resources

    Rules: internal procedures, legislation, and international standards

Critical Institutional Strengthening Components

    Capacity: staff, resource, and organizational capacities

Integrity: accountability mechanisms for management and operational practices

Sustainability: mechanisms for ensuring that planning for both human and other resources are developed.[37]

FIGURE 22
Joint Assessment Mission Matrix

	Personnel	Resources	Rules
Capacity			
Integrity			
Sustainability			

Source: Joint Assessment Mission, *Report*, 30.

According to the JAM report, the information was analyzed using the matrix in order to assess the current capacity of management structures, policies, systems, operations, professional development, training, and support services of the TLPS against the Terms of Reference Objectives that were set up in advance to the creation of the TLPS, considered as the benchmark information.[38]

EUJUST LEX Evaluation

In an interview, Alexander Blyth, EUJUST LEX, described his experience conducting an evaluation of an EU police training project in Iraq:

> In the spring of 2007, the PSC instructed the EUJUST LEX to conduct an evaluation of its work to date. No further clarification or definition was given by CPCC. EUJUST LEX conducted an evaluation case study (July–October 2007). The evaluation was also intended to assist PSC in its decision on whether or not to extend the tenure of the mission. To my knowledge, there was no general directive for this to happen for other ongoing European Security and Defence Policy (ESDP) missions. EUJUST LEX is an Integrated Rule of Law Mission facilitating training interventions for senior Iraqi police, judges, and penitentiary officers. Each discipline within the Iraqi CJS was evaluated separately, employing the same methodology (using the Kirkpatrick Model). Results were later amalgamated to produce a Mission Evaluation Overview Report.
>
> We used questionnaires, which were course specific. We enlisted the cooperation and assistance of the relevant Iraqi ministries. Students and

supervisors completed questionnaires in a private, closed session; then an extrapolation process occurred in closed face-to-face sessions. Respondents were forthcoming, due in part to the relationships that had been built between the students and trainers. They were also asked questions regarding their future aspirations. We came out with a "Santa Claus" type wish list. In other words, the list was extensive and very wide ranging.

There were three main conclusions, which led to new development of Iraqi courses: more practical than theory; more specialist courses; and inclusion of train-the-trainer courses. The lessons learned from the police evaluation served the mission in good stead for the judiciary and penitentiary evaluations which were to follow. The mission did the police evaluation in partnership with KAZE Management. In total, twelve to thirteen member states' experts were involved with the evaluation. This system of evaluation was groundbreaking for PSC, CIVCOM, and CPCC, and we now have it on record that our EUJUST LEX evaluations can be used as a template for other EU ESDP mission evaluations.[39]

Policing Success Indicators Project

A year after Blyth's evaluation was completed, the Australian Centre for Peace and Conflict Studies at the University of Queensland commenced their policing success indicators research project, which was initially designed and developed by Andy Hughes, former chief inspector of the Australian Federal Police (AFP) and head of their International Deployment Group (IDG) responsible for Australian police contributions to international peace support operations. Now led by Alex Bellamy, an internationally renowned peacekeeping scholar, the project seeks to identify the best indicators of policing success in peace support operations. Most of the background work – developing a typology of police missions and defining a distinct set of conflict environments – is being done by the support team with a focus on some new, different, better, and police-specific indicators and measures of police success in peace support operations.

According to project team member Charles Hunt, the project has developed a comprehensive list of possible indicators of success (both in relation to mandate-specifics and more abstract sustainable peace), throughout the time continuum of the war-to-peace transition and across the different mission types and objectives – all with associated benefits and limitations, cutting across different measurement methodologies and approaches. According to Hunt, the challenge is in the ordering, structuring, and weighting of these indicators in a way that extrapolates and presents tangible and ultimately useful reassurances of success for ongoing commitments, eventual exit strategies, and future deployments for police. The potential greater good of the project may be in applying the methodology as a decision aid for political decision-makers vis-à-vis peace support operations commitments.[40]

Peace-Building Sector

Participatory Methods and Consultations

According to the World Bank Operations Evaluation Department, participatory methods facilitate active involvement in decision-making by those with a stake in an intervention activity.[41] This method is proven to generate a sense of ownership – or "buy-in" – by local peoples who must live with the results of interventions long after the international community has exited. Common discourse among the security and defence sectors suggests that this method is time consuming and not objective enough, whereas those in the development sector find that the method enhances partnerships, learning, and quality of information for management decision-making.

Reflecting on Peace Practice Project

The *Reflecting on Peace Practice Project* (RPP) (2003) was a broad survey of the range of work conducted under the rubric of *peace work* that was becoming increasingly prominent in the early 1990s after the end of the Cold War. According to interview participant Lara Olson, University of Calgary, and co-researcher for RPP and co-author of the results of RPP in *Confronting War: Critical Lessons for Peace Practitioners*, RPP asked the questions: "What do we know about it? Does it work? Why?" In the three-year research process, RPP engaged over 200 agencies involved in peace work. "The intention was to capture their experience (the good and the bad, the warts and all) from a safe, internal perspective and *counter* the externally generated criticisms of the peace work industry of which agencies were feeling the negative results."[42]

> Case studies were confidential in order to build a high level of trust with the agencies that participated in the study. There was quite a lot of debate at the initial stages of the project of the definition of peace work. We decided to be general rather than specific about the definition in order to be more inclusive. The wider definition suggested that peace work included *track 1 diplomacy* to *transitional justice activities* to *inter-positional human rights work* like that conducted by Peace Brigades International. We focused upon the perceived and actual *peace dividend* of the activities and of institutions. The project wanted the agencies to be honest about their mistakes and problems – in effect asking agencies to *assess* themselves in order to improve

the industry of peace work – rather than being *evaluated* by outside critics in a top-down approach.

We discovered that there were no formalized mechanisms for capturing lessons learned or best practices from NGOs engaged in peace work, broadly defined. The net result of the study was that it ended up pushing the peace-building community to be more strategic about what they were doing, because the peace-building community is not very strategic about what they want to do or accomplish – their work, up until the study, was not localized, but narrowly focused on inputs and effects on participants in activities versus broader impacts on the environment. Often projects were successful in their own terms. Our role was to ask, "So what?"

1. So what if a project activity is reported as successful?
2. What are the longer term impacts of the activities?
3. How do we move beyond outputs and study impacts?

From this we introduced the notions of *peace writ large* to distinguish between the impact of specific initiatives for peace and broader impacts on the context that would actually support sustainable peace.

Reflecting on Peace Practice was groundbreaking in its focus on the *effectiveness* of peace work – other studies up until then focused on the *processes* of peace work. This caused the community to push itself and to constructively criticize itself in order to cause positive change in peace work. There was tension between practitioners, some of whom were critical of their years of efforts in conflicts which re-erupted and others who believed their particular programming approaches *must* work.

For example, there were some practitioners who believed that peace education in Bosnia was going to be the solution to all problems caused by the conflicts. However, others did not share this belief. Those that did hold the belief felt attacked by critical questions around broader impacts on peace or the notion of peace writ large.

We took thirty case studies and pulled out the criteria that visibly and tangibly showed positive impacts on peace. We then created a first-cut list of 100 criteria. We hosted dozens of international workshops to review and vet the draft criteria, to create a more focused list based on agency input. We then created a list of five criteria. There was general agreement on the criteria. The five *project effectiveness criteria* were distilled from the three-year research and consultative process, and were:

1. The effort (not a project focus per se) must stop a key driver of conflict;
2. The effort must result in people developing their own initiatives for peace (not dependent on outsiders or conveners);

3. The effort must result in the creation/reform of institutions (that is, be sustainable not just activity based);
4. The effort must prompt people to resist becoming involved in violence; and
5. The effort must increase security (both real and perceived) for the people.

This type of project effectiveness analysis is also dependent upon the elements of time and scale. Projects needed to be big enough (large scale, in tune with the scale of the conflict, not localized), fast enough (effects of projects must address the problem relatively quickly; projects which took a generation to see results were not fast enough by far in the project's view), and sustainable enough (the impact did not depend on continuing activities or initiatives from interveners). These factors were seen as showing significant impact on peace writ large. One of our key questions was "Are you really doing what you say you are doing?" Agencies claimed to be working for peace, so *peace* was used as the admittedly high bar to judge efforts against. We created a four-quadrant matrix (Figure 23) which helped agencies map out the impacts and underlying strategies of their peace work.

It was found that it was important for peace writ large for agencies to be working quadrants 3 and 4. The first quadrant was not found to be particularly significant at all, though many agencies start there and move down. We found that agencies/groups involved in the original RPP study were not aware of the driving principles behind their own programs and activities. Portions of this study were really uncomfortable for some because the study examined assumptions. *Theories of change* were relatively unexamined by agencies despite their importance as drivers of agency programs. The list of theories of change was captured through workshops and case studies (but not captured through direct questioning). In order to capture assumptions, we asked "Why are you doing what you are doing?" These things are often so implicit within an organizations that they are under-examined. There are no organizational policies that dictate assumptions.

We found a distinction between the level of sophistication in mapping intervention approaches and strategies. The conflict-resolution groups were very good at articulating strategies and the rationale for them, whereas the humanitarian and development organizations often were simply applying standard peace-building models they had been instructed to use.

There was a distinction between the perspectives taken to intervene:

- Assess causes of conflict and what needed to be done to address them – few organizations did this.

- Examine what approaches and methods an agency has in its own toolbox, and apply that tool in an intervention – mostly, agencies did this rather than starting with the question "What needs to be addressed in this setting and why?"

There were serious gaps in the ways agencies analyzed conflict and the relationship to intervention strategies that were then proposed/used in peace initiatives. Also, there were serious problems in measuring effectiveness of the initiatives undertaken, a big problem with attribution of impacts to any single initiative.

FIGURE 23
Reflecting on Peace Practice: Four-Quadant Matrix

		MORE PEOPLE	KEY PEOPLE
INDIVIDUAL / PERSONAL CHANGE	Healing/recovery Perceptions Attitudes Skills		
	Behaviour Individual relationships		
SOCIO - POLITICAL CHANGE	Group behaviour/ relationships Public opinion Social norms		
	Institutional change		
	Cultural or structural change		

Source: Adapted from Anderson and Olson, *Confronting War*, 48-9.

There used to be an emphasis upon inputs rather than impacts. Evaluation was a top-down process, imposition of development criteria, measuring of inputs versus measuring of impacts. There has been much that has come out of the RPP project to effect change in how we think about peace work and its effectiveness. NGOs use the tools that came out of the RPP study in workshops and implementation activities[43] to improve their activity impacts. The RPP research phase ended in 2002, and since then RPP has been used in a field implementation state, working with operational NGOs in the Balkans, West Africa, and the Great Lakes region. OECD DAC has adopted a guidance note on evaluation of peace-building that draws heavily on RPP.[44]

Compendium of Operational Frameworks for Peacebuilding and Donor Co-ordination

CIDA's *Compendium of Operational Frameworks for Peacebuilding and Donor Co-ordination* (1998) has been an ongoing methodological development of assessment tools and compendium of quantitative indicators. This CIDA project has contributed to thinking regarding the assessment of gaps and development of appropriate intervention strategies. Although this is an assessment tool, it is applicable to measuring success. The focus on measurable, number-based indicators is prevalent in the compendium.[45]

Science

Other substantive evaluation methods that come out of the social sciences as presented by Mosselman and Prince include effectiveness models such as goal attainment, side-effects, goal-free evaluation, comprehensive evaluation, client-oriented model, stakeholder model, policy commissions; economic methods such as cost efficiency, cost effectiveness, productivity model; and professional methods such as peer review.[46]

Many of these models have influenced the field of monitoring and evaluation. Project evaluation tools include cost-benefit and cost-effectiveness analysis. According to the World Bank, these tools are for assessing whether or not the costs of an activity can be justified by the outcomes and impacts. Used within the development sector, cost-benefit analysis measures both inputs and outputs in monetary terms, while cost-effectiveness analysis estimates inputs in monetary terms and outputs in non-monetary, quantitative terms such as improvements in literacy.[47] For projects that have benefits that are difficult to quantify, this method must be used with care. In addition, this measuring method is technical and requires specific data. Other monetary evaluations include the planning balance sheet method and the shade projection method.

There are many useful methods for evaluation that come from the sciences. Without going into details – leaving this task to the experts – it is a useful exercise to list some of the available quantitative methods for measuring success in peace operations and crisis management. Quantitative evaluation methods include explicit utility functions; expected utility function; restricted utility and *satisficing* analysis; hierarchical decision structures; goal programming; game theoretical methods; ideal point; and interactive decision. Discrete quantitative non-monetary evaluation methods include goal achievement matrix; expected value method; discrepancy analysis; concordance analysis; and graphic representation. Discrete quantitative numeric evaluation methods include ordinal concordance analysis; frequency; lexicographic ordering; permutation; eigenvalue; regime; multi-dimensional; metagame; mixed data (evamix); and trichotomic choice. Discrete qualitative non-numeric evaluation methods include score-card and key factor.

Other Mechanisms and Tools

Mapping

The *Zentrum für Internationale Freidenseinsätze* (ZIF), publishers of the now popular annual World Map of Peace Operations, which shows the footprint of international peace operations on a stylized world map, would suggest that success and progress are not easily charted. ZIF structure their world map so that mission size, length, and location are illustrated in a comparative sense.[48] (See Maps 1 and 2.) One look at the map and the breadth and depth of world operations can be easily determined – perhaps not assessed – in a "moment in time" intervention footprint. Mapping is a useful tool in determining our interventions; however, in a static publication, previous mission sizes, lengths, and locations can not be compared. One can see only what exists at the time of publication. Albeit, variations in size, length, and location are not necessarily indicators of progress or success: the US surge in Iraq comes to mind. (The online version of the World Map of Peace Operations can be accessed at http://www.zif-berlin.org.) However, this visual representation of the common tradespace within which the international community is functioning is a critical starting point for measuring peace operations and crisis management.

Mechanisms and Tools 117

MAP 1
ZIF Crisis Prevention and Peace Operations 2008

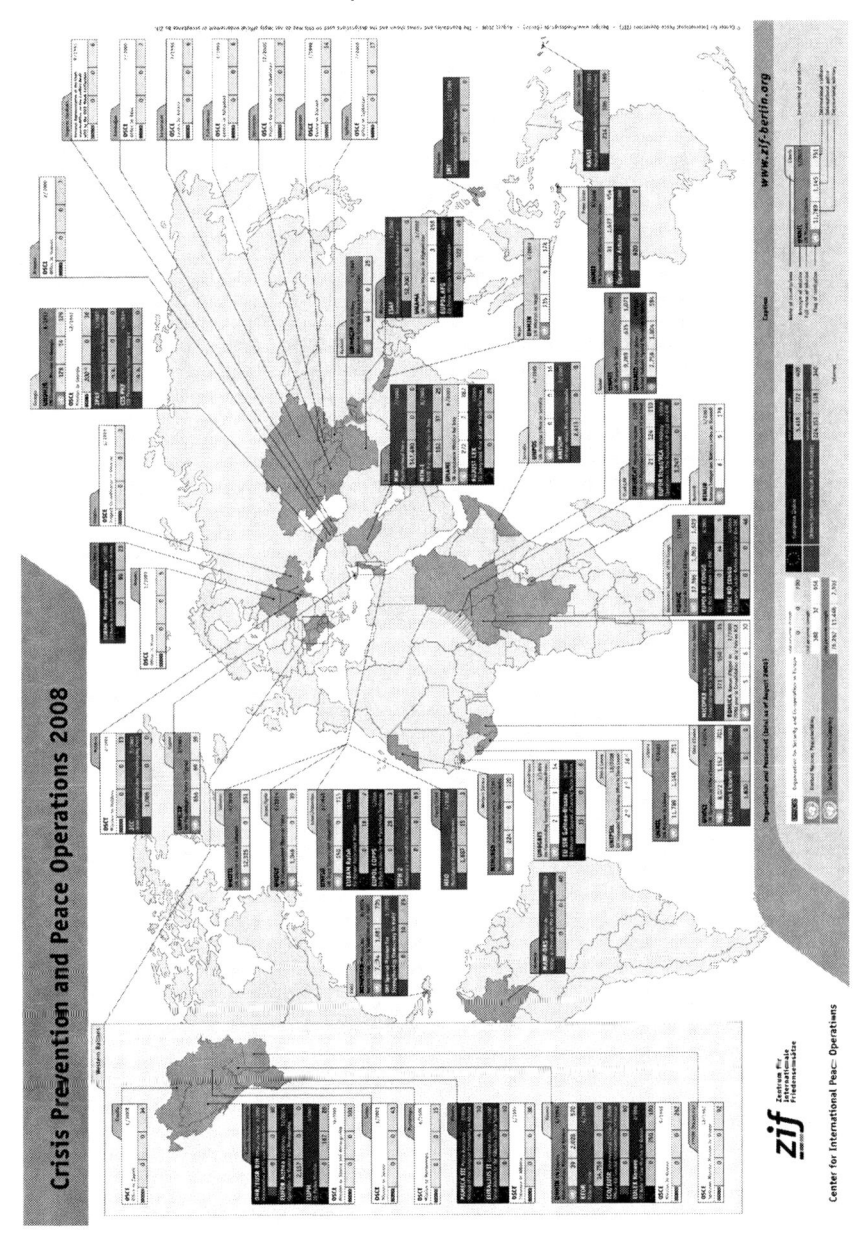

Source: ZIF Crisis Prevention and Peace Operations 2008. Copyright © 2008 by Zentrum für International Friedenseinsätze (ZIF). http://www.zif-berlin.org/en/home/html. Used with kind permission of the publisher.

MAP 2
A Detailed View of the ZIF Map

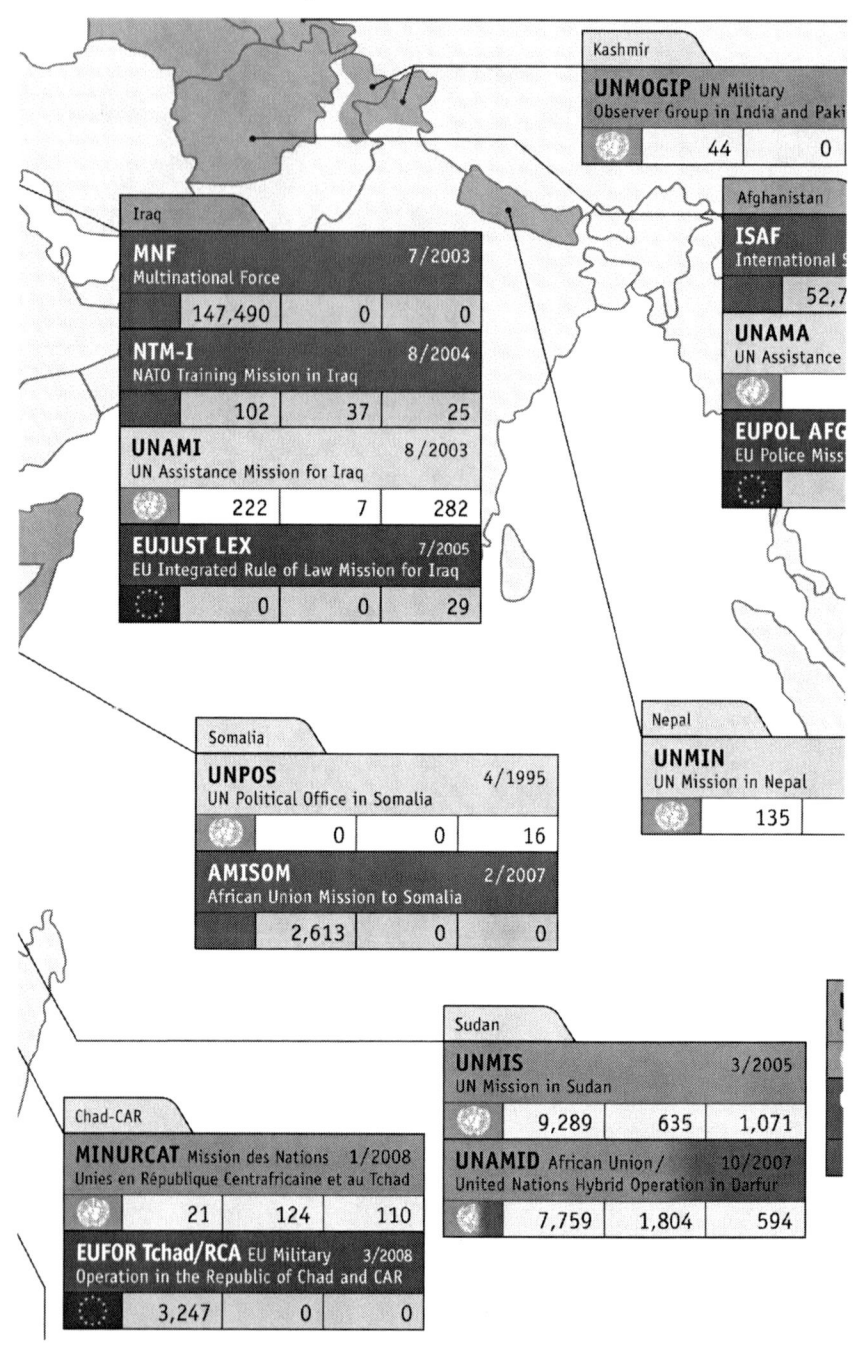

Kashmir
UNMOGIP UN Military Observer Group in India and Paki
| 44 | 0 |

Afghanistan
ISAF International
| 52,7 |

UNAMA UN Assistance

EUPOL AFG EU Police Miss

Iraq

MNF Multinational Force		7/2003
147,490	0	0

NTM-I NATO Training Mission in Iraq		8/2004
102	37	25

UNAMI UN Assistance Mission for Iraq		8/2003
222	7	282

EUJUST LEX EU Integrated Rule of Law Mission for Iraq		7/2005
0	0	29

Somalia

UNPOS UN Political Office in Somalia		4/1995
0	0	16

AMISOM African Union Mission to Somalia		2/2007
2,613	0	0

Nepal

UNMIN UN Mission in Nepal	
135	

Sudan

UNMIS UN Mission in Sudan		3/2005
9,289	635	1,071

UNAMID African Union / United Nations Hybrid Operation in Darfur		10/2007
7,759	1,804	594

Chad-CAR

MINURCAT Mission des Nations Unies en République Centrafricaine et au Tchad		1/2008
21	124	110

EUFOR Tchad/RCA EU Military Operation in the Republic of Chad and CAR		3/2008
3,247	0	0

Source: ZIF Crisis Prevention and Peace Operations 2008. Copyright © 2008 by Zentrum für International Friedenseinsätze (ZIF). http://www.zif-berlin.org/en/home/html. Used with kind permission of the publisher.

From even a cursory look at the ZIF map it becomes clear that the international community cannot create progress and significant measures of success in such a vast tradespace with the array of capacities available. If the map were expanded to include the other sectors and stakeholders involved in peace operations and crisis management, this tradespace includes additional capacities and capabilities to augment progress and success. The United Nations also publishes a map (Map 3) that visually depicts the locations, names, and dates of its missions.

The Center on International Cooperation (Figure 24) takes a slightly different approach to illustrate the types of missions, including their sponsoring organization, the number of troops and military observers committed, and the duration of missions.[49]

FIGURE 24
Military Deployments in Global Peace Operations

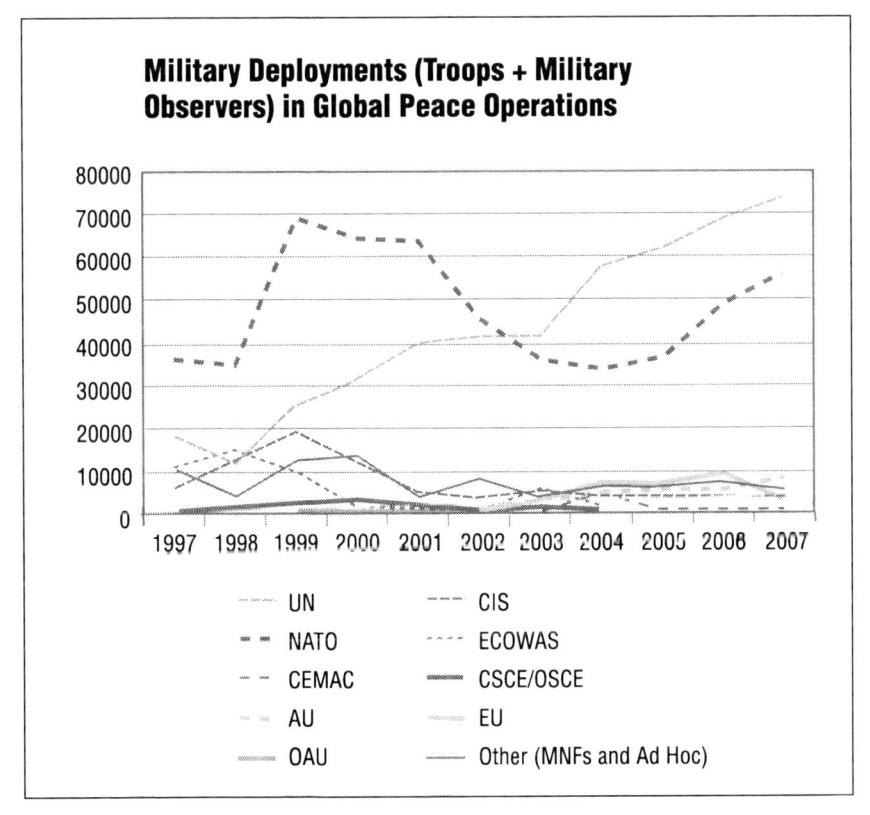

Source: Center on International Cooperation, *Annual Review*, 2. http://www.cic.nyu.edu/internationalsecurity/docs/Final2008briefingreport.pdf. Copyright © 2008 by Lynne Rienner Publishers, Inc. Used with permission.

120 *Measuring What Matters in Peace Operations and Crisis Management*

MAP 3
Mapping United Nations Missions

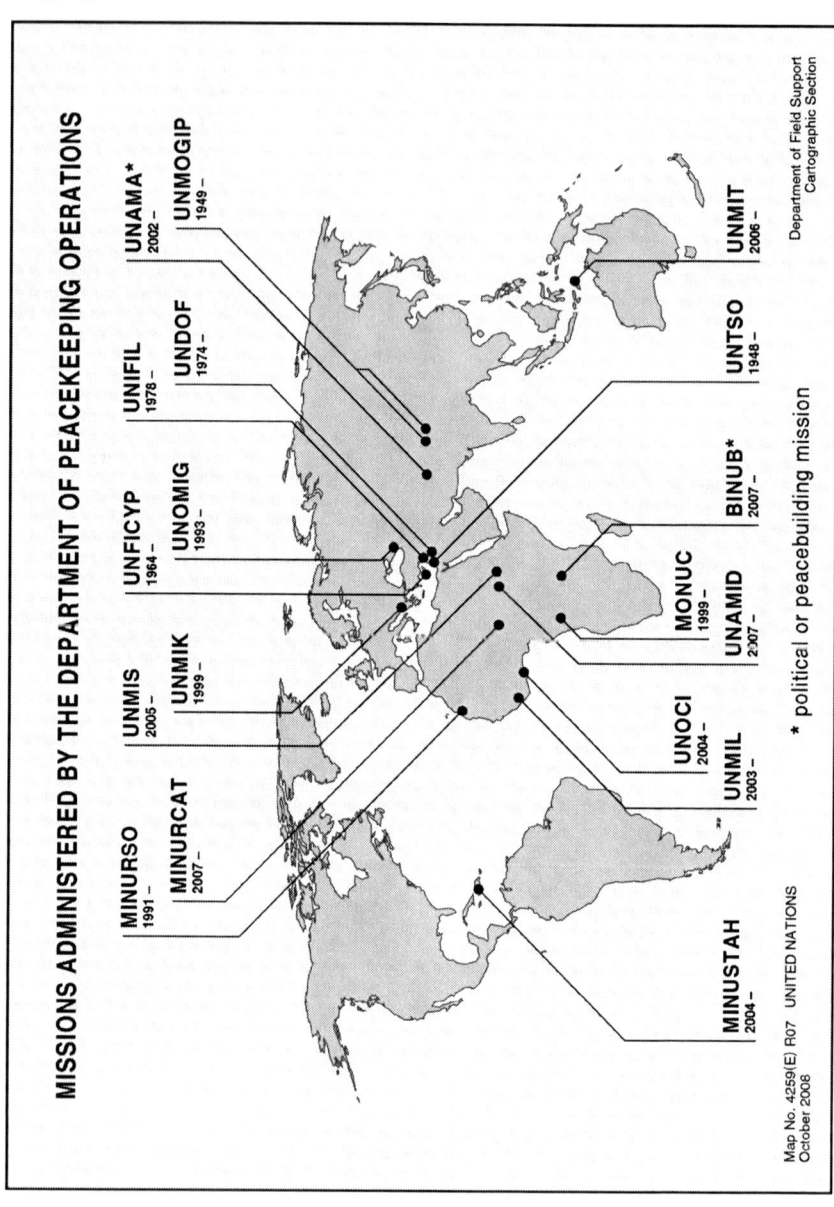

Source: The UN Cartographic Section. United Nations, New York, NY. 2008.

The World Bank Operations Evaluation Department indicates that "theory-based evaluation" lends itself to mapping: "By mapping out the determining or causal factors judged important for success, and how they might interact, it can then be decided which steps should be monitored as the program develops, to see how well they are in fact borne out."[50] The mapping of complex activities is also referred to as *Outcome Mapping* (Figure 25), which was pioneered by Canada's International Development Research Centre (IDRC).

FIGURE 25
IDRC's Outcome Mapping Approach

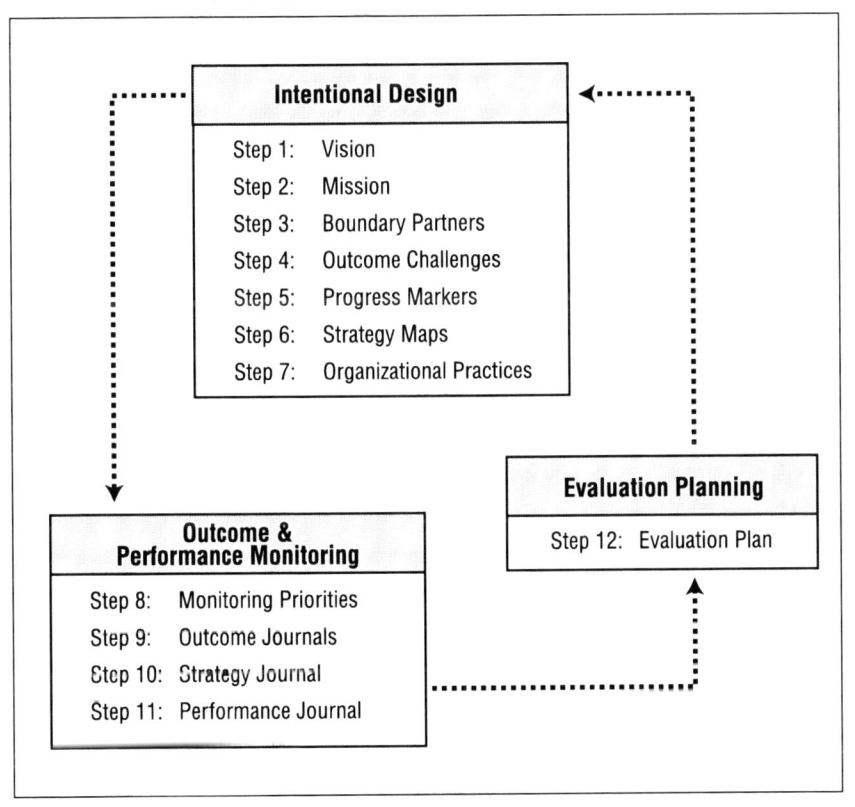

Intentional Design
- Step 1: Vision
- Step 2: Mission
- Step 3: Boundary Partners
- Step 4: Outcome Challenges
- Step 5: Progress Markers
- Step 6: Strategy Maps
- Step 7: Organizational Practices

Outcome & Performance Monitoring
- Step 8: Monitoring Priorities
- Step 9: Outcome Journals
- Step 10: Strategy Journal
- Step 11: Performance Journal

Evaluation Planning
- Step 12: Evaluation Plan

Source: Earl et al., *Outcome Mapping*. This figure is reproduced with the permission of Canada's International Development Research Centre (www.idrc.ca).

Mapping a scenario, however, can be a limiting factor, especially if it is overly complicated, the scale of the activities are very large, and an exhaustive list of factors and assumptions are fed into the mapping process.

Symbolism

Some stakeholders choose to present their measures and results with simulacra. Pictures that symbolize progress, peace, war, and profits (Figure 26), are commonly used in reports. For example, the International Crisis Group uses images of bombs and doves to depict changes in peace and stability in the regions where it focuses its analyses.

FIGURE 26
Bombs, Doves, Ups, Downs, and Sides

November 2008 Trends

Deteriorated Situations
India (non-Kashmir) (p.6)
Kashmir (p.6)
Nicaragua (p.10)
Nigeria (p.4)
Thailand (p.7)

Improved Situations
Bangladesh (p.6)

Unchanged Situations
Afghanistan (p.6), Algeria (p.12), Armenia (p.8), Azerbaijan (p.8), Basque Country (Spain) (p.9), Belarus (p.9), Bolivia (p.10), Bosnia (p.7), Burundi (p.2), Cameroon (p.4), Central African Republic (p.2), Chad (p.2), Chechnya (Russia) (p.8), China (internal) (p.5), Colombia (p.10), Côte d'Ivoire (p.4), Cyprus (p.9), Democratic Republic of Congo (p.2), Ecuador (p.10), Egypt (p.12), Ethiopia (p.3), Georgia (p.9), Guinea (p.4), Guinea-Bissau (p.4), Haiti (p.10), Indonesia (p.7), Iran (p.11), Iraq (p.11), Israel/Occupied Palestinian Territories (p.10), Kazakhstan (p.5), Kenya (p.3), Kosovo (p.8), Kyrgyzstan (p.5), Lebanon (p.11), Liberia (p.4), Libya (p.12), Macedonia (p.8), Mali (p.4), Mauritania (p.12), Moldova (p.9), Myanmar/Burma (p.7), Nagorno-Karabakh (Azerbaijan) (p.9), Nepal (p.6), Niger (p.4), North Caucasus (non-Chechnya) (p.8), North Korea (p.5), Pakistan (p.6), Peru (p.10), Philippines (p.7), Rwanda (p.2), Serbia (p.8), Sierra Leone (p.5), Somalia (p.3), Somaliland (Somalia) (p.3), Sri Lanka (p.7), Sudan (p.3), Swaziland (p.4), Syria (p.11), Taiwan Strait (p.6), Tajikistan (p.5), Timor-Leste (p.7), Turkey (p.9), Turkmenistan (p.5), Uganda (p.2), Ukraine (p.9), Uzbekistan (p.5), Venezuela (p.10), Western Sahara (p.12), Yemen (p.11), Zimbabwe (p.4)

December 2008 Watchlist

Conflict Risk Alerts
Bangladesh
Kashmir
Thailand

Conflict Resolution Opportunities
Bangladesh

Source: International Crisis Group (recreated from the ICG website) http://www.crisisgroup.org/library/documents/crisiswatch/cw_2008/cw64.pdf.

Thermometers depicting fundraising activities (Figure 27) are used in the social sector, for example, by the United Way.

FIGURE 27
Thermometer Imagery

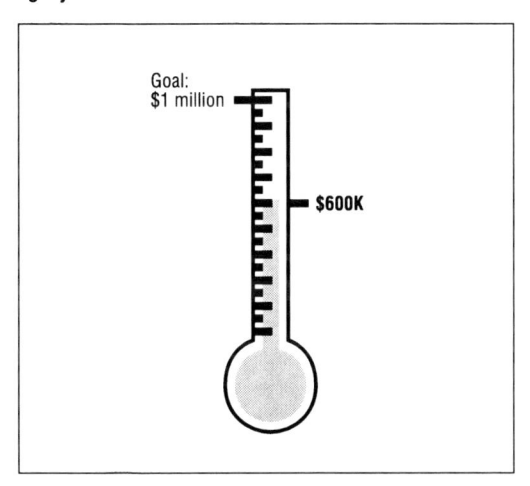

Another simulacra seen in the security and defence sector is the traffic light motif (Figure 28). It is used to illustrate changes in an environment that allow or impede operations, such as go (green), go carefully (yellow), and no go or stop (red).

FIGURE 28
Traffic Light Colour Coding (Red, Yellow, Green)

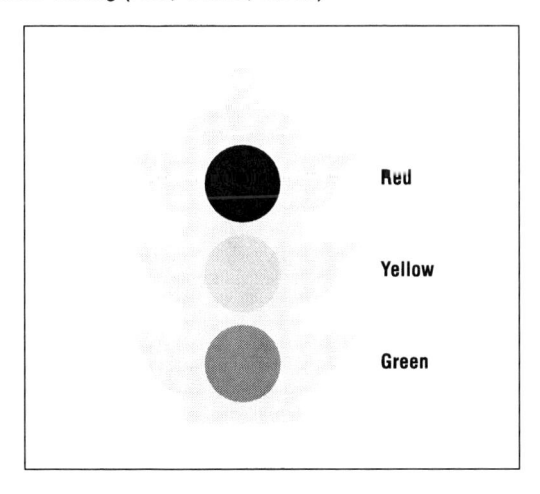

Symbolism of this kind has universal cachet and so is frequently used on multi-national missions when English or French is often the third or fourth language spoken by troop-contributing nations. Symbols and maps, however, oversimplify changes within the three-dimensional problem space of a complex peace operation, transforming them into two-dimensional info-bites. Symbols and maps have universal appeal, yet must be used with caution.

Digital Media/Video Methods

Although not considered a mainstream measurement tool, photo and video archiving of reconstruction activities is a powerful way to capture progress. A video is one of the best sources of evidence for decision-making.[51] Video archiving, linked with other digital media tools, is an underused progress-reporting mechanism. It requires little specialized training and is relatively objective compared to the more subjective measurement tools used in peace operations and crisis management reporting. As well, video archiving is less likely than traditional text-based reporting tools to be disputed or manipulated, and is a powerful way to engage most stakeholders and sectors involved in peace operations and crisis management.

During the post-conflict reconstruction of the Bridge of Mostar in Bosnia-Herzegovina, the Project Coordination Unit (PCU) tasked with reconstructing this culturally important site created a digital photo archive of reconstruction progress over time. The PCU uploaded the photo database to a publicly available web-based system. Viewers can scroll through the photo thumbnails and see the day-to-day building of the bridge. Some photo series show little progress, while other series show strong forward progress in short bursts of time. Factors such as climate and environment, donors and funding issues, political tensions, and other social forces can create challenges with speed or slow reconstruction activities. These phenomena can be cross-referenced with multi-media data such as photos or video to identify why progress was or was not being made.

Conclusion

Most mechanisms and tools oversimplify complex human conditions and tend to promote a false sense of overconfidence in the efficacy of international interventions. As well, analysis of impacts takes time and thoughtfulness – luxuries that are often diminished in peace operations and crisis management environments. Moreover, effectiveness is difficult to measure because it may occur over a long period of time. The act of measuring outputs and probable outcomes is further complicated because the identification of impacts and consequences is a subjective process. Cause-effect chains cannot be traced in linear fashion, and reliable indicators and/or baseline data applicable to MOEs are often absent in post-conflict environments. These issues have led to a general inability of the international community to explain activities, goals, and results to war-affected publics, as well as to tax-paying constituents back home. The central challenge remains that peace operations and crisis management environments are significantly complex to require different ways to think about measuring the effectiveness of activities.

In war-torn societies, the effectiveness of the measurable aspects of peace operations and crisis management activities is often decreased because of the unobservable non-linear dynamics causing observable effects in the operational space. We plan for a particular effect, for example, within a local community, yet the results are different from what we planned. Further, as a wider spectrum of stakeholders becomes more active in peace operations and crisis management activities, it is even more difficult to measure the effectiveness of their work because the principal agents do not share a worldview or ontology and must use alternative systems of measurement to show effectiveness.

Summary Points

- More suitable measuring mechanisms and tools balance quantitative and qualitative approaches to appropriately capture sustainable longer term activity results.

- The mechanisms and tools available for measuring tangible and intangible changes in intervention activities require further development to achieve sophisticated reporting, especially concerning intangible elements of activities.

- Visual measuring mechanisms are powerful tools for capturing progress and should be partnered with text-based mechanisms for informational balance.

Notes

[1] Pawson and Tilley, *Realistic Evaluation*.
[2] Sphere Project, "The Sphere Project," http://www.sphereproject.org/.
[3] These are: humanity, impartiality, informed consent, duty of care, witness, transparency, independence, neutrality, and complementarity. Refer to chapter 1 for a complete description.
[4] ALNAP, *Evaluating Humanitarian Action*, 14.
[5] Ibid.
[6] Mary Martin, personal communication, 2007.

[7] In December 2008 in Washington, DC, the United States Institute for Peace hosted a review meeting of a pilot study in which MPICE had been trailed. The field test had been conducted in Cite Soleil, Haiti. The results of the field test ran into obstacles including lack of baseline data against which to compare the MPICE progress indicators and lack of a consistent data-gathering methodology.

[8] Michael Dziedzic, personal communication, 2008.

[9] United States Institute for Peace, "Measuring Progress in Conflict Environments," 3.

[10] Channel Research, *Evaluation of ECHO's Humanitarian Intervention Plans*.

[11] CIDA, *Results-Based Management*.

[12] ALNAP, *Annual Review 2002*, 212.

[13] Ian Higginbotham, personal communication, 2008.

[14] Brad Bergstrand, personal communication, 2008.

[15] Bonventre, "Monitoring and Evaluation," 68.

[16] Ian Higginbotham, personal communication, 2008.

[17] Ibid.

[18] United Nations Development Group, *Inter-Agency Framework for Conflict Analysis*, 1.

[19] Ibid.

[20] The framework is from Orr, ed., *Winning the Peace*.

[21] USDS, *Post-Conflict Reconstruction Essential Tasks*.

[22] Orr, ed., *Winning the Peace*; USDS, *Post-Conflict Reconstruction Essential Tasks*; United Nations Development Group, *Inter-Agency Framework for Conflict Analysis*.

[23] Direction Générale de la Coopération Internationale et du Développement, *Fragile States and Situations of Fragility*.

[24] Stephan Massing, personal communication, 2008.

[25] Ibid.

[26] Lowe and Ng, "Effects-Based Operations," 61-2.

[27] Ibid.

[28] Smith, *Effects Based Operations*; Ho How Hoang, "Effects-Based Operations."

[29] Grossman-Vermaas, *The Effects-Based Concept*.

[30] Pusateri et al., *Assessment of Governance Quality Indicators*.

[31] Dortmans et al., "Analytical Approach," 885-91.

[32] Checkland, *Systems Thinking*.

[33] Ibid.; Checkland, "Achieving 'Desirable and Feasible' Change," 821-31.

[34] World Bank, *Monitoring and Evaluation*, 14.

[35] Mary Ann Zimmerman, personal communication, 2008.

[36] Last, "Rapid Assessment Process," 10.

[37] Joint Assessment Mission, *Report*.

[38] Ibid.

[39] Alexander Blyth, personal communication, 2008.

[40] Charles Hunt, personal communication, 2008.

[41] World Bank, *Monitoring and Evaluation*, 16.

[42] Lara Olson, personal communication, 2008.

[43] All RPP tools are available at http://www.cdainc.com/cdawww/project_profile.php?pid=RPP&pname=Reflecting%20on%20Peace%20Practice.

[44] Lara Olson, personal communication, 2008.

[45] CIDA, *Compendium*.
[46] Mosselman and Prince, *Review of Methods*.
[47] World Bank, *Monitoring and Evaluation*, 20.
[48] Visit ZIF to access the online version of the World Map of Peace Operations at www.zif-berlin.org
[49] Center on International Cooperation, *Annual Review*, 2.
[50] World Bank, *Monitoring and Evaluation*, 10.
[51] Berk, "Survey of Twelve Strategies," 52.

CHAPTER 5

Measuring Success in Bosnia-Herzegovina

Steve Flemming, a defence scientist with the Canadian Department of National Defence, began working on measures of effectiveness in 1997. He admits to having made every mistake in the book, but perhaps it is these learning opportunities that have made him one of the most credible voices on practical field applications of measuring progress in peacekeeping operations.[1]

In 1997 Flemming was a civilian scientist attached to the NATO-led Stabilisation Force (SFOR) in Bosnia-Herzegovina SFOR headquarters in Sarajevo. For two years he ran the measures of effectiveness project, which eventually became the SFOR Transition Strategy. At the beginning of his tenure with SFOR, when it became known that the UN had an MOE program, Flemming was sent to talk to the UN in the best interest of sharing the SFOR MOE system. Strategically, he was sent to the UN because he was one of the only civilians working in his area, and leaders at SFOR thought that the UN would be more receptive to a civilian than to uniformed military personnel. Perhaps strategizing along the same lines, the UN sent a military representative to the meeting on MOEs to best communicate with the SFOR rep. Ironically, Flemming and the UN military rep did not share the same way of communicating.

Communication was the least of Flemming's problems; the cultures of the organizations were also very different. The UN's system appeared to be entirely qualitative. "It was all about political reunification, about the disparate groups and the stresses among them, multi-ethnic groups, etc.," Flemming says. Both the UN and SFOR systems identified aspects of what could be called progress, but in neither case was the evidence linked to an overarching model of an end state, nor was progress linked to the activities of the international community. Both purported to tell only the story of how the intervention was progressing. While the SFOR MOE system was empirical and relatively sophisticated, with hundreds of indicators, the UN MOE system was purely narrative and qualitative, using intangible indicators in a report-based style. According to Flemming, these reports reached gargantuan sizes, often close to 300 pages. Each system contributed to understanding progress in Bosnia-Herzegovina; "However, neither system asked 'What is the international community trying to accomplish here?'" Flemming argues that this is the big question in measuring progress in peace operations and crisis management.

By the time Flemming left SFOR, the organization was tracking 300 indicators, and the military had created a system that would track change over time with the *traffic light* system of red, yellow, and green.

Flemming suggests that the predominance of indicators in the military planning field is based on the fact that planners – who typically produce initial MOE programs – are military engineers, and they tend to start at the wrong end – with what *can* be rather than what *should* be measured. Military officers always have the first crack at MOEs, which are then given to a civilian scientist who measures "the empirical positivist stuff, such as political and social factors, [which] is too messy and is too hard to measure, so it isn't measured. Everyone knows this now – but they didn't ten years ago. They thought they could and did measure everything that was important, and did attempt to generate empirical measures of some soft factors. What's really needed is a system that gets into the quantitative and qualitative."[2]

According to Flemming, the Dayton Accord (GFAP) was supposed to have created a list of indicators that could be fulfilled to measure progress in the peacekeeping operation. Dayton was essentially a bureaucratic exercise because the document did not address issues related to end state. Flemming reiterates that the first question to ask when designing MOEs and indicators is related to end states: "What are we really trying to accomplish here?" What we actually ask, he suggests, is: "What can we reasonably accomplish here?" The two possible end states are democracy (peaceful) and economy (people can eat). With these two end states comes the achievement of most benchmarks related to peace operations and crisis management. Interestingly, after he made this point, Flemming's pragmatic experience-hardened focus returned, and he stated that these end states have nothing to do with the "reality of the heart of darkness."

I could only assume that he was referring to the field realities inherent in all missions.

Measuring efforts need to step back from the measurement and indicator problem on the military side, because right now the military is consumed with

- data quantity
- counting
- methods
- rolling scores over time
- numbers

Based on the measuring frameworks being used, there is no link between what the military are actually doing and the progress being made in places like Bosnia or Afghanistan. The military has become focused on Effects-Based Approaches to Operations (EBAOs). Flemming maintains that EBAOs are not a sure-fire way of measuring progress, because of all sorts of kinetic and non-kinetic effects: "We don't know if these effects are in spite of our activities, or supported by our activities. We don't know what we don't know." Although EBAOs are a useful tool in tracking effects, they may not link activities with outcomes – the main tenet of measuring success. Flemming suggests, "We actually think that by measuring effectively, we are making that change." Military planners believe that if they can measure something, they can control it. Most stakeholders believe that if they can measure it, they have made that change.[3]

Flemming says sympathetically that the military is legitimately trying to do this within their worldview. They know that the cultural stuff is essential to the success of peace operations and crisis management activities in places like Afghanistan; however, they believe that security has to come first. As a result, Flemming thinks, the essential human factors absent from military MOE frameworks will be slow to come. The military does not want 300 page reports like those the UN has popularized.

In military decision-making circles, information is drawn from intelligence briefings and MOE briefings, but these two briefings are never joined up. Flemming observes, "The military intelligence folks think that MOE stuff is the soft stuff ... In an SFOR meeting, I witnessed a frustrated French two-star general get up and say he wanted a measurement of how much ethnic reconciliation was happening in his sector. This was impossible to give him. How do you measure ethnic reconciliation?"[4]

Flemming says during the time he spent in Sarajevo, he was able to make many changes to adjust for the need to see progress in the "soft" areas such as ethnic reconciliation. In the governance area, he began conducting content analyses of local print news to count iterations of "ethnic slurs." From this process he was able to extrapolate increases and decreases in ethnic tensions between and among some of the ethnic groups in SFOR regions. He began introducing qualitative aspects of measuring into the SFOR Transition Strategy by setting up a system that entailed collecting qualitative aspects that were reported quantitatively.

Based on his experience, Flemming suggests that military intelligence and measures of effectiveness briefings are best joined up to address the questions "What is working?" and "What hasn't worked?" These questions are the foundation for assessing any type of progress in a field situation.

When asked to consider measures of effectiveness in the context of peace operations and crisis management, Lieutenant General David Leakey, director general of the European Union Military Staff in the Council of the European Union, Brussels, deliberated on two main points.[5] The idea of MOEs is gaining currency at the European Union, he said, but as yet has no traction.[6] In addition, he argued that only some of the EU member states have a culture of military business planning. In his opinion, these member states include the Netherlands and the United Kingdom. A culture of business-style planning first needs to have traction in member states before it is applied to peace operations or to the way that the EU does business in Brussels.

Leakey goes on to suggest that it is not instinctively part of military culture to do business-style planning for peacetime – wartime, yes, but not during times of relative peace. Therefore measuring the effectiveness of peace operations and crisis management is not yet a part of operational theories. In Leakey's experience there are few "management plans" in the European Union defence sector because of the cultures that are a part of the EU – not just with ministries of defence but also the other ministries in Europe.

Leakey suggests that management plans are in essence MOEs, which assist with performance measuring. He notes that general management plans are uncommon in the EU: there are program and project plans, but no general plans, due to the absence of business planning cultures in EU institutions. "The business of performance measuring on operations is thin but gaining traction," he says. The UK has a sense of this and plans during times of peace and times of war. The UK Ministry of Defence (MOD) sets indicators for performance right down to the unit level.[7]

General Leakey served in EUFOR, Bosnia-Herzegovina, in 2004-05, and says that there was more performance measuring on this operation than any other he has been involved with. The Dayton Peace Accord had its own milestones that served as built-in indicators. Standards were set and were supposed to be met through IFOR and then through SFOR. Detailed *Instructions to Parties* (ITPs) for militaries only were a part of the Framework for Peace. "When I served there in 2004-05," Leakey says, "EUFOR was on Amendment 21 of the ITPs. They are constantly being met and then amended to create new indicators to reach." As the ITPs were modified, new targets were set by involved parties. The main target was the transfer of responsibility towards BiH authorities. Not only did the indicators come directly from the ITPs; so too did the records of the activities including all training and movement. "Everything was controlled. NATO archived all of the records."[8]

The High Representative, Paddy Ashdown, also developed his Mission Implementation Plan (MIP). The ITPs were military and the MIPs were civilian. The MIP had four parts: 1) economic reform, 2) rule of law/justice, 3) police, and 4) defence. Milestones were built into the MIP, and every few months Ashdown would report progress to the Peace Implementation Council (PIC). The mission was reviewed every six months in Brussels. "It seemed as if everyone involved accepted the ITPs and the MIPs as normal business," says Leakey. Performance was examined on many fronts and was not formulaic: it was an integral part of upholding the Dayton Peace Accord. Charles Call maintains that 60 percent of UN peacekeeping operations that ended their missions claiming to have fulfilled their mandate experienced no recurrence of even minor armed conflict within five years.[9] The fulfillment of a UN peacekeeping mandate has been a measure of success for military planners. This was indeed the case in Bosnia-Herzegovina.

Leakey describes the use of scientific opinion testing in Bosnia-Herzegovina (perhaps based on some of the seeds planted by Steve Flemming in his SFOR days) as a useful tool for gauging progress. The method was three-pronged:

1. human intelligence (HUMINT) that was evidence based
2. contact (matrix of liaison and observation teams reported on opinion trends)
3. blind opinion testing

Leakey stated that MOEs and performance measuring cannot be generalized, especially in permissive environments like Kosovo and Bosnia Herzegovina. In his view, permissive environments create "shades of grey" – nothing is clear. Comparatively, non-permissive environments are "black and white" and should not be viewed through the lens of performance and progress: "You are either being shot at, or not being shot at; therefore the non-permissive environment can be viewed as black and white when it comes to metrics and indicators."

A high-ranking EU military representative echoes this sentiment: "In non-permissive environments, a measure of success is NOT being shot. When you can walk around without getting shot, this becomes a measure of success."[10]

In the field the military uses a simple "red, yellow, green" system – as developed by Steve Flemming during his SFOR days in Sarajevo. However, Bergstrand, Flemming, and Leakey all believe that peace operations environments come in shades of grey (Figure 29).[11] Leakey cautions that in non-permissive environments, people are using their wits; to force measuring frameworks on them is inappropriate. However, once they emerge out of the black and white into the grey (more permissive environments), they do require performance indicators.[12]

Leakey reinforces this point by arguing the need for specific planning documents, as they had in Bosnia-Herzegovina (BiH) after the Yugoslav conflicts in the early 1990s. "If you do not have a campaign plan when you hit the grey permissive environment, you drift." He says that headquarters in UN missions appear not to have plans, and therefore there is much drift. He goes on to articulate "two caveats for setting performance measures: Do not do it in blackness (non-permissive environments); and be careful with setting indicators in grey areas (permissive environments), because the so-called geeks will become obsessed with the

FIGURE 29
Permissive, Non-Permissive, and Grey-Zone Environments of International Interventions

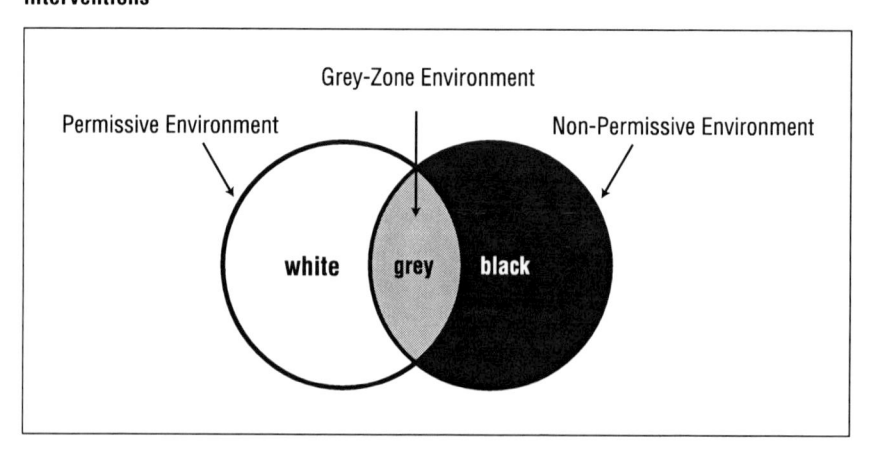

indicators rather than the principles of the operations and *real* achievements."[13] For Leakey, insecure and violent environments are non-permissive and therefore can be measured in black and white variables, while seemingly secure environments in which democracy and governance agendas are being fulfilled are permissive in nature but have rather woolly, so-called grey variables.

Colonel John Agoglia, former director of the US Army's Peacekeeping and Stability Operations Institute, raises an important point: "There is an assumption of a 'clear mandate' even though there may not be." He goes on to ask, "What is the impact of not having a clear mandate? What is the risk of not having a solid mandate?" For if a peace operation or civilian crisis management operation has a muddy mandate, it is near impossible to generate a campaign or operational plan that establishes a clear strategy, with requisite indicators and benchmarks fulfilling the overall strategy of a mission.[14]

Colonel Andre Harvey, Canadian Forces, points out that militaries are used to doing operational planning, and part of planning is measuring progress and effects through the "objectives" coming out of the ops plans. Measures of progress and, similarly, measures of success are also used to link activities to broader mission strategies, which are directly derived from mission mandates.[15]

David Beer, chief superintendent of the Royal Canadian Mounted Police, argues that "nothing really gets measured against a UN mandate. It is impossible to frame through a six-month mission. It takes two years to staff a mission; therefore, you don't have the expertise to conduct real measuring of progress or effectiveness. We are a long way from a business approach to peacekeeping operations."[16] In Beer's experience, such a lack of planning for measurement places police in a difficult position."The army does nothing in the field until they are ready to do it based on their mandate. They do not do anything until they get on the ground. On the ground, they often have weeks to prepare after they get there. The police are police the moment they arrive on the ground. Therefore the expectations of what the police can bring to the table and what they are actually bringing are worlds apart." He gives as an example a UN mission in Haiti:

> The UN mandate called for 1,700 police. They came from forty-five nations. The hybrid mandate had no executive authority but they wanted executive policing. There were twelve different languages spoken on mission, different religions, and no one was recruited for their expertise. There were no multi-lateral staff deployed [permanent UN employees to guide the mission]. It took a year to get up to 1,699 police – 65 percent were formed police

units to support the security portion of the mandate. The remainder were community police, and only 100 spoke French and Creole; therefore only one-sixteenth of the deployed police could communicate with the locals. With these practicalities, expectations could not be met. It was not the mandate's problem – rather, how these things were carried out. Expectations for police mandate are unattainable.

We only need a small core of people to lay out the plan, goals, and objectives to meet the mission mandate. There would be more clarity on what was working and not working from the outset of a mission.[17]

Glenn MacPhail, a retired member of the Royal Canadian Mounted Police, suggests that compliance issues are often at the heart of evaluating police programming because international standards can be "tampered with" by those in charge during each deployment.[18] In other words, MacPhail suggests, with each leader comes a different way to interpret standards against localized cultures of rule of law: "If we are not careful, if this tampering is not kept in check, it can really create havoc in a mission area three to four years down the line. Only [Police] commissioners can make local or regional changes to international standards. If there are changes – mission creep – these manifest over the course of years and the whole structure for police standards changes and is unrecognizable."[19]

MacPhail and Beer argue that assessments take a lot of time and money and are not done in every police mission. They are often begun years after the start of a mission – this is referred to as "assessment lag" – because the nature of police missions changes as time passes. Policing is not a discreet intervention activity, as is the case in various humanitarian projects; it is a mission or an element of an international mission. When new elements are introduced to a mission mandate, such as in 1998-99, when three new programs (including the targeting the reduction of organized crime and drug trafficking) came on line within the international community, there are new things to evaluate regarding police training functions and police operational functions. In places like Haiti, Bosnia, Kosovo, and Timor L'Este, these elements did not exist during the mission planning stages.

Like military personnel, most police personnel are not worried about the long-term effects of their work because they know they will be gone by the time their work takes effect in conflict environments: "We are seized with the concept of getting boots on the ground and reporting on progress; then we are long gone."[20] Sustainable change, however, requires security, time, money, human resources, and the political will to address challenges (Figure 30).

FIGURE 30
A Formula for Sustainable Change

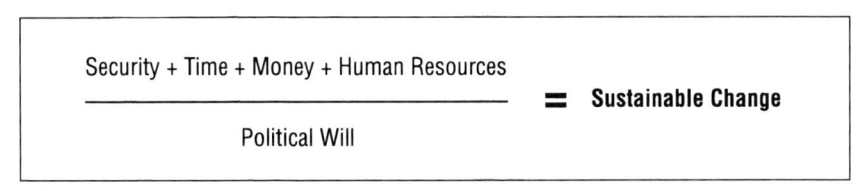

$$\frac{\text{Security + Time + Money + Human Resources}}{\text{Political Will}} = \text{Sustainable Change}$$

According to a high-ranking military representative of the Council of the European Union, the issue of measuring success is especially difficult when dealing with peace support operations. In this area, the military has no definitive way to measure success.[21]

> In the old fashion, war fighting was by some sense easier since one of the aims was the destruction of enemy forces. It was always possible to measure success by counting the number of deaths on our side and on their side, or relying heavily on statistics like was done in Vietnam (e.g., the number of bombs dropped in spite of their negative or unintended effects).
>
> Comparatively, in modern peace support operations, one of the indicators of success could be the number of contacts that are established with the locals, because a high number of contacts would mean equal trust. Trust towards our actions, in places like Afghanistan, is based on "contact" with locals. As an example, I can say that my action in Afghanistan was based upon building high levels of trust with locals in this respect.[22]

Olivia Setkic, a researcher with the Crisis Management Initiative in Finland, says that it is incumbent upon practitioners to manage expectations related to the outcomes of peace operations and crisis management activities. Like the high-ranking EU rep, Setkic maintains that this is especially important with locals in communities undergoing international interventions. When expectations regarding the efficacy of interventions are high, they are rarely met, which causes a loss of trust between crisis affected people and the international community stakeholders.[23]

The Butcher, the Baker, the Candlestick-Maker

In a small café in Brussels, Alexander Blyth, chief of staff, EUJUST LEX, told his story about evaluating a police training project in Iraq. In true British form, Alexander observed that to really get at evaluation, you must talk to "the butcher, the baker and the candlestick-maker" – meaning, the real citizens of a war-affected environment. These are the people who need to be engaged in measuring change.

In March 2007 the Pearson Peacekeeping Centre conducted field research in Bosnia-Herzegovina. The research was interview based and included locals involved in peace operation and crisis management as well as humanitarianism and development during and following the Yugoslav armed conflicts. A portion of the study focused on the effectiveness of the peace operations according to locals. The aim was to discover from their perspectives what they considered to be effective, what was ineffective, what worked well and was considered to be successful, and what was not worth repeating. Some participants comments on the short-, medium- and long-term effects of the peace operation in BiH.

Many of the people who lived out the war in BiH remain there. They are living with the results of the international community's experiment, including the successes and failures of intervention activities. According to one interview participant, "My Swedish OSCE boss said that Bosnia was an experiment for the international community. And he said that in all fact."[24] Seeds of negativity that were planted in Bosnia about the international community in the early 1990s are flourishing today – whether for good or for bad, for positive or negative progress. The people of Bosnia want the international community out.

The worldview of the locals affected by armed conflicts and resulting international community interventions are important to the critical assessment – measuring – of activities. Local opinions matter in the measuring formula, as they tend to illuminate issues and processes that are in the relative blind spot of those who intervene, driven by donor agendas and do-gooder paradigms. Locals provide a reality check. They can immediately identify what works and what does not work from the perspective of those who have to live in these postwar environments long after the international community has moved to other zones of conflict around the globe to repeat the same potential mistakes. Yet processes that work in one culture may not work in another; universal effectiveness measures, therefore, should not exist. What should exist is a way of thinking that can bring about best outcomes for conflict-affected people.

What follows reflects a localized perspective on the effectiveness of the peace operation in Bosnia-Herzegovina and the broader implications of the effectiveness of the international community to those who experience interventions first hand. The words are the participants' own, left in their original form to convey what matters to the people I spoke within Bosnia-Herzegovina in 2007.

Participant A[25]

Q: What have been the longer-term effects of the international community becoming involved in Bosnia?

A: Probably the security. Because twelve years after the war we don't really have any major violations of security in this country – and it's the most important.

Q: So it's a positive effect?

A: Of course. Everyone would say that.

Q: Are there any long-term negative effects of the international community becoming involved in Bosnia-Herzegovina?

A: Probably politicians will tell you that Dayton and constitution don't function and will lead to war in future of this country. Because the country is basically divided on the front lines, and not only that but the Bosnian government is weak. We cannot respond to our own citizens' needs, and the message is not sent from the top level of government to the local people.

Q: What could have made the international community and peace operation more effective here?

A: I think that the violence didn't bring anything to an end. The problem is that in the very beginning they should have tackled the strongest issues because today it's hard to change some things. It was easier after the war, because then the international community was really the controller. I mean they – common [motor vehicle] plates and common passports. The flag! Everything was – all of that was invention of international community.

Q: How would you measure the effectiveness of the international community in places like Bosnia-Herzegovina?

A: It depends on the situation and what you want to achieve – then you set up some criteria to measure. In this case, maybe there was no plan at all and nobody knew what to do. People were just following the events in the field. In this case certain principles should have been set up. Like, they said the former Yugoslav republic borders should not be violated. That was a principle. But then during the war we witnessed that all the time: the [BiH] border was in danger. Probably it was the media that perpetuated the violence, it was a human catastrophe. Probably no one saw death on that scale or violence like that.

Participant B[26]

Q: Were your needs met by the peace operation in the short term and medium term?

B: First of all, they stopped the war. That was the most important. And nobody else was capable in this country to do that, so that's the reality, that they did. And at that time when Dayton appeared, when Dayton was signed – you wouldn't worry, people felt, so like no more killing. That was the only important thing in the hearts of the people …

Not to be scared anymore, not to expect that something will happen – and that brought joy to everybody, depending on which area those people are living. During the war when they started to come they focused on reconciliation, between different communities – long-term process. That process went very slow at the beginning – there were many obstacles. It was really very tough. It worked slowly but it worked …

People felt most secure. First of all, and most important thing, was people were 100 percent sure that no more shelling, no more killing – that stopped. And that was very essential. Then economy is very important. If you have money – for example, I'm talking of myself, I have a good job, I have a good salary – I don't care who is going to be in power.

Participant C[27]

Q: In your opinion how effective was the international peace operation?

C: In many, many situations, they've been late, they've not been on time, and they never happened to be there where they are supposed to be. There was not any explanations or reasons why internationals could not afford food supply for people in Mostar, and not a lot of people to basically depend on the food that they brought. There has been proven that, at the time, internationals or NATO, during the bombardment or the siege area of Sarajevo, did not try to unblock the city. That is something that could be done anywhere else to get supply to people.

Participants D and E[28]

D: I watch CNN regularly and when I watch Sudan – even though we had things here, all the bloodshed and everything – it pains you to see those images of war because the same thing happened here years ago. But what hurts me the most, because I am a Muslim and I am liberal, that means I respect other religions. I read the Bible and I believe that all the books are practically saying the same thing. If every man upholds the Ten Commandments – even four of them! Don't kill, don't hate – then you know, it would be a good man. It really pains me to see that people are killing each other over some tribal issues. Those countries, those are really like tribal issues. I think that the international community needs to be more resolute about things. They need to be more effective – I know they have a lot of procedures that they need to follow, but they should really lessen their time investigating those kinds of events. Because they always form like dozens of committees for investigating, and it takes a lot of time for each of those to be evaluating, and a lot of people die.

Q: So act quicker?

D: Yeah. Because America especially is the most powerful country – if they want something, they will do, just like in Iraq. They didn't care what the rest of the world was saying. That's why I agree with him [referring to other student]: the wars can be prevented before they start. And I think if they want to prevent something, they can, especially in those countries where you have dictators, just like they did in Iraq.

Q: So let's talk about the international community again. You said they're going too fast, 100 miles an hour. How can the international community be more effective?

E: They need to prevent our politicians – because everything is business seniority, but now politicians really don't care. You know, under the table and status quo, as long as they all receive their paycheques, which are all large, and in this country they are not doing anything. If you see any of them on TV, there is a politician who always speaks eloquently but he doesn't say nothing. And I think it's odd, it's really odd, when you give ten or twenty sentences and you don't say anything.

D: Supporting education and economy. Education is really important and this is one of the ways to promote these international programs. I know that we will soon become part of European Union.

Participant F[29]

Q: How could the international community have been more effective here in your hospital in Sarajevo and the health sector in Bosnia-Herzegovina?

F: You know that at one time we had more than 400 NGOs in our region in the health sector – and all 400 wanted to implement their own ideas. And the wrongest approach is that you want to build a system in which [you] are experienced in another condition. They just want to broaden their models and by force put in the system which is completely different. They have a lot of ideas, they have experience, and they have models which they want to put in the BiH, which is really impossible without tiers. I always persuade them, you can have models but this model has to be tiered, this model has to suit us. You couldn't bring me the boots [size] 42 and I wearing 36. That was the very hard process to persuade them, and I had a lot of fights between international community, between representatives, between World Bank representatives, EU representatives, to show them that this is not South Africa, this is not Rwanda. This is the country which had system more developed than many western countries in which people were on insurance, in which people were completely covered with care and there were no need to pay anything at the spot of delivering care. And we were taught by the people in which [place] you have millions of uninsured people, segregated completely from the health care system. And they gave us lecture and I really – sometimes I enter into conflict with them. At first they recognized me as a conflict person, but at the end of meetings they recognized me as a key stakeholder and advisor and person who advocate in proper way, and I still continue to work this ...

Maybe one example is that people doesn't listen to the voice of the health professionals to protect division of the health by a constitution and the country. They have power, they can do this, and the time when Dayton was built, but they really didn't have feeling that they need to be more stronger involved in policy of how to design health sector. As a consequence of this, because international community allowed our politicians to fight for their own interests, to be small kings in small arenas, and they gave them authorization so they could cut, for example, education into pieces, they cut health into pieces, they cut social care into pieces. As a consequence of this, you now have thirteen ministries of health in BiH, thirteen health insurance funds, and thirteen small gods in health sector. The international community really didn't listen to the voice of those who were behind the politicians. That is the probably the time when international community lost the chance to design good state, and they listened more to politicians who were nationalists and who want to be in the power instead of translating best practice from other countries.

Participant G[30]

Q: In your opinion, how effective was the peace operation?

G: Well, not very effective, given the number of those that got killed, got expelled, or tortured ... who ended up in camps or prisons or – given the Srebrenica genocide and all this – not very effective."

Q: So in your opinion some of those atrocities and the genocide could have been stopped?

G: Yes.

Q: At the time, were your needs met and your family's needs met by the international community during the last part of the war and just after the war?

G: Well, when I think back about needs, we really didn't need a lot, so we were happy with little. And given that we kind of survived, I guess the needs were met, if you look at it like that. I'm not sure that they were actually – this is tricky question. I'm trying to look back and figure out whether they were there or whether they were met because of the internationals or because of the culture or because of the nature of the people here or because of the willingness to help. At this moment I'm not really sure what was the reason that certain needs were met at the time.

Q: So thinking back, the peace operation and the international community through particular methods may have met short-term needs through humanitarian aid and other assistance. Now think about the medium term and longer term needs that you have as a young professional family, maybe your parents or your larger family ... Did the peace operation and the international community meet the longer term needs that you have now?

G: Longer term needs ... I definitely think that there is a huge improvement in many areas of life since the war ended – well, in this sort of period of ten or twelve years. But there are also many other things where quality of living or quality of needs significantly dropped in comparison to the situation before the war, and this especially comes with regard between social and economic rights of people of Bosnia-Herzegovina. To certain extent, rights to education, social, and economic, and maybe education too. We're probably better refined and better settled now than they were before the war. When I look at my parents, they're retired now, and the quality of life or quality of living or the financial support or financial benefits that they get today is probably – certainly – less quality than it was before the war. We also have to include here the right to health care: it's also completely undermined in comparison to prewar period.

Participant H[31]

Q: Do you think that the international community met your short-term needs, for you and your family?

H: I think the short-term needs would be, at the wartime and shortly after the wartime, securing the peace and provide food and basic supplies. If you are talking about that part of the international roles – as a short one, that's definitely being met. If we're talking about the long-term needs, I don't know – I feel that a lot of local people believe that taking responsibility is the job of internationals. I personally do not believe that they should take all responsibility, but they also have to be aware that they've not been saints here.

Q: Do you believe that locals think the international community should take responsibility for politics, for economics?

H: Well it's easier – yeah, for politics, it's easier like that. We have to be aware of the system that was being previously present in these countries or in this country – such as a communist or socialist system.

Q: What about the humanitarian aspect of the international intervention?

H: Yes, that was an aspect that was well done, or done at the highest level possible for certain areas and places.

Q: Do other people share your opinion?

H: I believe so. I believe that everyone has to be aware that without humanitarian aid we would not survive hunger and the sieges. Did I agree with the politics and other things? No.

Participant I[32]

I: If the prime minister of Canada were to come to me and say "Ady, what's one thing that you would suggest my government to do internationally?" I would tell him, please, stop giving money to UN agencies. Stop giving them even one dollar.

Q: Stop the money to the UN? Why?

I: The work that they do is terrible. Within all of these project that they do, they have hundreds of project, and of course if you have hundred projects, you will find only two, three which are good. But if ninety-eight of them are terrible, then generally you raise the question: Is there a need to raise all of this money to these UN agencies? First of all, UN has a specific role. It is supposed to be this cream, the top of the peace, peace-keeping, peace-developing, whatever … well, UN is supposed to protect us. They failed in that role. UN example is Srebrenica, where it was UN-protected zone, and it was genocide …

In my opinion, I'll never forgive them that the UN protective zone was the place where at the end of the twentieth century the biggest genocide was committed. And they didn't protect these people. I know they had similar role in Sarajevo. They did nothing.

Q: Do other people share your opinion?

I: Definitely. I can say this now, on CNN if it's necessary – we hate UN. The work that they did after – it's … you would expect that they were supposed to do whatever it was in their mandate – the role that they have provides the possibility to do some really complete stuff. In my opinion, they failed ...

I can speak now from UN agencies which conduct health reform. Well, all of their work is this six-month thing – six month, one month, one year. About bunch of these guys that come from all over the world, so-called experts for this, experts for that ... I mean, I never saw – probably Bosnia was the country which was visited by biggest number of experts than any country ever in the world ...

When you turn on the TV or radio, you are visited by this experts or that experts ... all of these experts, and where are the outcomes of these experts? Statements are one thing. The concrete work are other thing.

Q: *So measuring the outcomes?*

I: I think the only way how you can measure some outcomes is concrete work. I can tell you now about everything what we do. About family medicine development, specialty programs and ... but when you ask me what concretely – and that's one thing that our people in Yugoslavia and I would say Europeans, we like concrete stuff ...

Every European person would ask me: "Okay but concretely, what do you mean, Ady, by 'development program'?" And then I would say, well, we opened up so many teaching centres, satellite, we reconstruct them, we train so many hundred of doctors, so many hundred thousand of nurses, so many students, you know.

Q: *They want numbers?*

I: Not necessarily numbers but concrete outcomes. Results. Let's say in two or three years, when some things could be measured. It's not fair to measure some results after six months or one year, because I told you, they can't do anything in that time. Even two years is too short period of time. I think that this small investment of foreign agencies should be really targeted for the long term, for developing things, and not for really vague "institutional capacity building" and all of that. Well, in environment such as Bosnia, it's just waste of time.

Q: *So, you are suggesting that it is better to have a longer period program – five, ten, fifteen years – that has a larger budget, a longer strategy, and fewer rotations of people?*

I: Definitely. It all depends on people.

Q: *And according to you, an unsuccessful system is the short, quick-impact projects run by the UN, and OHR – huge, monolithic organizations – with fast rotations of staff, so-called experts, and projects shorter than five years?*

I: Yes. You can't do anything, in my opinion, in the period shorter than five years. Nothing, except deliver humanitarian aid or fix some building. Any developing project less than five years is just waste of money.

Summary Points

- Bosnia-Herzegovina is a good case study to better understand the shift from measuring tangible results such as security to increasingly intangible outcomes related to ethnicity, democracy, and good governance.

- Recipient populations have a different ways of understanding intervention activities, and their opinions are critical to designing appropriate activities.

- Activities are too short in time to create sustainable results – especially intangible results – in recipient populations.

- The international community is able to create concrete results early on in intervention activities, but these are rarely lasting and there are few of the long-term results that matter to recipient populations.

Notes

[1] Steve Flemming, personal communication, 2008.
[2] Ibid.
[3] Ibid.
[4] Ibid.
[5] David Leakey, personal communication, 2008.
[6] He suggested that it will have soon, though.
[7] David Leakey, personal communication, 2008.
[8] Ibid.
[9] Charles T. Call, "Knowing Peace When You See It," 179.
[10] Anonymous, personal communication, 2008.
[11] Brad Bergstrand, personal communication, 2008; Steve Flemming, personal communication, 2008; David Leakey, personal communication, 2008.
[12] Steve Flemming, personal communication, 2008.
[13] David Leakey, personal communication, 2008.
[14] John Agoglia, personal communication, 2008.
[15] Andre Harvey, personal communication, 2008.
[16] David Beer, personal communication, 2008.
[17] Ibid.
[18] Glenn MacPhail, personal communication, 2008.

[19] Ibid.
[20] David Beer, personal communication, 2008; Glenn MacPhail, personal communication, 2008.
[21] Anonymous, personal communication, 2008.
[22] Ibid.
[23] Olivia Setkic, personal communication, 2007.
[24] Mirjana Sičaja, personal communication, 28 March 2007.
[25] Daut Bajramović, personal communication, 27 March 2007.
[26] Anonymous, personal communication, 21 March 2007.
[27] Murat Corić, Mostar city council president, personal communication, 26 March 2007.
[28] Medical students, personal communication, 21 March 2007. This group of interview participants were selected based on their age. They had been young children during the war in Bosnia-Herzegovina and served as blind study participants, not having prior experience with the international community attempting to recover an area from armed conflict. This group was the first of two such interview groups of students in their late teens and early twenties.
[29] Dr Bakir Nakaš, personal communication, 22 March 2007 in Sarajevo.
[30] Anonymous, personal communication, 22 March 2007 in Sarajevo.
[31] Adis Pašalić, personal communication, 30 March 2007 in Sarajevo.
[32] Adnan Mirojević, personal communication, 29 March 2007.

PART II

Measuring What Matters

An Epistemic Community

As the international community of states and organizations occupies a common tradespace of activities, standards, and praxis for peace operations and crisis management, the knowledge and solutions produced by an epistemic community become of utmost importance. The contributors highlighted in the following section are an *epistemic community*. This transnational, trans-sector, trans-functional network of knowledge-based practitioners helps to define the problems faced by the international community in respect to measuring effectiveness, progress, and success, and focuses on what decision-makers should do about these challenges. This epistemic community is made up of a disparate group of people who do not share a peace operations history but who search for a common practice for the international community in the hopes of making peace operations and crisis management more effective, or at the very least, of reducing the negative, unintended consequences of interventions.

This particular community represents diversity among sectors and approaches, worldviews and perspectives, motives and missions. Moreover, they think critically about intervention and the social order it impacts. They raise important issues rather than maintaining the status quo in their respective positions and institutions. And most importantly, they question the principles of progress and the value of success in peace operations and crisis management.

The authors of the eight chapters that follow are Rory Keane, John Borton, Keith Hauk and Stephen Mariano, Stuart Gordon, David Chuter, Emery Brusset, Kristiina Rintakoski, and Jake Sherman Typically, those who contribute to this body of knowledge are either theorists or practitioners. In this case, they are both, and were intentionally chosen because they bridge theory and practice with applied thinking. As well, individually they are able to face challenges bigger than themselves and have the confidence to stand in the difficult space of ambiguity. This approach is critical to understanding the realpolitik of measuring the success and progress of peace operations and crisis management. Throughout their vignettes the authors make linkages among dominant discourses, worldviews, and measuring mechanisms. Salient ideas, summarized in bullet points following each vignette, are analyzed and presented as policy options in chapter 14.

CHAPTER 6

Peace Operations and Crisis Management: Not Just Benign Tasks But Political Acts

RORY KEANE[1]

There is no such thing as a "neutral actor" or a "neutral policy" in peace operations and crisis management. Peace operations and crisis management (POps/CM) activities are often perceived as predominantly benign practices. While this may sometimes be true, it is also the case that such operations are *political acts*. Within this short article, I call for a stronger consciousness of the political elements of interventions by the theorists, the policy-makers, and the practitioners, so that peace operations can ultimately be more effective and *do no harm*.[2]

Increasing the level of political consciousness among stakeholders necessitates moving away from an understanding of POps/CM activities as solely benign acts of a technical nature. Rather, operatives in this field will be increasingly effective if they become more conscious of the political nature of peace-building, which requires international peace-building missions to address complex questions such as: How can local ownership and service delivery be simultaneously respected? How can the development of a cohesive state be ensured even if decentralized governance is a necessary part of reform?

International staff need to be more conscious of the fact that POps/CM activities have become much more political in recent years due to a complex post-Cold War international agenda, the nexus between security and development, and resulting broader peace-building agendas. Stakeholders involved in POps/CM activities are increasingly forced to accept that their success demands the reconfiguration of *Westphalian* notions of sovereignty,[3] the qualification of what is understood to be local ownership,[4] and the making of hard choices on a range of issues, such as the amnesty-impunity conundrum[5] or indeed effective, swift service delivery versus slower, less effective, but home-grown solutions (contracting out versus contracting in).

The Changing Political Focus in the Post-Cold War Era

The end of the Cold War set in motion a fundamental re-conceptualization of notions of security. The narrow stress on territorial security and weapons security was systemic of the Cold War. Developing countries were sometimes treated as pawns in a global game of geopolitics. Stability and status quo were the watchwords of the realist policy-makers. Today it is no longer just about stability, as issues relating to governance and redistribution have scaled upwards on the policy chart. In the context of developing countries, there is a recognized need for peace operations to take this into account and to place a greater focus on service delivery for citizens, sustainable development, peace-building, and a suitable state that may require a post-Westphalian configuration that decouples or at least fudges territoriality and sovereignty in the interest of some form of relative peace (for example, Northern Ireland, Bosnia-Herzegovina, Sudan).

We are now living in an age when the security of the state and the security of people are increasingly seen as mutually reinforcing. This reality is also strongly influencing the international community, as a growing *development approach* to security has emerged since the end of the Cold War period (as symbolized by notions such as *human security*[6]). It is no longer accepted – at least openly – to pursue the ideologically inclined, top-down approaches that formerly typified most military assistance.

The Cold War period produced distinct lines between sovereignty and intervention as understood by the western international community, and especially western militaries in some respects, as their political vision was based almost entirely on a *realist approach*. This international relations approach was informed by agendas of *stability* and *containment*. The post-Cold War period has blurred the lines informing this more traditional political vision. This period is made distinct by the coming together of security and development; the prioritization of people-focused peace-building above hard stability at all costs has meant that militaries are obliged to become more involved in security system reform (SSR), upstream conflict prevention (including early warning), and civil-military relations – in essence, more involved in pursuing the notion of *comprehensive security*.[7] Today, security is increasingly a question of governance – a question of development. Therefore, peace operations need to ensure that an appropriate donor institutional framework is developed and the requisite international human resource capacity is put in place to manage a crisis in a manner that conforms to complex political questions of democratic norms, local ownership, and sound principles of governance and development.

This growing nexus between security and development, along with the complexity of peace-building, has put issues such as civil-military relations centre stage. For example, in Afghanistan, the divisions of military and civilian tasks have started to slowly and unsurely cross-fertilize, as is evident through Provincial Reconstruction Teams (PRTs). This cross-fertilization – if more effectively pursued – can promote increased policy and implementation coherence between and amongst military and civilian stakeholders. However, more work is required to establish good international practices and shared international principles for conducting civil-military relations in Afghanistan and indeed elsewhere.

The Big Political Question: "What to Do about Ownership"?

The ever-broader remit for peace operations and crisis management activities has meant that peace-building has become the cornerstone of the international community's approach. Peace-building encompasses a large number of programs of both development and security related activities. However, linking security and development alone will not bring about peace-building unless the reforms are locally owned. Local-level ownership often increases when the international community aligns reform projects to local realities to address root causes of conflict and instability.

In this regard, ownership is a particularly challenging issue for peace operations to deal with, insofar as an international presence on the ground can be seen (by some) as a source that *erodes* local ownership and legitimacy. UN-mandated peace operations rightly aim to work through host nation governments in post-conflict and developing countries in order to increase ownership and legitimacy. A challenge arises in some cases when local governments are not representative of their people. In some post-conflict countries, the state is sometimes *neopatrimonial* in nature – a "big man" rules, and state functions and services for citizens remain poor. In these situations the international community – striving to build local capacities for ownership and legitimacy – needs to consider whether to support the neopatrimonial state (such as Zimbabwe) and risk contributing to the further legitimization of the system, or whether to disengage from these states and risk contributing to the further decline of functions and services intended for civilian populations, and to the eventual collapse of the state.

There is no easy way of addressing ownership. So-called *new liberal imperialists* such as Stephan Krasner[8] or Robert Cooper[9] argue that the focus should be on the moral responsibility to intervene on behalf of beleaguered citizens to protect human rights and democracy (the classic case of Kosovo 1999). Stronger and longer-term international engagement with democracy as a north star is thus at the heart of this approach. New liberal imperialism endorses a nexus between security and development, and is concerned with both legitimacy and efficiency. This doctrine seems to indirectly suggest that at times it may be necessary for the international community to disrespect the wishes of the government of the recipient state in order to deliver human security and service delivery. This approach – which may or may not fall under the criteria of the Responsibility to Protect doctrine – requires a strong commitment from western states, coupled with a robust military presence, if required.

The challenges faced in Afghanistan and Iraq have caused some to question new liberal imperialism and to revert to a more realist Cold-War era approach, where the global discourse on peace-building is replaced by a more calculated approach based on stability rather than ideational values. Such a reversion would tend to preference stability and narrow definitions of security over and above the human security approach. Other emerging approaches have taken an altogether different slant on peace-building and prefer to focus on traditional notions of governance. These critical approaches urge that we stop exporting western concepts (such as occidental notions of peace-building) and rather build on what exists locally (with a focus on understanding the context -specific dynamic between *gesellschaft* and *gemeinschaft*[10]) and accept that notions of statehood and governance will differ depending on tradition, culture, and history.

Concluding Remarks

When the international community intervenes in places like Afghanistan, it is important to have a clear political vision as well as a clear mandate. While peace operations tend to carry out specific niche actions in support of peace-building, it is important for international actors and national counterparts to have a clearly agreed upon understanding of how such actions support an overall political vision for peace-building. For example, does the overall vision prioritize local capacity-building? Local ownership? Alignment to local requests? If yes, do specific projects and programs respond in part to that jointly agreed-upon political vision? Do the theories of new liberal imperialism or the realism agenda have a bearing on the political vision? If yes, how so? This is not only an academic debate or a discussion to be had between the policy people at headquarters. Rather, all operatives on the ground need to understand the overall political goal, as without such vision a successful and sustainable implementation strategy is made all the more difficult to achieve.

There is no such thing as a "neutral actor" or a "neutral policy" in POps/CM. In this sense all peace operations and all crisis management activities are politically loaded. While this is not necessarily a negative fact, it is vital that all actors involved are conscious of the political ramifications of actions taken in order to be more effective and to do no harm. The necessity for political consciousness has become all the more urgent because the international community's focus on peace-building has heightened a number of challenges, most notably Westphalian notions of sovereignty and local ownership, and the new focus on civil-military relations.

Summary Points

- Peace operations and crisis management activities are *political acts* that *can do harm*.
- All stakeholders need to have political consciousness – the awareness that intervention activities are never neutral.
- Political consciousness assists in achieving a successful and sustainable implementation strategy.
- The complex peace and security environment has corresponding political demands – sovereignty, ownership, amnesty-impunity, service delivery questions, etc.
- The security of the state and the security of people are mutually reinforcing.
- New liberal imperialists intervene based upon moral responsibility, such as the protection of human rights and democracy.
- The realist approach to intervention is based on stability and status quo rather than ideational values like human security. This approach uses locally accepted notions of statehood and governance that respond to tradition, culture, and history.
- Local-level ownership often increases when the international community aligns reform projects to local realities that address root causes of conflict and instability.

Notes

[1] The opinions expressed in this article are subjective and do not necessarily in any way represent official OECD views or policy.

[2] For overview of the "do no harm' principle," see Anderson, *Do No Harm*.

[3] State sovereignty is not axiomatic but rather changes configuration over time and space. See Weber, *Simulating Sovereignty*.

[4] The Development Assistance Committee (DAC) of the Organization for Economic Co-operation and Development (OECD), in its seminal 1996 statement, "Shaping the 21st Century," asserts that sustainable development "must be locally owned" and that development cooperation has to be shifted to a partnership model in which donors' programs and activities operate within locally owned development strategies. Donors should "respect and encourage strong local commitment, participation, capacity development and ownership." The DAC then linked these arguments to a series of specific targets for poverty reduction, which formed the basis of the Millennium Development Goals adopted by the United Nations in 2000.

[5] While the fight against impunity needs to be at the centre of any sustainable peace-building initiative, it is also the case that peace negotiations sometimes directly or indirectly deliver amnesty to certain key political players. The question is whether a peace negotiated with amnesty provisions can ever hope to provide sustainable peace and transitional justice.

[6] For an overview of human security, see Maclean et al., eds., *Decade of Human Security*.

[7] This paradigm shift can be seen within NATO, which traditionally was an archetype realist Cold War structure. Nevertheless, in April 2008 NATO ministers endorsed a comprehensive approach to security and defence during the NATO Bucharest Summit.

[8] Krasner and Pascual, "Addressing State Failure."

[9] Cooper, "The Postmodern State."

[10] *Gemeinschaft* – often translated as "community" – is a relationship between individuals and a larger association, more so than to an individual's own self interest. Furthermore, individuals in *gemeinschaft* are regulated by common mores or beliefs about the appropriate behaviour and responsibility of members of the association, to each other and to the association at large. In contrast, *gesellschaft* – often translated as "society" or "association" – describes relationships in which, for the individual, the larger association never supercedes individual self-interest and lacks the same level of shared mores. Unlike *gemeinschaften*, *gesellschaften* emphasizes secondary relationships rather than familial or community ties, and there is generally less individual loyalty to society. See Tönnies, *Gemeinschaft und Gesellschaft (Community and Society)*.

CHAPTER 7

Trends and Challenges in Measuring Effectiveness in the Humanitarian System

JOHN BORTON[1]

Efforts to measure effectiveness within the Humanitarian System take place at different levels and employ a variety of approaches. For outside observers, the picture can appear complex and difficult to gauge. Drawing on the author's involvement in evaluation, learning, accountability, and capacity development efforts within the Humanitarian System over the last twenty-five years, and a recent study on performance assessment and measurement within the system, this chapter seeks to provide an overview of trends in the measurement of effectiveness within and of the Humanitarian System, and the challenges that confront such efforts.

The Humanitarian System

The Humanitarian System is variously defined, but in broad terms it comprises a multiplicity of international, national, and locally based organizations deploying financial, material, and human resources to provide assistance and protection to those affected by conflict and natural disasters, with the objective of saving lives, reducing suffering, and aiding recovery.

Drawing boundaries around the Humanitarian System is a considerable challenge in itself. To begin with, many of the organizations that comprise this system undertake development as well as humanitarian programs. Consequently, the drawing of lines *around* the system also requires drawing lines *through* organizations.

The range of activities undertaken as part of humanitarian responses has become extremely broad. While health services, water/sanitation and hygiene promotion, food security, nutrition, and food aid, shelter, settlement, and non-food items remain at the core of humanitarian responses, many humanitarian operations now include a wide range of other activities, including protection, education, agriculture, psycho-social/mental health support, income generation, infrastructure rehabilitation/reconstruction, human rights, and support to the re-establishment of the rule of law. In countries with ongoing peacekeeping operations, humanitarian agencies of the United Nations (UN) and international and national non-governmental organizations (NGOs) work alongside, and sometimes closely with, peacekeeping missions.

Related to these two points is the challenge of deciding which type of activity is counted as "humanitarian." Pre-disaster investment in disaster risk management and in reducing the vulnerability of at-risk communities is often a more cost-effective intervention than waiting until the disaster has struck. But does this mean that pre-disaster investment in cyclone shelters in Bangladesh or food security programs in Ethiopia should be included within the definition of the Humanitarian System? Many humanitarian agencies would argue that it should not.

Though these challenges create significant and sizeable grey areas around "humanitarian" expenditures that make measuring them difficult, valiant efforts have been made to do so. Expenditures on humanitarian assistance grew rapidly in the 1990s following the end of the Cold War. Global expenditures in 2006 were estimated to be US$14.2 billion, of which US$9.2 billion (65 percent) was official humanitarian assistance contributed by Organisation for Economic Co-operation and Development (OECD) donor countries, and an estimated US$2.3 billion (16 percent) was contributed by the general public and through voluntary contributions to NGOs, Red Cross/Red Crescent, and UN agencies. The US$9.2 billion contributed by OECD donors in 2006 represented 9 percent of the total overseas development assistance (US$102 billion) provided by them.[2]

An associated trend throughout the rapid growth of the 1990s was a proliferation of agencies, particularly NGOs, providing humanitarian assistance. Over 200 were estimated to have been involved in the response to the Rwanda emergency from 1994 to 1996. In the town and area around Goma, the site of a massive refugee influx and associated cholera epidemic in 1994, approximately 100 NGOs were present.[3] Ten years later the Tsunami Evaluation Coalition report on the December 2004 tsunami concluded: "There is general agreement that there were far too many agencies present in Indonesia and Sri Lanka."[4]

Principal Trends and Challenges in the Assessment of Effectiveness in the Humanitarian System

Separating out the principal trends over the last fifteen to twenty years in the assessment of effectiveness in the Humanitarian System is a challenge, but three particular trends are highlighted here.

The Rise of Evaluation

During the 1980s, evaluation units within bilateral donor organizations tentatively began to apply approaches developed in relation to the evaluation of *development programs* to the field of *humanitarian assistance*. Early examples of this application were the United Kingdom's Official Development Assistance (ODA) evaluation of its funding of responses to the mid-1980s African Food Emergency[5] and the Netherlands' Ministry of Foreign Affairs evaluation of the use of its funding in responses to the famine in Somalia.[6] Such early efforts demonstrated the benefits of applying evaluation to humanitarian programs and operations.

Much of the rapid growth in humanitarian expenditures in the early 1990s was funded by bilateral donor organizations in OECD countries. As the proportion of their budgets being allocated to humanitarian responses grew, so the public accountability requirements of bilateral donors made it necessary for them to report on and assess the effectiveness of such budget allocations. Evaluation provided a ready means of doing so, and from the early 1990s onwards the number of evaluations of humanitarian programs and operations steadily increased.[7]

The 1994 genocide in Rwanda and the scale and complexity of the humanitarian response resulted in an unprecedented collaborative evaluation process by donors and humanitarian agencies – the Joint Evaluation of Emergency Assistance to Rwanda (JEEAR) led by the Evaluation Unit of the Danish Ministry of Foreign Affairs. Follow-up to the JEEAR process resulted in

- the preparation of guidance materials on evaluating humanitarian assistance aimed at relief workers[8] and at evaluation managers in bilateral and multilateral donor organizations (OECD-DAC 1999)[9]
- the establishment, in 1997, of the Active Learning Network for Accountability and Performance in Humanitarian Action (ALNAP).

The combination of the pressure on humanitarian agencies to demonstrate their effectiveness, the availability of guidance on evaluating humanitarian assistance, and ALNAP's encouragement and facilitation of networking and the sharing of experience with evaluation processes resulted in a rapid increase in the use of evaluation within the Humanitarian System. At the beginning of the 1990s, evaluations of humanitarian assistance were rare, and the appearance of an evaluator or evaluation team at the field level often provoked responses from resentful field personnel along the lines of "We did our best under difficult circumstances. Who are you to come and question that?" A decade later it had become almost *de rigeur* that humanitarian programs would be subjected to some sort of evaluation process.

A Plethora of Accountability and Quality Initiatives

In parallel to the increased use of evaluation, the 1990s also saw the first in a long line of initiatives generally referred to as either "accountability" or "quality" initiatives (or both). Among the earlier initiatives, two were particularly significant:

- The Code of Conduct for the International Red Cross and Red Crescent Movement and NGOs in Disaster Relief was published in 1994 by the Steering Committee for Humanitarian Response (SCHR).

- The Sphere Project, launched in 1997 by the SCHR, brought together the United States, European, and global NGO umbrella organizations (InterAction, VOICE, and ICVA, respectively) to develop a set of universal minimum standards in core areas of humanitarian assistance (water/sanitation and hygiene promotion, food security, nutrition and food aid, shelter, settlement, non-food items, health services). The process involved a highly collaborative process, with wide (but not complete) buy-in across humanitarian NGOs. The first edition of the *Sphere Handbook*, published in 2000, has been translated into over twenty languages and is widely used.

Both these initiatives enjoyed high levels of participation and buy-in. They have since been followed by a large number of codes of conduct, statements of principles, and elaboration of standards at different levels of the Humanitarian System and in relation to different areas of activity. Some have achieved high levels of participation and buy-in and complemented the earlier initiatives; others have had the effect of confusing the picture as to which codes and standards are being applied in which context by which agencies and by which type of activity. The proliferation of agencies, their (perceived) need to protect their independence of action, and the lack of leadership within the Humanitarian System have all contributed to this confusing situation. Such factors, together with issues such as the interplay between national and international legal jurisdiction, have also served to deter the development of compliance mechanisms in relation to the principle codes and standards. While many elements of a normative framework for the Humanitarian System have been constructed, it would be wrong to say that such a framework actually exists, simply because it is so unclear as to who is seeing themselves as being accountable in relation to what.

Belated Attention to the Importance of the Views of Beneficiaries

An unattractive characteristic of the Humanitarian System over the last twenty years has been its neglect – arguably, wilful disregard – of the importance of seeking and responding to the views of its intended beneficiaries (which in many other systems, industries, or sectors would be referred to as "customers" or "clients"). The case for doing so was powerfully made in Harrell Bond's study *Imposing Aid: Emergency Assistance to Refugees* (1986). But too often humanitarian agencies have approached their task as though it were a package of known deliverables that have to be provided as quickly as possible, and hence there is little need to consult with the affected population. It is only in the last few years that impetus has been gathering for a change in approach.

A key development in this regard has been the Humanitarian Accountability Partnership (HAP), which has developed a quality assurance tool for humanitarian agencies to assess both their accountability to their intended beneficiaries and their quality management systems at the same time. The Humanitarian Accountability and Quality Management Standard, published in 2007, is made up of a set of accountability principles and benchmarks. The accompanying certification and accreditation system is seen as a means of realizing HAP's vision of an accountable humanitarian system through the accreditation of HAP-affiliated NGO networks and associations which have the authority to certify their own members as being compliant with the HAP accountability principles.[10]

Alongside HAP, the work of the Fritz Institute has demonstrated the feasibility and value of independently conducted questionnaire surveys of large samples of beneficiaries, and the Collaborative for Development Action's Listening Project has demonstrated the value of open-ended conversations with beneficiaries. ALNAP's recent commitment to carry forward and build on such mechanisms may affect change after this long period of neglect of recipient views.

Widespread Use of, but Difficulties with, Linear Models of Causality

During the 1980s donor organizations began to use the Logical Framework Approach (LFA) in relation to their development programs. Intended as a tool to help planners and managers design and manage projects and programs, the LFA relies on the detailed breakdown of the "chain of causality" in the project design stage from the overall goal down through the purpose, objectives, outputs, and inputs. During the 1990s its use was extended by donors to those humanitarian projects and programs they were helping to fund – thereby converting this useful *logic* tool into an *audit* tool. Consequently, for the last decade or so, most humanitarian programs have had to prepare a LogFrame at the outset of the program and then report against it. However, critiques of the LFA approach are becoming increasingly cogent.[11]

For a humanitarian agency to demonstrate the contribution of its interventions to the outcomes for a particular population presents a considerable challenge. Post-disaster and conflict-affected contexts are by definition disrupted, stressed, and fluid. Establishing causality and attribution, and correctly identifying changes that would have occurred in the absence of a particular project or program, are extremely difficult. This is especially so when account is taken of the number of agencies frequently working alongside each other in a camp or area and providing similar or closely related types of assistance. For instance, the outcomes of a health program are often highly dependent upon the effectiveness of interventions (often by other agencies) in the fields of food and nutrition, water and sanitation, and shelter and settlement. Separately identifying the contribution of a particular agency often cannot be achieved without significant expenditures on ongoing monitoring, surveys, and analysis. Given the pressure on available resources, it is a rare program that is able to accurately demonstrate the contribution of an individual agency to particular outcomes and impacts. When allowance is made for the personal and organizational biases inherent in reporting to donors (often the same donors that will be approached to provide follow-on funding), agencies' claims regarding their particular contribution to outcomes and impacts may not provide a sufficiently objective basis for assessing their effectiveness.

Inadequate Investment and Effort in Operation-Level Surveys

Humanitarian agencies involved in implementation are, as one would expect, focused upon the effectiveness of their own programs. Consequently, for most agencies the monitoring and surveys that they undertake invariably focus only upon "their" program areas and "their" target populations. Attempts have been made to collate such program-level information to generate a picture of the situation at a higher level – that of a whole operational area – partly to identify where additional effort should be concentrated and possibly to make inferences about the effectiveness of the collective effort. The best example of this approach is the Standardised Monitoring and Assessment of Relief and Transitions (SMART),[12] an inter-agency initiative launched in 2002 and focusing on the generation of basic public health information such as crude mortality rates and the nutritional status of children under five years of age. Considerable effort has been invested in the development and adoption of standardized methodologies, and it is now possible to directly compare the results of health and nutrition monitoring and surveys by the different agencies participating in SMART. However, because the surveys are patchy, covering only selected populations at different times, the extrapolation of overall mortality rates from a group of surveys is problematic. Often the results are subject to significant variation between their upper and lower estimates and thereby subject to differing interpretations.

An alternative approach to generating operation-wide information is to organize and undertake regular, operation-wide surveys. Though such surveys are undertaken in humanitarian operations, nowhere near enough of them are undertaken. For instance, over the last few years, retrospective mortality surveys indicating how many people have died over the preceding period and the likely cause of death have only been undertaken in five operations (Democratic Republic of Congo, Iraq, Afghanistan, Darfur, and northern Uganda) out of perhaps twenty to thirty operations for which such information is unavailable. The cost of such surveys is estimated to range from $100,000 to $300,000 per survey.[13] Considering that such operations may be costing several hundred million dollars each year, such costs probably represent a small fraction of 1 percent of the annual budget and could prove beneficial on a number of issues plaguing many operations. That the Humanitarian System spending around US$14 billion each year is unable to generate reliable annual estimates of the overall numbers of people who died in its areas of operation is quite remarkable and points to a lack of genuine political and organizational commitment to the assessment of effectiveness.

Reporting Overload on Agencies

Since the 1990s, donors funding the Humanitarian System have steadily increased the information they require from the organizations that they fund. Efforts to coordinate reporting requirements between donors have so far not been successful, and different donors continue to require different types of reporting. Humanitarian agencies seeking to maximize their funding sources and reduce their dependence upon a particular donor frequently have to report to ten or more different donors, placing a significant reporting burden on many humanitarian agencies. When this is combined with the proliferation of accountability and quality initiatives that require their own particular types of monitoring and reporting, and agency membership of particular groupings or federations, which also require particular types of information, personnel in humanitarian agencies increasingly talk of a "reporting overload."[14]

The costs of such reporting are difficult to ascertain as they are often embedded within program costs. Consequently, it is difficult to establish what proportion of program costs is being taken up with such reporting requirements and whether the data support the perceived increase in the reporting burden. However, the perception of the existence of a "reporting overload" by implementing agencies is of interest, especially when combined with the methodological difficulties of establishing attribution and causality at the program level (please refer to the information outlined above under "Widespread Use of, but Difficulties with, Linear Models of Causality") and the lack of regular operation-wide surveys (please refer to the details outlined above under "Inadequate Investment and Effort in Operation-Level Surveys"). Considering these concerns together suggests a need for a better balance of resources for monitoring and surveys between the program level and the operation level within humanitarian operations. It is quite conceivable that more regular surveys at the operation level would better equip the Humanitarian System to demonstrate its effectiveness at that level while simultaneously relieving individual agencies and their programs of a significant part of their current burden for monitoring and reporting.

Future Prospects

Based on these realities, the following points are offered regarding the future course of efforts to assess effectiveness and performance within the Humanitarian System.

First, evaluations have a well-established role within the system, and it is likely that they will continue to play a major role in efforts to assess effectiveness and performance for many years to come. Part of their attraction is that they can be tailored and focused on particular issues and needs. A trend towards more joint evaluations and more real-time evaluations[15] looks set to continue. ALNAP has committed itself to encourage and help facilitate more frequent system-wide evaluations of particular operations along similar lines to the JEEAR and Tsunami Evaluation Coalitions. However, evaluations do have a number of shortcomings. Variable quality and a lack of standardized approaches make it difficult to directly compare the results of one evaluation with the results of another. Aggregating results of multiple evaluations to compile an overall picture of performance for the whole Humanitarian System is not a realistic proposition. Evaluations are therefore limited in their ability to provide a solid basis for assessing the overall effectiveness and performance of the *whole* Humanitarian System or for establishing trends in *overall* effectiveness and performance over time.

Second, substantially more information on the views of beneficiaries, including their views on the effectiveness of humanitarian operations and agency performance, will be generated over the coming years. How such information is used and whether it substantially alters the current top-down nature of relief operations remains to be seen.

Third, the ability of the Humanitarian System to report on its overall effectiveness and performance on a regular basis looks to be a long way off. A combination of definitional challenges and methodological difficulties, as well as the challenge of generating a sufficiently broad consensus across donors, UN agencies, the Red Cross/Red Crescent Movement, and NGOs, makes it unlikely that the Humanitarian System will be able to report regularly and objectively on its overall effectiveness and performance in anything less than a decade. However, a coalition is being built to carry this agenda forward among ALNAP members and others, and it is hoped to achieve this vision sooner than 2018.

Summary Points

- The Humanitarian System is a multiplicity of international, national, and locally based organizations deploying financial, material, and human resources to provide assistance and protection to those affected by conflict and natural disasters with the objective of saving lives, reducing suffering, and aiding recovery.
- The range of activities undertaken as part of humanitarian responses has become extremely broad.
- The principal meta-trends in the assessment of effectiveness in the Humanitarian System include:
  - the rise of evaluation
  - a plethora of accountability and quality initiatives
  - belated attention to the importance of the views of beneficiaries

- widespread use of, but difficulties with, linear models of causality
- inadequate investment and effort in operation-level surveys
- reporting overload on agencies

- Evaluations have a well-established role within the Humanitarian System, and it is likely that they will continue to play a major role in efforts to assess effectiveness and performance for many years to come.

- Substantially more information on the views of beneficiaries, including their views on the effectiveness of humanitarian operations and agency performance, will be generated over the coming years.

- The ability of the Humanitarian System to report on its overall effectiveness and performance on a regular basis looks to be a long way off.

Notes

[1] The author wishes to acknowledge the benefit of previous work on humanitarian performance that was funded by the Active Learning Network for Accountability and Performance in Humanitarian Action (ALNAP) (www.alnap.org).

[2] OECD Development Initiatives, 2008, 2, 6.

[3] JEEAR, 1996.

[4] Telford and Cosgrave, *Joint Evaluation of the International Response*, 107.

[5] Borton et al., "Evaluation of ODA's Provision of Emergency Aid."

[6] Operations Review Unit, 1994.

[7] Wood et al., *Evaluating International Humanitarian Action*, 10-12.

[8] Hallam, *Evaluating Humanitarian Assistance Programs in Complex Emergencies*.

[9] Whereas the DAC criteria for the evaluation of development programs were efficiency, effectiveness, impact, sustainability, and relevance, these guidance materials for humanitarian assistance advocated the use of a modified and slightly expanded set of criteria that also included the criteria of coverage, coherence, and coordination.

[10] More information on HAP can be found on their website: http://www.hapinternational.org/default.aspx

[11] Wallace et al., *The Aid Chain*.

[12] More information on SMART can be found on their website: http://www.smartindicators.org/index.html

[13] Francesco Checchi, personal communication, 15 May 2008.

[14] Belinda Duff, personal communication, 20 August 2008.

[15] Beck and Buchanan-Smith, *Joint Evaluations Coming of Age?*

CHAPTER 8

The Art and Science of Assessing Iraqi Security Force Performance

KEITH HAUK AND STEPHEN MARIANO

Measuring and assessing the performance of the Iraqi Security Forces has been a subject of international and national attention. In the United States, the Congress requires the Department of Defense to describe progress every ninety days in a report titled "Measuring Security and Stability in Iraq." Increased Iraqi Security Force (ISF) capability has always been a part of the United States and Coalition reconstruction and stabilization strategy in Iraq, but it gained prominence when President Bush uttered the phrase, "As they stand up, we will stand down."

Though the US military has emerging doctrine for "security force assistance," the doctrine is new and still being tested. "Battle damage assessments" for conventional, kinetic operations do not lend themselves to simple adaptation for security force assistance operations. Typically, the military measures progress in terms of numbers of enemy killed or captured, vehicles destroyed or immobilized, and terrain seized and held. Though the term "effects based" has recently fallen out of US military doctrinal favour, its logic endures; using power to influence behaviour and attitudes, it asks the question, "Did our actions have the desired effect?" Due to the unconventional and unstructured environment in which the security force assistance mission in Iraq was functioning, we undertook a complex assessment effort, using a combination of disciplines. Developing the assessment framework turned out to be as much art as science.

The Scorecard

The mission of the Multi-National Security Transition Command – Iraq (MNSTC-I; pronounced *min-sticky*) is to assist the Iraqis in generating and replenishing their security forces, while simultaneously improving the quality of those forces and supporting ministerial-level institutions, in order to enable greater Iraqi capability (the standing up) and reduced coalition involvement (the standing down). Because of the unstructured Iraqi operational environment, we drifted away from doctrine and built a framework to assess the command's efforts in developing the ISF by using a *Balanced Scorecard* as a way to guide our work. Though we did not adopt the standard Harvard Business School Balanced Scorecard "perspectives," we did develop four mission-specific goals:

1. Generate the required Iraqi security forces;
2. Improve their capability to operate independently;
3. Improve the institutional performance of the security ministries; and
4. Strengthen the professionalism and reduce the sectarianism of those forces and ministries.

It was around these four goals that we built our assessment methodology and began to translate academic theory into joint and combined military practice.

Conditions, Objectives, Tasks

The command consisted of American and Coalition personnel, from all services, military and civilian members, active as well as reserve. Accordingly, we had to define our terminology and get agreement not only on what we were measuring but also on the language we would use to talk amongst ourselves and our higher headquarters, the Multinational Force – Iraq (MNF-I). Rather than sticking strictly to "effects-based" language, we redefined our framework in terms of *conditions* to be achieved, *objectives* required to create the conditions, and *tasks* to direct subordinate unit action. The MNSTC-I headquarters focused largely on the objectives to be achieved because they linked stakeholder requirements to task execution. Stakeholders drove our perspectives and were external to our headquarters; task execution was done largely by MNSTC-I subordinate headquarters and units. To explain our progress, we needed tasks and objectives that were measurable, whether using a scientist's graph or an artist's canvas.

We used a *conditions-objectives-tasks* taxonomy, which is fairly simple; it represents some of the *science* in our approach to assessing Iraq's security force development. Under the four conditions, we developed eighteen supporting objectives, each with an associated measurement. Nested in those objectives were dozens of tasks tailored to MNSTC-I subordinate units, where personnel actually mentored and trained military, police, and special operations forces and ministerial-level counterparts. While it would be difficult to describe the entire cascading framework in detail, a few examples are provided below.

Many force generation tasks were empirically measurable and had associated measurements. Are the numbers being generated and synchronized in accordance with a planned schedule? The institutional performance questions were similarly clear: Are security ministries executing their budgets in key areas – personnel pay and allowances, operations and maintenance, and capital investment? Some answers were easy and lent themselves to graphs, spreadsheets, or equations: v number of uniforms issued, w soldiers trained, x weapons issued, y bases built by z date. Synchronizing that activity, however, proved more difficult. Soldiers would graduate from a training program, for example, but not have a permanent base in which to live, vehicles to drive, or weapons to operate. At other times, equipment or weapons would be stockpiled in one ministry's warehouse while another ministry experienced critical shortages. The sub-optimal outcome was a delay in getting capable soldiers into the fight or police on the street at the right time.

We found that assessing the Iraqi force requirements process meant using more art than science. Once a national decision was made – to create an infantry division – it was relatively easy to ensure that it was injected into manning, training, equipping, and basing planning and execution processes. But national decisions were more political than mathematical, more subjective than objective. For example, Iraq's oil pipelines came under increasing attack and needed quick repair to keep oil revenues flowing. The requirement to protect the pipeline was clear, but there was little consensus on how to generate the capability – or who would foot the bill. Eventually, Coalition and Iraqi leaders generated engineer and infrastructure units with pipeline repair and protection capabilities as well as an agreed-to funding plan and timeline.

This example highlights a similar component of the "operate independently" condition, which required both empirical and quasi-empirical approaches. Over time, Iraq's basic military and police units were clearly growing, but they lacked component parts or *enablers* to sustain themselves. In part, this lack reflected a deliberate decision driven by the security environment at the time. The degenerating security situation on the ground necessitated the creation of an *unbalanced* force – one focused on combat units, vice combat support, and service support formations.

As the situation began to stabilize, we needed not only to grow the enablers required to balance the force but also to assess their growth – which could be objectively measured – and to address whether they were building the *right* enablers (i.e., those required to support the counterinsurgency mission).

The latter assessment was more subjective. For example, did the Iraqi Army have communications, intelligence, and logistics units required to support the generated number of infantrymen? Did air force capabilities adequately support critical ground counterinsurgency operations such as long-loiter close air support and intelligence, surveillance and reconnaissance operations? What ministry should own a riverine defense capability, and what type of platform was required? Did the police have the proper number and type of criminal investigators and supporting forensics capabilities? In some cases, mathematical force planning or bases of issue ratios were helpful, but in those instances where quality was as much a factor as quantity, simple mathematical measurements were less informative.

Other People's Data

In assessing MNSTC-I progress to increase Iraqi forces' professionalism and decrease their sectarianism, we took a more nuanced or artful assessment approach and one that ultimately relied on other people's data. For example, the Multinational Corps-Iraq (MNC-I) was the war fighting command and possessed transition teams that were embedded with ISF units. These teams assured Iraqi access to US and Coalition forces but also provided assessments of ISF unit ability to operate independently. Though not under MNSTC-I command, these teams' reports provided an essential feedback mechanism with which we could assess, and modify as required, the quality of basic and advanced training provided to the Iraqi forces. The reports themselves were a mix of quantitative and qualitative assessments, but the transition team commander made the ultimate score call based on his subjective judgment. In one report, for example, the transition team commander commented on the professional appearance of a unit: the uniforms were neat, the weapons well cared for, the base immaculate, and the soldiers beaming. He also noted, however, that the veneer of professionalism covered a deep-seated ethnosectarian hate that emerged in unit chants and marching songs. How does one assess the professionalism of a militarily capable but politically divisive unit?

Since a definition of military professionalism is subject to the population it protects, we also relied extensively on public-opinion polling data and focus-group interviews. Polling data provided answers to questions about the trustworthiness and corruption levels of ISF members. As with the transition teams, this data was not under direct MNSTC-I control but was managed by MNF-I and executed by a combination of US and Iraqi entities. Nonetheless, the polling data provided feedback to MNSTC-I commanders and directors on the quality of their "product" being provided to the war-fighting commander. MNSTC-I was able to work with other organizations to shape feedback mechanisms and have them incorporate considerations that underwrote the command's mission.

We also used focus groups to conduct self-assessments regarding the quality of our own efforts. Advisors commented freely on their own competence to advise their Iraqi counterparts. They noted the need for more cultural and language training, a better alignment of skill sets with their Iraqi partner, and shortfalls in translators, vehicles, and supplies. These views allowed commanders and directors to assess their preparation and assignment policies and to make choices about where to (re)apply resources.

Conclusion

Based on our experience in planning and assessing security force development activities, four insights are important. First, overly rigid or doctrinal approaches will not be helpful in political-military, multi-service, multi-national organizations. While the US Department of Defense has doctrine for just about everything, over-attachment to doctrine can be an obstacle to achieving progress. In this case, willingness to explore alternative assessment methodologies and integrate civilian and military ideas provided an understandable and workable framework. Use of the Balanced Scorecard was proposed by an Australian office, but it was introduced to the staff by a US army officer, well received by the British civil servants working in the security ministries, and understood by policemen working at the Baghdad police college and by staff officers in the Iraqi Joint Headquarters.

Second, unity of effort is key not only in planning but also in assessing progress. Initially, the MNSTC-I commander was uncomfortable using performance measures outside his direct control. To allay fears, we had to demonstrate unity of effort between three headquarters – by ensuring that our conditions and objectives were nested within the MNF-I theatre-level Joint Campaign Plan and showing complementarity with the MNC-I war-fighting framework. Eventually the MNSTC-I commander saw the utility of their data and accepted the risk. This approach was confirmed by March/April 2008 ISF operations against insurgent forces in Basrah, Baghdad, and Mosul. In the wake of those operations, both objective and subjective measures of ISF performance were used to adjust ISF training programs as well as to force development plans and timelines – especially for those aforementioned enablers. The more rigorous and integrated assessments of ISF capabilities eventually found their way into General Petraeus's congressional testimonies and became powerful influencers on public opinion and policy-makers.

Third, in the conditions-objectives-tasks approach, subordinate unit commanders must have the authority and flexibility to adjust tasks as required, provided that their efforts support mission accomplishment. They must also continually assess and communicate changes across the organization, particularly in a customer-provider relationship. In this regard, planners need to focus their efforts on ensuring that the conditions and objectives accurately describe what must be done to accomplish the mission, and subordinate units need to focus on building supporting tasks. As the plan is executed and assessed, some tasks simply will not provide the feedback or insight necessary to assess performance.

Finally, an advisory organization must have a strong *engagement plan* for how it intends to partner with supported forces and ministries. MNSTC-I's organizational effectiveness was measured on how well the Iraqis did at generating forces, building enablers, improving institutional performance, strengthening professionalism, and reducing sectarianism. Accordingly, an advisory organization should partner with the host-nation both as it writes the plan and assesses its execution. Convincing a supported government to *buy in* to a coalition plan is not enough.

One area for further exploration and development is host-nation data gathering and reporting processes that facilitate operational execution and assessment. Our experience in Iraq tells us that the issues in this area are far more cultural and political than technical. The end goal of any security assistance organization should be to work itself out of a job. As host nation capabilities mature, government forces and security ministries must be an integral part of plan execution and assessment – not simply a target of it.

Summary Points

- Traditionally, the US military has measured progress in terms of numbers of enemy killed or captured, vehicles destroyed or immobilized, and terrain seized and held.

- A modified version of the *Balanced Scorecard* informed US military assessment methodology and translated academic theory into joint and combined military practice.

- Because of the multi-functional, multi-national, and multi-sectoral nature of the command in Iraq, groups had to agree upon terminology, what they were measuring, and descriptions of progress.
- Measuring progress is as much an art as a science.
- In those instances where quality was as much a factor as quantity, simple mathematical measurements were less informative in assessing progress.
- Adopting a more *nuanced* or *artful assessment approach* ultimately relied on other stakeholder and sector data. Though they were not under MNSTC-I command, these teams' data and reports provided an essential feedback mechanism with which to assess and modify as required the quality of training provided to Iraqi forces.
- MNSTC-I was able to work with other organizations to shape feedback mechanisms and incorporate considerations that underwrote the command's mission.
- The use of focus groups was helpful to conduct self-assessments regarding the quality of MNSTC-I efforts. These views allowed commanders and directors to assess their preparation and assignment policies and make choices about where to (re)apply resources.
- Overly rigid or doctrinal approaches will not be helpful in political-military, multi-service, multi-national organizations.
- An over-attachment to military doctrine can be an obstacle to achieving progress.
- Unity of military effort is key not only in planning but also in assessing progress.
- In the *conditions-objectives-tasks approach*, subordinate unit commanders must have the authority and flexibility to adjust tasks as required, provided their efforts support mission accomplishment. They must also continually assess and communicate changes across the organization, particularly in a *customer-provider relationship*.
- Planners need to focus their efforts on ensuring that the conditions and objectives accurately describe what must be done to accomplish a mission, and subordinate units need to focus on building supporting tasks. As the plan is executed and assessed, some tasks simply will not provide the feedback or insight necessary to assess performance.
- The host-nation must be a partner in writing the plan and assessing its execution.

CHAPTER 9

Measures of Effectiveness: Examining the United Kingdom in Afghanistan

STUART GORDON

Measuring effectiveness and organizational performance has been most difficult when seeking to measure the least tangible benefits of peace – particularly governance, attitude change, and "confidence" in government and political leaders. In contrast, it is relatively straightforward to measure the effectiveness of more tangible projects such as the development of infrastructure, improvements in economic performance, and basic service delivery. This has been the experience of the United Kingdom's Provincial Reconstruction Team (PRT) in Afghanistan, which implements both tangible and intangible projects to contribute to peace and stabilization.

In 2006 the UK deployed a sizeable military and civilian presence to the southern Afghan province of Helmand as a part of the NATO-led International Security Assistance Force (ISAF). By 2008 this presence cost annually over £1.6 billion,[1] and comprised some 7,500 troops and nearly fifty civilians drawn from the Foreign Office (FO), the Department for International Development (DFID), and the Stabilisation Unit (the relabelled Post Conflict Reconstruction Unit), as well as the customs, prisons, and policing services and the legal profession. The civilian effort is largely managed within the framework of a UK Foreign Office-led PRT comprising a broadly equivalent number of UK military staff as well as a small number of development and diplomatic officials from the United States, Denmark, and Estonia. The PRT, based in Helmand's provincial capital, Lashkargar, alongside the military Task Force Headquarters, has the broad mission to "support the Government of Afghanistan to promote security, good governance, rule of law and economic and social development in order to establish a more developed, secure and stable Afghanistan." Given the political significance of the deployment, its multinational nature, and the scale of the resources invested, there is an understandably strong interest in measuring "effectiveness."

Measurements are not simply to identify which instruments contribute to political, security, and development objectives and provide value for money; inevitability they are linked to bureaucratic and political imperatives to demonstrate the effective *performance* of "military" and "civilian" delivery mechanisms. At times this results in a degree of confusion between measuring the *impact* of the diverse range of programs and activities and measuring *performance* in the management and application of resources.

Measuring *impact* has also been difficult due to the volatility of the Helmandi environment. The violence and consequent politicization of the operational environment seriously curtail the collation of baseline data (both in terms of infrastructure and governance structures) as well as access to projects, implementing partners, and beneficiary communities – making program monitoring and evaluation painfully difficult.

Conceptualizing progress has also been challenging. Initially, in 2006, development-type activities within Helmand tended to be evaluated by the PRT in terms of inputs (resources committed) and raw outputs (buildings created and the availability and volumes of public services). Increasingly, however, objectives have been defined in terms of higher order goals related to "stabilization" progress – conceptualized largely in terms of the protection of civilians and critical institutions, preventing the recurrence of violent conflict, and preparing for longer-term inclusive political processes and sustainable development. In a counter-insurgency environment, these have tended to converge on the idea of establishing a "political settlement" – a "tipping point" on the path to a self-sustaining peace (or what the US Institute of Peace describes as "viable peace") in which the institutional and societal capacities to constrain conflict drivers outweigh those drivers. Conflict drivers and institutional capacities to resist them, however, are inherently diverse and multi-dimensional, encompassing a bewildering array of political, social, economic, security, and rule of law factors. While several of these are obviously "measurable," many are highly subjective, abstract, and resistant to meaningful quantification, while attitude measures tend to be unreliable due to the politicization of responses caused by the conflict dynamic itself.

UK government ministries have differed significantly in their approaches to measuring "progress" – with the development ministry, DFID, focused more on traditional program and project monitoring/evaluation techniques, while the Ministry of Defence (MOD) and FO have been more concerned with identifying the broader political effects of military activities and civilian development/stabilization programs. The MOD has also tended to focus on the contribution made by civilian efforts to force protection, while the FO has sought to measure the political settlement that is intended to consolidate tactical military success. Both ministries have sought broad measurements of attitude change, both at a local level (with the MOD measuring "atmospherics" and perceived attitudes within, for example, a village) and at provincial and regional levels with much broader conventional attitude surveys. Both of these measures have suffered considerable methodological difficulties caused by the small sample sizes, the imprecision of questions (and reliability of data sets), the subjectivity of interpretations, the absence of baseline data, an inadequate understanding of tribal and ethnic boundaries (and their impact on sample sizes, results and interpretations of data), the perceived politicization of responses, and limited access to key communities.

Culturally both the MOD and, to a lesser extent, the FO have been less comfortable with traditional program management tools and the systems for measuring program performance that they entail, viewing these as burdensome and unnecessarily bureaucratic impediments to the pace of delivery. Contrastingly, the development community has tended to employ "logical frameworks" (or variants thereof) as the planning and program management tool of choice, stressing their potential to more clearly articulate objectives and strategic goals and their corresponding performance indicators, and to link these with specific causal activities and "inputs." However, the logical framework, or LogFrame, approach has not been easy to export beyond DFID to other UK departments. DFID has a trained staff that uses a common measurement approach enforced by a range of administrative and information technology processes augmented by career incentives that have been difficult to export to a multi-agency environment.

Furthermore, LogFrames remain largely unknown beyond the development community. In many ways this is a missed opportunity. Militaries, in particular those engaged in civil-military cooperation (CIMIC), have for over a decade unsuccessfully pursued the holy grail of "universal measures of effectiveness," ultimately alighting on two controversial and generally flawed measures: traffic light coding of progress by "sector" (i.e., making subjective judgments on whether a sector is "red," "amber," or green") and what has been labelled critically as the "Blue Peter spendometer"[2] analysis of projects started and completed.[3] The complexity of operational environments from the Balkans through to Afghanistan has tended to cause militaries to measure the most tangible elements of what they term "civil effect," particularly project "inputs" and "outputs" – i.e., money spent and buildings constructed rather than higher order "purpose" or "goals" – such as the impact of a "building" or "service" on a community's attitudes. Measuring inputs rather than outcomes has the advantage of being easy to compile and provides a simple vehicle for communicating conclusions, but it also has the potential to distort planning, encouraging the confusion of strategic progress with "resource inputs" and "raw" outputs. Partly as a consequence of dissatisfaction with the shortcomings of these approaches, the PRT and the UK military adopted the Tactical Conflict Assessment Framework (TCAF).

Tactical Conflict Assessment Framework (TCAF)

TCAF has been a useful, albeit imperfect innovation. Authored by USAID's James Derleth, it is rooted in the assumption that insurgencies are fuelled by grievances that can be identified and manipulated. By asking a community a simple set of four questions, it encourages a focus on what frustrates people, how they are mobilized, and who is able to manipulate them, helping intervening parties to support the development of the state and society's capacity to recognize and respond to destabilizing factors (see Table 3). Derleth argues that the TCAF process does this by:

- addressing societal grievances (causes)

- denying, limiting, or neutralizing resources that sustain IN/CON (means)

- identifying and diminishing vulnerabilities (opportunities)

- decreasing outside pressures that increase vulnerabilities (external influences).[4]

TABLE 3
Tactical Conflict Assessment Framework (TCAF) Questions

(1) Has the population of your village changed in the last 12 months?
(2) What is the greatest problem facing your village right now?
(3) Who do you trust to resolve your problems?
(4) Of your problems, what would you solve first?

The initial questions are followed by in-depth interviews of key leaders and representatives that seek to establish perceptions of the conflict and the capacity of the state and society to respond, together generating a statistical "narrative" that tracks changes in a population's sense of grievances and the agency with the greatest capacity to remedy them. This process enables the intervening parties to support the development of a more responsive governmental capacity to prioritize and address specific grievances and conflict drivers.

However, TCAF is not without weaknesses. Some populations have become "TCAF-weary," or have responded in ways that seem to be intended to deliver projects that will provide them with personal benefit rather than address what could be described as "insurgency generating grievances." Furthermore, because TCAF tends to be administered by the military, women and more marginalized or hostile elements of a community are systematically excluded from the TCAF process, reducing the capacity to identify their concerns. Lastly, TCAF provides only a list of perceived grievances rather than a mechanism for evaluating the intensity of each within and between geographical areas.

Perhaps the key conclusion from this short chapter is that measuring effectiveness and organizational performance is most difficult when seeking to measure the least tangible benefits of peace – particularly governance, attitude change, and "confidence" in government and political leaders. Measuring issues such as the development of infrastructure and improvements in economic performance and basic service delivery, however, is relatively straightforward. Applying a system such as TCAF allows better questions to be asked and answered at the beginning of projects in order to adjust how we measure the effectiveness of the UK PRT in Afghanistan.

Summary Points

- Measuring effectiveness and organizational performance has been difficult when seeking to measure intangible outcomes of peace operations activities.
- Measuring effectiveness has been relatively easy when seeking to measure tangible outcomes of peace operations activities.
- Given the political significance of the British PRT deployment in Afghanistan, its multinational nature, and the scale of the resources invested, there is an understandably strong interest in measuring "effectiveness."

- There is confusion between measuring the *impact* of the diverse range of peace operations activities and measuring *performance* in the management and application of resources.
- Volatility, violence, and the politicization of an operational environment curtail access to information, partners, processes, and projects, making measuring effectiveness difficult.
- Some elements of political, social, economic, security, and rule of law factors are obviously measurable; however, many are highly subjective, abstract, and resistant to meaningful quantification.
- LogFrames remain largely unknown beyond the development community; this may be a missed opportunity for measuring CIMIC-type activities.
- Measuring "inputs" rather than "outcomes" provides a simple vehicle for communicating conclusions, but it also has the potential to distort planning, encouraging the confusion of strategic progress with "resource inputs" and "raw" outputs.
- The Tactical Conflict Assessment Framework (TCAF) assumes that insurgencies are fuelled by grievances that can be identified and manipulated by asking a community four key questions.
- Applying a system such as TCAF allows better questions to be asked and answered at the beginning of projects in order to adjust how we measure the effectiveness of our activities in Afghanistan.

Notes

[1] The equivalent of EURO 2 billion, USD 2.9 billion, CAD 3.17 billion, and AUD 3.98 billion.

[2] The "Blue Peter Spendometer approach" is shorthand for an approach that measures raw outputs rather than their higher order and more meaningful objectives.

[3] These frameworks are used routinely by troops from NATO countries deployed in the Balkans, Iraq, and Afghanistan.

[4] James Derleth, personal communication.

CHAPTER 10

Measures of Effectiveness for Peace Operations and Crisis Management

DAVID CHUTER

This chapter examines some of the difficulties in measuring the effectiveness of peace operations and activities that are intended to manage crises. My argument is focused on government-level involvement in the United Nation's peace operations, both as separate actors and as members of international organizations, but briefly treats other actors as well.

Measures of effectiveness (MOE) can only be assessed against previously set objectives, which is where the difficulties begin. Few organizations deliberately set out to court failure, so there is always a temptation to set objectives that are either so vague that claims of success can never be disputed, or so limited and easy that they will almost certainly be accomplished anyway. Peace operations are expensive and not always popular, so it is hard for a government or international organization to admit failure if it occurs. This profoundly affects the way that objectives are set and measured.

Three levels of objectives can be distinguished against which effectiveness can theoretically be measured. The first is the objectives of a state, which thinks that it can largely, or at least preponderantly, settle a crisis itself. Solo crisis management is rare but not unknown. Generally, however, even major actors and regional hegemons will prefer to shelter behind regional organizations and international groupings – Nigeria and the Economic Community of West African States (ECOWAS) is a good example. A more common variant is the formation of a "contact group" for crisis management, which unites major external states (often self-appointed) with regional actors. Contact groups rarely have formal objectives; keeping close to the main players and trying to ensure the maximum realistic coordination in search of a settlement is usually the most that can be hoped for. Indeed, one of the functions of such a group is to reduce the collateral damage that results from different players following different agendas.

These agendas always exist, however, and imply different national objectives and different criteria for success. They frequently result from different analyses of the same situation or, alternatively, from different perceptions between regional and external actors, as was the case with the Ivory Coast, for example. They may also result from fundamental strategic differences, as between the United States and Russia over how to manage the Balkan conflicts.

The second level is that of international organizations. A complicating element is that most major nations are members of several different organizations, and there may well be competition among them to manage a crisis or control a mission. Large and powerful organizations may have institutional goals that differ from those of member states – the European Commission, with its political and financial independence, is one example. In most cases, however, the objectives publicly set by an international organization will be a compromise between what its major players want, or are prepared to go along with. International organizations have two sorts of objectives: external and institutional. Organizations of any size and importance will generally have policies and strategies for regions or thematic problems, and will in principle be willing to involve themselves in crisis management if they think that they can further these strategic and policy interests. The European Union's (EU) military involvements in African crises, therefore, have been in support, at least notionally, of its wider Africa policy. But the relationship is not mechanistic, especially when it comes to sending troops and financing missions. In the EU, to take the example further, many of the newer members have little previous experience or interest in Africa, and they have their own economic problems to worry about. A further group (Sweden, Germany, the Netherlands) see Africa more as a development issue, while the former colonial powers (France, Britain, Belgium, Portugal) may be more willing to contemplate military involvement but have other calls on their resources as well. On the other hand, newer members may want to prove their European credentials, while some countries may welcome experience of overseas deployments, and so forth.

There will then be institutional objectives, or rather objectives for the institution, which will again vary between nations. In most cases, nations will want the institution to prove its worth and look useful, which often means high-profile but not necessarily difficult or complicated interventions. Mandates and objectives resulting from this kind of process are often nuanced and limited, leaving behind them a trail of complex negotiations. They often mean, for example, that the missions will be relatively small and of short duration, with modest objectives. This kind of approach minimizes costs, strain on human and other resources, and the risk of failure. It may not, of course, do much to address the crisis itself, but that is usually a subordinate issue. Cooperation between organizations – the EU and the African Union (AU) is a good example – adds a further layer of complexity, especially when the main objective is to demonstrate that the organizations are capable of working together.

These factors bulk especially large in the case of UN missions. There is a fundamental difference of interest in the Security Council, depending on who will be paying what, and who will be contributing troops. It is easy to propose and demand expensive mandates when others will have to carry them out. Posturing and politicking are bound to be features of such a large, complex organization such as the UN, and very often the original objectives are lost sight of. This can result in complex and contradictory mandates for the actors implementing the Security Council Resolutions, and even mandates that are actually incapable of being implemented, let alone measured for their effectiveness.

This was arguably the case with the United Nations Protection Force (UNPROFOR) in Bosnia. Inasmuch as international actors were capable of formulating a political objective for the resolution of the crisis in Bosnia, it was that the former republic should become an independent unitary state, as some, but by no means all, of its population wanted, rather than split into separate components. As a political objective this was unachievable (and essentially remains so), and the resolutions and associated mandates were largely irrelevant in addressing the reality on the ground.[1] UNPROFOR, with its mandate and force structure, could do nothing to achieve this political objective. Rather, the situation would have called for a robust military campaign against separatist forces (no doubt supported from across the borders by Croatia and Serbia) and the occupation, at a minimum, of Banja Luka, Mostar, and Pale. Since such a military campaign was never remotely practicable, the professed objectives of the whole mission – as they constantly changed – never really corresponded to reality. The mandates were not reflected in the capacity deployed on the ground. After the suspension of hostilities, intermediate objectives such as elections were pursued, in the hope that somehow they would contribute to peace-building, and the establishment of a happily united country. Such projects had the advantage of being easier to organize, achieve, and measure, and therefore to justify as *progress*.

The UNPROFOR mission and mandates illustrate particularly starkly the risks involved in applying military campaign planning methods to peace operations. In the military planning discipline, there is an explicit assumption that the means provided to the commander, if correctly handled, will enable the mission to be accomplished and the political end state achieved. Success is therefore relatively easy to measure.

This outcome is much less obvious with complex peace operations. Often the reverse happens: objectives are retrospectively adjusted to reconcile with what can realistically be accomplished on the ground. Therefore, there is often no necessary connection between the mandate, mission objectives, and ability/capacity to measure effectiveness against these objectives.

To further complicate measuring effectiveness, nations have all sorts of motives for taking part in peace operations and crisis management that they never declare but that are nonetheless important in measuring perceptions of success. For some nations, it is a chance to earn money; for others, it is an opportunity to be noticed, or to provide troops and commanders with worthwhile experience. For these nations, rebuilding a hospital, or deploying an engineering company for six months without taking any casualties, can be objectives in themselves, irrespective of any larger purpose of the mission. Some nations, however, may see themselves as having a moral or political duty to take part or to provide funding, while others may have an eye on future economic advantage. Some nations – influenced very much by non-governmental organizations (NGOs) and the media, and influencing them in turn – also take a resolutely moralizing attitude to crises, arguing that there is a moral duty to intervene, involving, if necessary, extreme use of force. Such countries, as well as the organizations and media outlets that support them, do not generally provide much help themselves; the moral injunction "*We* must do something" usually means in practice, "*You* must do something." For such groups, intervention is an end in itself because it is the fulfillment of a moral duty, irrespective of the carnage that may result.

So a number of individuals and institutions have argued that, irrespective of the situation in the country today, the invasion of Iraq in 2003 was a success because it led to the overthrow of the regime of Saddam Hussein and thus fulfilled the moral duty to protect the Iraqi people from tyranny and oppression. Most governments, and certainly those who contribute troops, do not share this cold-blooded approach. They recognize that governments are responsible for what they do, and that those who mandate and conduct missions must bear the longer-term moral responsibility if things get broken.

Finally, there is a political tendency to assume that the resolution of the crisis and the success or failure of the mission are the same thing. In fact, wars may stop and start, and crises may emerge or be resolved – independently of the mission itself – making the measurement of effectiveness even more problematic than would otherwise be the case.

Summary Points

- Measures of effectiveness (MOE) can only be assessed against previously set objectives.
- Peace operations are expensive and not always popular, so it is hard for a government or international organization to admit failure if it occurs. This profoundly affects the way that objectives are set and measured.
- The increasing complexity of United Nations Security Council Resolution mandates influences the ability to implement the mandate and determines the capacity to measure the achievement of the mandate.
- Tangible activities have the advantage of being easier to organize, execute, and measure, and therefore make it easier to justify that *progress* is being achieved.
- All nations have different motives for being involved in peace operations and crisis management that they never declare but are important in measuring perceptions of success.
- The resolution of a crisis and the success or failure of a mission are not the same thing. Wars may stop and start, and crises may emerge or be resolved independently of the mission, making the measurement of effectiveness problematic.

Note

[1] Its defenders argue that UNPROFOR's deployment did something to reduce the level of violence in the country, although it is hard to know how much of that reduction would have occurred anyway. Its detractors argue that UNPROFOR's deployment had the practical effect of lengthening the war and increasing the final death toll.

CHAPTER 11

Significance of Impact Assessment: A New Methodology

EMERY BRUSSET

The essence of the international community's evaluation methodology for conflict prevention and peace-building programming (CPPB) focuses on cause/effect relationships in order to create ideal conditions for peace. The focus combines an emphasis on personal qualities and planning to overcome chance and adversity to reach the ideal state. This Greek or western way of planning is distinct from the worldview of other cultures, such as that of the Chinese. In the Chinese worldview there is no ideal world to strive for, only a constant search for ways of making the environment come, of its own accord, to conditions that are optimal for the most artful planner.

This chapter argues that conflict analysis-based evaluation is more important than the typical method of reviewing intervention strategies and assessing theories of change (these theories aim to explain the assumptions made as to why a particular intervention will lead to a particular outcome). It also describes how verification is more feasible than measurement, and, even more importantly, what kind of contribution to the dynamics of conflict is more important than actually ascribing a cause to an effect – in other words, attributing impact to a specific CPPB activity.

This chapter offers a way to overcome difficulties that conflict-prevention practitioners face in operationalizing their analysis in a reliable and verifiable way. It has implications for the current methods used in performance monitoring and evaluation, namely the *Effects Diagram*, *Outcome*

Mapping and the *Logical Framework*, and can be seen as a potential future trend in evaluating CPPB activities.

Our small operation, Channel Research, is a consulting company that works predominantly with the evaluation units of the bilateral aid ministries of the Organization for Economic Co-operation and Development (OECD) countries. As such, Channel Research completes forty evaluation projects per year on interventions in conflict settings, of which roughly two or three concern conflict prevention and peace-building (CPPB).

We have found that there are at present few developed methodologies for the evaluation of CPPB. The OECD Development Aid Committee has created a working group to discuss these issues and is in the process of developing guidelines for the evaluation of CPPB.[1] As we shall see, these guidelines do not offer some of the specific advice needed to overcome some key challenges. They do, however, underline the importance of conflict analysis, stating that the findings need to be translated into action and influence evaluation processes.

A Perennial Problem

A perennial problem of evaluations is that they attempt to relate a particular change to a particular approach. To do this, most planning in international aid and cooperation uses the *Logical Framework* (LogFrame) as a planning tool, with a pyramid of results going from the activities to the most general objectives. However, while it is possible to assess the effectiveness at the lower levels of the LogFrame, it becomes more difficult the higher one goes, as other influences become prevalent. This is often labelled the *micro-macro problem* or *attribution problem*: How can we prove that a change in the status of peace and conflict can be traced back to a specific intervention or project?

The LogFrame routinely presents a leap between the specific objective (for example, to support the demobilization of paramilitary groups) and the overall objective (for example, to contribute to an environment conducive to peace). The movement from the actual achievement of the specific objective to the general one is often an act of faith. Good LogFrames deal with this gap by tightening the connections between levels (looking for more immediate effects with fewer risks of achievement), but this then leaves open the question of the value of an intervention in the broader picture.

The most argued response to the disconnect between results achieved and impact on peace or conflict has been the *Effects Diagram* developed by the European Commission for the evaluation of its External Relations.[2]

As illustrated in Figure 31, the Effects Diagram is a cascade of objectives, which can represent complex interconnections between different levels of intervention, from the project-specific to the global. However, the final stages that link an intervention to the reduction of poverty and then to the achievement of greater stability make a very significant leap, based on important assumptions.

One response to the problem has been to analyze the theories of change that could link the top levels of the effects chain, as stated in the OECD DAC Working Guidance:

> Where the theory is not clearly stated it is possible for an evaluator to elicit or discern the logic behind the activity as part of the evaluation process, especially in discussions with the implementation team. In either case, the evaluation will "unpack" and map out the inputs, outputs and desired future outcomes – and the expected connection between these – in order to evaluate whether the strategy being used is logical and effective.[3]

Yet testing these theories is a narrative, highly contentious explanation of the conflict. It is relatively easy for a critical reviewer of the evaluation to question the validity of the interpretation, and it is even more difficult for the evaluator to defend this validity. Assumptions and interpretations muddy the evaluation process, and it becomes unclear as to what degree being effective in the top levels of the intervention is indeed significant for impact.

This *black box* between cause and effect is exacerbated in the evaluation of CPPB programs because they experience a series of particular constraints. These include:

- The balance between direct peace-building objectives and other objectives is rarely made clear by aid organizations;
- The standard use of objectives as benchmarks of performance is weakened because conflict programming requires a response to constraints and opportunities as they arise. These cannot be planned for in advance and therefore present considerable difficulties for evaluators;
- It is difficult to separate the impact of peace-building projects from other impacts on conflict;
- Selecting indicators of change demands a shared understanding of the conflict and a shared use of verification methods that are applicable in a conflict situation;
- No common defining terms such as *peace* and *conflict* exist among evaluators and evaluations; and

FIGURE 31
Effects Diagram, Afghanistan Evaluation

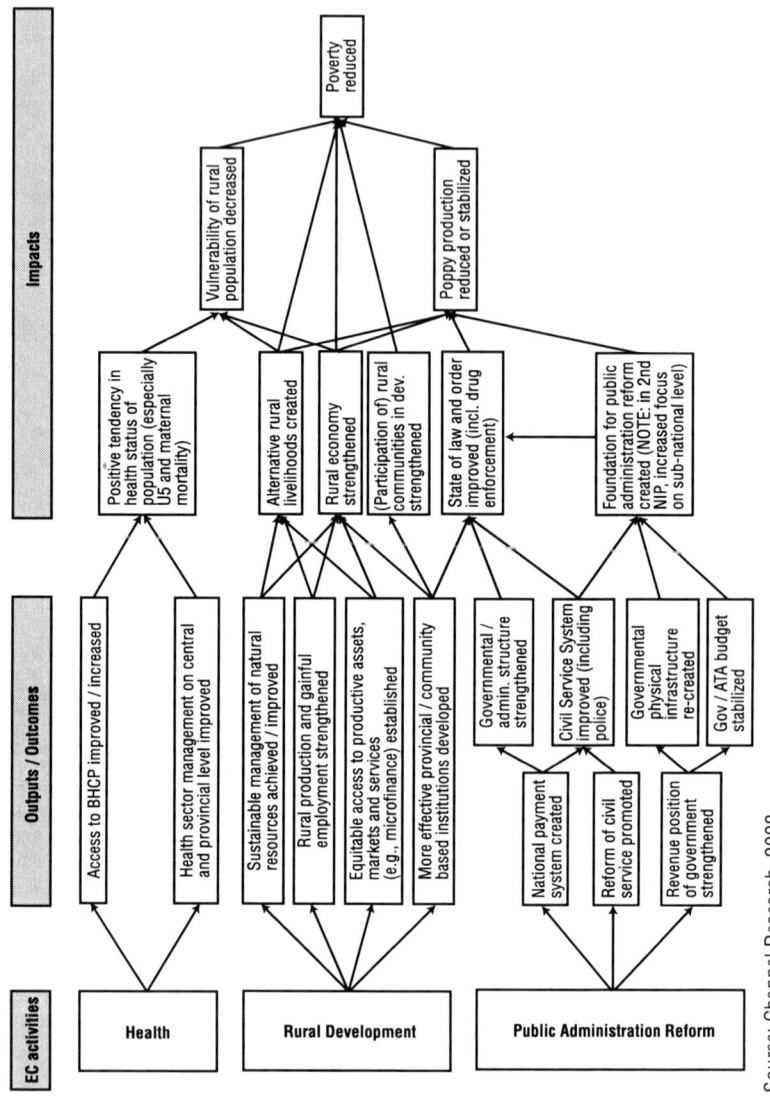

Source: Channel Research, 2008.

- Conflict prevention and peace-building programming often depend on the identification of an end state. The value given to this end state may not be shared by all stakeholders or even those within a single program or organization.

The black box is represented in Figure 32.

FIGURE 32
The "Black Box" in Impact Evaluations

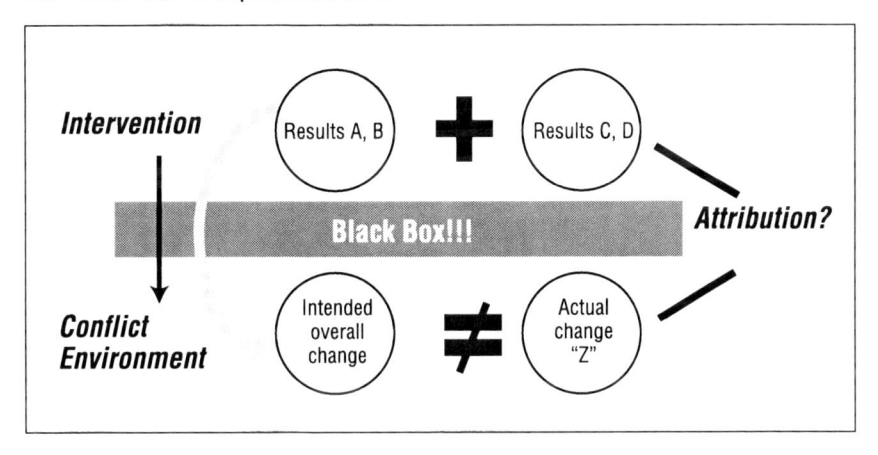

Source: Channel Research, 2008.

It is difficult to extrapolate the effect of intervention (a set of outcomes) on the overall situation – in terms of intention (why we think change will occur), but even more so in terms of attribution: to conclude that A, B, C, and D have caused Z. The black box decreases the validity of many methods of evaluations of CPPB. Such constraints cause practitioners to apply the *diagram of effects* methodology or to reconstruct complex theories of change, because of the complexity and informality of their CPPB objectives. Without another approach at hand, the diagram of effects methodology becomes the default method of evaluation.

Another possibility is presented by *Outcome Mapping*, developed by the International Development Research Council of Canada (IDRC). However, this methodology requires an *intentional design* of the intervention, which has to be patterned after the methodology. In other words, this system has to be built into the initial planning of an intervention. Real world limitations suggest that this is impossible, yet the methodology does not allow for retroactive application. It must be used at the beginning or not at all.

To overcome these limitations, and to capture the frequent occurrence of what we could refer to as *unintentional design* – confluence of informal objectives, improvization in funding systems, and dynamics of conflict – Channel Research has developed an alternate methodology called *Significance of Impact*.

Significance of Impact Methodology

The tools described here are those developed from the point of view of our evaluation company. Rather than a new method of social science research, they represent a cost-efficient method that can be used in adverse situations. Channel Research has developed participatory and verifiable methodologies for the evaluation of interventions in conflict environments and has focused in particular on a conflict analysis approach to define the significance of an aid contribution, drawing in some ways on the constructs of environmental impact assessment, and in others on effects based mapping.

The framework uses the following definitions of key analytical tools, which are broadly aligned to the terminology of the OECD Development Assistance Committee (DAC):

- *Output*: A product, usually a definable quantity (most easily monitored over time and space). This could be a report, a conference, or the establishment of a stable relationship with key actors in a conflict.

- *Outcome*: The short-term or medium-term effects of an output. These are changes in the behaviour, relationships, activities, and/or actions of a boundary partner that can be logically linked to a program (although they are not necessarily directly caused by it). We generally advocate a slightly more specific meaning, which is "how an output is used." Equating outcome to utilization of output allows the analyst to situate the concentric circles more precisely.

- *Impact*: The intended or unintended consequences of the outcome. The impact of an outcome can be verified in terms of the relevance of an outcome to an issue area (or priority sector: for example, the police force in a conflict situation), the extent of the effect of this outcome on that issue (for example, the numbers of police-force personnel exposed to that influence), and, finally, the duration of that influence (less than a year, recurrent, many years, extending after the end of a program, etc.). Impact can be instantaneous or can take years to occur. It can be local, national, or global.

These categories are drawn from the predominant language in the field of aid and development.[4] The *Significance of Impact* method has developed since 2005 when we first fully tested it in an evaluation on behalf of USAID in Casamance (Senegal). It has since been peer-reviewed through four specialized seminars and five separate evaluations.[5] It focuses more particularly on the contribution of a program to a CPPB situation and incorporates a *significance mapping* process in order to verify contributions.

The significance mapping methodology includes three stages as illustrated in Figure 33. Step 1 analyses the context in which a CPPB initiative takes place, in terms of how the main drivers – *events* and *trends* – interplay with one other. This stage can be complemented by a mapping of actors. This analysis is based on our own participatory method or on authoritative conflict analyses. Generally, there are few authoritative conflict analyses,[6] which suggests that information must be supplemented by papers written by UN missions, and by our own methods.

Step 2 is a search for evidence on the manner in which the outcomes have affected the issues. This evidence corresponds to the three rows in Figure 33, namely "conflict causes," "actors," and "dynamics and trends."

FIGURE 33
Evaluation Concept Overview

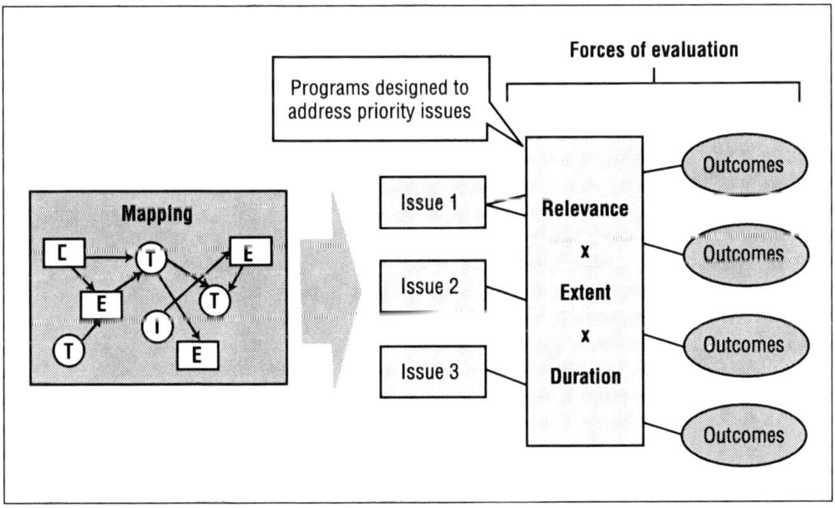

Source: Channel Research, 2008.

Step 3 reviews the key outcomes or objectives delivered by the CPPB programs in their given region or general context. This allows an analysis of the effects of different interventions with similar aims, or at least similar effects, in a unified manner, without falling into the trap of carrying out many small-scale evaluations that do not allow us to generalize to Mary Anderson's "peace writ large" concept:

> In this third and final stage we assess the interplay or relationship between these clearly defined "issues" or drivers of the situation, and the similarly verifiable outcomes/objectives. We seek to test the strength of this relationship by finding the evidence that exists concerning the relevance, extent, and duration of the outcomes in relation to the drivers.[7]

The main innovation in Channel Research's Significance of Impact methodology is that it shifts away from typical *theory-based evaluation* – methods that seek to reconstruct the logic of intervention – towards *conflict analysis-based evaluation* that focuses on the design of a CPPB intervention. It supports a noted shift away from evaluating the achievement of so-called objectives towards verifying the process and ideal conditions for change.

This shift is a way of avoiding a deeper hermeneutical issue: the interpretation of performance in conflict prevention does not depend on the identification of an end state, an explanation of the conflict, that would yield an overall objective defining the content of peace. Evaluations have to explain the achievement (or not) of this end state. For this to be done, the theory of what is "peace" – and of its most desirable characteristics – must be made explicit. At best, this is often perceived by CPPB stakeholders as taking sides, and at worst, as naïve and ill-informed. The evaluation findings are only agreed upon by those who share the same vision of peace. Those who wish to invalidate the findings – because it threatens their reputation, for example – just have to question the theory of peace.

Assessing the relationship between drivers of the conflict (the "issues" to be addressed) and outcomes is not attributing impact. It is about assessing whether or not a contribution has been significant. The criteria for assessment that we propose are drawn from the OECD DAC guidance exclusively and relate to the qualities of the relationship from outcome to issue:

1. How focused is this relationship?
2. How broad or intense is it?
3. How long does the influence last?

In Figure 33 the issues (policy aims, or drivers of the conflict) are drawn from a general analysis of the CPPB situation through the significance mapping process, either from a pre-existing evaluation or done for this evaluation.[8]

In step 3, interventions are examined by exploring three aspects that allow verification of the *significance* of the contribution. These are:

1. *Relevance* (R): This is defined by the evaluation question 3, and by the DAC, as the alignment of outcomes, needs, and priorities. Under this definition, we ask whether the outcomes achieved by partners are aligned to the priority issues in the conflict and peace dynamics as well as the key actors.

2. *Extent* (E): This relates in crude terms to the number of key actors covered, or the degree to which they have assimilated the CPPB activity outcome. This could, for example, be the size of the audience for public information campaigns, or the high-quality appreciation of a small number of negotiators.

3. *Duration* (D): This relates to the dimension of time, and timing, and is defined as the period over which the interaction of outcomes with key needs take place. We ask how prolonged and synchronized an outcome's influence has been on an issue. Sustainability in this approach is directly related to duration and is defined as the ability of outcomes to continue after the end of activities financed under a program. We also explore whether there has been continued use of aid outputs.

Extent (E) and Duration (D) form the overall criteria of coverage. These tests of influence constitute the significance of outcome, and are open to independent verification. We provide evidence along these broad areas of influence, using the evaluation questions, which are often given at the outset of our assignments.

The method allows us to explain why, or why not, relevance was achieved, without entering into a description of the myriad individualized strategies of intervention used by personnel on the ground. It also allows the use of qualitative as well as quantitative evidence, to avoid the trap of seeking only to measure impact itself.

In assessing the influence and significance of outcomes through the process illustrated in Figure 33, our evaluations explore the chain shown in Table 4: Inputs, Output, Outcome, and Significance of Impact Chain, using the example of the evaluation of Norwegian researchers' contribution to peace-building.

TABLE 4
Inputs, Output, Outcome, and Significance of Impact Chain

Inputs	Output	Outcome	Significance of Impact
Amounts allocated to this case study, divided into types of outcomes. For example, how much was spent on programs that contributed to the development of networks of trust in a given country? Who are the researchers, commissioners, and beneficiaries of the research?	What were the services and products that contributed to a given outcome? For example, what conferences, research projects, or visits contributed to the strength of ties to researchers in a given country?	What are the consequences of the combined outputs in a given country? For example, what material evidence is there of a meaningful use of the relations between Norwegian academic personnel and personnel involved in research in a given country for track 2 diplomacy?	What evidence is there of the relevance, extent, and duration of the influence of an outcome on the key drivers of a conflict, or on the key Norwegian foreign policy priorities in a given country? For example, was track 2 diplomacy involving the right people, were the right persons exposed deeply interested in the initiative, and how long were they involved?

Source: Channel Research, 2008.

The essence of the Significance of Impact approach is that it seeks to move away from Greek and European modes of thought, as represented by the end result, ideal world, or the ubiquitous evaluation objectives. Our approach focuses on ideal conditions – rather than end results – and the combination of personal qualities and techniques to overcome chance and adversity to reach this ideal state. Channel Research suggests that the worldview of other cultures such as that of China may provide an alternate option for the international community involved in CPPB activities. In the Chinese worldview, there is no ideal world to strive for, only a constant search for ways of making the environment come of its own accord to conditions that are optimal for the artful planner. Yet even the most artful planner, when looking back through the process of evaluation, stumbles on the most basic problem: what framework should be used to analyze performance? Are art, improvization, and judgment not the ultimate references? And what if the "ideal peace" towards which one is striving is not shared by the users of the evaluation conclusions and recommendations? The evaluator, who is more often independent from the planner and manager of the intervention, must use another mode of reference.

In this "other" mode, the emphasis is not on lining up outputs but on identifying the conditions that will determine change, or rather, will lead to the desired change without much apparent effort. To make the environment generate this change, small and well-targeted interventions, or mere passivity, should suffice. The challenge lies in understanding and seeing the world in its dynamics and unpredictability.

Conclusion

The prevailing notions of evaluation are based around references to planning and the definition of an ideal end state: the activities are linked to results, specific objectives, and general objectives. These general objectives are often phrased in general terms and either do not lend themselves well to performance assessment or, when they are made specific, are not realistic (the end state is often very different from what was foreseen) or are highly controversial.

In a related but different vein, the evaluation of impact in peace-building seeks to attribute impact to intervention but never succeeds. This is because the connections among activities, results, and objectives are loose, and many other factors and agencies cut across with their own particular influence on the overall dynamics. The ability to attribute CPPB cause and effect relationships remains a myth.

The Significance of Impact methodology, on the other hand, allows the evaluator to conclude on the value of a particular intervention. It is only possible to conclude on the significance of this contribution, but, we would argue, it is also sufficient to do so. Assessing the significance of an effect within a dynamic context also allows for adjustment – which is the fulfillment of the goal of evaluation.

Summary Points

- The international community's evaluation methodology for conflict prevention and peace-building programming (CPPB) focuses on cause/effect relationships in order to create ideal conditions for peace and is based on the Greek worldview of "ideal state."
- Worldviews of other cultures, such as that of the Chinese, may provide an alternate option for the international community involved in CPPB activities.
- Conflict analysis-based evaluation is more important than the method of reviewing intervention strategies and assessing theories of change.
- Evaluations that focus on verification are more feasible than those that focus on measurement.
- It is impossible to prove that a change in the status of peace and conflict can be traced back to any one intervention activity.
- The standard use of objectives as benchmarks of performance is weakened because conflict programming requires a response to constraints and opportunities as they arise. These cannot be planned for in advance and therefore present considerable difficulties for evaluators.
- It is difficult to separate the impact of peace-building projects from other impacts on conflict.
- Selecting indicators of change demands a shared understanding of a conflict and a shared use of verification methods that are applicable in a conflict situation.
- Conflict prevention and peace-building programming often depend on the identification of an end state. The value given to this end state may not be shared by all stakeholders or even those within a single program or organization.
- Channel Research's Significance of Impact methodology shifts away from typical theory-based evaluation towards conflict analysis-based evaluation that focuses on the design of an intervention. It supports a noted shift away from evaluating the achievement of so-called objectives towards verifying the process and ideal conditions for change.

- The Significance of Impact approach moves away from Greek and European modes of thought, as represented by the end result, ideal world, or the ubiquitous evaluation objectives and focuses on ideal conditions – rather than end results.

Notes

[1] OECD-DAC, *Guidance on Evaluating Conflict Prevention and Peacebuilding Activities*.

[2] European Commission, "Evaluation of Afghanistan Country Strategy," 14.

[3] OECD-DAC, *Guidance on Evaluating Conflict Prevention and Peacebuilding Activities*, 36.

[4] OECD-DAC, *Glossary of Key Terms*.

[5] INCORE Summer School, University of Ulster, June 2006 and 2007, La Converserie Seminar, September 2006 and 2007. Methodology applied for the evaluation of peace-building activities in Senegal (USAID), of the Northern Uganda Peace Initiative (USAID), of the Cross-Border Peace-Building Measures in Northern Ireland (EU), of the Collaborative for Development Action / Collaborative Learning Projects of Mary Anderson (SIDA), Evaluation of Norwegian R&D for CPPB for Norad, 2008.

[6] For example, in the Democratic Republic of Congo, we note in particular that the DFID 2007 Strategic Conflict Assessment that was led by a consultant with whom we often work, Tony Vaux, is practically the sole available conflict analysis done by a bilateral donor. This evidence was collected in the course of the OECD DAC / French Ministry of Foreign and European Affairs commissioned stock-taking study on human rights and conflict policy, 2008.

[7] Anderson, *Do No Harm*.

[8] Channel Research is particularly careful to recognize the partnership-driven approach of CPPB in many conflict environments. Achieving the outcome belongs very much to the partners as well as the funders.

CHAPTER 12

An Organizational Perspective on Measuring the Effectiveness of Crisis Management

KRISTIINA RINTAKOSKI

As crisis management and peace operations grow ever more complex and as the number of external interveners increase in crisis management, emphasis upon a comprehensive system-wide evaluation will come to the fore. Learning organizations such as the Crisis Management Initiative (CMI) are advancing themselves and their partnerships through a reliance upon *collective lessons learned and best practices* rather than on the traditional single stakeholder approach to learning from activities in crisis environments. As a small actor, CMI supports *communities of practice* and wants to improve transmission of best practices within and among international NGOs and local civil society organizations. This chapter emphasizes the learning evolution related to monitoring and evaluation experienced by CMI to highlight a successful approach to making our work more effective for both locals and our funders.

Crisis Management Initiative (CMI) is a non-governmental organization working on crisis management and conflict resolution. It develops and tests more effective approaches and tools for mediation, state-building, mission support capabilities, and evaluation. When established in 2000, CMI was more of a policy and advocacy organization, and since 2005 it has become more operational in the field, both in peace mediation and state-building activities. As of 2008, CMI did not have a systematic evaluation practice. However, since 2006 it has been developing an evaluation practice and training staff members on practices and methods. Through this evolution, CMI has recognized the need to build its capacity in monitoring and evaluating of its activities in conflict environments, where conflict sensitivity and sustainability are of vital importance. Systematic monitoring and evaluation are of greatest use to a peace-building NGO such as CMI, whose interventions occur throughout the many phases of conflict. Monitoring and evaluation at an early enough stage in our activities provide CMI with the requisite information to adapt strategies accordingly and improve the likelihood that a project or program will achieve its goals while at the same time avoiding some of the unintended consequences of crisis management. In very practical terms, our ability to better verify the contribution that CMI is making in a particular crisis environment will provide CMI with solid grounds to justify future funding, attract potential clients, and identify findings to share with others working in similar areas, thus building the collective capacity of NGOs in peace-building. In addition, this practice will contribute to the ability of NGOs to work effectively and transparently with other multilateral stakeholders such as EU institutions, member states, other international NGOs, and local civil society.

CMI has attempted to capture key *lessons learned* from peace mediation processes it has been involved with, particularly from the peace talks between the Indonesian government and the Free Aceh Movement in 2005. CMI was asked to share these lessons – what worked and why – with local peace facilitators in other conflict regions. CMI has also been involved in a European Commission funded program, Initiative for Peacebuilding, where one of the aims was to develop understanding and methods of evaluating mediation interventions.

In parallel, CMI works with partners to develop a standardized evaluation framework suitable for assessing crisis management activities, particularly the European Union's civilian operations. Although we are evolving our own evaluation system and working collaboratively to improve broader civilian operations, CMI has commissioned external evaluations to assess the impact of our work in different fields and activities. This has been paramount to our growth and development.

CMI considers evaluation as a key component in transparent and constructive dialogue and cooperation between key stakeholders of peace-building programs, including host communities and multilateral partners, to maximize their joint impact. A key assumption CMI holds regarding evaluation and monitoring is that these processes and methods provide our organization with a better understanding of the short- and long-term impacts of our programs on host countries' societies. CMI is committed to ensuring accountability and transparency of our programs with host societies.

Terminology

CMI employs the term *evaluation and monitoring progress* (or *impact*) rather than *measuring progress*. Monitoring is an activity to assess ongoing projects, and *evaluation* is an activity to assess projects after they have been completed. Evaluation examines impact and sustainability of activities. In conflict environments, progress can be difficult to measure, yet verification of progress is more easily addressed. Monitoring is normally carried out by CMI staff as a part of our own project management cycle, while evaluations of our projects are conducted by an external third party and are budgeted into all of our projects.

Through evaluation and monitoring, CMI attempts to capture *best practices* and *lessons learned* to improve project management and organizational practices. In parallel, CMI works with the concept of good or best practice in state building and develops methods on how these practices could be shared and replicated in other state building processes.

Evaluation Criteria and Useful Frameworks

Many of the key concepts and objectives that are central to CMI's work in crisis management and conflict resolution are reflected in the work of the Development Assistance Committee of the Organisation for Economic Co-operation and Development (OECD DAC) evaluation guidelines as evaluation criteria. One of the key concepts underpinning CMI evaluations of our activities and interventions is *conflict sensitivity*. Conflict sensitivity refers to the ability of an organization

- to understand the context in which it operates;
- to understand the interaction between its intervention and the context; and,
- to act upon the understanding of this interaction, in order to avoid negative impacts and maximize positive impacts.[1]

Another key concept underpinning the CMI evaluation framework is local ownership and sustainability. In CMI's view, local actors are central to any peace-building work, and external actors are there to help. CMI has adopted the term *quality of peace processes* to make sure that women and minorities are presented in fora that are discussing a country's future. Through this example CMI shows other stakeholders that locals matter in the process towards peace.

CMI is a small organization with limited resources for internal development and therefore tends to utilize existing evaluation templates and models developed by other organizations and adjust them to our specific needs. It is important to note that our primary evaluation criteria – based on the OECD DAC guidelines – must be the focus of any evaluation template or model that we use in our own evaluations. There are an increasing number of guidebooks on designing and evaluating NGO projects and programs in conflict environments.[2] CMI also uses the evaluation guidelines and criteria developed by the OECD DAC[3] and EuropeAid evaluation online handbook as references,[4] as these methods are thoroughly tested and include logical tools that allow flexibility in their application.

Evaluation questions generally focus on a limited number of key points, thus allowing better reflection on judgment criteria, more targeted data collection, more in-depth analysis, and a more useful report. Examples of key questions are:

- *Extent*: To what extent has a certain activity contributed to generating effect X?

- *Sustainability*: To what extent has the intervention generated effect X with a strong probability of survival of effects after the end of the aid?

- *Relevance*: When the intervention generates effect X, to what extent does it correspond to the needs of the population concerned?

- *Value Added*: When the intervention generates effect X, to what extent does it add value compared to a similar intervention implemented by other actors?

At CMI, an evaluation is intended to provide information that is both credible and applicable. It is performed in such a way as to satisfy the need for adequate information for decision-making at both the operative and strategic levels. The value of the evaluation depends on the follow-up: that is, on how the information produced affects future decisions.

Challenges

A key internal challenge for CMI is to establish systematic organizational practice and evaluation policies to ensure institutional learning. Some key external challenges in evaluating activities are the nature of the processes of peace negotiations, peace-building, and crisis management. Sometimes the rather short duration of operations and the fact that many impacts are visible only after a longer period of time make evaluation challenging. CMI projects and programs also take place in countries where there are numerous other actors, and it is difficult to distinguish the impact of one particular operation from the converging and often competing impacts of other projects. However, in general, organizations implementing activities in conflict areas have only limited control over the impact their activities will have.

As crisis management and peace operations grow ever more complex, and as the number of external interveners continues to increase, the evaluation of contributions of single organizations is no longer a useful activity. Such an individualized evaluation method does not adequately verify whether a broader set of activities collectively contributes to making a difference in a crisis. As part of our work in the field of *comprehensive crisis management,* CMI has been involved in discussions on how to develop methods to assess *system-wide* impacts in crisis management. A future trend in evaluation may be more emphasis on system-wide evaluation, as well as increased focus on qualitative verification instead of a dependence upon quantitative approaches.

As CMI continues to develop our capacity in monitoring and evaluation, it is important to learn from other organizations' experience and practice. A key interest is to continue to develop systematic approaches that draw useful comparisons and make peer learning easier. CMI remains interested in broader experiences and methods in assessing and evaluating operations rather than single organizational or programmatic missions in crisis environments. The improved evaluation practices being developed by CMI are building our capacity to assess what we are doing well, and helping us learn from past experiences. Thus, evaluation is used in a broader extent at CMI for institutional learning as an input for planning and training.

Summary Points

- Emphasis on a comprehensive system-wide evaluation framework is coming to the fore as crisis management and peace operations grow ever more complex and as the number of external interveners increases in crisis management.

- As NGOs better verify the contribution they make in an intervention, they are able to provide justification for future funding, attract potential clients, and identify findings to share with others working in similar areas, thus building the collective capacity of NGOs in peace-building.

- The value of evaluation depends on how the information produced affects future decisions and activities.

- Commissioning external evaluations to assess the impact of activities is paramount to stakeholder growth and development.

- Monitoring and evaluation of processes and methods provide a more comprehensive understanding of short- and long-term impacts of intervention activities upon war-affected societies.

- Monitoring and evaluation capture *best practices* and *lessons learned* that can be shared and replicated in other crisis activities.

- The OECD DAC guidelines and EuropeAid evaluation handbook provide methods that are thoroughly tested and include logical tools that allow flexibility in their application.

- Small organizations with limited resources for measuring progress can adopt existing evaluation frameworks developed by other organizations and adjust them to specific needs.

- Stakeholders implementing activities in conflict areas have only limited control over the impact their activities will have.

- There is increased focus on qualitative verification instead of a dependence upon quantitative approaches to measuring progress.

Notes

[1] ConflictSensitivity.org, *Conflict-Sensitive Approaches*.

[2] Church and Rogers, *Designing for Results*; Lederach et al., *Reflective Peacebuilding*; Conflict Prevention and Post-Conflict Reconstruction Network (CPR Network), *The Peace and Conflict Impact Assessment Handbook*.

[3] OECD, Guidance on Evaluating Conflict Prevention and Peacebuilding Activities.

[4] Available at http://ec.europa.eu/europeaid/evaluation/methodology/methods/mth_ccr_en.htm.

CHAPTER 13

Measuring Effectiveness in Peace-Building and State-Building

JAKE SHERMAN

The United Nations, across its work in conflict prevention, peace operations, and peace-building, is increasingly grappling with the question of how to effectively and sustainably deliver on its goals. Mission mandates have grown increasingly multi-dimensional, incorporating a range of tasks outside the remit of "traditional" peacekeeping operations – from security sector and public administration reform to promoting good (political and economic) governance and the rule of law. Today, across the organization's departments, measurement is becoming more and more a part of planning, implementation, and learning. The Security Council is requesting the Department of Peacekeeping Operations (DPKO) to develop benchmarks, and the department's capstone doctrine on peacekeeping now makes explicit reference to them. The Peacebuilding Support Office (PBSO) is strengthening post-conflict planning tools and developing guidance on peace consolidation benchmarks.

The differences in organizational culture that exist across diplomacy, defence, and development in government are reflected in the development, military, and policing arenas of the UN system as well. The nature and extent of current measurement practices vary from the UN Development Programme (UNDP) – the institutional culture of which includes monitoring and evaluation, albeit often at an output level – to the Department of Peacekeeping Operations (DPKO), with its tradition of planning, but often focused on task lists and characterized by sensitivity over security objectives. A central issue, therefore, is how to lift benchmarking at output level to the outcome level, and to do so in a holistic manner. While there is no lack of ideas on how to achieve this, there is a lack of consensus. Moreover, the many initiatives underway – not just within the UN but among other multilateral and bilateral actors – are not necessarily engaged with one another.

The Center on International Cooperation's (CIC)'s interest in measurement stems from recently initiated work examining the "state of the state" of several countries attempting to recover from war with assistance from the international community, including Afghanistan, Burundi, and Haiti.[1] In November 2008, CIC convened a meeting of policy-makers and practitioners from the UN, the US government, the OECD/DAC, the US Institute of Peace, interested member states, and others to discuss the needs of different actors in terms of metrics for conflict prevention, conflict management, and conflict resolution. They examined a range of different measurement initiatives – including the US Institute of Peace and Army Corps of Engineers' "Measuring Peace in Conflict Environments (MPICE) framework," the DPKO Rule of Law Indicators Project, and PBSO's aforementioned project on peace consolidation benchmarking – and their complementarities.

Several themes emerged over the course of the discussion. First, there is diverse understanding – if not a lack of clarity – of what "state-building" and "peace-building" actually mean, both conceptually and by extension in terms of policies, planning, and programming. Both the Human Development Indicators and the Millennium Development Goals have established a framework under which the UN and, indeed, most development organizations work, but neither is a useful tool for engagement in fragile states. Attempts have been made at constructing common frameworks for post-conflict recovery, but there is still no consensus on what these should look like. The lack of clarity influences what different actors are pursuing not only in terms of goals but also in how they judge and measure progress. In the absence of clarity on high-order goals, it often remains easier for departments to focus on individual outputs rather than on their collective outcome. Additionally, the lens with which one understands these goals – be it security, rule of law, or development – may influence priorities in terms of good governance, local ownership, legitimacy, sustainability, or other principles. Nonetheless, as the call for "state of the state" analysis suggests, the lack of clarity may in fact be reflective of the complexity and variation across countries, in turn challenging the merits of any single authoritative set of core metrics.

Second, metrics systems need to be developed by (and for) organizations in such a way that they are recognized as a positive tool rather than a hindrance. There is a need to make sure that the investment in civilian capacity is sufficient to the task at hand. This requires not only human and financial resources (not least, posts for strategic planning and for monitoring and evaluation at field and headquarters), but also receptive leadership. A key question that emerged was whether to focus on developing the capacity for undertaking measurement (the process) or on getting the metrics "right'" (outcome). This applies both to the UN and to the countries in transition that it is supporting. Indeed, as a participant from DPKO asked, if one does not have the capacity to undertake quality measurement – to identify indicators and collect, analyze, and interpret data, should one do so at all?

Third, while there was broad agreement among participants on why local ownership over metrics is important (i.e., for sustainability and legitimacy), there were different views on the manner, timing, and sequencing of this process. Who decides what the priorities are, how they are measured, and when the outcome is *good enough*? There is tension between, on one hand, the early inclusion of local stakeholders in decision-making, including the design of metrics systems (the identification of priorities and benchmarks and indicators thereof) and, on the other, the potential risks of including local power brokers lacking capacity, if not legitimacy. Some participants argued that it was better to accept a few flaws as the result of a nationally agreed process than to risk rejection. Others emphasized that while partnership and eventual transfer to local actors is a worthy goal, the reality of national capacities and motivations often dictates an unequal relationship in which internationals must, in fact, lead while national capacities are strengthened. How one balances international goals with local goals is a challenge.

A related issue is accountability: in Afghanistan and elsewhere, "compacts" between donors and government have been agreed upon for achieving high-level benchmarks. Compacts have proven useful in identifying a common vision on a least a few priorities. But while compacts are based on a principle of mutual accountability, in reality the benchmarks they contain are often driven by the political imperatives of donors, resulting in goals that are unrealistic in content and difficult to measure. And while there are reasons why a host country would subject itself to increased scrutiny, there is little real recourse for host governments when international actors fall short.

Finally, the international community is not external to the process of state-building and peace-building. Its presence affects how local actors engage and the decisions that they take; it may artificially buoy outcomes that will be undone by its eventual withdrawal. Nor can one escape from the interconnectedness between the goals – and contradictions – of different international actors' strategies. Thus, its impact, good and bad, needs to be measured. More work is needed to ensure that metrics measure local perceptions of the international community and its efforts as part of the monitoring process.

Summary Points

- The United Nations is increasingly grappling with the question of how to effectively and sustainably deliver on its goals.
- UN mission mandates are increasingly multi-dimensional, incorporating a range of tasks outside the remit of "traditional" peacekeeping operations.
- Measurement is becoming an important part of planning, implementation, and learning at the UN.
- Governmental cultural divisions between diplomacy, defence, and development also occur at the UN between military, police, and development.
- There is a lack of consensus on how to elevate benchmarking at the output level to the outcome level.
- There are many measuring initiatives underway at the UN and among other stakeholders; however, they are not engaged with one another.
- Lack of clarity on the meanings of "state-building" and "peace-building" may challenge the merits of any single, authoritative set of core metrics.
- The lens with which one understands security, rule of law, and development influences priorities in terms of good governance, local ownership, legitimacy, sustainability, or other principles.
- Metrics systems need to be developed by and for organizations in such a way that systems are recognized as a positive tool rather than a hindrance.
- "Compacts" are based on principles of mutual accountability, yet the benchmarks they contain can be driven by the political imperatives of donors, resulting in goals that are unrealistic in content and difficult to measure.
- Local ownership over metrics is critical for sustainability and legitimacy.
- Questions remain around priorities, how they are measured, and when the outcome of activities is good enough.

- The presence of the international community in war-affected environments may artificially buoy outcomes that are then undone by the eventual withdrawal.
- There is both interconnectedness and contradiction between the goals of different international actors' strategies, the impacts of which need to be measured.
- More work is needed to ensure that metrics measure local perceptions of the international community and its efforts as part of the monitoring process.

Note

[1] CIC is an independent think tank that works with the UN and member states on issues related to international peace and security. As part of CIC's program on state-building, the Organisation for Economic Cooperation and Development's Development Assistance Committee (OECD/DAC) commissioned CIC to draft a framing paper on donor engagement in fragile states. The resulting paper, "From Fragility to Resilience: Concepts and Dilemmas of Statebuilding in Fragile States," called for state-building policy and strategy in a given country to be based on "a specific, historically informed assessment of the state of the state." See Jones and Chandran with Cousens, Slotin, and Sherman, *From Fragility to Resilience*.

CHAPTER 14

Practitioner Perspectives and Policy Options

The practitioner perspectives highlighted in the previous chapters serve to identify at least six sectoral worldviews informing multi-functional peace operations and crisis management regarding measuring progress and success. In addition to illustrating particular approaches within the common tradespace, these practitioner perspectives allow a series of policy options to emerge. This chapter examines these practitioner worldviews in more depth and identifies the policy options that stem from them.

The final chapters and the conclusion will amalgamate practitioner policy options with the policy options emerging from the overall findings highlighted in this book.

Practitioner Perspectives

As development economist Amartya Sen observes, "Well-meaning attempts at pursuing global peace can have very counterproductive consequences when these attempts are founded on a fundamentally illusory understanding of the world of human beings."[1] Not only are our perspectives illusions of the world around us, but those illusions inform how we pursue global peace and how we attempt to measure success and progress towards our goals. All stakeholders – whether police, humanitarian, military, governmental, scholar, developmental, or private industry – have a dominant worldview that colours the way they do business in the common tradespace of international interventions. In peace operations and civilian crisis management, "some stakeholders have developed alternate modalities through which to identify, while others remain fixed on outdated identities that may no longer serve their work."[2]

According to David Leakey, director general of the European Union Military Staff in the Council of the European Union, Brussels, humanitarians are by nature reactive and bound by the principle of local ownership, which offers legitimacy to the humanitarians for being there. Militaries too are bound by the same mantra of local ownership, and this accounts in part for slow progress in operations in Kosovo and Afghanistan. For the UNHCR, performance indicators are numbers of repatriations within the "framework of resettlement." There are no incentives to create indicators. NGOs are there doing business to stay in business.[3] They are "hostages of fortune," says Mary Ann Zimmerman, US SCRS, offering that the development sector views the purpose of assessment of their activity effectiveness as, first, to do more good; and second, to get more money to do more good.[4] Jason Ladnier agrees that humanitarians "do it to get more money to do it."[5]

Many stakeholders do not understand other stakeholder worldviews as well as they think they do, and research reveals that each group has a strong idea of what the *others* are, and they tend to generalize about one another: "Perhaps, given the realities of the operational space in which these stakeholders are working, there is a concern that these groups are too entrenched in their own identities to create alternative roles and responsibilities that respond to the changed space and to each other ... The challenge, then, lies in the willingness and ability of the major stakeholders to be wrong about their assumptions of the other."[6] Eugene Bonventre suggests that the cooperation necessary for interventions may increase each stakeholders' knowledge of other principles and techniques and take them a step closer to a holistic, systems-wide approach to addressing critical intervention issues such as measuring effectiveness, progress, and success.[7]

In his contribution, Rory Keane maintains that interventionists need to be far more aware of the political nature of intervention. His view, that all interveners are political tools, is an important one because it highlights the oppositely held worldview by some that they can do no harm at all and that they are neutral – or, as Keane suggests – benign actors in the spectrum of intervention.

John Borton indicates how the humanitarian system has developed ways of measuring performance at the project and organizational level and is now tentatively beginning to grapple with the challenge of measuring its collective performance. This may suggest that self-assessment is critical to intervention and takes a high level of maturity. Interestingly, Keith Hauk and Stephen Mariano have come to this realization themselves based on their experience as planners in Iraq, recommending to commanding officers that they seek out truthful assessments of operations in order to adjust activities to best respond to an ever-changing cultural and political context. With this recommendation, Hauk and Mariano highlight the oppositely held worldview by most militaries, which is that it is best to avoid external feedback and to forge ahead with a "get 'er done" attitude: achieve the mission mandate at all costs.

Stuart Gordon makes it clear that assessment and appropriate measurement are predicated upon asking better questions prior to the design and implementation of an intervention. Better questions can equal better results. For militaries involved in non-permissive environments such as Afghanistan and Iraq, asking better questions of recipients of reconstruction and stabilization may augment progress and success. These suggestions again illustrate the perspective identified by Hauk and Mariano, which is that militaries tend to ignore or discount recipient perspectives as they are considered external to the realization of a mission mandate or the achievement of campaign planning goals and objectives.

David Chuter advises that the moral imperative worldview is not the only reason to intervene and that it can actually do harm. He thereby articulates the perspective that intervention is motivated by factors other than moral ones, including economic and political factors. Emery Brusset argues that the widespread fixity upon end goals by intervention stakeholders causes blindness to the appropriate processes possibly employed to achieve goals. He offers that the worldview of Chinese philosophy could better inform interventions in complex environments, and that this perspective could inform a more appropriate approach to evaluating and verifying the success of interventions.

Kristiina Rintakoski brings a scholarly learning perspective to understanding intervention. She offers that for organizations to learn, they must evaluate their activities and feed lessons back into an organizational cycle to contribute to knowledge growth. For Rintakoski, there are logical connections between learning, organizational improvement, and successful implementation. Rintakoski's *learner worldview* seeks to improve activities for the wider spectrum of sector and populations affected by activities. Jake Sherman also presents a scholarly learning perspective, and is less interested in the polarities of right and wrong, success and failure, than in multiple approaches to problems from differing perspectives. Stakeholders with this worldview are more easily able to think about ambiguity and do not necessarily require clearly defined answers to the challenges facing peace operations and civilian crisis management.

Other distinct practitioner perspectives were distilled from the interviews in support of this research project. They describe a definite pattern within the international community that could inform the policy options for measuring what matters in peace operations and crisis management. These worldviews include, but are not limited to, those compiled in Table 5:

TABLE 5
Intervention Worldviews

• Learners • Get 'er done • Do no harm • Political agency • Pacifism • Do good • Linear thinkers (right and wrong, black and white) • Non-linear thinkers (shades of grey) • Process-oriented • Goals-oriented • Policy-driven	• Profit-driven • Agenda-driven • What's in it for me • Spoilers (stakeholder, sectoral, recipient-local) • Imposing a world order (the right way, the answer) • West is best • Moral imperative • Predatory opportunism, anarchists, conflict capitalists	• Adrenalin junkies (bring it on!) • Authoritarian power • Bureaucratic, process-driven, over-systemized, bean-counters • Laissez-faire • Scientific, empiricist • Diaspora • Victim mentality • Individualistic • Synergistic

There are many other worldviews that inform the work of the international community, many others still that inform the worldviews on measuring progress and success, and many more again that inform the mechanisms and tools for measuring effectiveness, progress, and success. Intervention worldviews held by stakeholders are not static; they change over time, causing stakeholders' approaches to intervention to be transformed. It is problematic at best when only two or three sectors, each holding different worldviews, share the space within an intervention environment and attempt to implement their activities. As stakeholders within various sectors learn and develop, and as the context in which they work changes, their worldviews also shift; some shift ever so slightly, while other changes represent a sea change.

When multiple worldviews show up in the common tradespace of international interventions, a series of knock-on effects need to be addressed. The first is the requirement to broaden the understanding of participating stakeholder worldviews to better comprehend *why* other sectors do what they do. The second is the requirement for standards of sector success within this shared space. The worldviews discussed in this chapter are but a few that can help deepen the understanding of stakeholders and inform standards of success as they begin working within a common tradespace of international interventions.

The following section further distills the practitioner perspectives on measuring what matters. Peace operations and civilian crisis management activities are *political acts* that *can do harm*. Moreover, the context in which practitioners measure and evaluate progress of such activities is by nature political. Addressing the multiple aspects of challenges caused by crises calls for multi-stakeholder approaches. Given the political significance of most interventions (the UK PRT deployment in Afghanistan, for example), their multi-national nature, and the scale of the resources invested, there is an understandably strong interest in measuring "effectiveness." The lens with which one understands security, rule of law, and development influences priorities in terms of good governance, local ownership, legitimacy, sustainability, or other principles. Practitioners bring their unique sets of values, principles, and assumptions to their work and engage in measuring and evaluating progress in equally unique ways. Priorities are rarely shared among stakeholders; this statement is equally true regarding worldviews and conceptual understandings of interventions writ large.

New liberal imperialists intervene based upon moral responsibility such as the protection of human rights and democracy, suggesting that the security of the state and the security of people are mutually reinforcing. The realist approach to intervention is based on stability and status quo rather than ideational values like human security. This approach uses locally accepted notions of statehood and governance that respond to tradition, culture, and history.

Both interconnectedness and contradiction exist between the goals of stakeholder strategies, which have impacts that are equally interconnected and contradictory. Volatility, violence, and the politicization of an operational environment curtail access to information, partners, processes, and projects, which makes measuring effectiveness even more difficult.

All stakeholder activities are funded by donors, most of which require progress reporting of the interventions they are funding. Stakeholders involved in peace operations and civilian crisis management invest resources, money, and time into measuring the impact of their activities. The scope, scale, and consistency of reporting vary.

Moreover, the complex peace and security environment has corresponding political demands – sovereignty, ownership, and the amnesty-impunity nexus. The worldviews framing intervention, and therefore framing measuring progress, may be best understood through the lenses of *comprehensive security, new liberal imperialism,* and *realism.*

The reality of practitioners is that they function at the international, national, and locally based levels deploying financial, material, and human resources to provide assistance and protection to those affected by conflict; their various objectives include saving lives, establishing human and state-level security, reducing suffering, and aiding recovery through various mechanisms such as rule of law, governance, and human rights. The remit of the peace operations and civilian crisis management practitioner is broad. Often it is difficult for resource-poor stakeholders – which make up the majority of the civilian humanitarian sector – to advance the evaluation agenda. Although evaluation is on the rise and there is a commitment to accountability and quality, this effort is hampered by a reporting overload on agencies and inadequate investment and effort in activity-level measuring of success. Commissioning external evaluations to assess the impact of activities is paramount to stakeholder growth and development. The value of evaluation depends on how the information produced affects future decisions and activities.

Intervention activities include tangible and intangible elements. Traditionally, it has been easier to measure the tangible outcomes of peace operations and civilian crisis management activities. Although elements of political, social, economic, security, and rule of law factors are obviously measurable, most are highly subjective, abstract, and resistant to meaningful quantification. Progress of peace operations and civilian crisis management is controvertible. Because operations are expensive and not always popular, sponsoring governments and international organizations are reticent to admit negative progress or failure. This reticence has affected the methods through which activity objectives are set and measured. More often than not, measuring progress is a political exercise in reporting positive, incontrovertible target achievement and is outcome based. Although it offers a simple vehicle for communicating conclusions, it also has the potential to distort planning, encouraging the confusion of strategic progress with "resource inputs" and "raw" outputs. Consensus is lacking on how to elevate benchmarking at the output level to the outcome level.

Tangible activities have the advantage of being easier to organize, execute, and measure, and therefore they can more easily be used to justify that *progress* is being achieved. To further complicate measuring progress, all stakeholders have different motives for being involved in peace operations and civilian crisis management which they never declare but which are important in measuring perceptions of success.

Many practitioners working in the field of peace operations and civilian crisis management grapple with how to effectively and sustainably deliver on goals. Stakeholder interventions are increasingly multidimensional, politicized, and difficult to assess; yet measuring is becoming a part of planning, implementation, and learning within organizations. On the one hand, true measuring of impacts is improbable; on the other hand, it is necessary, as it is a learning tool that informs planning and implementation. Monitoring and evaluation of processes and methods provide a more comprehensive understanding of the short- and long-term impacts of intervention activities on war-affected societies. As stakeholders – and whole sectors – better verify the contribution they make in an intervention, they are more able to provide justification for future funding, attract potential clients, and identify findings to share within sectors.

Further, there is confusion among stakeholders between measuring the *impact* of activities and measuring the *performance* of the management and application of resources to support such activities.

The increasing complexity of peace operations and civilian crisis management mandates influences the ability to implement the mandate and determines the capacity to measure the achievement of a mandate. Moreover, the resolution of a crisis and the achievement of a mandate are not the same thing. Conflicts may stop, start, or be suspended, and crises may emerge or be resolved independently of a peace operations mission itself, making the measurement of progress problematic. Similarly, stakeholders implementing activities in conflict areas have a limited control over what impact their activities have and whether their intended impacts work in concert with or against other stakeholder activity impacts or effects. Compacts such as the Afghan Compact are based on principles of mutual accountability, yet the benchmarks they contain can be driven by the political imperatives of donors, resulting in goals that are unrealistic in content and difficult to measure. Local ownership over metrics is critical for sustainability and legitimacy Like mandates, compacts must be practical, sustainable, and legitimate, and measuring their effectiveness can only be assessed against previously set objectives.

Different capabilities and capacities to evaluate and measure exist within sectors and are distinct among stakeholders within each sector. The ability to report on overall sectoral effectiveness and performance on a regular basis may be a long way off. However, various measuring mechanisms exist within sectors, to a varying level of support: LogFrames remain largely unknown beyond the development community; evaluations have a well-established role within the humanitarian sector; metrics and measures of effectiveness play a leading role in military performance evaluation. Emphasis upon a comprehensive, system-wide framework is coming to the fore as civilian crisis management and peace operations grow ever more complex and as the number of external interveners increase in civilian crisis management. Yet even though there are many measuring initiatives underway at the UN and among other stakeholders, they are not engaged with one another. This stove-piped approach does not lend itself to synergy and conciliation, and reflects the competitive and often antagonistic nature that is a part of the international community system.

Selecting indicators of change demands a shared understanding of a conflict, and a shared use of verification methods, that are applicable in a conflict situation. Conflict prevention and peace-building programming often depend on the identification of an end state. The value given to this end state may not be shared by all stakeholders or even those within a single program or organization. Perhaps contributing to the lack of engagement in ongoing projects is the disagreement around definitions of activities such as state-building and peace-building. There is little agreement among stakeholders around these terms, which may challenge the merits – or possibility – of any single, authoritative set of core metrics against which to measure progress, success, and effectiveness.

Most approaches within the international community's evaluation methodology focus on cause/effect relationships in order to create ideal conditions for peace. Across sectors there is widespread use of – but difficulties with – linear models of causality. It is impossible to prove that a change in the status of peace and conflict can be traced back to an intervention activity. It is difficult to separate the impact of peace-building projects from other impacts on conflict.

Time frames have been found to be unrealistic and inappropriate in relation to achieving intervention activity planning projections and actual outcomes. Too little time is allocated to achieve outcomes; thus benchmarks need to be established that are realistic and appropriate to the country context in which the reconstruction activities are based. There is a clear focus on qualitative verification rather than on quantitative approaches to measuring progress; and questions remain around priorities, how they are measured, and when the outcome and impacts of activities are *good enough*.

Better questions need to be asked and answered at the beginning of projects in order to adjust notions of *good enough*. Because of the belated attention given to the importance of the views of beneficiaries across all sectors in assessments, planning interventions, and inclusion in evaluations, there are now growing opportunities to include locals in measuring what matters in peace operations and civilian crisis management.

Traditionally, most westernized militaries have measured progress in terms of numbers, scores, and measures. It requires an ontological shift in thinking to move beyond numbers to narratives and what may matter more in peace operations and civilian crisis management. There are some methods, such as the Balanced Scorecard approach, that apply academic theory to military practice. When multiple national militaries, cultures, and professions join up to conduct peace operations, it is critical that there is some training to establish a deeper comprehension of the *other*. Such training helps to create a common understanding of the approaches and language used in measuring the success and progress of the fulfillment of a mandate.

Military commanders and civilian leaders – such as the Special Representative of the Secretary General (SRSG) and police commissioners – need to adopt the use of feedback focus groups in mission. Although it takes courage to be assessed, the use of feedback is helpful in conducting evaluations regarding the quality of intervention activity efforts. Militaries can adopt more flexible approaches to measuring activities and be mindful of an over-attachment to military doctrine, because this can be an obstacle in achieving progress.

Although the traditional military method of fulfilling a mandate has been somewhat inflexible, it is better to allow subordinate leadership to have the authority and flexibility to adjust intervention tasks as the context requires, provided their efforts support mission accomplishment. Militaries must understand that peace operations are a relationship between interveners and a host nation. The nature of these types of operations, therefore, is based upon a customer-provider relationship. This is a reciprocal relationship, not one-sided, and must be acknowledged to enable sustainable change within the environment of a peace operation. The host nation is a partner in the success and progress of peace operations and crisis management.

Policy Options

Many pressures influence the policy options for measuring what matters in peace operations and civilian crisis management. There are other demands, too, including those affecting decision-makers and bureaucrats working at the mercy of the linear, causal reporting and auditing systems of most governments and international organizations.

The following policy options are recommended for the development of an approach to measuring success, progress, and effectiveness in multi-stakeholder, multi-functional peace operations and civilian crisis management with the goal of contributing to the guidance, doctrine and policy of a common tradespace.

Cross-Cutting Themes

1. Recognize that the host nation and affected recipient populations are partners in the success and progress of peace operations and civilian crisis management.
2. Apply consistent measuring methods to multi-sectoral, multi-functional peace operations.
3. Based upon the hallmark conventions and processes of the 1990s and 2000s, continue progressive development and agreement among the United Nations, NATO, European Union, African Union, and other stakeholders on the scope, scale, actors, and remit of the international community regarding international invention, sovereignty, and the human security doctrine.
4. Coordinate and make available to the public all peace operations and crisis management evaluations and reports on progress, success, and effectiveness.
5. Provide hard-copy synopses and multimedia oral presentations of evaluations and reports to recipient populations within the environment of peace operations.
6. Design a peace operation and civilian crisis management measuring, reporting, and evaluation web-based repository accessible to the public. No membership required.
7. Focus on asking better questions regarding intervention goals rather than identifying better metrics and indicators. If the identification of metrics is the only default position, emphasis should be placed on local perceptions of the international community, effectiveness, progress, and performance.

Strategic Measurement

1. Include the multiplicity of stakeholders and sectors as well as the recipient populations in the assessment and planning stages of interventions;
2. Educate stakeholders regarding political consciousness – the awareness that intervention activities are never neutral. Political consciousness can assist in achieving successful and sustainable intervention strategies.

Practitioner Perspectives and Policy Options   225

3. Donors must adopt a flexible reporting mandate to allow for field realities to be accounted for, rather than rigidly meeting objectives that may no longer be valid. Although cause and effect linear methods of measuring have their use in financial auditing, embracing non-linear dynamics into systems of measuring is more useful in the complex environment of peace operations.

4. The standard use of objectives as benchmarks of performance may no longer be a valid approach to measuring what matters. Instead, finding a balance between quantitative and qualitative reporting methods that shifts away from organizational performance, towards addressing positive sustainable changes in the peace operations environment can become a normative method of measuring.

5. Develop and implement a structured training and education approach to understand the worldviews of the involved stakeholders and sectors. Training and education should be implemented prior to intervention activities. Training should be ongoing to support learning about involved stakeholders and sectors while functioning within a common tradespace. Training and education should be subsidized through the international community of states to encourage participation in underrepresented sectors such as humanitarians, civilian NGOs, and recipient populations.

6. Adopt the method and logic of an effects-based approach to operations with sustainable peace, rather than winning and goal-attainment, as the effects to achieve. EBAOs provide an approach to map outcomes and intended impacts of peace operations and civilian crisis management, which moves beyond the capacity of the existing outcome mapping tools in the development sector. EBAOs embrace non-linear dynamics and are not performance measurement systems.

Ontological Shifts

1. Focus on ideal conditions rather than end results.
2. Measuring tools should verify the process and ideal conditions for change. Evaluations that focus on verification are more feasible than evaluations that focus on measurement.
3. Measuring tools should include a balance of both quantitative and qualitative information such as social and cultural narratives and numbers and scores.
4. Locals (recipient populations) must be revisited and asked to identify measures of effectiveness from their perspectives.

5. Adopt and further develop the OECD DAC guidelines as the underpinning guidelines of measuring frameworks for peace operations and civilian crisis management.

6. The United Nations should develop an appropriate peace operations and civilian crisis management donor reporting framework.

7. The international community must ensure that the requisite international human resource capacity is put in place to manage a crisis in a manner that conforms to complex political questions of democratic norms, local ownership, and sound principles of governance and development.

8. Encourage the use of feedback focus groups regarding success, effectiveness, progress, and performance of the sectors and stakeholders involved in a peace operation or civilian crisis management. This type of ongoing feedback is helpful to assess the quality of intervention activity efforts.

9. An ontological shift in thinking is required among military, police, and civilians to move beyond numbers and linear models of measuring towards narratives and what may matter more in peace operations and civilian crisis management.

10. The implementation of measuring mechanisms should help stakeholders do their jobs better, rather than be a hindrance to fulfilling their role in peace operations and civilian crisis management.

11. Incentives can be used to encourage stakeholders with limited resources to adopt the existing measuring mechanisms and adjust it to their specific needs.

12. In-mission training should be provided to underscore the approaches, language, and terminology used in multi-national, multi-cultural, multi-sectoral, and multi-functional peace operations and civilian crisis management. This training will increase understanding of measuring success and progress in support of fulfilling mandates.

Notes

[1] Amartya Sen, *Identity and Violence*, 12.
[2] Sarah Meharg, "Clash of the Titans," 116.
[3] David Leakey, personal communication, 2008.
[4] Mary Ann Zimmerman, personal communication, 2008.
[5] Jason Ladnier, personal communication, 2008.
[6] Meharg, "Clash of the Titans," 130-1.
[7] Bonventre, "Monitoring and Evaluation," 72.

PART III

Entering a Common Tradespace

CHAPTER 15

Measuring Success in a Common Tradespace

Among the indications that a common tradespace has evolved is the focus on a *comprehensive* approach to operations. This emerging thinking sees international operations as joined up, harmonized, coordinated, clustered, and integrated in order to improve their overall effectiveness. A compendium of guidance, doctrine, and theory continues to be developed to inform comprehensive praxis. Distinguishing when a comprehensive approach – and therefore comprehensive measuring – is to be employed is a question for further study. This chapter focuses on the comprehensive intervention approach intended to increase the effectiveness of international interventions in the common tradespace, and the measuring challenges within the comprehensive approach.

The comprehensive approach has many different definitions throughout the sectors involved in peace operations and multinational crisis management operations. According to Friis and Jamyr, researchers at the Norwegian Institute of International Affairs (NUPI), "the comprehensive approach concept should be understood in the context of an increasingly complex and interdependent international conflict management system."[1] NATO, the EU, the United States, and Canada understand *comprehensive* as distinct from coordinated, commanded, controlled, harmonized, joined-up, 3D, whole of government, inter-agency, hybrid, and integrated approaches to operations. The comprehensive approach, literally, can be understood as the planned application and coordination of specialized capacities and powers of stakeholders in various autonomous, yet hinged, sectors, to a failing or failed environment through a coherent, efficient, sustainable, and legitimate agenda of activities, outcomes, and intended impacts to underpin long-term peace and security. In plain terms, because crisis environments are so complicated, it takes a concert of actors and capacities to achieve international peace and security goals – hence, the comprehensive approach. Growing from increasingly competitive and antagonistic agency rivalries working at cross-purposes, vying for funding, duplicating efforts with sub-optimal economies of scale, the comprehensive approach is touted as a solution to the continued poor success rates of interventions as measured in the sustainability of the systems produced as a result of these international interventions.[2]

Interestingly, mechanisms and tools have been developed to achieve greater harmonization and synchronization, yet there is no empirical evidence that a comprehensive approach will ensure a successful intervention. What the international community has discovered, however, is that incompatibilities, paradigm blindness, and competitiveness can indeed undermine the achievement of intervention goals. Whether it is true that no one agency can be successful alone in its intervention activities is irrelevant to the philosophy driving the comprehensive approach. What is relevant is the advent within the international community of a comprehensive approach paradigm that is competing against other intervention paradigms, in particular those of hegemonic powers such as the United States and China, as well as the autonomous humanitarian sector made up of unique, often divergent and competitive agencies.

National government departments and agencies have additional capacities to lend to the multi-dimensional characteristic of such operations. The idea of planning among government departments to improve intervention activities has been introduced variously as the *whole of government, interagency, joined up*, and *3D* approaches.[3] For example, the whole of government approach in Canada is operationalized by teaming up the Canadian International Development Agency (CIDA), Foreign Affairs and International Trade (DFAIT), and the Department of Defence, to bring their experience to bear in planning and executing peace operations and crisis management in deployment-specific activities. Even humanitarian stakeholders have bought into this logic, with the creation of the cluster approach.

This section reveals some of the underlying dynamics that constrain comprehensive approach synergies regarding measuring effectiveness, progress, and success.

An interview participant with the Council of the European Union joked that the term *joint* (as in joint action, joint approaches, and joint doctrine), despite being only five letters long, is too huge and difficult a process to achieve among stakeholders involved in peace operations and crisis management. John Borton, the founder of ALNAP, suggests there are various difficulties and challenges but also opportunities in developing a comprehensive – or joint – approach to measuring what matters. As each sector is in a transformational process of establishing sector-wide approaches, it is almost logical that it be sorted out and tested in order for sector maturation to occur. It may be premature to launch into a comprehensive approach to measuring what matters *prior* to maturation within each sector regarding why and how to measure their work. However, will each sector mature at the same rate and collectively adopt a comprehensive approach? Not likely.

In addition, no rigorous empirical evidence exists to substantiate the utility of a comprehensive approach to peace operations and crisis management in relation to other approaches. Only with empirical evidence suggesting that the comprehensive approach improves the quality of lives of the recipient populations will it be accepted as a valid approach by the humanitarian and development sectors involved in field operations. And this acceptance may not occur sector wide, as each sector remains heterogeneous in its policies, practices, and prejudice. There are no homogenous security or humanitarian sectors, just as there are no homogenous recipient populations in an affected area.

Scholars identify two schools regarding the comprehensive approach: integration and coordination. Each addresses the idea of comprehension in different ways. In the integrated approach,

> the aim is to develop systems, processes and structures that will ensure that all the different dimensions are integrated into one holistic effort. Such an effort will pursue integration at all levels, starting with concepts and principles. Once the various agents have a common vocabulary and understanding of the concepts (which implies developing new concepts together), they can start working together on a common understanding of their overall theory of change and operational doctrine. They will undertake an integrated assessment, do integrated planning, manage the implementation together and monitor and evaluate progress against pre-agreed indicators of progress.[4]

In this approach, sector-specific perspectives inform what is done, how it is done, and how it is measured. Jared Rigg, program officer, United Nations Security Sector Reform, says that because of the onset of the comprehensive approach, there may be undue pressure upon practitioners to use one set of comprehensive metrics or indicators for peace operations and crisis management. This may not be the best option: Rigg argues that it may weaken the process of measuring success in that there may be one lens through which to view the impacts of a comprehensive approach to operations.

The coordinated approach adheres to many of the integrated approach principles, yet requires far less integration and assuages Rigg's concerns.

> Instead, the coordinated approach favours utilizing the diversity of the actors as a way to manage the complexity, whilst pursing coherence through brining the various dimensions together at the country level. This approach values the advantages of independent action, and seeks to coordinate among them, rather than integrating them into a single, larger entity. The coordinated approach does not pursue coherence at all levels – only at the strategy country level, where there is a facilitated initiative to formulate common objectives and goals. It then encourages each agent to undertake its own operational or implementation planning, according to its own principles, mandates and resources, but in a coordinated fashion.[5]

Humanitarian and non-governmental stakeholders support the coordinated approach because it allows for freedom of action and independence, which is representative of their intervention worldviews. The security and defence sectors are familiar with command and control structures and are proponents of the integrated concept of the comprehensive approach.

Synergies between Stakeholders

Keane argues that there is a drive towards the *whole of government* approach, and therefore a requirement for integrated mechanisms that underpin the strengthening and formalization of synergies between stakeholders. However, he is quick to note that there are three fundamental challenges with the whole of government approach that are not yet clearly mapped out. They are *structural, cultural,* and *financial.*

Structurally, all departments and agencies that make up the whole of government approach have distinct systems and structures through which they make decisions and implement programs, projects, and activities. These systems are not shared among departments, and often cause divergence in attempts to work together. For example, the ways in which a department of foreign affairs makes its decisions is wholly different than how a defence department functions. According to Major General Mike Ward, Canadian Forces, "When we [Department of National Defence] sit down with DFAIT and do planning, the bottom line is that we all share the agenda of making good in the world. We need to be careful to subordinate our respective departments' interests to the greater whole of government/comprehensive approach. It doesn't always work that way. The comprehensive approach takes humility and patience. There are always tensions between the departments, but you can get to work effectively together."[6]

The challenge of subordinating agendas to forward a comprehensive approach is exacerbated at the level of the international community interventions, such as NATO's International Security Assistance Force (ISAF). Colonel Andre Harvey, Canadian Forces, argues this point: "Before crisis management operations, the military was the master in the theatre of operations. This has transformed, and the military is no longer in the seat of power and no longer makes all the decisions. Using ISAF as an example, it is not a military operation but requires all actors, who all have their own responsibilities, and also a shared responsibility to the operation. How do you measure success or effectiveness in this type of operation?"[7]

Each stakeholder also has an inherent set of indicators for success. Diplomacy indicators are not comparable to judicial indicators, and the time scales at which these indicators are measured are not inter-operable or inter-sectoral. Culturally – which is proving to be the biggest challenge to approaching harmonized problem solving and implementation– each stakeholder within the whole of government approach has a distinct worldview and concomitant intervention set of expectations, which cause antagonism, fear, and sometimes even hatred. Some stakeholders have developed alternate modalities through which to identify, while others remain fixed on outdated identities that may no longer serve their work in contemporary crisis and calamity environments, and further increase tensions, especially the perceived competition between sectors such as humanitarians and military professionals.

Not surprisingly, this clash of worldviews and expectations informs national department agendas. For Ian Higginbotham, government departments contributing to the same international intervention project have very different objectives to meet, and this impacts the ways in which synergies can be formalized or systematized. For example, says Higginbotham, "in Canada, the Department of National Defence is involved in Afghanistan to win hearts and minds and gain consent, which comes directly from counter-insurgency theory. The Canadian International Development Agency is mandated to improve the quality of the lives of Afghans, while the Department of Foreign Affairs and International Trade is involved in governance and promoting democratic values." Although they are partners in the whole of government approach, each seeks to get something different out of each project they are collectively involved in (Figure 34).

FIGURE 34
Government Departments Approach Interventions from Different Perspectives

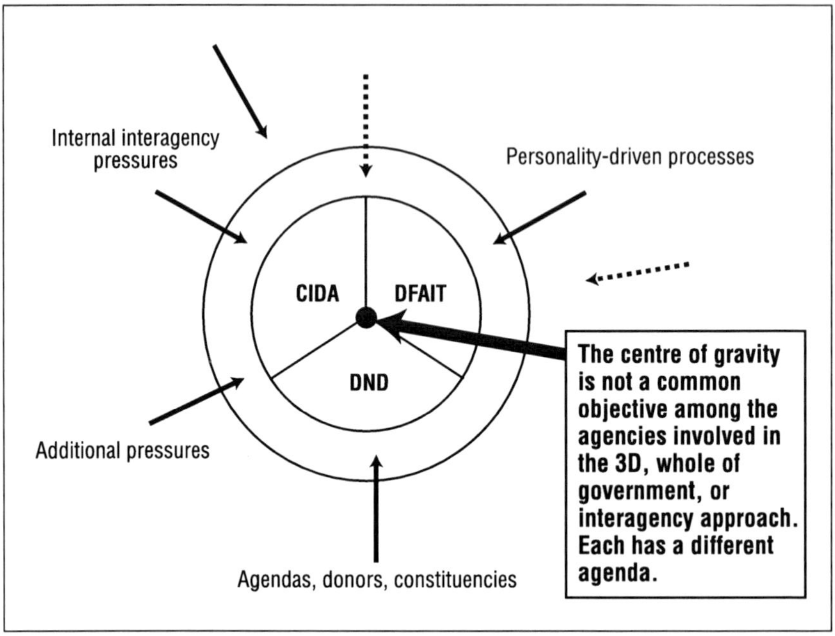

- Internal interagency pressures
- Personality-driven processes
- CIDA
- DFAIT
- DND
- Additional pressures
- Agendas, donors, constituencies
- The centre of gravity is not a common objective among the agencies involved in the 3D, whole of government, or interagency approach. Each has a different agenda.

Higginbotham says that in measuring results, it is easier to track one discreet aspect of a project than the whole. This parsing out "offers each partner a clearer perspective on their work as they go about measuring their results."[8] However, it is not clear whether measuring the parts informs the results of the whole. Moreover, the complicated nature of interventions, and the complexity of outcomes and impacts, suggest that the successes of sector-specific activities *do not equal* the success of a sector-wide comprehensive approach and the cumulative success of this approach in terms of sustainable peace and security. Rather, the efficacy of the comprehensive approach must be measured through a sector-wide lens.

For one high-ranking European Union interview participant, "the problem is that synergies are still a personality-driven process and humans are very poor at this; synergies are very related to personal interests (ego). Even Mother Theresa pointed this out in her own life."[9]

Yet successful comprehensive interventions are thought to be underpinned by synergies between stakeholders – both at the strategic organizational level and the tactical, person-to-person level. Synergies are understood as those behaviours and practices – formal, informal, or spontaneous – that improve coordination, cooperation, harmonization, and collaboration between and among the stakeholders active in interventions. Comprehensive operations assume that synergies are in place to strengthen mandates, missions, and objectives. However, there is so far little if any empirical evidence to substantiate the notion that comprehensive operations are indeed more effective than more traditional non-integrated operations. The international community is placing great emphasis on the efficacy of comprehensive operations; however, there is no evidence (except anecdotal) that suggests this is the best option for contemporary international interventions. A high-ranking European Union interview participant suggests with a hint of sarcasm that synergy is somehow *implied* in joint action within military forces. The notion of joint forces is in itself a worldview, and this is the difficulty referred to by this interview participant.

Strategic Level Synergies

At the strategic level, understood as headquarters or national level, there are ways in which synergies among stakeholders are building regarding measuring comprehensive, or joined-up, intervention activities. According to a UN political officer, processes and approaches related to United Nations Integrated Missions, such as coordination and harmonization, tend to derail the requirement to measure and evaluate missions.[10] It seems that this is not a unique phenomenon, and that it exists at the national level, too. For example, "each one of the US Government agencies is so interested in self-assessments that they tend to compete as opposed to cooperate."[11]

Canada's Stabilization and Reconstruction Task Force (START) has developed the use of video-conferencing with its European Union counterparts to share information and informally report on progress in field operations. Although START shares information with the United States's S/CRS and the United Kingdom's SU, and EU Crisis Management organizations,[12] there appears to be no clear inter-operable system of assessment between Canadian departments involved in the 3D approach to operations.

By nature, international interventions have a higher level of complexity than those of national government departments or organizational headquarters. David Chuter suggests this is because there are a greater number of actors with competing agendas and mission caveats constraining potential synergies.[13]

Synergies can be undermined at the agreement level of peace and conflict interventions, but as Rory Keane points out, there were positive synergies among the "development stakeholders regarding the European Union's Cotonou Agreement, the EU African Strategy (which is like a compact), United Nation's In Larger Freedom, the Millennium Declaration (which was never operationalized) and the Millennium Development Goals (MDGs) which are clear indicators of progress and success that are cross-cutting among and between stakeholders."[14] However, according to Keane, the Afghan Compact does not cover peace operations or stability operations and so cannot be a synergistic rallying point for NATO partners and collaborators. There are no indicators coming out of the Afghan Compact that are relevant to NATO. Thus NATO has had to function outside of the Compact framework and develop their own indicators of progress and success. Even so, the documents and agreements cited by Keane and others indicate a growing compendium of guidance that directs the common tradespace and the comprehensiveness of our activities there.

Colonel Brad Bergstrand, Canadian Forces, suggests: "There are lots of discussion and exchanges of information, but no formal system because I believe that each country would want the raw data and to do their own analysis, or at least get analyses from more than one source. Measurement results provided by a certain country may reflect a certain national bias that may not be helpful in making national decisions."

The French Ministry of Foreign Affairs engages with other stakeholders through the European Union engagement exercises on implementation of the EU Council Resolution on Fragile States. This helps to increase synergies with other stakeholders such as the EU, OECD, and UNDP.[15]

It appears from these observations that there are fewer synergies at the strategic level than expected.

Field Synergies

According to some field practitioners, synergies do not really exist in practice, except for those that are informal and personality driven.[16] Some practitioners are not aware of any formal synergies with measuring systems in the field,[17] which indicates that the various military forces use their own measuring systems, while police, humanitarians, and developers are indeed working with their own intra-sector measurement frameworks. At the organizational level, there are mechanisms for working together to share information about progress and success. The International Crisis Group, for example, is a member of the European Peacebuilding Liaison Office (EPLO), where it has access to approximately twenty-five other NGOs with whom they share membership and collaborate, at least on a superficial level.[18] In addition, the ICG distributes its reports free of charge because staff want other stakeholders to use them to inform their own frameworks for measuring their activities. After ICG releases its monthly and annual reports, staff attempt to find synergies with other stakeholders, in order to advocate for various levels of intervention in conflict societies. ICG is the first to admit that it is tricky to be sharing field information before the formal public release of field reports. They do keep reports private and internal prior to formal release.

Another way that the ICG creates synergies in the field is through the field consultation process that is integral to their research and report writing. The purpose of consistent field consultations is to meet with stakeholders including military and civilian police, officials, local population, and international workers to better understand their perspective on the localized peace and conflict dynamics upon which ICG regularly reports. According to ICG representatives, the various stakeholder representatives involved in their field reporting often deliberate openly what they cannot say internally to their own organizations. The ICG sees its role as that of a third party gathering information to provide a more comprehensive view of the peace and conflict dynamics in a particular region.[19] However, other field practitioners are quick to point out that the ICG is critical of stakeholders, be they the UN, NATO, EU, or non-state actors, whose role in a specific conflict situation could be improved.[20]

Some practitioners complain that the ICG does not capture the entire picture in its reports, and despite attempts to improve interventions, some that have been highlighted by the ICG as not doing enough in the face of the conflict dynamics in a particular country are reticent to share information with the ICG in future. This reaction impacts the potential synergies that the ICG has created over the years building networks in the field through their regionally based analysts. ICG analysts are hired because of their local expertise, language, writing skills, prior publications, and peer review. The organization now conducts ICG annual training in Brussels for new analysts to learn about report writing, how to conduct interviews, how to track information, how to maintain knowledge levels, and how to conduct day-to-day reporting methods that contribute to their monthly reports.[21]

Others see no synergies among the stakeholders in mission areas.[22] An Italian general who served in Afghanistan observes, "[In the field] I think there is a disconnectedness that is rather frightful and this is because there is no overarching leadership within the international community and in certain cases not even within national ones."[23]

A high-level civilian NATO planner suggests there needs to be a "super-envoy" to create the necessary synergies to coordinate the plans and the measures for an integrated stakeholder approach. This would formally shape behaviours and practices and provide centrally focused measures of effectiveness. Sandy Blyth, chief of staff, EU JUST LEX, echoes the NATO planner's argument. He suggests that in Bosnia-Herzegovina, High Representative Paddy Ashdown created coherence and a level of synergy between the multiplicity of key actors involved in the mission area through the Office of the High Representative (OHR).[24] In the view of Anthony Cordesman, a US security strategist, there is no central authority in many operational environments that provides comprehensive reporting on progress.[25] Blyth argues that the mechanism of a super-envoy should be adopted whenever possible in all mission areas of operations to create better communication across the spectrum of stakeholders, and perhaps lend itself to measuring progress and success. This type of systemization of communication would help to create better, more coordinated, and coherent synergies between the key actors in theatre and ultimately should make for better economic development, reconstruction, institution building, and even should help in the fight against the pervasiveness of all aspects of major and organized crime that so often impact crisis-torn areas.[26]

Tony Sheridan, former head of International Policing, UK Ministry of Defence Police, says that he is not convinced that there is a comprehensive approach to crisis management with the logical systematic synergies to support such an approach. To drive his point home, Sheridan explains that "there are no less than four databases in Kosovo alone just for capturing intelligence; so there is no comprehensive approach." Synergies are about trust, he says, and when trust does not exist in the field, then potential synergies are lost.[27] A high-ranking interview participant reiterates Sheridan's point by suggesting that it is imperative to employ local companies in reconstruction efforts because this creates trust and improves synergies.

According to international affairs expert Cedric de Coning, the underpinning principle driving the comprehensive approach is "get together so we can do things better." Yet while a comprehensive approach is relatively easy from a theoretical perspective, it is not so from a practitioner's approach[28] because there is a "policy-reality" gap in the comprehensive approach: inappropriate management philosophies, processes, and tools despite the policy drive for cohesion, synergy, and comprehension.[29] "Comprehensive" means better, more efficient and effective operations, equalling more impact.[30] This approach can be thought of as an *interdependent* system of *independent* stakeholders causing collective and cumulative effects that build momentum for peace over time. However, the obstacle remains that a comprehensive approach is easy from a theoretical perspective, but not from a practitioner's. Perhaps, then, a comprehensive approach is about *awareness* of other actors, even if they cannot coordinate or work with one another – in effect, "understanding each other so you can do things better."

If a planned comprehensive approach is on the horizon (versus a reactive one), what are the incentives – rather than the costs – for coordination under this rubric? This begs the question of how comprehensive should the comprehensive approach be, and for whom is the comprehensive approach intended. If it is merely to create increased efficiencies within the international community of states and organizations, then a sector-wide approach can be considered. If such an approach is intended to increase the efficacy of peace and stability writ large, the approach must include host nations and recipient populations. It follows that the international community would need to think very seriously about how comprehensive achievements are to be assessed and by whom. The question of true inclusion of recipient populations in the planning, implementation, and measuring of the comprehensive approach is salient to the ongoing development of this approach.

Comprehensive Policy Options

Perhaps, then, *intra*-sector approaches to assessing overall effectiveness, progress, and success may equally apply to *inter*-sector comprehensive approaches to peace operations and crisis management. Expanding John Borton's humanitarian-specific analysis to encompass the full spectrum of sectors (military, police, government, civilian, private industry, academics, etc.) suggests that a common measuring mechanism and concomitant vocabulary of effectiveness, progress, and success could potentially provide inter-sector benchmarks against which stakeholders could compare their own performance within a broader, performance-based approach.[31] Moreover, the process of developing an inter-sectoral (or comprehensive) mechanism could improve connections between sectors and highlight gaps in activities in a more holistic approach. In addition, it could serve to clarify those issues and areas that are within the control and influence of a sector and those that lie outside its purview, or that overlap other sectors, as in the case of the shared military and humanitarian space.[32] Similar challenges arise in the potential development of an intra-sector performance measurement.

According to John Borton, the methodological and technical challenges of collating and handling different sources of information and data for measuring efficacy could prove too difficult within a sector, let alone in an inter-sector approach. Such a costly process would have political hurdles to overcome in all of the sectors involved in operations, and not all stakeholders in the common tradespace would be willing to participate. Thus the mechanism could be obliged to proceed with incomplete information and/or support within a sector. Consensus around the comprehensive approach could be lost during the development process, thereby reducing utility of the mechanism, quality of the available data and information, and funding to support the use of the mechanism. However, some of these challenges could be avoided by applying a similar logic as the Humanitarian Accountability Partnership's Standard in Humanitarian Accountability and Quality Management, a comprehensive verification approach to success, progress, and effectiveness. This system uses a simple but effective inter-sector quality management system that can be adopted by all stakeholders. It is rooted in a set of peace and security principles that drives and shapes the comprehensive approach of its adherents and by which they voluntarily elect to be held to account.[33]

The Technology Horizon

If an inter-sector approach to measuring macro success in peace operations and crisis management is valid, it will require systems to support inter-agency linkages among stakeholders, organizations, and other members of the international community.[34] Microsoft Word is a useful example to highlight a point made by Jason Ladnier, of the US State Department. In the early to mid-1990s, it was common to receive email attachments that were indecipherable. The only system to open these word processing documents was in a Plain Text format on a PC. In my own experience at the Royal Military College of Canada, I would receive a document via email from a colleague in France and not be able to view it except as a series of symbols and signs that made no sense whatsoever. I would send my attachment to the poor souls in IT services, who would attempt to make sense of the document by opening it in successive word programming softwares including WordPro, Macintosh for Windows, Linux, and PDF. Over time, it became logical that people and institutions adopt a single operating system – or at least systems that could fluidly inter-operate with one another. Only with the widespread acceptance of a common operating system – Microsoft Word[35] – did this problem eventually disappear. The system allowed all users to communicate using the same language, format, and speed. With variations on a theme, users became able to choose their preferences within the common operating system and were still able to share documents despite their preference differences. This operating platform is now globally accepted and increases the effectiveness of our computer work. Microsoft Word and its compendium of tools such as Excel, Outlook, and others provide a comprehensive solution to written communications born from problems of incompatibilities.

Cheaper, more flexible, IT-based systems (perhaps open source) may be on the nearer horizon, which would mean that all organizations, no matter how resource poor, would be able to harmonize and align within their own sectors consistently over time to add to the quality and quantity of data against which they can measure their activity successes and shortfalls.

In the end, *connections* and *understanding* between and among sectors – whether touted as comprehensive, synchronized, harmonized, integrated, coordinated, clustered, inter-agency, whole of government, or joint – improve the efficacy and sustainability of peace operations and civilian crisis management and permit transparent measuring processes. To abandon the task of improving the comprehensive approach and other interoperable structures would make useless the billions of dollars already invested in the process of achieving sustainable peace. To leave this work unfinished would cost trillions of dollars in real costs. By improving interventions through the efficiencies lauded in the comprehensive approach, the international community can finally offer true protection to the world's citizens.

Notes

[1] Friis and Jarmyr, eds., "Comprehensive Approach," 11.
[2] de Coning, "Coherence and Coordination," 5.
[3] The three "Ds" are understood as the departments of defence, diplomacy, and development and include other departments and agencies such as Justice, Corrections, and Police.
[4] de Coning, "Coherence and Coordination," 5; Friis and Jarmyr, eds., "Comprehensive Approach," 15.
[5] de Coning, "Coherence and Coordination," 5; and Friis and Jarmyr, eds., "Comprehensive Approach, 15.
[6] Mike Ward, personal communication, 2008.
[7] Andre Harvey, personal communication, 2008.
[8] Ian Higginbotham, personal communication, 2008.
[9] Anonymous, personal communication, 2008.
[10] Ibid.
[11] Mike Ward, personal communication, 2008.
[12] Brad Bergstrand. Personal communication, 2008.
[13] David Chuter, personal communication, 2008.
[14] Rory Keane, personal communication, 2008.

[15] Anonymous, personal communication, 2008.
[16] Emery Brusset, personal communication, 2008.
[17] Brad Bergstrand, personal communication, 2008.
[18] Neil Campbell, personal communication, 2008.
[19] Ibid.
[20] Anonymous, personal communication, 2008.
[21] Ibid.
[22] Timothy Lannan, personal communication, 2008.
[23] Anonymous, personal communication, 2008.
[24] Alexander Blyth, personal communication, 2008.
[25] Cordesman, *Armed Nation Building*, 3.
[26] Alexander Blyth, personal communication, 2008.
[27] Tony Sheridan, personal communication, 2008.
[28] Anonymous, personal communication, 2008.
[29] Cedric de Coning, personal communication, 2008.
[30] de Coning, *The United Nations and the Comprehensive Approach*.
[31] Borton, "Inventory of the Principal Projects."
[32] For an in-depth analysis of the shared military and humanitarian space, see Sarah Meharg, ed., *Helping Hands and Loaded Arms*.
[33] Borton, "Inventory of the Principal Projects."
[34] Jason Ladnier, personal communication, 2008.
[35] Although there are many who do not subscribe to the economic and political agenda of Microsoft, and use other intuitive operating platforms such as Macintosh Windows, this argument remains valid.

CHAPTER 16

Emerging Trends in a Common Tradespace

It is relatively easy to determine success of peace operations at the macro level.[1] Lives are being saved, or they are not. Stability is either present, or it is not. And it is either facilitating democratic transformation, or not. However, perceiving operational success as black and white progress towards peace and stability seems overly simplistic, especially in the global security environment, categorized by most theorists and practitioners as incalculably complex.

Pessimism about the trends affecting peace operations and crisis management is high. When asked what future trends they saw on the near horizon, many interview participants were caught short. Some made wild suggestions about the collapse of the global system of states, while others were so neutral about the emergence of change that there was reason for speculation on my part. Some participants, however, made attempts to home in on the challenges and opportunities that await the next mission, the next deployment, and the next development project. These are highlighted in the next few pages.

Civilian Policing

According to Vic Josey, superintendent, Royal Canadian Mounted Police, pre-project technical assessments must be a future requirement to determine strength and number of personnel a mission should have.

Currently these pre-project assessments are not as efficient and complete as they should be. Within civilian police deployments, there is a requirement to conduct thorough needs analysis to determine what is needed and in what numbers to best effect change in failed states.[2] According to Josey, "Quality should trump quantity every time – there is a belief that 80 percent of the work [on a mission] is completed by 20 percent of the personnel, and of that, about 80 percent of the work completed is for internal purposes and only 20 percent to serve external needs. Some of this is unavoidable, but there is a lot of room for improvement to ensure that a larger percentage of time is committed to tasks that assist indigenous police services."[3]

Glenn MacPhail, a retired member of the Royal Canadian Mounted Police, concurs, suggesting that real assessments will be a necessity in the future as the face of policing changes.[4] Police missions are growing in number, size, complexity, cost, and time to complete.[5] MacPhail believes that the current UN predilection for high numbers of police contributed, rather than the quality of those same police, will be the downfall of future missions. For MacPhail, the quality, not the quantity, of police on a United Nations mission is the critical element for sustainable success.[6] As Dave Beer, chief superintendent, RCMP, says, it is easy to teach police how to handcuff a person; the hard part is teaching them to handcuff the right person. "This isn't rocket science," says Beer. "It's policing!"[7] With this comment, Beer listed off the key components required for training post-conflict police, including the general skills, the specific skills, language, and culture, and the time required to achieve learning objectives. With authority steeped in experience, he observed, "This stuff should be basic and prescriptive, but it is painfully obvious that it is not working."[8]

The United Nations, with the influence of key police practitioners and theorists, is becoming more concerned that the quality of policing will be reduced within more complex and complicated environments because of the types of police being deployed. Police deployments require improvements in many aspects. To address improvements, better performance measuring – perhaps adopted from military experience – will be useful in deploying the right police to the right areas to do the right things in culturally appropriate contexts.

Beer says that there are some bright ideas influencing the ways in which civilian police are deployed to the world's hot spots. According to Beer, Mark Krocker, former senior political advisor at UNDPKO, proposed a smart plan for a UN permanent staff group of two teams of twenty-five personnel to start up every mission. If the mission was to be stood up, the experts were sent in to develop the policing programs, procedures, goals, and objectives. This was a great concept and would have been much more efficient in that it would reduce to a few days/weeks what normally takes months to complete with a multi-national team. Beer maintains that it would create a start and end of a mission as an accountability mechanism, which is the most important missing factor in police missions. Krocker's floating team would cycle through the roster of UN missions and steer things and get things on track. "It was a brilliant idea," says Beer. "The first problem was that he tried to implement this at the UN and therefore was only permitted to go half-way on the development of the idea. Five years later, the system still wasn't implemented." Yet Beer says, "We can't blame the UN, because it is the only mechanism that we have. No one can do it all by themselves."[9]

Military

Tim Lannan, a retired Canadian Forces officer currently working for a regional security organization, suggests that in the future, militaries involved in reconstruction and stabilization should adopt the time frame for change relevant to development. Adjusting our short-term gains lens of success and progress towards longer-term sustainable peace is a sea change for militaries involved in reconstructing Afghanistan. "Every unit goes into theatre wanting to make their own mark, and then they leave and the next rotation arrives wanting to make their own mark," says Lannan. "This does not correlate with the plan. Sometimes there is no plan." He is prescient of future trends when he frames commander success criteria as a pitfall of short rotations in areas in which development time frames are required for real change to occur. According to Lannan, each new commander arriving in theatre sets "Mission Success Criteria" in order to motivate the troops to do something that puts their own mark on that rotation. Unfortunately, these criteria are not necessarily a part of the plan for reconstruction and stabilization and are often established to raise troop morale and allow commanders to put their stamp on their rotation – to make it their own. Worse, work that may have been accomplished by a previous commander often is not pursued or built upon by new commanders. Despite these obstacles, Lannan sees holistic, inclusive approaches to measuring effectiveness of missions as the key to improving the lives of recipient populations.[10] Measuring the effectiveness of the overall mission plan in places like Afghanistan is undermined by variances to the plan; however, plans require adjusting during the process of implementation to achieve flexibility, adaptability, survivability, scalability, modifiability, and robustness.

Major General Mike Ward, Canadian Forces, suggests that there will be a trend and tendency towards the comprehensive approach and improved civil-military cooperation. In his view there will be more shocks to the global system of systems, which will affect the ways in which militaries undertake missions: "We need to deduce alternate futures. Evaluation and validation is using the best information from current operations to project forward; then trying to apply metrics and measures of effectiveness, such as time, distance, speed, and precision. These are the precise parameters that become measures to ensure that the Canadian Forces are flexible and multi-purpose twenty to thirty years out from now."[11]

Civilian

For a UN political adviser with deep field experience, the changing face of missions from traditional to hybridized is a transference of power for the UN. "We don't know how to evaluate the mission [in Darfur] because the start-up (mission launch phase) has been difficult because we are integrating the African Union and the UN systems. At some point an evaluation will have to be completed (for the headquarter level)."[12] This interview participant, with some frustration, suggested that the UN does not know how to measure these new missions. Is it their efficiency that should be assessed, or the harmony between the two converging elements of the African Union and the UN? "We are pushed to do a hybrid mission. Will we ever have another hybrid mission? When there are two command structures, such as the AU and UN mission in Darfur, what are the issues of command and control? What is the chain of command? What is the reporting structure?" For this political adviser, the typical ways in which the UN deploys – even to the world's worst environments – are not valid in Darfur, which eventually impacts the ways in which the UN measures its effectiveness in Darfur. "Darfur is a very hostile environment. How do we settle our UN staff in such an insecure environment? There is no logistical support from member states. There is no water, no accommodation for people. How do we make this mission more effective? We really need to ask ourselves how."[13]

Such hostile environments, non-permissive by their very nature, are difficult places for the civilian components of peace operations and crisis management to function and be effective in achieving their objectives, let alone in measuring their processes and achievements for their donors. Ian Higginbotham, Canadian Department of Foreign Affairs and International Trade, suggests that governments will soon look at their development work in hostile environments with formative and summative evaluations at the project level: "As peace and security programming has found its groove at the international level, they will begin to have more standards for evaluation and auditing."[14] For others, measurement frameworks should be flexible tools that come from the grassroots of an operation. A delegate of the French Ministère des Affaires

Etrangères et Européennes offers, "This ground-up approach engages our people in the field who are aware of the realities of the intervention activities. We are convinced that the strategic thinking must come from the ground – and that this is a necessity in measuring the success of our activities."[15]

For Rory Keane, Organisation for Economic Co-operation and Development, a key question underpinning the quest to better measure the effectiveness of peace operations is whether the international community is engendering peace or stabilization. Keane suggests that these are two very different concepts that require variations in processes, means, and ways. Of utmost concern to Keane is the dearth of qualitative approaches, as well as some of the reasons supporting this dearth: "The UN quantitative approach to MOEs supports the UN getting more money to stay in countries longer. More qualitative measures need to be injected into the quantitative MOEs for peace operations. We need to establish co-measurement tools with partner governments in the field (in the whole of government approach). This will inject field realities into the MOE process."[16] Rory Keane and Stephan Massing suggest that a common tradespace could be further strengthened by increasing joint-partner projects and jointly monitoring progress with partnering countries. The mutuality and jointness of the tradespace they outline seeks out equilibrium between sectors and stakeholders.

As the international community continues to place emphasis on state building, Keane points to the *state-society interface*, observing that a state can exist for service delivery to its citizens, or exist for power. Keane suggests there will be massive urbanization over the next few years – 50-75 percent mass migration to cities around the world – which may cause new *city states* to emerge. These city states may exist to serve their citizens, but may attempt to flex power and even deny international interventions to save lives. Keane asks: "Will we shift to a pre-Westphalian understanding [of sovereignty]? How will donors work with interventions into these new city states?"[17] Sovereignty then becomes important in emerging missions as the world's population recalibrates itself to the new unit of statehood: the urban powers.

Missions Are Doing Too Much

Based on the interviews conducted for this project, peace operations missions are trying to achieve too much. Missions have been asked to be *all-encompassing* – and are expected to include all scales and elements of state building – yet there are rarely enough *means* contributed to meet the political objectives, and the ways to achieve these objectives are often misdirected or misapplied. Although the Report of the Panel on United Nations Peace Operations, released in 2000 and dubbed the "Brahimi Report," represents a positive shift in thinking regarding linking up means and ends of peacekeeping missions, the recommendations remain difficult to operationalize, let alone measure. Chuter argues: "Mission objectives must always be agreed upon at the political level and linkages made between the political end state and the mission means. We may be at the point where the pendulum is swinging back towards simpler operations, and the activities that are difficult to measure will be dropped from the mandate."

Measuring systems have not kept ahead of day-to-day operational imperatives within the context of peace operations and crisis management. Ad hoc and under-funded measuring of effectiveness, progress, and success is the norm. Moreover, there is no clear understanding between and among stakeholders of what are effective and successful peace operations. In addition, there is little transference of traditional financial auditing frameworks normed against the longer-term behavioural, attitudinal, and quality of life changes in recipient populations. Most sectors have been slow to acknowledge the importance of the views and opinion of its clients – the populations affected by conflicts and natural disasters. Although the so-called "bean-counters" have not made any obvious shift, there have been shifts in some sectors that move the so-called *beneficiaries* or *affected populations* to the centre of the decision-making and implementation process.

According to Colonel Brad Bergstrand, Canadian Forces, there are ways in which a rebalance can occur. The Multi-National Experimentation process (MNE), a coordinated and thematic bi-annual experiment among NATO nations, is proving to provide some solutions to this issue. The MNE process, now in its sixth biannual cycle, builds close international cooperation; however, Bergstrand is hesitant to suggest whether such cooperation will yield any changes. He further points out that cooperation will not extend to real measures of effectiveness: "We are most likely going to slide back into measuring the easy stuff. When we go to ask for more money, [quantitative] indicators are the easy numbers to support our requests. In a way we get stuck, because we have to present a case for funding (with aims and objectives for our activities) before we are on the ground. The up-front plan is based on the best information that we have access to at the time to justify expenditure of resources. However, this plan may not relate to the realities on the ground. We in effect set up the goals and objectives up front. There is a process to update the plan when we assess the resources or need to request additional funding/resources."

While UN and other peace operations missions continue to attempt to do too much through wide-lens mandates, other stakeholders are adopting the "do-more" approach in the ever-competing space of peace operations and crisis management. Crisis-affected environments mean less precise boundaries between stakeholders and their roles – soldiers are humanitarians, developers are doing post-conflict reconstruction, diplomats are working in development. David Chuter uses a Christmas tree analogy to describe the effects of this growing competition and overlap: "Everyone wants to put an ornament on the Christmas tree. This becomes lethally dangerous when it happens all at the same time. This causes fratricide between the various mission elements because there is too much competition all at once, and the tendency is to kill the other rather than work with the other."[18]

While the means and ends may not be aligned, and mandates may not be fully supported by political will, another expectation expressed by stakeholders is a core challenge: time.[19] Expectations are high regarding what can be accomplished on mission, but there is never enough time to meet the expectations described in the mandates. We collectively expect to establish tenable peace and security in war-affected environments, yet these expectations are too high. Rarely has the international community achieved peace writ large.

Measuring Actual Effectiveness

Although measuring *actual* effectiveness is a relatively unmined activity, measuring has been attractive to stakeholders for two reasons. Based on an interview with an high-ranking European Council representative, honest measuring can lead to improving situations and effects – and less-than-honest measuring may lead to increased funding or budget allocations. Indicators can be misleading or be falsely set up to make intervention activities appear to be successful. The proper use of statistics is a real issue in measuring success; measuring without a proper interpretation of results risks leading to black and white conclusions. To avoid this, a measuring system is required that is scientific but has human intuition built into it. There must be a balance between science and intuition.[20] Many of these points are further underpinned by Mary Ann Zimmerman, US Department of State's Office of the Coordinator for Reconstruction and Stabilization, who argues that the development world has a tendency to "tick boxes" when reporting and measuring. It is output oriented and based on report writing. What is harder is the *analysis* of the data that is gathered. Data analysis is not fed into the management of activities; rather, it is fed up the food chain in the form of reporting.

Analysis is not linked to management of projects, and there is a dependency on "near-term outputs."[21]

The development and implementation of measures of effectiveness for peace operations may have to be done by the military despite the constraints this puts on the production of knowledge in the area of progress, success, and effectiveness.[22] Western militaries have a decidedly developed capacity in this area of expertise. Military planners will have to expand their thinking regarding the social and cultural effects of peace operations and crisis management activities, because the operational environment is rapidly changing and developments are moving faster than ever before.[23] Perhaps the lynchpin for the military regarding measuring the social and cultural effects of intervention activities is effects-based thinking. In Effects-Based Approach to Operations (EBAO), everything that the military inputs into the model has an impact; the significance of impact, however, is not necessarily calculated using EBAO, yet it creates a map of potential impacts across the spectrum of operations. If other sectors began using the same sort of model, this could result in the ability to map the wider impact of the minutiae accomplished through peace operations and crisis management. As in the evaluation of science experiments, when conducting evaluations of intervention activities only a small aspect of a problem is examined. This, as most scientists suggest, can lead to a fictitious but well-structured representation of the problem under examination.[24] It is not possible to measure all aspects of an intervention activity because not all outcomes, impacts, and effects can be identified during the planning stages of an intervention. There is widespread acknowledgement that it is improbable to be able to measure the *actual* longer-term impacts in the field due to the inability to examine the whole, resulting in a recalibration towards readiness and capacity rather than effects.[25] What is needed is an integrated way of thinking about effects across the spectrum of conflict and intervention.[26]

Next Steps

As understanding between and among stakeholders increases, a way forward can be based on opportunities rather than historical, ideological, political, or identity constraints. Some stakeholders are seen by other stakeholders as inflexible within the complicated environment of peace operations and civilian crisis management, especially regarding measuring interventions. In addition, any measuring synergies between stakeholders is chalked up to be personality driven rather than caused by standardized, duplicatable measuring approaches. One high-ranking official at the European Union said, "I do not think there are any synergies between international actors regarding measuring success; on the contrary, I think there is a disconnectedness that is rather frightful and this is because there is no overarching leadership within the international community, and in certain cases, not even within national ones. The problem is that synergies are still a personality-driven process and humans are very poor at this; synergies are *very* related to personal interests (ego). Even Mother Theresa pointed this out in her own life."[27]

As western defence structures such as the US military, the Canadian Forces, and EU member militaries continue to shift their perspectives in response to the changing nature of international community interventions, so too there is a shift in how they measure effectiveness, progress, and success. Militaries are now concerned with effectiveness beyond their own performance. This is a shift away from the auditing approach towards a more inclusive worldview of the sectors involved in operations, not just those of the traditional military and defence actors.

In contrast, the humanitarian sector is not viewed by other stakeholders as adapting itself to the complicated intervention environment, or to the ways in which its organizations measure their activities. Unfortunately, what is perceived by other stakeholders suggests that humanitarian organizations are functioning with outdated understandings of operational realities that impede their ability to serve recipient populations in peace operations and civilian crisis management.

The humanitarian community has an opportunity to better inform other stakeholders of progress made by adopting new frameworks for measuring overall performance (rather than merely placating individual donors). As well, humanitarian agencies and organizations have the opportunity to demonstrate greater flexibility working alongside defence and security actors in the changing operational environment.

To further complicate comprehensive progress, the security and defence sectors often perceive NGOs as unorganized, lacking leadership, and being without a clear voice or guidelines. These perceptions exist despite the challenges that face humanitarian stakeholders regarding measuring their multi-faceted intervention activities – which are rarely as clearly defined as military and security activities. Humanitarians are viewed as a homogenous group of actors, while in reality this sector is the most disparate of all those involved in interventions. Some of their challenges include functioning within the often violent context existing in pre- and post-conflict societies; the multiple multi-national, multi-functional, and competitive stakeholders in theatre; political and economic agendas of the international community; perceived "takeover" agendas of the military; and a lack of inter-and intra-organizational communication and coordination standards within the humanitarian sector as a whole.

Yet the other stakeholders face some of the same challenges in theatre. The other stakeholders, however, are more homogeneous because they come under a more centralized command during interventions. Although a UN mission can have seven hundred police from forty-four nations, they are under unified command within a formalized hierarchical structure. Even so, these stakeholders still cannot adequately measure their success in missions. What hope, then, does the heterogeneous humanitarian sector have?

It has become clear that a comprehensive approach to operations requires an ontological shift in training and education. Multi-sector, multi-functional training supports the common tradespace in which interventions occur. No longer will it be acceptable to function within this space with blinders on – whether known or unknown. It is rare to talk to soldiers, peace-builders, or humanitarians who are aware of the organizing agencies of their counterparts. For example, most officers and soldiers do not know of ALNAP, the Humanitarian Code of Conduct, or International Humanitarian Law, while police deployed to theatre do not understand the role of the UN's SRSG; the humanitarians and peace-builders do not fully understand NATO's role, nor do they understand national caveats that outline military functions in peace operations. If international community interventions are to effect change, a new way to develop the wide scope of operational awareness must be a foundation block supporting the doctrine, guidance, and policies within the common tradespace of operations.

Humanitarian organizations' principles dictate that they maintain neutrality and independence to effectively deliver aid to recipient communities. Such principles are grounded in a well-developed humanitarian philosophy of neutrality, impartiality, and protection that has evolved since the 1880s. These principles limit the ways that humanitarian actors interact with defence and security stakeholders in peace operations. There are major concerns among humanitarians of being *contaminated* by the military and stigmatized by other humanitarian organizations as being *embedded* with the military and contributing to winning the hearts and minds of local populations. The fear of being seen as a part of the formal military structure, or even as an extension of a *"hearts and minds"* or *trust and confidence* campaign has prompted humanitarian organizations largely to distance themselves from militaries. Hearts and minds campaigns are seen as psychological effects-based operations by humanitarians, and most organizations will likely maintain their distance from such activities. This affects the ways in which measuring progress occurs in the field. Although this reality exists, humanitarian agencies and organizations have the opportunity to increase their understanding of security and defence sector worldviews by involving themselves in comprehensive-approach conferences and training opportunities and contributing to the ways in which progress and success are measured in peace operations and civilian crisis management.

In addition, the traditional guidance, doctrine, protocols, and policies guiding peace operations require a retooling to calibrate stakeholder roles, responsibilities, funding, and measuring operations within the common trade space of intervention. Stakeholders involved in international interventions are now questioning whether traditional conventions, protocols, and guidelines remain relevant to all stakeholders active in the common trade space. As well, policy-makers need to understand how these emerging protocols represent the new space that is being developed.

Stakeholders need to set aside competitive approaches to interventions and be open to educating themselves on other worldviews to maximize open communication regarding intervention activities and measuring what matters in international interventions. The understanding and acceptances of stakeholder worldviews – even if they are counterintuitive or considered wrong – allow the development of a common tradespace for intervention activities. The effectiveness, progress, and success achieved in future comprehensive interventions will be predicated upon attitudinal shifts to know and accept the "other" – whether the other is a sector, stakeholder, or, more importantly, a recipient population. Worldviews inform roles, attitudes, and behaviours. Further understanding these views will cause a recalibration of success – and the achievement thereof – within the common tradespace.

Notes

[1] Center on International Cooperation, *Annual Review of Global Peace Operations 2006*.
[2] Victor Josey, personal communication, 2008.
[3] Ibid.
[4] Glenn MacPhail, personal communication, 2008.
[5] David Beer, personal communication, 2008.
[6] Glenn MacPhail, personal communication, 2008.
[7] David Beer, personal communication, 2008.
[8] Ibid.
[9] Ibid.
[10] Timothy Lannan, personal communication, 2008.
[11] Mike Ward, personal communication, 2008.
[12] Anonymous, personal communication, 2008.
[13] Ibid.
[14] Ian Higginbotham, personal communication, 2008.

[15] Anonymous, personal communication, 2008.
[16] Rory Keane, personal communication, 2008.
[17] Ibid.
[18] David Chuter, personal communication, 2008.
[19] Alexandra Novosselof, personal communication, 2008.
[20] Anonymous, personal communication, 2008.
[21] Mary Ann Zimmerman, personal communication, 2008.
[22] Steve Flemming, personal communication, 2008.
[23] Ibid.
[24] Curtis et al., "'Doing the Right Problem,'" 1304.
[25] Emery Brusset, personal communication, 2008.
[26] Steve Flemming, personal communication, 2008.
[27] Anonymous, personal communication, 2008.

Conclusion

Since there is no empirical proof that intervention activities 1) permanently alleviate human suffering; or 2) cause sustainable peace, then intervention activities have not yet got it right. In fact, *interventions are experiments*, because collectively the international community continues to test intervention theories on various primary stakeholders in conflict environments, with varying results.

In scientific experimentation, results of an experiment can be retested by different scientists using the same methodology, conditions, and variables as the original. In international interventions, we have not reached the point when we can duplicate the methods, conditions, and variables of an intervention and get the same results. It is important to recognize, too, that when humans are involved as subjects of a study (vis-à-vis a physical or biochemical study), the same methodology, conditions, and variables can not necessarily be duplicated, resulting in different results from the original activity impacts. Therefore, since people are involved in intervention activities, as implementers, recipients, beneficiaries, or political proponents and/or spoilers, it becomes impossible to duplicate results in peace operations and crisis management. We simply continue to experiment on other states' populations with varying results. Although we are collectively experimenting with other populations, the experiments are not *duplicatable*, and we do not know how to measure the significance of our impacts in a meaningful way. To suggest that an activity was successful because x amount of people were fed, or x number of dollars were spent that were committed, or x number of minutes of media coverage was calculated is nugatory at best. However, after the dust settles on a project, the numbers outlast the narratives and inform the next series of projects in a chain of reductionism.

With the new peace operations and crisis management trend in post-conflict environments comes the requirement to measure the effectiveness of these types of activities – for the recipient populations of such interventions, the groups planning and implementing the activities, and the groups and agencies financially supporting the activities. Civil servant bean-counters may be happy with measuring, but just because you can measure an activity and its perceived impacts does not mean that the activity is effective.

Although some of the performance measurement systems emerging from the development sector address components of operations, they require further advancement to be applicable to peace operations and crisis management activities. In addition, difficulties arise when the international community puts undue emphasis on the utility of military-centric indicators and metrics, which are useful in combat operations but do not transfer to peace operations and crisis management activities. Militaries, as well as other sectors sharing the common tradespace, are by nature instrumentalist and bureaucratic and this has been problematic in measuring interventions in Bosnia, Haiti, Iraq, and Afghanistan, that are not instrumentalist by nature. Misapplied or inappropriate technologies create a different type of problem in a different type of world, necessitating a different ontology for considering effectiveness, success, and progress. New methods and strategies based on qualitative inquiry are required, based on this shift in assumptions.

The international community will need to discard typical and outmoded indicators and metrics as defined mostly by the defence sector and allow indigenous populations to identify their own considerations of effectiveness over time. There is room to include social and cultural narratives – as well as numbers and scores – in emerging measurement tools to better understand the effectiveness of peace operations and crisis management activities, especially if intervention trends continue. Moreover, it is incumbent upon the international community to revisit recipient populations after interventions have ended, to identify measures of effectiveness from peoples' perspectives to better comprehend the *significance of impact* of peace operations and crisis management.

Managing Knowledge

If the end of the twentieth century was known as the information age, the first part of the twenty-first century will become known as the knowledge management age. With the onslaught of information – and onslaught it has been for those around the globe with access to the Internet – came the overwhelming need to manage it. It is an easy claim to make to say that no one is keeping up with the production of knowledge and information in their field of expertise. For trained scholars, there are traditional methods to follow and stay abreast of advances in their respective fields. These methods include access to indices and journal articles, attendance at annual conferences of learned societies, and publication of research. This system is no longer fully valid, and the expectations for our research have shifted towards applicability rather than research for research's sake.

In my own experience in scholarly and applied research endeavours, the halls of academe have a hushed silence. No longer is the hum of collegiality heard in the corridors of universities and colleges I frequent, but rather there is a silenced fear as we professors and researchers burrow away at the stacks of reading on our buried desks. Foreheads creased, we scan RSS feeds, blogs, journal articles, indices, and other sources of relevant information that allow us to maintain our knowledgeable positions in our field of study. Most scholars focus on a hair's-breadth of a specialization, and build careers upon having the knowledge that allows us to be *the* expert in that field. These slivers of specialization are shrinking, as it becomes impossible to know everything in our chosen field of study. We chose smaller areas to study so we can be confident of keeping abreast of emerging information. Yet, fear's mocking voice has invaded the consciousness of most scholars. The rules have changed as information is available to everyone. The privileged position of the scholar in society is no more.

This problem is not only that of scholars. Studies suggest that as soon as students graduate from technical school, the skills and information they learned in the first two years of their program have already become out of date and are no longer applicable to their trade. For scientists, the problem is worsened as more and more scientific journals go online. Much redundancy is now exposed as scientists discover, for example, that the very projects they have been working on in Germany are being finalized in Canada and results published.

It seems that anyone can be an expert these days. We seem to be only one Google search away from information that allows us to forfeit research in the name of cursory analysis. To worsen matters, much information available – especially on the Internet – is rehashed journalistic information popularized by media sensationalism and accepted as factual. The glut of information may be even more problematic for western civil servants who are challenged with distilling large amounts of details into sound bites at the request of their bosses and politicians who frequently ask for "quick and dirty" analyses. The task for the staffer becomes adding the most current or significant information in such an analysis by leaving out the critical nuances that inform and educate. Because the quantity of information on the Internet grows exponentially – rather than geometrically – as more and more of the world's population goes online, hope dwindles of being in the know or having a full awareness of the scope and breadth of a subject matter and the interconnections between subjects.

This, however, leads to an opportunity. The information challenges are representative of validity, scope, currency, duplication, significance, and trans-connectivity. These challenges signify a shift in our needs concerning information. It has been said that information is just that – information, not knowledge. Just because it is available on the Internet does not make it correct or transform it into knowledge. Yet as we get smarter about our information needs, we begin to manage the onslaught through frameworks based on interests, requests, and requirements. Some well-known information management frameworks are Google Alerts, RSS feeds, Linked-In, and other online communities. These frameworks retrieve the information we want from the global commons of information. They bring us what we need to fulfill the requests that we intentionally manage through these systems. The information in-gathered does not always fit our requirements, and the frameworks for gathering are rudimentary. Moreover, the glut of information is ever growing, even as our management frameworks seek to catch up.

To counteract information degradation, comprehensive-type operations require primary field research, credible and alternate information-sharing approaches, and measuring systems. Thought needs to be given to sharing information more effectively with less classification. Information can be shared in multiple ways: within government departments, across government departments, and with partnering governments. These habitually remain information-sharing divides. For information to be shared across these divides requires levels of relationship and trust as well as software systems. We are now taking baby steps in this direction.[1]

Information management is several steps away from knowledge management. Not only do the frameworks need to catch up but so too must there be a shift in thinking from the *utility of information* (as an end in itself) towards *creation of knowledge* leading to its application. Although the distinction may seem insignificant, the application of decisions based on information differs greatly from those based on knowledge.

Knowledge in international interventions is representative of scope, currency, duplication, significance, and trans-connectivity. As information is iteratively plotted through an open-source, web-based hub by engaged stakeholders and sectors, knowledge is created. Information regarding scope of operations (who is involved, where, and what they are implementing), currency of operations (the changing environment and the flexibility of interventions to address the changes), duplication of operations (what are the typologies of interventions, are there overlaps, where are the synergies), significance of operations (budgets, funding, spending, attributed results, non-attributed results, tangible and intangible changes in societies), and trans-connectivity (between and among stakeholders, sectors, convergent strategies, plans, policies, doctrine, systems, approaches, results, impacts) can be iteratively input into a globalized framework of operations available to all. This, in short, becomes the collective commons of interventions in which data regarding individual stakeholders' involvement is self-regulated, uploaded, and updated, along with their successes and failures, budget requirements and donor funding. Google Reporting is born and the common tradespace is visually mapped for collective understanding of the scope, currency, duplication, significance, and trans-connectivity of our activities.

Unlike other sectors such as education and health, international interventions still lack the appropriate baseline data against which to measure their own progress. The next steps will be to develop web-based software and databases for the various sectors involved in peace operations and crisis management to input data consistently over time. Data can be collected through a web-based system accessible to the various sectors involved in operations. To ensure that quality and quantity benchmarks are achieved, a series of questions referring to the data required can be made available on the web. The provision of a data framework individualized for each sector could be made available for downloading from the web-based, transparent system to serve in gathering consistent data over a continuous period of time. Data collected by involved stakeholders could then be uploaded to serve as appropriate baseline data in future operations. This process would be open source, and would become part of the collective commons of peace operations and civilian crisis management. It may address issues related to the dearth of baseline data appropriate to the intervention sector, challenges of consistent institutional memory in participating sectors, and incentives to improve operations.

Data related to the views of beneficiaries/locals/recipients could also be part of the data collected, including their views on effectiveness of activities, intervention agency performance, and longer-term significance of impacts. Such a database could also provide consistent institutional memory over the long term and counteract the issue related to consistency across rotations in and out of the field by particular sectors, especially the military.

Academic research has growing importance in the cycle of progress and success of peace operations and crisis management. The development of knowledge occurs through reflective and applied research. A direct and timely injection of this knowledge into the spectrum of intervention allows more lessons to be learned and increased application of theories to praxis. If we are to experience increases in progress and success, it becomes incumbent upon the international community to link scholars to field practitioners, and field practice back to academia. This moves beyond knowledge management to an ever-evolving cycle of knowledge acquisition – in other words, to true learning. Connections between academia and field practice are forged through government programs, think-tank initiatives, private funding, and web-based knowledge sharing. Applying theory and lessons learned from past interventions to future operations is complex, yet no stakeholder of peace operations and crisis management is better suited than academia to support the transition from the information age to the knowledge age.

The environment of complex operations is akin to the three-dimensional chessboard analogy posited by Joseph Nye.[2] The bottom board – representative of transnational power – is influenced by myriad factors that arise in the aftermath of violent conflicts, including continued hostilities, corrupt opportunism, political upheaval, ethnic divisions, insurgencies, transnational terrorism, intelligence community agendas, mass exploitation, pandemics, climate change, and drug and human trafficking. On this board, power and influence are chaotically distributed. No longer do the omnipotent states of the twentieth century retain their power and exercise their wills to thwart threats against their national interests. This environment suggests that power is displaced and difficult to understand using the same perspectives of power that were used in recent history. Power hierarchies have shifted in the operational environment in which the international community attempts to intervene and to measure its interventions. The environment is not within the influence or control of the international community, and measuring merely offers the illusion of control to stakeholders. Measuring the ever-present and ever-changing human condition may be beyond our current collective competencies; however, with technological applications and knowledge-age thinking, a more promising prospect is on the near horizon. The ability to see the whole picture of international interventions is within our collective grasp and can generate a much-neglected learning continuum in the common tradespace. To see this whole picture, as Jason Ladnier points out, technology will be the next step – if it is not inhibited by political agendas.[3]

The rules have changed regarding information and power. No longer are the plutocrats and magnates the sole keepers of information, used to exercise power over people for often selfish gains. People are now being introduced to their ability – albeit limited, in some areas around the globe – of taking the remit of political power away from those who kept it to bend the will of the people. Now, the people of the world can plot intervention activities in a way that permits a glimpse of the ability to generate sustainable peace and prosperity through our actions.

With the iterative plotting of information by stakeholders involved in peace operations and civilian crisis management, the scope and breadth of an intervention become visible. Humans think in pictures and images, not words and numbers. As we develop more advanced imaging approaches to our intervention activities, we are better able to see the natural conclusion of interventions as comprehensive and synchronized. So too will the clients of interventions be able to see the scope, intentions, and breadth of the activities, to better understand the intention to achieve sustainable peace and prosperity.

As indicators emerge identifying where we are, we begin to understand where we are going. If we remain unclear of our intervention aims, we will have trouble measuring the results of intervention. When intervention objectives remain unstated or unknown, the management of interventions remains eclipsed. Common objectives are more useful than discrete stakeholder objectives in a common tradespace. We require a much more rigorous differentiation of what is being measured on operations, as well as concerted efforts to measure at different levels in order to try to triangulate effectiveness.[4] New technologies allows us to do two types of measuring: sector and tradespace performance measurement, and significance of impact evaluation. By understanding where we are going, the measuring of impact becomes possible. Without this understanding, we are merely intervening. Because we *collectively* do not know what we are measuring, or for whom, we have no way of mapping effectiveness, success, and progress. In order to measure, we must have an understanding of where we have come from. The conclusion remains that there are structural and systemic problems with the management process of peace operations and crisis management because there is yet no way to see the bigger picture of these massive undertakings in the public interest.

Effectiveness, efficiency, accountability, and sustainability have become the measurement and reporting meta-narratives of twenty-first century peace operations and crisis management. As these are public enterprises, they require international standards that keep them honest and accountable and in the public interest. Although measuring cannot stop corruption,[5] the transparency of technologies like Google Reporting can serve to highlight it, which is not the current state of affairs. The new liberal imperialism – concerned with legitimacy and efficiency – is a harbinger of operational effectiveness, success, and progress to come.

We will continue to be confronted with the challenge of using two-dimensional knowledge management systems to determine non-linear dynamics in the complex environment of operations. New technologies, however, offer an increasingly comprehensive perspective on the trans-connectivity of the common tradespace.

This book contends that understanding *thinking* becomes a way of planning, and therefore provides the ability to measure effectiveness, success, and progress. The new complex environment seeks our understanding, and a quantum leap of faith to generate the forward momentum urgently required to measure sustainable results. Leadership may be invaluable in shedding outdated thinking and adopting new thinking appropriate to the complex environment. New technologies can help map stakeholder and sector worldviews as well as concomitant failures and successes regarding international interventions in a way that can elicit the sea-change required to strengthen weakened states, prevent bloodier violence, and promote tenable peace in our interconnected, complex world. A transparent environment can lead to change.

Then, and only then, will the international community have come of age.

Notes

[1] Jason Ladnier, personal communication, 2008.

[2] Nye, "Commentary: Hard Times, Soft Power." In Nye's analogy, the three-dimensional chessboard represents levels of power and US hegemony. On the first chessboard, military power, the US is the only superpower. On the middle board, economic power, there is no clear hegemon but a consortium of power players. On the bottom board, transnational power (which is influenced by myriad factors that arise in the aftermath of violent conflicts, including continued hostilities, corrupt opportunism, political upheaval, ethnic divisions, insurgencies, transnational terrorism, mass exploitation, pandemics, climate change, and drug and human trafficking), power and influence are chaotically distributed. Although Nye was referring to US power, the analogy of the bottom board is useful in understanding the context of international interventions.

[3] Jason Ladnier, personal communication, 2008.

[4] Stuart Gordon, personal communication, 2008.

[5] Many participants interviewed in support of this research suggested that corruption is increasing in international intervention activities. Corruption is a complex issue not to be passed over. To date, Paddy Ashdown's exposé on corruption in postwar Bosnia remains the most practical and serious. See Ashdown, *Swords and Ploughshares*.

APPENDIX A

Summary of Interview Questions

The following questions were part of the interview process in 2008 on measuring effectiveness:

1. What principles, concepts, values, or philosophies guide the development of measures of effectiveness? What guidance is there (i.e., doctrine, policy or strategy papers)? What guidance or policies are needed? What would be helpful?
2. In your experience, what effects are measured? Why should these effects be chosen? How are these effects measured? When should they be measured?
3. What terminology does your organization use to describe measurement activities?
4. Are there synergies between international stakeholders and their measuring systems (US inter-agency, UK, NATO, UN, EU, OECD-DAC, OSCE, other IOs, and NGOs, etc.)?
5. What time frame does your organization work to when measuring its activities? How is that time frame harmonized with other stakeholders?
6. What measurement methods are the most appropriate in crisis environments?
7. Why should the various stakeholders involved in "integrated" peace operations and/or crisis management measure the effectiveness of their activities?

8. How would you counsel your successors/counterparts regarding measures of effectiveness (MOEs) in their deployments?
9. Can you identify any future trends in the area of measurement?
10. Are you aware of other work in this area? What gaps exist in this field? What would be helpful to you or your organization?

The following questions were part of the interview process conducted in Bosnia-Herzegovina in 2007 on effectiveness according to local recipients of an international intervention:

1. Are you currently working?
2. What is your job?
3. Did you live in the former Yugoslavia before 1990?
4. Are you currently living in Bosnia-Herzegovina?
5. Has your life improved here? Why/why not?
6. Do you identify with a particular ethnic community? If yes, which one(s)?
7. What is your postwar experience of the international community?
8. In your opinion, did you have a say in the postwar reconstruction of Bosnia-Herzegovina?
9. What would you have suggested to the international community to help with the reconstruction of Bosnia-Herzegovina?
10. What was it like here before the war?
11. Why was it like that?
12. Was it always like that?
13. When was that?
14. In what way did you experience this? (Through what means? How did you experience pre-war life?)
15. Do other people you know share your opinion on what it was like before the war? Why/why not?
16. Were you living here during the war? (BiH)
17. Did you experience the war?
18. How did you experience it?
19. When was that?

20. Where was that?
21. What did your community look like during the war?
22. What changes occurred here during the war?
23. How did your quality of life change during the conflict?
24. What resources were you able/unable to access during the conflict?
25. Were you here between 1991 and 2001 when the international community was involved on a large scale?
26. What was that like?
27. In your opinion, how effective was the peace operation?
28. What were your needs at that time?
29. Were your needs met by the peace operation in the short term?
30. If yes, how were your needs met?
31. If no, why were your needs not met?
32. Were your needs met by the peace operation in the medium to long term?
33. If yes, how have your needs been met?
34. If no, why have your needs not been met?
35. What do you remember the most about the international peace operation?
36. Why does that stand out in your memory?
37. At the time, did you understand the efforts of the international community here in Bosnia?
38. What parts did you understand most? Why?
39. What parts did you understand the least? Why?
40. How did the international community involve you or your community?
41. If you were involved, was this important to you? Why?
42. Remembering back to this time, what were the short-term effects of the international community becoming involved in Bosnia?
43. How did these effects impact your life (for example, your places, your community, your culture, your groups/families)?

44. What have been the longer-term effects of the international community becoming involved in Bosnia?
45. How will these effects impact your life (for example, your places, your community, your culture, your groups/families)?
46. Is there a difference between reconstructed places and newly constructed places?
47. If yes, what is the difference?
48. In your opinion, what is the most successful reconstruction project?
49. Who uses it?
50. Why is it successful?
51. Will it remain successful? Why/why not?
52. In your opinion, what is the most unsuccessful reconstruction project?
53. Why is it unsuccessful?
54. Will it remain unsuccessful?
55. Why/why not?
56. Could it become successful? If yes, how?
57. What are some other examples of reconstruction projects?
58. What is your experience of your reconstructed places? (include people, community, and culture if appropriate)
59. How is this different from your memories before the war of your places? (Include people, community, and culture if appropriate.)
60. Have these differences affected you? How?
61. In your opinion, what is the most successful new construction project?
62. Who uses it?
63. Why is it successful?
64. Will it remain successful? Why/why not?
65. In your opinion, what is the most unsuccessful new construction project?
66. Why is it unsuccessful?
67. Will it remain unsuccessful? Why/why not?
68. Could it become successful? How? (For whom?)

69. What is your experience of your newly constructed places? Culture?
70. How is this different from your memories before the war of your old places? (Include people, community, and culture if appropriate.)
71. How long do you think the war will affect you?
72. How long do you think the postwar reconstruction and construction projects, activities, and programs will affect you?
73. How long should the international community be involved in Bosnia-Herzegovina? Why?
74. What could have made the international peace operation more effective for you?
75. Is your life better or worse from the peace operation?
76. How would you measure the effectiveness of international intervention on you and your life, people, places, community, and culture?
77. What messages/advice do you have for other populations experiencing international interventions (such as in Iraq, Sri Lanka, Sudan, Afghanistan, Haiti, Congo)?
78. If an international intervention was to happen all over again here, what would you change or do differently? Why?
79. What messages/advice do you have for the international community intervening in other places, such as in Iraq, Sri Lanka, Sudan Afghanistan, Congo, and Haiti?
80. What messages/advice do you have for recipient populations (locals) in other conflict areas, such as in Iraq, Sri Lanka, Sudan Afghanistan, Congo, and Haiti?
81. Are there particular values that civilians should have who are working in the peace profession to best serve locals?
82. What skills and competencies should civilians have who are working in the peace profession in order to best serve locals?

APPENDIX B

The White Man's Burden[1]

RUDYARD KIPLING

Take up the White Man's burden–
Send forth the best ye breed –
Go bind your sons to exile
To serve your captives' need;
To wait in heavy harness,
On fluttered folk and wild –
Your new-caught, sullen peoples,
Half-devil and half-child.

Take up the White Man's burden –
In patience to abide,
To veil the threat of terror
And check the show of pride;
By open speech and simple,
An hundred times made plain
To seek another's profit,
And work another's gain.

---

[1] Kipling, R., "The White Man's Burden," *McClure's Magazine*, 1899. http://www.journalism.wisc.edu/mpi/shah/burden.pdf.

Take up the White Man's burden –
The savage wars of peace –
Fill full the mouth of Famine
And bid the sickness cease;
And when your goal is nearest
The end for others sought,
Watch sloth and heathen Folly
Bring all your hopes to nought.

Take up the White Man's burden –
No tawdry rule of kings,
But toil of serf and sweeper –
The tale of common things.
The ports ye shall not enter,
The roads ye shall not tread,
Go mark them with your living,
And mark them with your dead.

Take up the White Man's burden –
And reap his old reward:
The blame of those ye better,
The hate of those ye guard –
The cry of hosts ye humour
(Ah, slowly!) toward the light: –
"Why brought he us from bondage,
Our loved Egyptian night?"

Take up the White Man's burden –
Ye dare not stoop to less –
Nor call too loud on Freedom
To cloak your weariness;
By all ye cry or whisper,
By all ye leave or do,
The silent, sullen peoples
Shall weigh your gods and you.

Take up the White Man's burden –
Have done with childish days –
The lightly proferred laurel,
The easy, ungrudged praise.
Comes now, to search your manhood
Through all the thankless years
Cold, edged with dear-bought wisdom,
The judgment of your peers!

Bibliography

Active Learning Network for Accountability and Performance in Humanitarian Action (ALNAP). *Annual Review 2002*. London: Overseas Development Institute, 2002.
– *Evaluating Humanitarian Action Using the OECD-DAC Criteria: An ALNAP Guide for Humanitarian Agencies*. London: Overseas Development Institute, March 2006.
Amponin, K., and I. Hope. *Strategic Assessment for the Reconstruction of Afghanistan*. Unknown publisher. Unknown date.
Anderson, M., and P. Woodrow. *Rising from the Ashes: Development Strategies in Times of Disaster*. Boulder, CO: Westview Press, 1989.
Anderson, B. *Imagined Communities: Reflections on the Origin and Spread of Nationalism*. New York: Verso, 1983.
Anderson, M.B. *Do No Harm: How Aid Can Support Peace or War*. Boulder, CO: Lynne Reinner Publishers, 1999.
Anderson, M.B., and L. Olson. *Confronting War: Critical Lessons for Peace Practitioners*. Cambridge, MA: Collaborative for Development Action, 2003.
Aoi, C., R.C. Thakur, and Cedric De Coning, eds. *Unintended Consequences of Peacekeeping Operations*. New York: United Nations University Press, 2007.
Ashdown, P. *Swords and Ploughshares: Bringing Peace to the Twenty First Century*. London: Weidenfeld & Nicolson, 2007.
Banerjee, N. "Development for Afghans: Missing Measurements and Missed Opportunities." Centre for International Policy Studies Policy Brief No. 4 (February 2009).
Barakat, S., C. Cockburn, and M. Kojakovic, eds. *Post-Conflict Reconstruction and Conservation in Croatia: Study Tour and Conference Report*. York, UK: Post-War Reconstruction and Development Unit, University of York Press, 1992.
Barnes, Trevor. "Placing Ideas: Genius Loci, Heterotopia, and Geography's Quantitative Revolution." *Progress in Human Geography* 28, no. 5 (October 2004): 565-95.

Barton, F., B. Crocker, and M.L. Courtney. *In the Balance: Measuring Progress in Afghanistan*. Washington, DC: Center for Strategic and International Studies. Special Report, 18 July 2005.

Baylee, J.S. Maximizing the Use of Evaluation Findings: Asian Development Bank. Operations Evaluation Department Occasional Paper.

Bebbington, A. "NGOs and Uneven Development: Geographies of Development Intervention." *Progress in Human Geography* 28, no. 6 (December 2004): 725-45.

Beck, T., and M. Buchanan-Smith. *Joint Evaluations Coming of Age? The Quality and Future Scope of Joint Evaluations: ALNAP Seventh Review of Humanitarian Action*. London: Overseas Development Institute, 2008.

BERCI International. *Peacekeeping Operations in the Democratic Republic of the Congo: The Perception of the Population*. New York: United Nations Press, 2005.

Bergstrand, B. *Success in Peacekeeping*. Paper submitted to Dr J.T. Jockel in compliance with War Studies 526, Royal Military College, 1992.

Berk, R.A. "Survey of 12 Strategies to Measure Teaching Effectiveness." *International Journal of Teaching and Learning in Higher Education* 17, no. 1. (2005): 48-62.

Bonventre, E.V. "Monitoring and Evaluation of Department of Defense Humanitarian Assistance Programs." *Military Review* 88, no. 1 (January-February 2008): 66-72.

Boone, J. "World News: Afghan Aid 'Wasteful and Ineffective.'" *Financial Times*, 25 March 2008, front section, European ed.

Borton, J. *Concept Note: The ALNAP Humanitarian Performance Project*. Unknown publisher, 2008.

– "The Literature on Performance Measurement and Performance Management." Extract from an unpublished paper by John Borton, April 2008.

– "Inventory of the Principal Projects, Initiatives and Approaches Which Are Relevant to Overall Performance Assessment of the Humanitarian System." *ALNAP HPP Inventory Draft for Correction and Comment*. London: Overseas Development Institute, 6 March 2008.

– "Summary of the Emerging Results from the ALNAP Humanitarian Performance Project: Exploratory Phase." Paper presented at the 23rd ALNAP Biannual Meeting, Madrid, 4-5 June 2008.

Borton, J., R. Stephenson, and C. Morris. "Evaluation of ODA's Provision of Emergency Aid to Africa, 1983-86." *Evaluation Report EV425*. London: Overseas Development Administration, 1988.

Brailsford, M. "Better Programming Initiative: The International Federation of Red Cross and Red Crescent Societies Approach to Peace and Conflict Impact Assessment." MA thesis, University of York, UK, 2004.

Bruce, R. "Barriers Fall as New World Order Fast Emerges." International Accountancy: Financial Times Special Report. *London Financial Times*, 25 March 2008: 2.

Brusset, E. "Evaluation of Conflict Prevention and Peace Building." Paper presented at the Crisis Management Initiative Workshop, Brussels, 7 November 2007.

Brusset, E., J. Brett, T. Vaux, and N. Olesen. "Collaborative Learning Projects: Final Report." *SIDA Evaluation 07/11*. Stockholm: Swedish International Development Cooperation Agency, 2007.

Bulmer, M., and D.P. Warwick, eds. *Social Research in Developing Countries: Surveys and Consensus in the Third World.* Chichester, UK: John Wiley & Sons, 1983.
Call, C.T. "Knowing Peace When You See It: Setting Standards for Peacebuilding Success." *Civil Wars.* 10, 2. (June 2008): 173-94.
Campbell, P.L. "Measures of Effectiveness: An Annotated Bibliography." *Sandia Report SAND2004-2902.* Albuquerque, NM: Sandia National Laboratories, 2004.
Canadian International Development Agency. *Results-Based Management in CIDA: Policy Statement.* Ottawa: CIDA Publications, 1996.
– *Compendium of Operational Frameworks for Peacebuilding and Donor Co-ordination.* Ottawa: CIDA Publications, 1998.
– *A Results Approach to Developing the Implementation Plan: A Guide to CIDA Partners and Executing Agencies.* Ottawa: Government of Canada, 2001.
– *The Guide for Preparing a Country Development Programming Framework: The Performance Measurement Framework.* Ottawa: CIDA Publications, 2002.
– *Canada's Development Commitment for Afghanistan.* Ottawa: CIDA Publications, 2005.
Center for International Peace Operations (ZIF). *Facts and Figures.* Berlin: ZIF, 2007.
Center on International Cooperation. *Annual Review of Global Peace Operations 2006.* Boulder, CO: Lynne-Rienner Publishers, 2006.
– *Annual Review of Global Peace Operations 2007.* Boulder, CO: Lynne Rienner Publishers, 2007.
– *Annual Review of Global Peace Operations 2008.* Boulder, CO: Lynne Rienner Publishers, 2008.
Channel Research. *Evaluation of ECHO's Humanitarian Intervention Plans in Afghanistan and Assessment of ECHO's Future Strategy in Afghanistan with Reference to Actions in Iran and Pakistan.* Brussels: European Community Humanitarian Aid (ECHO), 2004.
Chapman, A. *Maslow's Hierarchy of Needs: Original Five-Stage Model.* Leicester, UK: Alan Chapman Consultancy, 2004.
Checkland, P. *Systems Thinking, Systems Practice.* Chichester, UK: John Wiley & Sons, 1981.
– "Achieving 'Desirable and Feasible' Change: An Application of Soft Systems Methodology." *Journal of Operational Research Society* 36 (September 1985): 821-31.
– *Systems Thinking, Systems Practice: Includes a 30-Year Retrospective.* Chichester, UK: John Wiley & Sons, 1999.
Church, C., and M. Rogers. *Designing for Results: Integrating Monitoring and Evaluation in Conflict Transformation Programs Manual.* Washington, DC: Search for Common Ground, United States Institute for Peace, and Alliance for Peacebuilding, 2006.
Cohen, C. "Measuring Progress in Stabilization and Reconstruction." Stabilization and Reconstruction Series. Washington, DC: United Nations Institute of Peace, March 2006.
"Conference Report: Rebuilding Wartorn Societies." Report of the Workshops on the Challenge of Rebuilding Wartorn Societies and the Social Consequences of the Peace Process in Cambodia. Geneva, 27-30 April, 1993.

Conflict Prevention Network. *Conflict Impact Assessment: A Practical Working Tool for Prioritising Development Assistance in Unstable Situations.* Brussels: Conflict Prevention Network, 1999.

Conflict Prevention and Post-Conflict Reconstruction Network (CPR Network). *The Peace and Conflict Impact Assessment Handbook of the Conflict Prevention and Post-Conflict Reconstruction Network*, Version 2.2. New York: CPR Network, United Nations Development Programme, September 2005.

ConflictSensitivity.org. *Conflict-Sensitive Approaches to Development, Humanitarian Assistance and Peacebuilding: A Resource Pack.* http://www.conflictsensitivity.org/node/51. Africa Peace Forum, Center for Conflict Resolution, Consortium of Humanitarian Agencies, Forum on Early Warning and Early Response, International Alert, and Saferworld, 2004.

CONOPS. *The Effects-Based Operations Process Version 0.61.* Joint Forces Command Joint Experimentation Directorate EBO Prototyping Team. 4 November 2004.

Cooper, R. "The Postmodern State." In *Re-ordering The World: The Long-Term Implications of September 11th.* Edited by Mark Leonard. London: Foreign Policy Centre, 2002.

Cordesman, A. "The Missing Metrics of 'Progress' in Afghanistan (and Pakistan)." Working draft paper presented at the Conference on Peacebuilding in Afghanistan: Taking Stock and Looking Ahead. Ottawa, 10-11 December 2007.

– *Armed Nation Building: The Real Challenge in Afghanistan.* Washington, DC: Center for Strategic and International Studies, November 2007.

Crocker, B., ed. *The Post Conflict Reconstruction Project, "Progress or Peril?" Measuring Iraq's Reconstruction.* Ottawa: Center for Strategic and International Studies, 2004.

Curtis, N.J., P.J. Dortmans, and J. Ciuk. "'Doing the Right Problem' versus 'Doing the Problem Right': Problem Structuring within a Land Force Environment." *Journal of the Operational Research Society* 57, no. 11 (November 2006): 1300-12.

Davies, H., S. Nutley, and I. Walter. "Assessing the Impact of Social Science Research: Conceptual, Methodological and Practical Issues." Research Unit for Research Utilisation (RURU), University of St Andrews, Edinburgh, Scotland, 2005.

de Coning, Cedric. "Coherence and Coordination in United Nations Peacebuilding and Integrated Missions: A Norwegian Perspective." *Security in Practice* 5. Oslo: Norwegian Institute of International Affairs, 2007.

– *The United Nations and the Comprehensive Approach.* Copenhagen: Danish Institute for International Studies, 2008.

Defence Intelligence. *Defence Intelligence Assessment: Afghan Attitudes: Results from Wave One of Opinion Polling in Eight Afghan Provinces.* Canberra, Australia: Defence Intelligence Organization, Department of Defence, 2005.

Department for International Development (DFID). *Afghanistan: Provincial Reconstruction Teams, Project Memorandum.* London: DFID, 2003.

– *Interim Strategy for Afghanistan, 2005-2006.* London: DFID, 2004.

Development Initiatives. *Global Humanitarian Assistance, 2007/2008.* Wells, UK: Development Initiatives, 2008.

Direction Générale de la Coopération Internationale et du Développement. *Guide to Evaluations.* Ministère de Affaires Étrangères. Paris: Government of France, 2005.

– *Fragile States and Situations of Fragility: France's Policy Paper.* Paris: Government of France, 2007.
Dortmans, P.J., N.J. Curtis, and N. Tri. "An Analytical Approach for Constructing and Measuring Concepts." *Journal of Operational Research Society* 57 (August 2006): 885-91.
Earl, S., F. Carden, and T. Smutylo. *Outcome Mapping: Building Learning and Reflection Into Development Programs.* 2001. IDRC. http://www.idrc.ca/en/ev-28377-201-1-DO_TOPIC.html. Accessed 9 December 2008.
EIM Business and Policy Research. *Review of Methods to Measure the Effectiveness of State Aid to SMEs: Final Report to the European Commission.* Zoetermeer, Netherlands: EU Publications Office, 2004.
Embrey, J. "R.E. GEN Mattis on Effects (UNCLASSIFIED)." E-mail message to author, 2008.
European Commission. "Evaluation of Afghanistan Country Strategy." Team led by Martin Steinmayer, PARTICIP GmBh, 2008.
"First Conference on Reconstruction: Strategies and Challenges beyond Rehabilitation." Hargeisa, Somaliland, 20-24 October 1998.
Flavin, W. *Civil Military Operations: Afghanistan. Observations on Civil Military Operations during the First Year of Operation Enduring Freedom.* Washington, DC: Peacekeeping and Stability Operations Institute, US Department of the Army, 2004.
Friis, K., and P. Jarmyr, eds. "Comprehensive Approach: Challenges and Opportunities in Complex Crisis Management: NUPI Report." *Security in Practice* 11. Oslo: Norwegian Institute of International Affairs, 2008.
Goodhand, J., and P. Bergne. *Evaluation of the Conflict Prevention Pools: Country Case Study 2, Afghanistan Study.* Department for International Development (DFID) Evaluation Report EV 647. London: DFID, 2004.
Gordon, S. "Chapter 3: The Changing Role of the Military in Assistance Strategies." *Humanitarian Policy Group Report 21.* London: Overseas Development Institute, 2006.
Government of Canada. *Canada in Afghanistan: The International Policy Statement in Action.* http://www.Canada-afghanistan.gc.ca/IPS-in-action-en Ottawa: Government of Canada Publications, July 21, 2005.
– *Preparing and Using Results-Based Management and Accountability Frameworks.* http://www.tbs-sct.gc.ca/eval/pubs/RMAF-CGRR/guide/guide_e.asp. Ottawa: Treasury Board of Canada Secretariat, Government of Canada Publications, 2005.
Gregory, D. *The Colonial Present: Afghanistan, Palestine, Iraq.* Oxford: Blackwell, 2004.
Griffiths, L., and M. Meyer. "After the Conflict, the Reconstruction." *Guardian Weekly*, 27 September 2001. http://www.guardian.co.uk/world/2001/sep/27/balkans.socialsciences.
Grossman-Vermass, R. *The Effects-Based Concept, MNE 3 and NMOs: An Experimental Analysis.* Ottawa: Strategic Analysis Research Team, Operational Research Division, Department of National Defence, Government of Canada, 2003.
– *Hastening the Day.* Defence Analysis/Operational Research Division Department of National Defence. Montreal: McGill University Press, 1-2 April 2005.

Hallam, A. *Evaluating Humanitarian Assistance Programmes in Complex Emergencies*. London: Relief and Rehabilitation Network and Overseas Development Institute, 1998.

Hart, G. "Geography and Development: Critical Ethnographies." *Progress in Human Geography* 28, no. 1 (February 2004): 91-100.

Harrell-Bond, B.E. *Imposing Aid: Emergency Assistance to Refugees*. Oxford: Oxford University Press, 1986.

Hatfield, J.M. "Developing Performance Measures for Criminal Justice Programs." *Assessment and Evaluation: Handbook Series No. 2*. Washington, DC: Bureau of Justice Assistance State Reporting and Evaluation Program, US Department of Justice, United States Government, 1994.

Hawkins, D.R. *Power vs. Force: The Hidden Determinants of Human Behaviour*. Carlsbad, CA: Hay House, 2002.

Herndon, R.B., J.A. Robinson, J.L. Creighton, R. Torres, and L.J. Bello. "Effects-Based Operations in Afghanistan." *Field Artillery* (January-February 2004): 26-30.

Hoffman, M. "Peace and Conflict Impact Assessment Methodology." *Berghof Handbook for Conflict Transformation*. Berlin: Berghof Research Center, 2004.

Ho How Hoang, J. "Effects-Based Operations Equals to 'Shock and Awe'?" *Pointer Journal of the Singapore Armed Forces* 20, no. 2 (2004).

Humanitarian Accountability Project. *HAP 2007 Standard in Humanitarian Accountability and Quality Management*. Geneva: HAP International, 2007.

International Federation of Red Cross and Red Crescent Societies. *Code of Conduct*. Geneva, Switzerland: IFRCRCS. http://www.ifrc.org/publicat/conduct.

International Organization for Standardization. *ISO/IEC Guide 2: 1996, Standardization and Related Activities – General Vocabulary*. Geneva: International Organization for Standardization, 1996.

– *ISO/IEC Directives, Part 2: 2001, Rules for the structure and drafting of international standards*. Geneva: International Organization for Standardization, 2001.

Jobbagy, Z. *Literature Survey on Effects-Based Operations: A Ph.D. Study on Measuring Military Effects and Effectiveness*. The Hague: Netherlands Organization for Applied Scientific Research, 2003.

– *From Effects-Based Operations to Effects-Based Force*. Netherlands Organisation for Applied Scientific Research – Physics and Electronics Laboratory (TNO-FEL), Defence Staff. Brussels: TNO-FEL, March 2004.

Joint Assessment Mission. *Report of the Joint Assessment Mission Carried Out by the Government of Timor-Leste, UNMISET, UNDP and Development Partner Countries for the Timor-Leste Police Service*. Geneva: Joint Assessment Mission, January 2003.

Joint Evaluation of Emergency Assistance to Rwanda (JEEAR). *The International Response to Conflict and Genocide: Lessons from the Rwanda Experience*. Copenhagen: Steering Committee of the JEEAR, Royal Danish Ministry of Foreign Affairs, Government of Denmark, 1996.

"Joint Progress toward Enhanced Aid Effectiveness." *Paris Declaration on Aid Effectiveness*. Paris: OECD. March 2005. http://www.oecd.org/document/18/0,2340,en_2649_3236398_35401554_1_1_1_1,00.html

Jones, B., and R. Chandran, with E. Cousens, J. Slotin, and J. Sherman. *From Fragility to Resilience: Concepts and Dilemmas of Statebuilding in Fragile States*. Paris: Fragile States Group, OECD-DAC, March 2008.

Jones, S.G., J.M. Wilson, A. Rathmell, and K.J. Riley. *Establishing Law and Order after Conflict.* Santa Monica, CA: RAND Corporation, 2005.

Junne, G., and W. Verkoren, eds. "Chapter 1: The Challenges of Postconflict Development." *Postconflict Development: Meeting New Challenges.* Boulder, CO: Lynne Rienner Publishers, 2004.

Kaldor, M. *Human Security: Reflections on Globalization and Intervention.* Cambridge, UK: Polity Press, 2007.

Keeney, R.L. *Value-Focused Thinking: A Path to Creative Decision-Making.* Cambridge, MA: Harvard University Press, 1992.

Keith, M.W. "Force Size for the Post-Westphalian World." *Orbis* no. 49, 4 (autumn 2005): 649-62.

Klein, Jacques Paul. *Peace in the 21st Century: Between the Supranational and the Grassroots United Nations and Diplomatic Aspects.* Wageningen, Netherlands: United Nations Press, 2000.

Krasner, S.D., and C. Pascual. "Addressing State Failure." *Foreign Affairs* 84, no. 4 (July/August 2005).

Kumar, K., ed. *Rebuilding Societies after Civil War: Critical Roles for International Assistance.* London, UK: Lynne Rienner Publishers, 1996.

Last, D.M. "Rapid Assessment Process (RAP) and Security Sector Reform." Prepared for the proceedings of Cornwallis X, Analysis for New and Emerging Society Conflicts. Royal Military College, Kingston, Canada, 21-24 March 2005.

Lederach, J.P. *Preparing for Peace: Conflict Transformation across Cultures.* Syracuse, NY: Syracuse University Press, 1995.

Lederach, J.P., R. Neufeldt, and H. Culbertson. *Reflective Peacebuilding: A Planning, Monitoring and Learning Toolkit.* Mindanao, Philippines: Joan B. Kroc Institute for International Peace Studies, University of Notre Dame, and Catholic Relief Services, 2007.

Lee, J., M. Ong, R. Singh, A. Tay, Y.L.Weng, J.J. Garstka, and E.A. Smith, Jr. *Realising Integrated Knowledge-Based Command and Control: Transforming the SAF.* Singapore: Pointer Monograph 2, Singapore Armed Forces, 2003.

Litovsky, A., S. Rochlin, S. Zadek, and B. Levy. "Investing in Standards for Sustainable Development: The Role of International Development Agencies in Supporting Collaborative Standards Initiatives." *AccountAbility.* London: AccountAbility, December 2007.

Lowe, D., and S. Ng. "Effects-Based Operations: Language, Meaning and Effects-Based Approach." Paper presented at the Command and Control Research and Technology Symposium, The Power of Information Age Concepts and Technologies. Canberra, Australia, 2004.

Maclean, S.J., D.R. Black, and T.M. Shaw, eds. *A Decade of Human Security: Global Governance and New Multilateralisms (Global Security in a Changing World).* Hampshire, UK: Ashgate Publishing, 2006.

Maley, W. "Chapter 16: The Reconstruction of Afghanistan." In *Worlds in Collision: Terror and the Future of Global Order,* ed. Ken Booth and Tim Dunne. New York: Palgrave MacMillan, 2002.

Meharg, S.J. *Afghanistan Campaign Plan Measures of Effectiveness.* Ottawa: Department of National Defence, Canadian Forces Joint Operations Group, 2006.

– 2007. *Helping Hands and Loaded Arms: Navigating the Military and Humanitarian Space.* Cornwallis, Canada: Canadian Peacekeeping Press, 2007.

- "Measuring the Effectiveness of Reconstruction and Stabilization Activities." *Pearson Papers,* vol. 10:1. Cornwallis, N.S.: Canadian Peacekeeping Press, 2007.
Mosselman, M., and Y. Prince. *Review of Methods to Measure the Effectiveness of State Aid to SMEs: Final Report to the European Commission.* Brussels: European Commission, 2004.
Munck, R., and P.L. de Silva, eds. *Postmodern Insurgencies: Political Violence, Identity Formation, and Peacemaking in Comparative Perspective.* London, UK: Macmillan Press, 2000.
New Partnership for Africa's Development (NEPAD). *The New Partnership for Africa's Development: The African Peer Review Mechanism.* Johannesburg, SA: NEPAD, 2003.
Nye, Joseph. "Commentary: Hard Times, Soft Power." *Globe and Mail,* 16 February 2009.
OECD-DAC. *Guidance for Evaluating Humanitarian Assistance in Complex Emergencies.* Paris: OECD-DAC, 1999.
- *Glossary of Key Terms in Evaluation and Results Based Management.* Paris: OECD-DAC, 2002.
- *Guidance on Evaluating Conflict Prevention and Peacebuilding Activities: Working Document for Application Period.* Paris: Development Assistance Committee, OECD, 2007.
Office of the Special Inspector General for Iraq Reconstruction (OSIGIR). *Review of the Effectiveness of the Provincial Reconstruction Team Program in Iraq, SIGIR-07-015.* Arlington, VA: OSIGIR, Government of the United States, 18 October 2007.
O'Hanlon, M.E., and N. Kamp. *Afghanistan Index: Tracking Variables of Reconstruction and Security in Post-Taliban Afghanistan.* Washington, DC: The Brookings Institution (updated) 15 September 2005.
Operations Review Unit. *Humanitarian Aid to Somalia.* The Hague: Operations Review Unit, Ministry of Foreign Affairs, Government of the Netherlands, 1994.
Orr, R.C., ed. *Winning the Peace: An American Strategy for Post-Conflict Reconstruction.* Washington, DC: Center for Strategic and International Studies, 2004.
Owen, T., and P. Travers. "3D Vision: Can Canada Reconcile Its Defence, Diplomacy, and Development Objectives in Afghanistan?" *The Walrus* (July-August 2007): 45-9.
Nordic Consulting Group and Channel Research. *Evaluation of the Norwegian Emergency Preparedness System (NOREPS): Evaluation Report 1.* Oslo: Nordic Consulting Group and Channel Research, 2008.
Pawson, R., and N. Tilley. *Realistic Evaluation.* London: Sage Publications, 1997.
Poon, J.P.H. "Quantitative Methods: Past and Present." *Progress in Human Geography* 28, no. 6. (December 2004): 807-14.
Potter, J. "Discourse Analysis and Constructionist Approaches: Theoretical Background." In *Handbook of Qualitative Methods of Psychology and the Social Sciences,* ed. J.T.E. Richardson, 125-40. Leicester, UK: British Psychological Society, 1996.
PricewaterhouseCoopers LLP. *A Monitoring and Evaluation Framework for Peace Building.* Draft final report. Belfast: Special European Union Programmes Body, European Union. December 2006.

Pugh, Michael. *Post-Conflict Rehabilitation: The Human Dimension*. Proceedings of the 3rd International Security Forum workshop. Switzerland: ISF Workshop, 19-21 October 1998.
Pusateri, A., D. Thompson, M. Donlin, C. Oldre, and W. Kruft. *Assessment of Governance Quality Indicators (AGQI) in Afghanistan: Initial Assessment in Three Afghan Cities Using a Standardized Assessment Tool and Potential for Application of AGQI in Future Operations*. Fort Bragg, NC: Civil Affairs and Psychological Operations Command, United States Army, June 2005.
Reychler, L., and T. Paffenholz. *Conflict Impact Assessment: Peace and Conflict Impact Assessment Systems (PCIAS)*. Unknown publisher, 2005.
Reynolds, P. "Blair's 'International Community' Doctrine." *Global Policy*. New York: Global Policy Forum, 6 March 2004.
Rose, G. *Visual Methodologies: An Introduction to the Interpretation of Visual Materials*. London: Sage Publications, 2001.
Rossi, P.H., M.W. Lipsey, and H.E. Freeman. *Evaluation: A Systematic Approach*. 7th ed. Thousand Oaks, CA: Sage Publications, 2003.
Royal Canadian Mounted Police. *Canadian Police Involvement in a Provincial Reconstruction Team (PRT) in Afghanistan*. http://www.rcmp-grc.gc.ca/po-mp/afghanistan-eng.htm. August 2005. (updated) February 2008.
Royal Danish Ministry of Foreign Affairs. *The Power of Culture: The Cultural Dimensions in Development*. Copenhagen: Nielson & Krohn, 2000.
Saferworld and International Alert. *Developing an EU Strategy to Address Fragile States: Priorities of the UK Presidency of the EU in 2005*. London: Saferworld and International Alert, June 2005.
Salomons, D. "Chapter 2: Security: An Absolute Prerequisite." In *Postconflict Development: Meeting New Challenges*, ed. Gerd Junne and Willemihn Verkoren. Boulder, CO: Lynne Rienner Publishers, 2004.
Sandia National Laboratories. "Measures of Effectiveness: An Annotated Bibliography." *Sandia Report SAND2004-2902*. Albuquerque, NM: Sandia National Laboratories, 2004.
Sawhill, J., and D. Williamson. "Measuring What Matters in Nonprofits." *McKinsey Quarterly*. www.mckinseyquarterly.com. May 2001.
Schein, E.H. "Kurt Lewin's Change Theory in the Field and in the Classroom: Notes toward a Model of Managed Learning." *A2Z Psychology Online*. http://www.a2zpsychology.com/articles/kurt lewin's_change_theory.htm Accessed: 9 October 2008.
Sedra, M., and P. Middlebrook. *Afghanistan's Problematic Path to Peace: Lessons in State Building in the Post September 11 Era*. Washington, DC: Foreign Policy in Focus, March 2004.
Sen, A. *Identity and Violence*. New York: W.W. Norton, 2006.
Smiley, M.A. "Planned Change in Organizational Development." Term paper for MG456, Emporia, 2001. http://academic.emporia.edu/smithwil/001fmg456/eja/smiley.html#Theories%20of%20Planned Accessed: 9 October 2008.
Smith, E.A. *Effects Based Operations: Applying Network Centric Warfare in Peace, Crisis, and War: Command and Control Research Program*. Washington, DC: Department of Defence, Government of the United States, 2002.
Sproles, N. "Getting the Measures of Test and Evaluation." *Journal of Electrical and Electronics Engineering* 17, no. 2. (April 1997): 95-101.

– "Measures of Effectiveness: How Will I Recognize That I Have Succeeded?" Proceedings of INCOSE UK Fourth Annual Symposium. Hendon, UK: INCOSE UK (1-2 June 1998): 95-102.
– "Coming to Grips with Measures of Effectiveness." *System Engineering* 3, no. 1 (February 2000): 50-8.
– "The Difficult Problem of Establishing Measures of Effectiveness for Command and Control: A Systems Engineering Perspective." *System Engineering* 4, no. 2 (May 2001): 145-55.
Storey, D. "Six Steps to Heaven: Evaluating the Impact of Public Policies to Support Small Business in Developed Economies." *International Journal of Entrepreneurial Education* 1, no. 2 (2002): 181-202.
Swisspeace. *FAST Update: Afghanistan. Semi-Annual Risk Assessment, December 2004 to May 2005*. Berne: Swisspeace, 2005.
Telford, J., and J. Cosgrave. *Joint Evaluation of the International Response to the Indian Ocean Tsunami*. London: Tsunami Evaluation Coalition 2006.
Tonnies, F. *Gemeinschaft und Gesellscaft (Community and Society)*. 1887. Translated by Charles P. Loomis. New York: Dover 2002.
Tucker, J. "Types of Change: Developmental, Transitional and Transformational." *Business Management*. August 2007. http://businessmanagement.suite101.com/article.cfm/types_of_change Accessed: 9 October 2008.
United Nations Development Group. *Inter-Agency Framework for Conflict Analysis in Transition Situations*. http://www.undg.org/index.cfm?P=150. New York: United Nations, November 2004.
United States Department of State (USDS), Office of the Coordinator for Reconstruction and Stabilization (OCRS). *Post-Conflict Reconstruction Essential Tasks*. Washington, DC: OCRS, USDS, April 2005.
United States Government Accountability Office (USGOA). *Afghanistan Reconstruction: Despite Some Progress, Deteriorating Security and Other Obstacles Continue to Threaten Achievement of US Goals: GAO-05-742*. Report presented to Congressional Committee, July 2005.
United States Institute for Peace. "Measuring Progress in Conflict Environments (MPICE)." *Metrics Framework for Assessing Conflict Transformation and Stabilization*. Washington, DC: United States Institute of Peace, February 2008.
– "The Cycle of Theory and Practice." *PeaceWatch* 14, no. 2 (June 2008): 4-5.
United States Joint War Warfighting Center. *Commander's Handbook for an Effects-Based Approach to Joint Operations*. Joint Concept Development and Experimentation Directorate, Standing Joint Force Headquarters, 2006.
Venetoklis, T. *Methods Applied in Evaluating Business Subsidy Programs: A Survey*. Vatt-Discussion Paper no. 236. Helsinki: Government Institute for Economic Research, December 2000.
Waldman, M. *Falling Short: Aid Effectiveness in Afghanistan*. ACBAR Advocacy Series. Kabul, Afghanistan: ACBAR, March 2008.
Wallace, T., with L. Bornstein and J. Chapman. *The Aid Chain: Coercion and Commitment in Development NGOs*. London: Practical Action, 2006.
Weber, C. *Simulating Sovereignty, Intervention, the State and Symbolic Exchanges*. Cambridge, UK: Cambridge University Press, 1994.

Wiharta, S., H. Ahmad, J.-Y. Haine, J. Löfgren, and T. Randall. *The Effectiveness of Foreign Military Assets in Natural Disaster Response*. Stockholm: Stockholm International Peace Research Institute, 2008.
Williams, G.H. *Engineering Peace: The Military Role in Postconflict Reconstruction*. Washington, DC: United States Institute of Peace, 2005.
Winchester, H.P.M. "Qualitative Research and Its Place in Human Geography." In *Qualitative Research Methods in Human Geography*, ed. Iain Hay. Oxford, UK: Oxford University Press, 2000.
Wood, A., R. Apthorpe, and J. Borton. *Evaluating International Humanitarian Action: Reflections from Practitioners*. London: Zed Books/ALNAP, 2001.
World Bank. "Reconstruction and Development Program in Bosnia and Herzegovina: Progress Update." World Bank Group, Country Office Bosnia and Herzegovina. Sarajevo. www.worldbank.org/ba . June 2002.
– *Monitoring and Evaluation: Some Tools, Methods and Approaches*. Washington, DC: Operations Evaluations Department, Evaluation Capacity Development World Bank, 2004.
– *Influential Evaluations: Evaluations That Improved Performance and Impacts of Development Programs*. Washington, DC: Operations Evaluations Department, Evaluation Capacity Development, World Bank, 2004.
– *Country Assistance Evaluations: CAE Methodology*. http://www.worldbank.org/oed/countries/cae/cae_methodology.html. 2005.

Further Websites

Development Gateway. Accessible Information on Development Activities. www.developmentgateway.com.
Economic Reconstruction and Development in South East Europe. www.seerecon.org.
European Bank for Reconstruction and Development. www.ebrd.com
Sphere Project. http://www.sphereproject.org.
Theory of Change. http://www.theoryofchange.org/.
World Bank. http://www.worldbank.org.

Author Biography

SARAH JANE MEHARG, PH.D.

Dr Meharg is the senior research associate in the Department of Research, Education and Learning Design at the Pearson Peacekeeping Centre (PPC), Ottawa, Canada.

In her position at the PPC, Dr Meharg manages research projects on issues related to global peace and security. She has planned, coordinated, and implemented field research programs in Bosnia-Herzegovina, Belgium, and Canada, as well as managed and directed multi-national field research teams. She also represents the PPC at international conferences, where she presents primary research on peace operations.

Dr Meharg conducts ongoing research and advisement on simulation exercises, course materials, and learning products for multi-national and multicultural adult learners who are involved with the PPC. She has extensive writing and editing experience and has published chapters and journal articles in peer-reviewed journals, including the book *Helping Hands and Loaded Arms: Navigating the Military and Humanitarian Space* (2007).

She is a leading post-conflict reconstruction theorist and specializes in the study of the intentional destruction of culturally symbolic places during contemporary armed conflict and the reconstruction of these important places in post-conflict theatres. Her unique theory of conflict – identicide (1997) – defines the attacks perpetrated against people and their cultural places (e.g., the Bridge of Mostar, the Bamiyan Buddhas, historic libraries, the World Trade Towers). Dr Meharg achieved top honours in innovative doctoral research at Queen's University, Canada, and has received numerous awards for research, writing, and conference presentations. She has a regional focus on the Balkans and is currently researching the environment of peace operations, military geography, and identicide.

Dr Meharg is an adjunct professor at the Royal Military College of Canada and serves as a research fellow with the Centre for Security and Defence Studies and the Canadian Defence and Foreign Affairs Institute. She is president of Peace and Conflict Planners Canada Inc., a firm that specializes in economic and cultural reconstruction in conflict-affected areas as well as new-use technology applications for post-conflict reconstruction.

An avid outdoorsperson, she enjoys canoeing, camping, hiking, skiing, riding, and tennis with her husband and family.

Contributors

John Borton

After working as the planning officer for the Government of Botswana's National Drought Relief, John Borton has devoted the last twenty-five years to research, evaluation, networking, and capacity development within the field of international disaster mitigation and humanitarian action. From 1991 to 2002 he was a research fellow at the Overseas Development Institute in London where he established and led the ODI Relief and Rehabilitation Network (now Humanitarian Practice Network), led Study III of the Joint Evaluation of Emergency Assistance to Rwanda (JEEAR), established the Active Learning Network for Accountability and Performance in Humanitarian Action (ALNAP), and served as coordinator for its first five years.

Emery Brusset

After a career in the United Nations agencies (UNHCR, UNDP) serving in Iraq, Sudan, and Rwanda, Emery Brusset specialized in conflict prevention, human rights protection, and humanitarian aid. He has carried out a number of donor-based regional evaluations of humanitarian assistance and conflict programs, most recently an evaluation of Norwegian research in conflict prevention and peace-building, and an OECD study on linkages between human rights and conflict programming. He often coordinates complex teams in the field, as out of a total of ninety-one short-term assignments undertaken since beginning consulting work between January 1995 to 2009, he has undertaken fifty-one evaluations (57 percent of all consulting assignments); for thirty of these evaluations, he was the team leader for the entire assignment (for all studies, and 38 percent of all consultancies), responsible for the quality and delivery of the report to the client. His core client base is that of the OECD DAC Evaluation Working Group (Nordics, France, Belgium, UK, US, Canada), plus the United Nations, Red Cross, and non-governmental organizations. He has carried out commissioned research on behalf of the extractive industry as well as the French Ministry of Defence.

David Chuter

Based in Paris, David Chuter specializes in issues such as the reform of the security sector, pre- and post-conflict issues, and the link between security and development and civil-military relations around the world. From 1976 to 2008 he worked for the UK Ministry of Defence, primarily in the international area. He was responsible for issues such as arms control, the development of European defence, the support of exports to Asia, and Balkan war crimes and transitional justice issues. From 2005 to 2008 he worked in the French Ministry of Defence. Since the early 1990s he has had a parallel academic career, including spells at the Centre for Defence Studies at London University and the International Institute for Strategic Studies. He is the author of three books (a fourth in preparation) and numerous articles, all related to security issues. In 1993 he became involved on a personal basis with the defence transformation process in South Africa and has written extensively on the subject as well as lecturing in Africa and in Europe and acting as an informal consultant to several governments.

Stuart Gordon

Stuart Gordon is an academic in the Department of Defence and International Affairs at the Royal Military Academy, UK. He is also a research fellow at Reading University and a member of the Board of International Advisers to Liverpool Hope University's Centre for War and Peace Studies. He is currently the program director for the Academy's Measuring the Effectiveness of Stabilisation Operations Programme and a part of a research project, based in Tuft's University's Feinstein Center, that is exploring the use of development assistance in conflict environments. He specializes in the politics of conflict and has written widely on various aspects of strategic studies – principally military strategy, UN peacekeeping, and the securitization of development assistance. He has conducted research in Afghanistan, Iraq, Nepal, Sudan, Eritrea, Ethiopia, Somalia, Cyprus, Croatia, and Bosnia-Herzegovina. During 2003 he was the operations director for the US/UK's Iraq Humanitarian Operations Centre in Baghdad. He has taught at the Joint Services' Command and Staff College and at Reading University.

Keith B. Hauk

Keith B. Hauk is a US Army colonel currently assigned to Headquarters, Department of the Army G-3, as chief of the Resource Analysis and Integration Division. An infantryman by training, he has commanded both light and mechanized infantry units and has served as an embedded advisor with the Royal Saudi Land Forces. His current area of specialization is operational planning and assessment. Previous assignments include deputy chief of Strategic Planning and Assessments at the Multinational Security Transition Command – Iraq; senior operations officer, Directorate for Operations, J-3, the Joint Staff, in Washington DC; and deputy chief of Current Operations, XVIII Airborne Corps and Coalition/Joint Task Force-180, in Afghanistan. He holds a bachelor's degree in engineering from the US Military Academy, West Point, and master's degrees in economics from the Colorado School of Mines, Golden, Colorado, and national security studies from the US Naval War College, Newport, Rhode Island.

Rory Keane

Rory Keane (Ph.D.) is a former Marie Curie Research Fellow on European Security and Defence Policy. He was stationed in Belgrade from 2000 to 2003, firstly with the Civic Education Programme at the University of Belgrade and later with the OSCE. Subsequently, he worked for the European Commission, specifically on security sector reform in the Democratic Republic of the Congo and demilitarization, demobilization, and reintegration in the Great Lakes Region. He currently leads work relating to security system reform, armed violence reduction, and the security and development interface at the OECD's International Network on Conflict and Fragility (INCAF). He has published broadly on matters relating to security and development and participates regularly in international fora on these matters.

Stephen Mariano

Stephen J. Mariano is a US Army colonel currently assigned to the US Army Southern European Task Force as the chief of Strategy, Plans and Policy. He was a visiting defence fellow at the Queen's Centre for International Relations, Kingston, Ontario, and is a doctoral candidate in war studies at the Royal Military College of Canada. His previous assignments include chief of Strategic Planning and Assessments at the Multinational Security Transition Command – Iraq in Baghdad; military advisor to NATO's Senior Civilian Representative in Afghanistan; strategic planner at the NATO Headquarters in Brussels; chief of Coalition Plans at the US European Command in Stuttgart; and professor of military strategy and comparative military systems at the US Military Academy, West Point. He holds a bachelor's degree in mathematics and economics from the University of California, Santa Barbara, and a master's degree in national security affairs from the Naval Postgraduate School, Monterey.

Kristiina Rintakoski

Kristiina Rintakoski is the director for programs, Crisis Management Initiative (CMI), Helsinki. She is responsible for overseeing the content development and fundraising of CMI's programmatic activities. Her areas of specialization are European security, crisis management, state-building, and use of information technology in crisis management. She is coordinating a multi-year participatory foresight process on European security (FORESEC) and leading a European level expert group on foresight and scenarios under European Security Research and Innovation Forum. She joined CMI in October 2000 and worked as a security policy adviser for President Martti Ahtisaari. Previously she worked in the OSCE Mission to Bosnia and Herzegovina as a democratization officer. Her other placements included the Political Department of the Finnish Ministry for Foreign Affairs, External Relations Directorate in the European Commission, and European organizations representing small and medium-sized enterprises (EUROPMI, Belgium 1995 and CNA, Italy 1996). She holds a master's degree in international relations from Tampere University, 1997, and a European master's degree in human rights and democratization from the University of Padova, Italy, 1998.

Jake Sherman

Jake Sherman is associate director for Peacekeeping and Security Sector Reform at New York University's Center on International Cooperation. As a senior fellow at CIC, he also contributes to work on state-building and peace-building. During 2008 he was seconded to the secretariat of the Independent Panel on Safety and Security of UN Personnel and Premises. From 2005 to 2007 he was a consultant on peace-building issues in Cambodia with Oxfam GB, American Friends Service Committee, and the Alliance for Conflict Transformation, a local NGO. Previously, he worked for the United Nations Assistance Mission in Afghanistan as a political officer in the Office of the Special Representative of the Secretary-General and in the mission's northeast regional field office; as a program officer with the International Peace Academy; and with Physicians for Human Rights in the Balkans. He holds a bachelor's degree in anthropology from Tufts University and a master's degree in international affairs from the School of International and Public Affairs, Columbia University.

Index

academia, 7, 260
AccountAbility, 87n82
accountability, 51–52. *See also* Humanitarian Accountability Partnership
 and Center on International Cooperation, 211
 donor requirements for, 161, 165–66
 gaps in, 90–91
 initiatives, 162–63
 and international standards, 91, 163, 240, 261–62
 and measuring, 10, 11, 74, 162–63
 Results Based Management and Accountability Framework, 97
Active Learning Network for Accountability and Performance in Humanitarian Action (ALNAP)
 establishment of, 90, 161
 evaluation typology of, 76, 77(table), 78
 feasibility study of assessment mechanisms, 90
 and recipient views, 163
 and system-wide evaluations, 166
additionality, 58–59
affected people. *See* beneficiaries; recipient populations
Afghan Compact, 236
Afghanistan. *See also* provincial reconstruction teams

Afghanistan
 Agency Co-ordinating Body for Afghan Relief, 35
 behavioural change in, 85n5
 Canadian objectives in, 18n25, 233
 and CIDA, 233
 civil-military relations in, 155
 and International Security Assistance Force, 18n25
 Manley Report on, 18n25
 measuring effectiveness in, 36, 177–78, 182n3; auditing, 79; "Blue Peter spendometer" analysis, 179–80, 182n2; developing measures, 17n8; effects diagram, 192(fig); government reports, 6–7; holistic approach to, 245; indicators, 105, 236; local trust levels, 137; LogFrames, 58; results-based, 93; Tactical Conflict Assessment Framework, 180–81
 mortality surveys in, 165
 peace-building approaches in, 29, 156
 Quick Impact Projects in, 17n8
 synergies between stakeholders, 233, 237
 UK presence in, 177–78, 180–81
Africa, 115, 161, 184, 185, 236, 246
African Food Emergency, 161
African Union, 246

Amnesty International, 7
applicability, 106
association. *See* gesellschaft
auditing, 10, 79

"badges." *See* police sector
Balanced Scorecard, 71, 170
Balkans, 93, 179–80, 182n3
baseline data, 97, 259
behavioural change, 45, 85n5
belief systems, 47, 131
benchmarks. *See also* goals; *specific sectors*
  for assessing overall effectiveness, 222, 239
  changing, 12
  definition of, 81
  and evaluations, 78, 84
  realistic, 222
  of United Nations, 81, 209–10
  using objectives as, 191
  in war-affected environments, 98, 100
beneficiaries, 41–42, 107–8, 163. *See also* recipient populations
BERCI International, 42
best practices, 11, 51–53, 67, 75–76, 204, 205
Blair, Tony, 30, 53, 54
"Blue Peter spendometer" analysis, 179–80, 182n2
"boots." *See* military sector
Borton, John, 87n68, 159–68, 285
Bosnia-Herzegovina
  field research in, 138–46, 147n28, 264–67
  Instructions to Parties, 133
  measuring success and performance in, 129–34, 264–67
  Mission Implementation Plans, 133
  NATO Stabilisation Force Transition Strategy in, 129–30, 132
  peace education in, 112
  photo archive of progress in, 124
  stakeholder synergies in, 238
  UN Protection Force in, 185–86, 187n1

Brahimi Report, 248
Brusset, Emery, 61, 76, 189–200, 285–86. *See also* Channel Research; significance-of-impact methodology

Canada
  and comprehensive approach, 229–30, 232–33
  Department of Foreign Affairs and International Trade: measuring and reporting, 96–97, 235; objectives in Afghanistan, 233; Stabilization and Reconstruction Task Force, 96–97, 235; success of, 97
  Department of National Defence, 232–33; measuring effectiveness, 17n8, 64
  inter-departmental assessments, 235
  Manley Report on Afghanistan, 18n25
  and NATO, 18n25
  planning future interventions, 35
Canadian Forces, 17n8, 79
Canadian International Development Agency (CIDA), 49, 93–94, 233
CARE, 7, 10, 73
cause-and-effect mechanisms for measuring. *See* Logical Frameworks; measures of effectiveness; results-based measuring
cause-and-effect relationships, 58–60, 59(fig), 67–71
Center for Strategic and International Studies, 6
Center on International Cooperation, 119(fig), 210–12, 213n1
change management theories, 47–49
change theory, 46–47, 49
Channel Research, 40, 61, 76, 190, 194, 201n8
Chuter, David, 151–52, 183–87, 286
clients, 41. *See also* beneficiaries; recipients

codes of conduct, 38–39, 44n17, 162
coherence, 52, 78–79
Collaborative for Development Action, 163
colonialism, 28–29, 43n4
communities, imagined, 43n2
community. *See* gemeinschaft
compacts, 211, 221, 236
Compendium of Operational Frameworks for Peacebuilding and Donor Co-ordination, 115
comprehensive approach to interventions, 229–41
  assessing effectiveness in, 239–41, 242n35
  challenges to, 230–31, 232–33, 234
  cluster approach of, 230
  coordinated approach of, 231, 232
  definition of, 229–30, 238–39
  degrees of, 239
  integrated approach of, 231–32
  inter-agency approach of, 230
  and International Security Assistance Force, 233
  joined-up approach of, 230, 231
  mechanisms and tools for, 230
  policy-reality gap in, 238–39
  as solution to poor success rates, 230
  synergies among stakeholders in, 234–39
  3D approach of, 230, 241n3
  training and education on, 252
conditions-objectives-task taxonomy, 170–71
conflict, 4(fig), 93, 98, 178
conflict-analysis approach. *See* significance-of-impact methodology
conflict prevention, 51, 191
conflict resolution, 51
conflict sensitivity, 53, 205
Congo, Democratic Republic of, 165, 201n6
contact groups, 183–84
coordination, 52
corruption, 262n5
Cotonou Agreement, 236

crisis management, 33, 47, 153–56, 183–84, 185
  measuring the effectiveness of, 203–7
  and policy, 14
  as political acts, 219
Crisis Management Initiative, 75–76, 203–7
cultural assumptions, changing, 47

DARA's Humanitarian Response Index, 81
Darfur, 165, 246
data sets. *See also* information management
  access to, 33
  baseline, 97, 259
  in government reports, 6–7
  host-nation gathering of, 174
  in measuring effectiveness, 62–63, 63(fig), 64, 249–50
  transferability of, 13
  usability of, 6
Dayton Peace Accord, 130, 133
defence sector. *See* 3D approach; military sector
Denmark, 161
dependency theory, 46
developed country, definition of, 54n2
development sector. *See also* 3D approach
  as an industry, 16n3
  benchmarks, 78
  change management in, 49
  evaluations in, 78
  goals and mandates of, 8–9
  linear planning method in, 51
  measuring, 5, 11, 256
  mechanisms and tools, 58, 93–96, 95(fig), 107–8, 111, 179
  on provincial reconstruction teams, 17n8
  recommended good practices, 52
  and stakeholder incompatibilites, 7
  and standards for sustainable development, 87n82
  worldviews, 43, 216

development theory, 45–46
diplomacy sector, 2(fig), 7. *See also* 3D approach
displacement, 58–59
doctrine of international community, 30–33, 51–53, 54, 90–91
donors
  accountability requirements of, 10, 161
  Compendium of Operational Frameworks for Peacebuilding and Donor Co-ordination, 115
  and fragile states, 88n96, 213n1
  and local ownership, 158n4
  and Logical Framework Approach, 164
  project methodology adopted by, 94–96, 95(fig)
  reporting to, 9, 83, 165–66, 219, 225, 226
duration, 197

effectiveness, 51–52, 61, 261–62. *See also* measures of effectiveness (MOEs)
effects-based approach to operations, 63, 63(fig8), 101, 102–5(figs), 104–5, 131, 169, 225, 250
effects diagram, 192(fig)
efficiency, 34–35, 51–52, 71, 261–62
end-users. *See* beneficiaries
epistemic community, 151–52
ethnic reconciliation, measuring progress of, 131–32
EuropeAid handbook, 206, 208n4
European Union
  in Africa, 184, 185, 236
  on comprehensive approach, 229–30
  and development stakeholders, 236
  EUJUST LEX evaluation, 109–10, 137
  European Commission, 93, 190, 204
  European Security and Defence Policy, 64–66
  Integrated Rule of Law Mission, 109–10
  and International Financial Reporting Standards, 79
  on lessons learned, 67
  measuring effectiveness and performance, 65–66, 93, 132
  member state objectives, 184, 185
  planning future interventions, 35
evaluating. *See also* evaluation methodologies; evaluations
  challenges to, 220
  criteria for, 205, 206
  definition of, 74, 205
  at early stages of activities, 204
  effective method of, 84–85
  future trends in, 207
  growth of, 161
  and objectives, 199
  in post-conflict interventions, 34
  process of, 74–75, 75(fig)
  at project level, 246–47
  questions asked in, 206
  and stakeholders, 204–5
  typology of ALNAP, 76, 77(table), 78
  value of, 221
evaluation methodologies, 84–85, 189–201
  cause and effect, 189, 191, 193, 193(fig)
  and Chinese worldview, 189
  conflict analysis-based evaluation, 189
  diagram of effects methodology, 190–91, 192(fig), 193
  guiding principles of, 76, 80
  in humanitarian sector, 67, 76, 77(table), 78, 91
  language of, 78–79
  Logical Framework, 190
  numbers vs narratives in, 84–85, 116
  and OECD-DAC guidelines, 190, 226
  outcome mapping, 193
  significance-of-impact methodology, 194–99, 195(fig), 198(fig), 200, 201n5
  and theories of change, 191
  theory-based, 121
  using templates, 206

Index 293

and worldview of other cultures, 199
evaluations, 74–79, 84, 221
  "black box" in, 193(fig)
  influence of initiatives, 105, 105(fig)
  public repository of, 224
  role of, 166
  typology of, 77(table)
extent, 197, 206

feasibility, 80, 90, 106
finance sector, 7
first-order effects, 84
Flemming, Steve, 8, 50, 129–32
focus-group interviews, 172–73, 223, 226
fragile states, 29, 55n12, 88n96, 213n1
Fragile States and Situations of Fragility: France's Policy Paper, 54n3
fragility, assessing levels of, 100–101
France, 52, 54n3, 55n12, 70–71, 100–101
  Paris Declaration on Aid Effectiveness, 51–53
Fritz Institute, 163
"From Fragility to Resilience: Concepts and Dilemmas of Statebuilding in Fragile States," 213n1

gemeinschaft, 156, 158n10
gesellschaft, 156, 158n10
goals, 78, 170, 211, 217, 224
Gordon, Stuart, 58, 83, 151–52, 177–87, 286
Governance Indicators, 81, 105–6
government sector, 2–3, 6–7, 16n3, 49. *See also* whole-of-government approach; whole-of-government sector
Great Lakes region, 115
Grid of Fragilities, 100–101
Guinea, Republic of, 93

Haiti, 74, 93, 126n7, 135–36
harm, doing, 51, 53, 80–81, 219. *See also* displacement
Hauk, Keith, 151–52, 169–75, 287
Health Canada, 82

health information, generating, 165
hostile environments, 133–35, 134(fig), 217, 246–47
host nations, 7, 41, 155–56, 174, 223, 224
human condition, 5, 9, 30–31, 72, 124
Human Development Indicators, 210
Humanitarian Accountability and Quality Management Standard, 163, 240
Humanitarian Accountability Partnership, 38, 90–91, 163, 168n10
Humanitarian Charter and Minimum Standards in Disaster Response, 90
humanitarianism, 16n3, 37–38, 38(fig), 125n3
Humanitarian Practice Network, 87n67
humanitarian sector
  activities of, 160
  alliances, 44n12
  approaches to interventions, 9, 35, 40, 230, 232
  benchmarks, 91, 92
  change management in, 49
  definition of, 159
  evaluations in, 67, 76, 77(table), 78, 91
  on "hearts and minds" campaigns, 252
  measuring, 8–9, 11, 36, 58;
    challenges to, 33–34, 164–67, 251;
    human condition, 5; trends in, 161–63, 166–67
  mechanisms and tools, 40–41, 89–92; capturing lessons learned, 67; Logical Framework Approach, 58, 164; performance indicators, 16n3; performance measurement, 73, 216–17; surveys at operation level, 164–65, 166
  motivations of, 10, 38
  objectives of, 159
  and People in Aid, 89–90
  and pre-disaster investment, 160

humanitarian sector (cont.)
  principles of, 37–38, 40, 216, 252
  on security companies, 10
  on self-assessment, 217
  and stakeholders, 7, 160–61
  standards in, 38–39, 80, 89–90
  as viewed by others, 2–3, 10, 251, 252
  worldviews of, 37–41, 43
human resources, 73, 226, 243–44
human rights, 30
human security, 31, 140, 154
  Human Security Project, 42, 92
  Human Security theory, 31–32
  Responsibility to Protect policy, 31–32

impacts, 70–71. *See also* significance-of-impact methodology
  assessing, 76, 207
  conceptual impacts, 70
  definition of, 70–71, 194
  evaluations of, 76, 193(fig), 199
  impact indicators, 81
  instrumental impacts, 70
  longer-term impacts, 250
  marginal impacts, 70
  measuring, 80, 178, 221
  total impacts, 70
Imposing Aid: Emergency Assistance to Refugees, 163
indicators, 81–82
  and challenges to reporting, 34
  Governance Quality Indicators, 81, 105–6
  Human Development Indicators, 210
  impact indicators, 81
  incomparability between sectors, 233
  indices of, 80, 81–82
  for measuring effectiveness, 105, 236
  outcome indicators, 81
  of performance, 16n3, 80, 81–82
  of policing success, 110–11
  of progress, 236
  realistic, 82
  selecting indicators of change, 222
  and United Nations, 216

Indonesia, 161, 204
inefficiency, definition of, 71
influence of initiatives, 105, 105(fig)
information age, 13, 46
information management, 257, 258–59, 261
inputs, 71, 180
institutional learning, 206, 207
Instructions to Parties, 133
intangibles, measuring of, 34, 34(table), 59–60, 177, 181, 220
InterAction, 162
Inter-Agency Framework for Conflict Analysis in Transition Situations, 98
International Committee of the Red Cross, 58, 81, 121(fig)
International Council of Voluntary Agencies, 44n12, 162
International Crisis Group, 236–37
International Development Research Centre, 121
International Federation of Red Cross and Red Crescent Societies, 39, 58
International Financial Reporting Standards, 79
International Humanitarian Law, 38
International Organization for Standardization, 79
International Red Cross and Red Crescent Movement and NGOs in Disaster Relief, 39, 162
International Security Assistance Force, 18n25, 233
interventions. *See also* comprehensive approach to interventions; *specific sector approaches to*
  balance of forces in, 47
  designing, 94–96, 95(fig), 217, 224
  as experiments, 255
  as form of neo-colonialism, 28–29
  goals of, 224
  for humanitarian purposes, 30, 31–32
  and in-mission training, 226
  logic of, 58
  motivating factors of, 217
  new liberal imperialists' approach to, 219

political nature of, 216
post-conflict, 34
realist approach to, 219
spectrum of operations in, 3–4, 4(fig)
trying to achieve too much in, 247–49
worldview of, 218(fig)
intervention stakeholders. *See* beneficiaries; recipient populations
intervention theories. *See* theories of intervention
Iraq
  "Blue Peter spendometer" analysis, 179–80, 182n2
  capacity-building problems in, 17n8
  government reports on progress in, 6–7
  imposition of westernized practices on, 29
  Iraqi Security Forces, 169–74
  "Measuring Security and Stability in Iraq," 169
  moral duty in, 186
  mortality surveys in, 165
  and Multi-National Security Transition Command mission, 170
  and Office of the Special Inspector General for Iraq Reconstruction, 17n8
  peace-building approaches in, 156
  police training project in, 137
  protecting oil pipelines of, 171
  success of invasion of, 186
  US overspending in, 35

joint approach. *See* comprehensive approach to interventions
Joint Committee on Standards for Educational Evaluation, 80
Just War theory, 31

Keane, Rory, 151–52, 153–57, 287
knowledge management, 256–61
Kosovo, 216

leadership, 16, 262
Lessard, Marc, 18n25

lessons identified, interim, 67
lessons learned, 11, 67
  capturing, 67, 204, 205
  contributing to knowledge growth, 217
  as critical to improving missions, 67
  and military measures of effectiveness, 67
  process in US Army, 68(fig)
  web-based approach, 69(fig)
linear planning method, 51
local ownership. *See also* recipient populations
  and donors, 158n4
  military principle of, 216
  and new liberal imperialism approach, 156, 261–62
  OECD on, 158n4
  over metrics, 221
  of peace-building programs, 155–57, 248
  in peace process, 205
locals. *See* beneficiaries; recipient populations
logic, linear chain of, 59(fig)
Logical Framework Approach, 58, 94–96, 95(fig), 164
Logical Frameworks (LogFrames), 58, 94–96, 95(fig), 164, 179, 190, 221

macro-operations, assessing, 98–100, 99(fig)
mandates, 133, 135–36, 209, 221
Manley Report on Afghanistan (2008), 18n25
mapping, 116–22
  of mission types, 119(fig)
  of outcomes, 121, 121(fig), 193
  significance mapping process, 195–97, 195(fig)
  of UN missions, 119, 120(map)
  World Bank on, 121
  World Map of Peace Operations, 116, 117(map), 118(map), 119, 127n48
  of worldviews, 262
Mariano, Stephen, 151–52, 169–75, 287–88

Maslow's hierarchy of needs, 31, 32(fig)
measures of effectiveness (MOEs), 61–67
 data in, 64, 187, 249
 definition of, 61–62
 designing, 17n8, 35–36, 50, 64, 130, 132
 of disarmament, demobilization and reintegration, 63(fig7)
 focus of, 131
 identifying interim lessons, 67
 inputs vs. outcomes, 180
 internal measurement methods, 66–67
 language in, 58
 local perceptions of, 36, 138–46
 as military modalities, 8, 63–64, 66–67
 against objectives, 183–86
 in permissive and non-permissive environments, 133–35, 134(fig)
 qualitative approaches to, 247
 of reconstruction delivered, 36
 reporting on overall sectoral effectiveness and performance, 221–22
 rolling process, 66, 66(fig)
 of security incidents, 36
 and stakeholder motives, 186
 systems used in Bosnia-Herzegovina, 130
 Tactical Conflict Assessment Framework, 180–81, 180(table)
 tangible vs. intangible benefits of peace, 177
 and typical mission analysis process, 104–5, 104(fig)
 using traffic light coding, 179–80, 182n3
measures of performance (MOPs), 11, 62. *See also* performance measuring
measures of progress, 61–67
measuring
 modalities of, 62(fig)
 policy options for developing, 223–26
 requirements for, 60
 scope of, 60
 value of, 221

measuring effectiveness
 challenges to, 33–35, 36, 124–25, 219
 and common language of, 58
 future challenges and opportunities in, 249–50, 251
 interview questions on, 263–64
 Multi-National Experimentation process of, 248
 of peace operations, 33, 112, 132, 135, 137
 standardization of, 35
measuring mechanisms and tools, 5–6, 7, 8, 11, 12, 89–125, 219, 224. *See also* mapping; presentation of measures and results; *specific sectors*
 adapting, 226
 arising from social sciences, 115–16
 Assessment of Governance Quality Indicators, 81, 105–6
 attribution and influence levels, 105, 105(fig)
 challenges to, 124–25
 combat-centric perspective, 11
 Compendium of Operation Frameworks for Peacebuilding and Donor Co-ordination, 115
 cost-benefit and cost-effectiveness analyses, 115–16
 effects-based approach, 101, 102–5(figs), 104–5
 EUJUST LEX evaluation, 109–10, 137
 Evaluation of Humanitarian Action, 91
 Grid of Fragilities, 100–101
 Humanitarian Accountability Partnership, 38, 90–91, 163, 168n10
 Human Security Project, 42, 92
 implementation planning, 94
 Inter-Agency Framework for Conflict Analysis in Transition Situations, 98
 Joint Assessment Mission, 108–9, 109(fig)
 linear, 51
 Logical Frameworks, 58, 94–96, 95(fig), 164, 179, 190, 221

Index 297

measuring mechanisms and tools (cont.)
  Metrics Framework for Assessing Conflict Transformation and Stabilization, 92–93
  mission analysis process, 104(fig)
  nonlinear dynamics, 50
  operational research methods, 105(fig), 106–7
  participatory methods, 111
  policing success indicators project, 110–11
  Post-Conflict Reconstruction Essential Tasks, 98–100, 99(fig)
  Rapid Assessment Process, 107–8
  Rapid Rural Appraisals, 107
  Reflecting on Peace Practice Project, 111–15, 114(fig)
  results-based, 7, 49–51, 93
  Soft Systems Methodology, 106–7
  Sphere standards, 80, 89–90, 162
  and stakeholder values, 8
  technical limitations of, 5
  for testing concepts, 106
"Measuring Security and Stability in Iraq," 169
Mercy Corps, 7
metrics, 80–81. *See also* measures of effectiveness
Metrics Framework for Assessing Conflict Transformation and Stabilization, 82, 92–93, 126n7
metrics systems, 92–93, 210–11
Microsoft Word, 240–41
military power, 262n2
military sector. *See also* effects-based approach to operations; lessons learned; measures of effectiveness
  ability to measure success, 8, 9, 137
  approaches to measuring, 8, 9, 10, 11, 35–36, 57, 73, 131
  approaches to operations, 38, 38(fig), 232
  audit trail, 79
  best practices, 67
  challenges to measuring, 33
  change management in, 49

military sector (cont.)
  consulting with recipients, 217
  deployments in peace operations, 119(fig)
  "doing the right problem vs. doing the problem right," 64, 65(fig)
  future challenges and opportunities in, 245–46
  and host nations, 223
  on humanitarians, 10
  indices of indicators used, 81–82
  measuring mechanisms and tools, 101–7; Assessment of Governance Quality Indicators, 105–6; cost-benefit and cost-effectiveness analyses, 115–16; effects assessment reports, 102(fig); evaluating the influence of initiatives, 105, 105(fig); lines of operations using effects, 103(fig); mission analysis process, 104(fig); operational research methods, 106–7; participatory methods, 111
  motivations in humanitarianism, 38, 38(fig)
  and other sectors, 2–3, 245–46, 252
  planning in, 58, 64, 67, 132
  presentation of results, 102(fig), 123, 123(fig28)
  Quick Impact Projects (QIPs), 17n8
  and stakeholder incompatibilites, 7, 8
  and traffic light coding system, 102(fig), 123, 123(fig), 130, 134, 179
  worldviews, 35–36, 43, 216
Millennium Declaration and Development Goals, 210, 236
Mission Implementation Plans, 133
modernization theory, 45–46
monitoring, 16n3, 74, 75, 204–5, 221, 247. *See also* Standardized Monitoring and Assessment of Relief and Transition
moral duty, 186
mortality rates and surveys, 165
Multi-National Experimentation process, 248

narratives vs. numbers, 7, 82–85, 116, 221–23, 226
needs, hierarchy of, 31, 32(fig)
neo-colonialism, 28–29
neopatrimonial states, 155–56
Netherlands, 161
new liberal imperialism, 220
non-governmental organizations, 8–9, 10, 39, 112, 115, 162, 251. *See also* Crisis Management Initiative; humanitarian sector
Nordic Consulting Group, 40
North Atlantic Treaty Organization (NATO)
  approach to interventions, 28–29, 158n7, 233
  Canada's commitment to, 18n25
  International Security Assistance Force, 18n25, 233
  measuring progress and effectiveness, 18n25, 35, 129–30, 236, 248
  Military Committee Conference (2007), 18n25
Norway, 197, 198(fig)
not-for-profit organizations, 8–9
numbers vs. narratives, 82–85, 116

objectives, 220
  in hostile environments, 246–47
  incompatible between sectors, 10
  levels and types of, 183–86
  measuring against, 60, 183–86, 191
  and project planning, 94–96, 95(fig)
  used in evaluation, 199
operations, spectrum of, 3–4, 4(fig)
Organisation for Economic Co-Operation and Development (OECD)
  cost of its humanitarian assistance, 160
  Development Assistance Committee: criteria for interventionists and evaluators, 39–40, 60, 226; on evaluating, 115, 161, 168n9, 190; on local ownership, 158n4; *Principles for Good International Engagement in Fragile States*, 51–52; and theory of change, 191

outcomes. *See also* significance-of-impact methodology
  definition of, 70, 194
  and impacts, 67–71
  indicators, 81
  mapping, 121(fig), 193
  measuring, 9, 145, 180
  modalities for, 11
  relationship between issues and, 195(fig), 196
outputs, 70, 71, 194
Overseas Development Institute, 87n67
Oxfam, 7

Paris Declaration on Aid Effectiveness, 51–53
peace
  ideal of, 199
  peace vs. stabilization, 247
  stakeholder paradigms of, 57–58
  tangible vs. intangible benefits of, 177
  theories of, 51, 196
  writ large, 112, 113
peace-building, 3–4. *See also* peace operations
  costs of, 16n3
  EU Initiative for Peacebuilding, 204
  evaluating, 115, 191, 193
  and international community, 211–12
  lack of understanding of, 50, 210
  and local ownership, 155–57, 248, 261–62
  objectives of, 153, 156–57, 191
  research contributions to, 197, 198(fig)
  standards in, 80
  and theory of peace, 196
peace-building sector, 16n3, 50, 93, 111–15, 114(fig), 126n43
peace economy, 3, 16n3, 36
peacekeeping, 16n3. *See also* peace operations
Peacekeeping and Stability Operations Institute, 68(fig)
peace operations
  activities of, 33

future challenges and opportunities of; in civilian policing, 243–45; in civilian sector, 246–47; comprehensive approach, 252; measuring effectiveness, 249–50, 251; in military sector, 245–46; operational awareness between sectors, 252–53; relevancy of traditional approaches, 253; trying to achieve too much, 247–49
goals of, 33, 47, 186
locals on effectiveness of, 138–46
monitoring and evaluation modalities, 16n3
and policy, 14
as political acts, 153–54, 219
political focus of, 154–55, 158n5
peace work, 111, 112
Pearson Peacekeeping Centre, 20–21
field research in Bosnia-Herzegovina, 138–46, 147n28, 264–67
interview questions on measuring effectiveness (2008), 263–64
People in Aid, 89–90
performance measuring, 6, 71–74, 72(fig13), 133–35, 134(fig), 171, 256
performance monitoring, 93–94
performance reporting, 93–94, 221–23
Philippines, 93
photograph archiving, 124
play space, 1. *See also* tradespace
police sector
ability to measure success, 8–9, 10, 33–34, 136
assessment of Timor-Leste Police Service, 108–9, 109(fig)
change management in, 49
as evaluated by locals, 42
evaluation of EU police training project, 109–10
measuring in, 57–58, 74, 135–36
and other sectors, 2–3, 252
policing as international mission element, 136
policing success indicators research project, 110–11

and Rapid Assessment Process, 107–8
stakeholder incompatibilities, 7
and sustainable change, 136–37, 137(fig)
training post-conflict police, 244
policy-makers, tools for, 93
policy options for developing an approach to measuring, 223–26
political decision-makers, tool for, 110–11
populations affected. *See* beneficiaries; recipient populations
post-conflict environments, 34, 244, 256
Post-Conflict Reconstruction Essential Tasks, 98–100, 99(fig)
power, types of, 262n2
predictability, 52
presentation of measures and results, 122–24. *See also* mapping
primary stakeholders. *See* beneficiaries
private sector, 2–3, 7, 10
problem-solving, approaches to, 217–18
progress. *See* success
progress measuring, 53, 220, 221
progress reporting, 11, 13, 34, 34(table), 235
provincial reconstruction teams, 17n8, 58, 105, 155, 177–78, 180–81
public-opinion polling, 172–73

qualitative measuring, 83–84, 107, 225, 226
quality initiatives, 162–63
quantitative measuring, 83, 84, 116, 225
questioning, process of, 107
Quick Impact Projects, 17n8

RAND Corporation, 6, 11
rapid appraisal methods, 107–8
recipient populations
and comprehensive approach to interventions, 239, 245

recipient populations (cont.)
  creating trust in, 137, 238
  definition of, 41
  and designing interventions, 217
  on effectiveness of peace operations, 42, 138–46, 225, 256, 259
  engaged in measuring, 111, 137, 221, 222–23
  engaged in program planning and implementation, 51, 155–57, 204–5, 211–12, 248
  future of women and minorities in, 205
  and impact evaluations, 76
  long-term behavioural changes in, 59
  managing expectations with, 137
  measuring attitudes of, 179, 180, 212
  qualitative information gathering from, 83, 107
  and "quality of peace" processes, 205
  sharing evaluations with, 42, 224
  tracking changes in grievances of, 181
recipients, 41. *See also* non-governmental organizations
reconstruction, reporting on, 93–94, 124
Reflecting on Peace Practice project, 50, 93, 111–15, 114(fig), 126n43
relevance, 78–79, 197, 206
religious agenda, 7
reporting on overall sectoral effectiveness and performance, 221–23
research contributions to peacebuilding, 197, 198(fig)
resiliency, 100–101
resilient states. *See* fragile states
result, definition of a, 70–71
results-based measuring, 49–51, 93
Rintakoski, Kristiina, 64, 151–52, 203–7, 288
rule of law, 30, 76, 109–10
Rwanda, 90–91, 160, 161–62

"sandals." *See* humanitarian sector
scientific method. *See* Logical Frameworks

security, 12, 154–56, 220. *See also* human security
security sector, 2–3, 76, 154–55. *See also* military sector
Sherman, Jake, 151–52, 209–12, 288
significance-of-impact methodology, 194–99, 195(fig), 198(fig), 200, 201n5
social contract theory, 51
social science methodologies, 105–6, 115–16
Soft Systems Methodology, 106–7
Somalia, famine in, 161
sovereignty, 29–30, 158n3
Sphere Project and standards, 80, 89–90, 162
Sri Lanka, 161
Stabilisation Force Transition Strategy, 129–30, 132
stability, 12, 46, 100–101, 178
stakeholders, 3, 7–8, 10, 11, 15, 225. *See also* donors; host nations; recipient populations; *specific sectors*
  political consciousness of, 153–54, 157, 224
  synergies among, 185, 233, 234–39, 250–53
Standardized Monitoring and Assessment of Relief and Transition (SMART), 81, 165, 168n12
standards, 79–80
  applied vs. imposed, 31
  of human condition, 30–31
  in humanitarian sector, 38–39, 80, 89–90
  Joint Committee on Standards for Educational Evaluation, 80
  of sector success, 219
  Sphere Project, 80, 89–90, 162
  and sustainability, 261–62
state, definition of a, 29, 30
state-building, 205, 210, 211–12, 247
"state of the state" analysis, 210
state theory, 46
status-of-forces agreements, 73

status quo behaviour, 47
success, 3, 4, 5–6, 11–12, 15, 16n4, 97
  measuring, 4, 11, 15, 97, 131
Sudan, 93
"suits." *See* diplomacy sector
surveys, 83, 163, 164–65, 166, 179
sustainability, 51–52
  and evaluations, 205, 206
  and international standards, 261–62
  as key in verification, 78–79, 197
  as measure of success, 74
  sustainable change, 136, 137(fig)
synergies among stakeholders, 185, 233, 234–39, 250–51

Tactical Conflict Assessment Framework, 180–81, 180(table)
tangibles, measuring, 34, 34(table), 59–60, 177, 181, 220
theories of intervention, 45–54
  change management theories, 47–49
  change theory, 46–47, 49
  conflict prevention, 51
  conflict resolution, 51
  conflict sensitive approach, 53
  dependency theory, 46
  development theory, 45–46
  Do No Harm, 51, 53
  modernization theory, 45–46
  principles informing, 51–53
  social contract theory, 51
  state theory, 46
  theories of peace, 51
  theory of change, 47, 49–51, 94, 191
  world systems theory, 46
theory of change, 47, 49–51, 94, 191
Thompson, Denis, 35–36
3D approach, 2, 2(fig), 17n8, 241n3
Timor-Leste police service, 108–9, 109(fig)
trade-offs, 1
tradespace, 1–2, 3, 32
transition management, 47–49, 98, 172
transparency, 74, 79
Tsunami Evaluation Coalition, 161

Uganda, mortality surveys in, 165

United Kingdom
  Department for International Development, 6
  measuring effectiveness, 64, 132, 161, 179–80
  Official Development Assistance evaluation, 161
  and political fallouts of failed operations, 35
  presence in Afghanistan, 177–78, 180–81
United Nations (UN)
  approaches to intervention, 28–29, 32, 185–86
  in Bosnia-Herzegovina, 129–30, 133, 144–45, 185, 187n1
  and Center on International Cooperation, 210–12
  change management in, 49
  in Darfur, 246
  donor-reporting framework, 226
  evaluating new missions, 246
  mapping missions, 119, 120(map)
  measuring: as basis for planning, 35; and benchmarks, 81, 209–10; comprehensive intervention activities, 235; current practices of, 209; against mandates, 133, 135–36; opinion of recipient populations, 42; and performance indicators, 216; qualitative approach of, 129–30; quantitative approach of, 247
  Millennium Declaration and Development Goals, 52
  mission mandates, 133, 209
  objectives, 155–56, 185, 248
  proposed permanent staff group, 244–45
  on provincial reconstruction teams, 17n8
  on quick impact projects, 17n8
  Report of the Panel on United Nations Peace Operations, 248
  synergies among stakeholders, 185, 236
  unified command in missions, 252
  UN Refugee Agency, 216

United States
  and comprehensive approach to operations, 229–30
  and humanitarian assistance, 36
  and Iraq mission, 35, 169
  measuring effectiveness: Government Accountability Office recommendations, 11; Inter-Agency Framework for Conflict Analysis in Transition Situations (2004), 98; military construct of, 64; *Post-Conflict Reconstruction Essential Tasks*, 98–100, 99(fig)
  Overseas Humanitarian, Disaster and Civic Air programs, 36
  planning future interventions, 35
  and political fallouts of failed operations, 35
United States Army
  Commander's Emergency Response Program, 17n8
  lessons learned process, 68(fig), 69(fig)
United States Institute of Peace, 92–93
unity of effort, 173–74
universal rights and freedoms, 30
urbanization, 247

value added, 206
value-focused thinking, 8
value imperialism, 31
verification, 78–79, 197, 204, 207, 225
viability, 106
video archiving, 124
VOICE, 162

war-affected publics, 9, 42. *See also* recipient populations
weltanschauungen. See worldviews
Westphalia, Treaty of, 29
"White Man's Burden," 28, 269–70
whole-of-government approach, 230, 232–34, 234(fig)
whole-of-government sector, 92–107
  Grid of Fragilities, 100–101

whole-of-government sector (cont.)
  Inter-Agency Framework for Conflict Analysis in Transition Situations, 98
  Logical Framework Approach, 94–96, 95(fig)
  Metrics Framework for Assessing Conflict Transformation and Stabilization, 92–93
  Post-Conflict Reconstruction Essential Tasks, 98–100, 99(fig)
  results-based management in, 93–94, 97
  Results Based Performance Framework, 96–97
World Bank
  on better assessments, 35
  and Governance Indicators, 81
  on LogFrames, 96
  on mapping and theory-based evaluation, 121
  on participatory methods, 111
  on performance indicators, 81
  on rapid appraisal methods, 107
World Disasters Report, 81
World Map of Peace Operations, 116, 117(map), 118(map), 119, 127n48
world systems theory, 46
worldviews, 27–43. *See also specific sectors*
  charity, 28
  Chinese, 189, 199, 217
  colonialism, 28–29
  colouring stakeholder activities, 215–16
  cultural imperialism, 29
  definition of, 27
  and doctrine of international community, 30–33
  effects of sector worldviews, 215–16, 220
  Eurocentric, 28
  Greek, 189
  imposing on other regions, 28
  informing measurement, 218
  on intervention, 218(fig)

worldviews (cont.)
  learner, 217
  linear, 15
  local, 41–42, 43
  mapping of, 262
  of non-governmental organizations, 216
  shifting of, 218
  sovereignty, 29–30
  and stakeholder differences in, 27–28, 216, 218–19, 225, 253
  on standards of human condition, 30–31
  understanding, 16

Yugoslavia, former, 42

zero-order effects, 84

About the Pearson Peacekeeping Centre

Peace operations have evolved significantly since the first deployment of peacekeepers over 50 years ago. Today's global environment requires states to mobilize whole-of-government resources to secure peace and reconstruct failed states. In this effort, it demands effective and unprecedented levels of synchronization among civilians, military and police.

The Pearson Peacekeeping Centre (PPC) integrates civilians, military and police in an open and collegial learning environment. This, coupled with years of experience in activity-based education and training, has earned it an international reputation for excellence in peace operations research-led training, education, and capacity development.

The Pearson Papers

The Pearson Papers provide a forum where researchers and practitioners can openly explore the complexities of evolving peace operations. The journal is peer reviewed and brings together theorists and practitioners in an interdisciplinary venue.

The topics covered in each issue are developed based upon emerging trends within the international peace operations community.

Occasional Papers

From time to time, the PPC publishes *Occasional Papers* on topics of interest which fall outside a given theme or scope of the current volume of *The Pearson Papers*. *Occasional Papers* include field contributions, research articles, and/or topical reviews examining emerging trends in peace operations.

Our Courses*

The PPC has a wide array of foundational, operational and strategic courses that can be delivered anywhere in the world. Our courses are for civilian police, military, humanitarians, government employees, and most importantly, stakeholders involved in peace operations.

Governments and institutions around the world can request to have the PPC deliver a custom-tailored course that meets specific objectives and requirements. PPC courses are not offered to the general public. Our learning products reflect an integrated, multi-dimensional approach to accommodate adult learning styles and cultural requirements.

Core Competencies for Police in Peace Operations Course

This course is a United Nations police pre-deployment training designed to increase the operational effectiveness of international police officers participating in the African Union (AU) and United Nations (UN) Hybrid Mission in Darfur. Participants are provided with mission-specific information and competencies to fulfill their mandate while deployed on mission.

Sexual- and Gender-based Violence (SGBV)

This course aims to strengthen the capacity of United Nations police officers who work with Government of Sudan police on sexual- and gender-based violence in Darfur by further developing effective mentoring and reporting competencies.

Planning for Integrated Missions (PIM)

This course supports the development of a strong understanding of the various dimensions of complex peace operations, and how each contributes to the overall functioning of a multi-disciplinary/multi-dimensional integrated peace operations mission. Targeted participants are mid-level career officers in the police or military (senior Captain to Lieutenant Colonel or equivalent), or humanitarian or development workers in middle-leadership positions.

Advanced Planning for Integrated Missions (APIM)

This course reinforces/enhances the understanding of the critical issues in planning and leading complex peace operations. The focus is on exploring key questions pertaining to security, humanitarian operations, legal and ethical issues, and mission credibility and success. Targeted participants are upper-level career officers in the police or military (Lieutenant Colonel to Colonel or equivalent) or humanitarian or development workers in middle-leadership positions.

United Nations Integrated Mission Staff Officers Course (UNIMSOC)

This six-week course is a major defence-diplomacy initiative of the Canadian Department of National Defence's Military Training Assistance Program (MTAP). It shares Canadian culture, values and approaches with selected intermediate and senior military officers from MTAP countries, while preparing them to fill key staff positions in a UN integrated mission headquarters.

Senior Management Course on Integrated Peace Missions (SMC)

This course is a major defence-diplomacy initiative of the Canadian Department of National Defence's Military Training Assistance Program (MTAP) in which it shares Canadian culture, values and approaches with selected senior military officers from MTAP countries while preparing them to fill key staff advisory positions within peace operations or within their home governments.

Candidates must be fluent in English to participate in most of the courses listed. We also have a series of courses for French- and Spanish-speaking clients.

For more information on the Pearson Peacekeeping Centre, our courses, and how to order them, please contact us at info@peaceoperations.org, or visit www.peaceoperations.org.

Queen's Policy Studies
Recent Publications

The Queen's Policy Studies Series is dedicated to the exploration of major public policy issues that confront governments and society in Canada and other nations.

Our books are available from good bookstores everywhere, including the Queen's University bookstore (http://www.campusbookstore.com/). McGill-Queen's University Press is the exclusive world representative and distributor of books in the series. A full catalogue and ordering information may be found on their web site (http://mqup.mcgill.ca/).

School of Policy Studies

International Migration and the Governance of Religious Diversity, Paul Bramadat and Matthias Koenig (eds.), 2009. Paper 978-1-55339-266-8 Cloth ISBN 978-1-55339-267-5

In Roosevelt's Bright Shadow: A Collection in Honour of the 70th Anniversary of FDR's 1938 Speech at Queen's University and Marking Canada's Special Relationship with America's Presidents 1938 to Present Day, Arthur Milnes (ed.) 2009.
Paper ISBN 978-1-55339-230-9 Cloth ISBN 978-1-55339-231-6

Economic Transitions with Chinese Characteristics: Thirty Years of Reform and Opening Up, Arthur Sweetman and Jun Zhang (eds.), 2009.
Paper 978-1-55339-225-5 ($39.95) Cloth ISBN 978-1-55339-226-2 ($85)

Economic Transitions with Chinese Characteristics: Social Change During Thirty Years of Reform, Arthur Sweetman and Jun Zhang (eds.), 2009.
Paper 978-1-55339-234-7 ($39.95) Cloth ISBN 978-1-55339-235-4 ($85)

Who Goes? Who Stays? What Matters? Accessing and Persisting in Post-Secondary Education in Canada, Ross Finnie, Richard E. Mueller, Arthur Sweetman, and Alex Usher (eds.), 2008. Paper 978-1-55339-221-7 Cloth ISBN 978-1-55339-222-4

Politics of Purpose, 40th Anniversary Edition, Elizabeth McIninch and Arthur Milnes (eds.), 2009. Paper ISBN 978-1-55339-227-9 Cloth ISBN 978-1-55339-224-8

Dear Gladys: Letters from Over There, Gladys Osmond (Gilbert Penney ed.), 2009.
ISBN 978-1-55339-223-1

Bridging the Divide: Religious Dialogue and Universal Ethics, Papers for The InterAction Council, Thomas S. Axworthy (ed.), 2008.
Paper ISBN 978-1-55339-219-4 Cloth ISBN 978-1-55339-220-0

Immigration and Integration in Canada in the Twenty-first Century, John Biles, Meyer Burstein, and James Frideres (eds.), 2008.
Paper ISBN 978-1-55339-216-3 Cloth ISBN 978-1-55339-217-0

Robert Stanfield's Canada, Richard Clippingdale, 2008. Cloth ISBN 978-1-55339-218-7

Exploring Social Insurance: Can a Dose of Europe Cure Canadian Health Care Finance? Colleen Flood, Mark Stabile, and Carolyn Tuohy (eds.), 2008.
Paper ISBN 978-1-55339-136-4 Cloth ISBN 978-1-55339-213-2

Canada in NORAD, 1957–2007: A History, Joseph T. Jockel, 2007.
Paper ISBN 978-1-55339-134-0 Cloth ISBN 978-1-55339-135-7

Canadian Public-Sector Financial Management, Andrew Graham, 2007.
Paper ISBN 978-1-55339-120-3 Cloth ISBN 978-1-55339-121-0

Emerging Approaches to Chronic Disease Management in Primary Health Care, John Dorland and Mary Ann McColl (eds.), 2007.
Paper ISBN 978-1-55339-130-2 Cloth ISBN 978-1-55339-131-9

Fulfilling Potential, Creating Success: Perspectives on Human Capital Development, Garnett Picot, Ron Saunders, and Arthur Sweetman (eds.), 2007.
Paper ISBN 978-1-55339-127-2 Cloth ISBN 978-1-55339-128-9

Reinventing Canadian Defence Procurement: A View from the Inside, Alan S. Williams, 2006.
Paper ISBN 0-9781693-0-1 (Published in association with Breakout Educational Network)

SARS in Context: Memory, History, Policy, Jacalyn Duffin, and Arthur Sweetman (eds.), 2006. Paper ISBN 978-0-7735-3194-9 Cloth ISBN 978-0-7735-3193-2 (Published in association with McGill-Queen's University Press)

Dreamland: How Canada's Pretend Foreign Policy has Undermined Sovereignty, Roy Rempel, 2006. Paper ISBN 1-55339-118-7 Cloth ISBN 1-55339-119-5 (Published in association with Breakout Educational Network)

Canadian and Mexican Security in the New North America: Challenges and Prospects, Jordi Díez (ed.), 2006. Paper ISBN 978-1-55339-123-4 Cloth ISBN 978-1-55339-122-7

Global Networks and Local Linkages: The Paradox of Cluster Development in an Open Economy, David A. Wolfe and Matthew Lucas (eds.), 2005.
Paper ISBN 1-55339-047-4 Cloth ISBN 1-55339-048-2

Choice of Force: Special Operations for Canada, David Last, and Bernd Horn (eds.), 2005.
Paper ISBN 1-55339-044-X Cloth ISBN 1-55339-045-8

Force of Choice: Perspectives on Special Operations, Bernd Horn, J. Paul de B. Taillon, and David Last (eds.), 2004. Paper ISBN 1-55339-042-3 Cloth 1-55339-043-1

New Missions, Old Problems, Douglas L. Bland, David Last, Franklin Pinch, and Alan Okros (eds.), 2004. Paper ISBN 1-55339-034-2 Cloth 1-55339-035-0

The North American Democratic Peace: Absence of War and Security Institution-Building in Canada-US Relations, 1867-1958, Stéphane Roussel, 2004.
Paper ISBN 0-88911-937-6 Cloth 0-88911-932-2

Implementing Primary Care Reform: Barriers and Facilitators, Ruth Wilson, S.E.D. Shortt and John Dorland (eds.), 2004. Paper ISBN 1-55339-040-7 Cloth 1-55339-041-5

Social and Cultural Change, David Last, Franklin Pinch, Douglas L. Bland, and Alan Okros (eds.), 2004. Paper ISBN 1-55339-032-6 Cloth 1-55339-033-4

Clusters in a Cold Climate: Innovation Dynamics in a Diverse Economy, David A. Wolfe and Matthew Lucas (eds.), 2004. Paper ISBN 1-55339-038-5 Cloth 1-55339-039-3

Canada Without Armed Forces? Douglas L. Bland (ed.), 2004.
Paper ISBN 1-55339-036-9 Cloth 1-55339-037-7

Campaigns for International Security: Canada's Defence Policy at the Turn of the Century, Douglas L. Bland and Sean M. Maloney, 2004.
Paper ISBN 0-88911-962-7 Cloth 0-88911-964-3

Understanding Innovation in Canadian Industry, Fred Gault (ed.), 2003.
Paper ISBN 1-55339-030-X Cloth 1-55339-031-8

Delicate Dances: Public Policy and the Nonprofit Sector, Kathy L. Brock (ed.), 2003.
Paper ISBN 0-88911-953-8 Cloth 0-88911-955-4

Beyond the National Divide: Regional Dimensions of Industrial Relations, Mark Thompson, Joseph B. Rose and Anthony E. Smith (eds.), 2003.
Paper ISBN 0-88911-963-5 Cloth 0-88911-965-1

The Nonprofit Sector in Interesting Times: Case Studies in a Changing Sector, Kathy L. Brock and Keith G. Banting (eds.), 2003.
Paper ISBN 0-88911-941-4 Cloth 0-88911-943-0

Clusters Old and New: The Transition to a Knowledge Economy in Canada's Regions, David A. Wolfe (ed.), 2003. Paper ISBN 0-88911-959-7 Cloth 0-88911-961-9

The e-Connected World: Risks and Opportunities, Stephen Coleman (ed.), 2003.
Paper ISBN 0-88911-945-7 Cloth 0-88911-947-3

Institute of Intergovernmental Relations

Canada: The State of the Federation 2006/07: Transitions – Fiscal and Political Federalism in an Era of Change, vol. 20, John R. Allan, Thomas J. Courchene, and Christian Leuprecht (eds.), 2009. Paper ISBN 978-1-55339-189-0 Cloth ISBN 978-1-55339-191-3

Comparing Federal Systems, Third Edition, Ronald L. Watts, 2008.
Paper ISBN 978-1-55339-188-3

Canada: The State of the Federation 2005: Quebec and Canada in the New Century – New Dynamics, New Opportunities, vol. 19, Michael Murphy (ed.), 2007.
Paper ISBN 978-1-55339-018-3 Cloth ISBN 978-1-55339-017-6

Spheres of Governance: Comparative Studies of Cities in Multilevel Governance Systems, Harvey Lazar and Christian Leuprecht (eds.), 2007.
Paper ISBN 978-1-55339-019-0 Cloth ISBN 978-1-55339-129-6

Canada: The State of the Federation 2004, vol. 18, *Municipal-Federal-Provincial Relations in Canada,* Robert Young and Christian Leuprecht (eds.), 2006.
Paper ISBN 1-55339-015-6 Cloth ISBN 1-55339-016-4

Canadian Fiscal Arrangements: What Works, What Might Work Better, Harvey Lazar (ed.), 2005. Paper ISBN 1-55339-012-1 Cloth ISBN 1-55339-013-X

Canada: The State of the Federation 2003, vol. 17, *Reconfiguring Aboriginal-State Relations,* Michael Murphy (ed.), 2005. Paper ISBN 1-55339-010-5 Cloth ISBN 1-55339-011-3

Canada: The State of the Federation 2002, vol. 16, *Reconsidering the Institutions of Canadian Federalism,* J. Peter Meekison, Hamish Telford and Harvey Lazar (eds.), 2004. Paper ISBN 1-55339-009-1 Cloth ISBN 1-55339-008-3

Federalism and Labour Market Policy: Comparing Different Governance and Employment Strategies, Alain Noël (ed.), 2004. Paper ISBN 1-55339-006-7 Cloth ISBN 1-55339-007-5

The Impact of Global and Regional Integration on Federal Systems: A Comparative Analysis, Harvey Lazar, Hamish Telford, and Ronald L. Watts (eds.), 2003.
Paper ISBN 1-55339-002-4 Cloth ISBN 1-55339-003-2

John Deutsch Institute for the Study of Economic Policy

The 2006 Federal Budget: Rethinking Fiscal Priorities, Charles M. Beach, Michael Smart and Thomas A. Wilson (eds.), 2007.
Paper ISBN 978-1-55339-125-8 Cloth ISBN 978-1-55339-126-6

Health Services Restructuring in Canada: New Evidence and New Directions, Charles M. Beach, Richard P. Chaykowksi, Sam Shortt, France St-Hilaire, and Arthur Sweetman (eds.), 2006.
Paper ISBN 978-1-55339-076-3 Cloth ISBN 978-1-55339-075-6

A Challenge for Higher Education in Ontario, Charles M. Beach (ed.), 2005.
Paper ISBN 1-55339-074-1 Cloth ISBN 1-55339-073-3

Current Directions in Financial Regulation, Frank Milne, and Edwin H. Neave (eds.), Policy Forum Series no. 40, 2005. Paper ISBN 1-55339-072-5 Cloth ISBN 1-55339-071-7

Higher Education in Canada, Charles M. Beach, Robin W. Boadway, and R. Marvin McInnis (eds.), 2005. Paper ISBN 1-55339-070-9 Cloth ISBN 1-55339-069-5

Financial Services and Public Policy, Christopher Waddell (ed.), 2004.
Paper ISBN 1-55339-068-7 Cloth ISBN 1-55339-067-9

The 2003 Federal Budget: Conflicting Tensions, Charles M. Beach, and Thomas A. Wilson (eds.), Policy Forum Series no. 39, 2004.
Paper ISBN 0-88911-958-9 Cloth ISBN 0-88911-956-2

Canadian Immigration Policy for the 21st Century, Charles M. Beach, Alan G. Green, and Jeffrey G. Reitz (eds.), 2003. Paper ISBN 0-88911-954-6 Cloth ISBN 0-88911-952-X

Framing Financial Structure in an Information Environment, Thomas J. Courchene and Edwin H. Neave (eds.), Policy Forum Series no. 38, 2003.
Paper ISBN 0-88911-950-3 Cloth ISBN 0-88911-948-1

Our publications may be purchased at leading bookstores, including the Queen's University Bookstore (http://www.campusbookstore.com/), or can be ordered online from: McGill-Queen's University Press, at
http://mqup.mcgill.ca/ordering.php

For more information about new and backlist titles from Queen's Policy Studies, visit **http://www.queensu.ca/sps/books** or visit the McGill-Queen's University Press web site at: **http://mqup.mcgill.ca/**